LOURDES COLLEGE LIBRARY

D0208327

The Letters of

SAMUEL JOHNSON

SAMUEL JOHNSON

by Sir Joshua Reynolds, 1769 (The Lord Sackville)

The Letters of

SAMUEL JOHNSON

VOLUME I · 1731–1772

Edited by

BRUCE REDFORD

PRINCETON, NEW JERSEY

PRINCETON UNIVERSITY PRESS

MCM·LXXXXII

PUBLISHED BY PRINCETON UNIVERSITY PRESS, 41 WILLIAM STREET
PRINCETON, NEW JERSEY 08540

LIBRARY OF CONGRESS CATALOGING-IN-PUBLICATION DATA

JOHNSON, SAMUEL, 1709–1784. [CORRESPONDENCE]
THE LETTERS OF SAMUEL JOHNSON / EDITED BY BRUCE REDFORD
P. CM.
INCLUDES BIBLIOGRAPHICAL REFERENCES AND INDEX.
CONTENTS: V. 1. 30 OCTOBER 1731 TO 15 DECEMBER 1772.
ISBN 0–691–06881–X (V. 1)
1. JOHNSON, SAMUEL—1709–1784—CORRESPONDENCE.
2. AUTHORS, ENGLISH—18TH CENTURY—CORRESPONDENCE.
3. LEXICOGRAPHERS—GREAT BRITAIN—CORRESPONDENCE.
I. REDFORD, BRUCE. II. TITLE.
PR3533.A4 1992 828′.609—dc20 [B] 90–8806

PRINCETON UNIVERSITY PRESS BOOKS
ARE PRINTED ON ACID-FREE PAPER, AND MEET THE
GUIDELINES FOR PERMANENCE AND DURABILITY OF
THE COMMITTEE ON PRODUCTION GUIDELINES
FOR BOOK LONGEVITY OF THE COUNCIL
ON LIBRARY RESOURCES

PRINTED IN THE UNITED STATES OF AMERICA
BY THE STINEHOUR PRESS, LUNENBURG, VERMONT

1 3 5 7 9 10 8 6 4 2

CONTENTS

ILLUSTRATIONS

PREFACE

SAMUEL JOHNSON's letters have been slow to take their rightful place at the center of his oeuvre and of the eighteenth-century epistolary tradition. Johnson himself is partially responsible for this neglect: his peremptory, dismissive, and ambiguous comments on "the great epistolick art" have reinforced his general strictures on letter writing in the *Life of Pope*;[1] together these mixed or negative signals have helped to create the misleading impression of an *épistolier malgré lui*. A further obstacle to just assessment is that highly charged individual masterpieces—chief among them the letters to Lord Chesterfield and James Macpherson—have tended to forestall acquaintance with the full range of Johnson's achievement. The resulting anthologist's-eye view, moreover, has distracted attention from the actual trajectory of Johnson's epistolary career. From his early twenties to his late fifties, Johnson most often employed the letter as a functional instrument of communication—a stopgap method of conducting business, requesting a favor, answering an invitation, or perpetuating a friendship. In the late 1760s, however, this utilitarian approach receded as Johnson grew into an epistolary vocation. Indeed the final phase of his literary career can be defined in terms of two great achievements: the *Lives of the Poets* and the sequence of letters that begins *c.* 1770 and extends through the opening years of the 1780s.

Behind this claim lies my belief that the distribution of the recovered letters reflects in its general shape the number of letters Johnson actually wrote. As the volumes of the Hyde Edition document at a glance, approximately three-quarters come from the final twelve years of his life. R. W. Chapman has suggested that the relative *copia* of the later years can be attributed to the "leisure and security" Johnson enjoyed.[2] I

1. See To James Boswell, 8 Dec. 1763; To Hester Thrale, 27 Oct. 1777; 11 Apr. 1780; *Johnson's Lives of the English Poets*, ed. G. B. Hill, 1905, III.206–8.

2. *The Letters of Samuel Johnson, with Mrs. Thrale's Genuine Letters to Him*, ed.

would argue that post-pension freedom from financial anxiety was a contributing but not a causal factor. Rather, we can observe Johnson turning aside from strenuously public commitments and investing himself in the cultivation of a form that, in the earlier phases of his career, had seemed of peripheral importance.

One important catalyst for Johnson's belated discovery of a vocation was his close friendship with Hester Thrale, who elicited his most sustained, painstaking, and multifaceted letters. From Boswell to Chapman, however, commentators have slighted the bond and the letters that defined, complicated, and finally dissolved it. Chapman speaks for many when he declares, "Though they [Johnson's letters to Hester Thrale] are never patronizing they are limited by her power of appreciation" (p. xix). Quite the opposite is true: in his correspondence with the Mistress of Streatham Park, Johnson learns what the familiar letter, and the familiar letter alone, can accomplish. He renews and extends himself by celebrating the private and the occasional. He cultivates nuance. He combines utmost economy with utmost resonance. He succeeds in modulating his voice, in perfecting networks of allusion, in enlivening authority with ease and tempering ease with authority.

The Hyde Edition aims ultimately to provide the materials for a fresh assessment of Samuel Johnson, man of letters. Its immediate rationale can be summed up concisely: new letters, more accurate texts, and up-to-date annotation. Fifty-two previously unknown letters or parts of letters have come to light since the publication of R. W. Chapman's three-volume set. Outstanding in biographical significance are the twelve to Charlotte Lennox; outstanding in literary merit is the letter of consolation to Mary Cholmondeley (6 May 1777). This letter adheres closely to Johnson's customary formula: first, a declaration of fellow feeling, based on shared or anticipated experience; second, a steady look at the hard facts of human mortality; third, an invocation, implied or explicit, of shared beliefs;

R. W. Chapman (Oxford: Clarendon Press, 1952), p. xvii. Subsequent references to this work appear parenthetically in the text.

and finally, an injunction to activity, to reimmersion in "the business of life." These attributes, though predictable, supply a benchmark by which to gauge the changes in Johnson's "epistolick art." In contrast to earlier messages of consolation (e.g., To James Elphinston, 25 Sept. 1750), which resemble quasi-public homilies of a sententious amplitude, the letter to Mary Cholmondeley achieves a telling simplicity of manner and directness of feeling. Such qualities permit Johnson to enact—instead of merely prescribing—a transition from raw grief to poised acceptance. The perpetual moralist is present, yet he no longer speaks distantly *ex cathedra*.

It should be emphasized that such "new" letters are scarcely more important than those for which only inferior printed texts or copies of varying reliability had previously been recovered. The Hyde Edition offers scores of texts transcribed for the first time from the original documents; one significant example is Johnson's letter of thanks to Lord Bute (20 July 1762). In the case of Johnson's letters to Hester Thrale, I have been able to transcribe from holographs forty-two letters that had been known only in the corrupt text of *Letters to and from the Late Samuel Johnson, L.L.D.* (1788). Furthermore, in many instances I have substituted complete letters for brief extracts from auction catalogues (e.g., To John Taylor, 9 Dec. 1779). Four letters included in Chapman's edition have been dropped from the canon: two (Nos. 57.1, 712.1) because I strongly doubt their authenticity; another (No. 1136) because it appears to have been written for Henry Thrale; and a fourth (No. 1126) because internal evidence establishes that it has been attributed to the wrong "Dr. Johnson."

R. W. Chapman declares in his introduction, "My prime ambition has been to furnish an accurate text" (p. vii). Chapman was indeed an expert student of Johnson's often difficult hand. Nevertheless, his transcripts are far from immaculate: while correcting the mistakes of previous editors, he commits blunders of his own. For example, in Johnson's letter to Henry Bright of 24 May 1770, Chapman creates a ghostly Mr. "J. Combe" out of the name of Henry Thrale's nephew, Ralph

Plumbe. Given the difficulties inherent in decipherment—difficulties compounded by the mutilated state of many of the manuscripts—no editor can claim to have achieved transcriptions of spotless accuracy, particularly in matters of capitalization and punctuation. I do believe, however, that the Hyde Edition represents an improvement over its predecessors.

For the first time, moreover, textual notes supply a record of substantive deletions. It is intriguing to discover, for instance, that the line from Johnson's epitaph for Hogarth, "If Merit touch thee, shed a tear," originally read, "If History touch thee, shed a tear"; or that, in writing to the pious and sickly Hill Boothby, Johnson changed "It has pleased God to make me much better" to "It has pleased God to permit me to be much better." Quite often these first or second thoughts—what was scratched out or erased or written over—give us intimate knowledge of Johnson's stylistic procedures, mental habits, and chains of association.

In the headnote to each letter the Hyde Edition records, also for the first time, information that will promote access to and study of the recovered letters. Even at the time of publication, Chapman's ownership credits were often decades out of date. This fact is especially true of what he called "transatlantic transfers" (p. xiv)—letters that had left England for public and private collections in the United States. With the generous help of scholars, collectors, booksellers, and librarians, I have done my best to chart transfers of every kind. Inevitably the locations of a few letters have proved elusive. With these exceptions, however, the ownership credits document the current disposition of the manuscripts.

Johnson's own declaration in his "Preface to Shakespeare" has guided the annotation of these volumes: "I have endeavoured to be neither superfluously copious, nor scrupulously reserved, and hope that I have made my authour's meaning accessible to many who before were frighted from perusing him."[3] Forty years of important work by various scholars on

3. *Johnson on Shakespeare*, ed. Arthur Sherbo, vol. 7 of *The Yale Edition of the Works of Samuel Johnson*, 1968, p. 103.

Johnson and his period have enabled me to solve a wide variety of problems, or at the very least to suggest possible solutions. Johnson was a highly allusive letter writer with an astonishing variety of correspondents, and the task of explaining his cryptic references often sends one dashing from Juvenal to Junius, politics to publishing history, law to medicine, lexicography to genealogy. Though it is difficult to single out individual contributions from the array of groundbreaking scholarly studies, I would like to pay special tribute to the work of L. F. Powell, J. L. Clifford, and J. D. Fleeman.

"We talked of Letter-writing," Boswell tells us. "JOHNSON. 'It is now become so much the fashion to publish letters, that in order to avoid it, I put as little into mine as I can.' BOSWELL. 'Do what you will, Sir, you cannot avoid it. Should you even write as ill as you can, your letters would be published as curiosities.' "[4] Boswell was right: they have been published, they will go on being published. But not as mere "curiosities": Johnson was incapable of putting "little"—of himself or any other topic—into his letters. At their most cursory and casual, they are never less than precious biographical documents. A significant number, however, mirror, define, and re-create what Carlyle calls "a spirit-speaking likeness"[5]—the likeness of a consummate man of letters.

4. *Boswell's Life of Johnson*, ed. G. B. Hill, rev. L. F. Powell, 1934–64, IV.102.

5. "Boswell's Life of Johnson," in *The Works of Thomas Carlyle: Centenary Edition*, 1896, XXVIII.75.

ACKNOWLEDGMENTS

THIS edition would not have been possible without the extraordinary vision, knowledge, and generosity of Mary Hyde Eccles. She laid its foundations and contributed to its every part. As joint creator of the Hyde Collection, Lady Eccles has formed an archive of incomparable rarity and coherence; as discerning scholar and benefactor, she has played a crucial role in the development of Johnsonian studies. I speak for many in adapting these words from one of Johnson's own dedications: "From Flattery, my Lady, either of the Dead or the Living, I wish to be clear, and have therefore solicited the Countenance of a Patron, whom, if I knew how to praise her, I could praise with Truth, and have the World on my Side; whose Candour and Humanity are universally acknowledged, and whose Judgment perhaps was then first to be doubted, when she condescended to admit this Address from, THE EDITOR."

Editions of this scope are necessarily collaborative ventures, dependent upon the energy, expertise, and goodwill of many people. A complete roll of honor would resemble Homer's Catalogue of Ships; I must therefore be content with singling out those whose contributions have been central to the enterprise.

I have been fortunate in working with two gifted students of the eighteenth century, John Whittier-Ferguson and Marcia Wagner Levinson, both of whom began as assistants but developed rapidly into colleagues. Without their keen eyes, sharp minds, and patient dispositions, the long journey would have been immeasurably more taxing.

Those who assisted importantly in the launching of this project include Herbert Bailey, Viscount Eccles, Marjorie Sherwood, and the late William Shellman. At Princeton University Press, the support of Robert Brown, Mike Burton, and Walter Lippincott continues to prove indispensable. I am deeply grateful to the Press's managing editor, Janet Stern, for her rare discernment and dedication. Mark Argetsinger has done visual justice to Johnsonian utterance.

From the beginning Princeton University Library has played a crucial role in the daily life of this edition. I have come to depend—shamelessly but gratefully—on the expert advice and boundless goodwill of Alfred Bush, Mark Farrell, Stephen Ferguson, Mary Ann Jensen, William Joyce, Donald Koepp, John Logan, Richard Ludwig, Glendon Odell, and William Stoneman. Their manifold kindnesses buttress the enterprise. At Yale the staff of the Boswell Office has gone out of its way to assist a needy alumnus; special thanks, as always, are due to Rachel McClellan. The Beinecke Library remains the most accessible of treasure houses, thanks in large measure to Vincent Giroud and Stephen Parks. At Harvard, Hugh Amory, Rodney Dennis, and Roger Stoddard gave generously of their time and knowledge. I have received every courtesy at the Berg Collection (New York Public Library), the Huntington Library, the Pierpont Morgan Library, the Folger Library, the Free Library of Philadelphia, the Historical Society of Pennsylvania, the Rosenbach Library, the Boston Public Library, the Yale Center for British Art, the University of Rochester Library, and Texas Christian University Library.

In Great Britain my path was smoothed by the staffs of the British Library; the National Portrait Gallery; the Royal Academy of Arts; the Guildhall Library; Johnson House (London); the Wellcome Institute; the Cambridge University Library; the Fitzwilliam Museum; the Bodleian Library; the Library of Pembroke College, Oxford; the John Rylands University Library; Birmingham Public Library; Sheffield City Library; the William Salt Library; the National Library of Scotland; and Aberdeen University Library. At the Johnson Birthplace Museum, G. W. Nicholls has been a vital resource.

I have benefited from the learning and generosity of The Club of Johnson Scholars, chief among them Edward Bloom, Lillian Bloom, O M Brack, Thomas Curley, Robert DeMaria, Stephen Fix, J. D. Fleeman, Gwin Kolb, John Riely, Howard Weinbrot, and Richard Wendorf. Allen Reddick transcribed most of the manuscript letters in Volume II, and contributed generously to the annotation of 1773 and 1774.

For assistance of various kinds I am indebted to the following: Frank Baker, Roger Barrett, Robert Barry, Elizabeth Beatson, Alan Bell, David Bevington, G. W. Bowersock, the Hon. Mrs. Brooks, Iain Brown, D. H. Burden, James Caudle, Patricia Coke, Lady Margaret Colville, Rupert Colville, John Comyn, Margaret Conable, Aileen Douglas, John Edgcumbe, Christopher Edwards, Robert Ferguson, Priscilla Parkhurst Ferguson, Janet Ing Freeman, Gerald Goldberg, Joanne Gottlieb, the late Robert Halsband, Frances Harris, Kimball Higgs, the late Arthur Houghton, Paul Hunter, Christopher Jones, Neill Joy, Dennis Katz, Siobhan Kilfeather, H. W. Liebert, David McKitterick, Colin McLaren, Rose McTernan, Sarah Markham, Glenise Matheson, Ernest Mehew, Leslie Morris, Daisuke Nagashima, Robert Nikirk, Arthur Pennant, Sir John Riddell, C. S. Rogers, Allen Rosenbaum, Loren Rothschild, the Earl of Shelburne, Francis Sheppard, Thomas Tanselle, Veronica Tritton, Earl Waldegrave, Marion Waller, Peter White, Thomas Wright, K. K. Yung.

"We all live on this condition that the ties of every endearment must at last be broken" (To Mary Cholmondeley, 6 May 1777). I can no longer anticipate the pleasure these volumes would have given to five who were present at the creation: Elizabeth-Ann Knapp, Louis Landa, Robert Rosenthal, William Shellman, Willard Thorp. *Alle Seelen ruhn in Frieden.*

BRUCE REDFORD

PRINCETON, NEW JERSEY
JUNE 1990

EDITORIAL PROCEDURES

POLICIES of annotation and transcription have been modeled on the style sheet for the Yale Research Edition of the Private Papers of James Boswell. The most detailed version in print appears in the front matter to *The Correspondence of James Boswell with David Garrick, Edmund Burke, and Edmond Malone*, ed. P. S. Baker et al. (1986). The statement that follows adheres closely to this version.

THE TEXTS

Choice and Arrangement of Letters

The letters are presented in chronological order. Letters written for others, as well as public dissertations in the guise of letters, have been excluded. Undated letters that cannot be assigned with confidence to a specific year appear in Appendix I, where they are ordered alphabetically by correspondent. Appendix II gathers together the evidence for letters whose texts have not been recovered. Translations of Johnson's letters in Latin appear in Appendix III.

The copy-text has been the MSS of letters sent, whenever such MSS were available. In the absence of originals, we have used MS copies. When no MSS at all have been recovered, we have used printed texts as copy.

Transcription

In accordance with the policy of the Yale Research Series, "manuscript documents in this edition have been printed to correspond to the originals as closely as is feasible in the medium of type. A certain amount of compromise and apparent inconsistency seems unavoidable, but change has been kept within the limits of stated conventions."

The following editorial conventions are imposed silently: *Addresses*. Elements appearing on separate lines in the MS are run together and punctuated according to modern practice. On franked covers, handwriting is that of the franker unless otherwise specified.

Datelines. Places and dates are joined at the head of the letter regardless of their position in the MS. Punctuation has been normalized.

Salutations. Abbreviations are expanded. Commas and colons after salutations are retained; in the absence of punctuation, a colon is supplied.

Complimentary closes. Abbreviations are expanded. Punctuation has been normalized. Elements appearing on separate lines in the MS are run together. Complimentary closes paragraphed separately in the MS are printed as continuations of the last line of text.

Endorsements. Handwriting is that of the recipient unless otherwise specified.

Punctuation. At the ends of completed sentences periods may replace commas or dashes and are always supplied when omitted. A sentence following a period always begins with a capital letter.

Changes. Substantive additions and deletions in Johnson's hand are recorded in the notes.

Lacunae. Words and letters missing through a tear or obscured by a blot are supplied within angle brackets. Inadvertent omissions are supplied within square brackets. Non-authorial deletions are not reported unless the reading is in doubt.

Abbreviations, contractions, and symbols. The following abbreviations, contractions, and symbols, and their variant forms, are expanded: abt (about), acct (account), agst (against), Bp (Bishop), cd (could), compts (compliments), Dr (Dear), Ld (Lord), Lop (Lordship), Ly (Lady), Lyship (Ladyship), recd (received), sd (should), Sr (Sir), wc (which), wd (would), yr (your), & (and), &c (etc.). All retained abbreviations and contractions are followed by a period. Periods following ordinals have been removed.

Superior letters. Superior letters are lowered.

Brackets. Parentheses replace square brackets in the text, brackets being reserved for editorial use.

Spelling. The original spelling has been retained, except for obvious inadvertencies, which are corrected in the text and recorded in the notes.

Capitalization and paragraphing. Original capitalization and paragraphing have been retained.

ANNOTATION

Headnotes. Postmarks, although partly illegible on some letters, are left unbracketed when not in doubt. Marks on the wrappers other than addresses, postmarks, endorsements, and stamped and written franks have been ignored.

Footnotes. When an abbreviated source is given, the full citation may be found in the list of cue titles and abbreviations on pp. xxvii–xxix. All other reference titles in the footnotes are sufficiently complete to enable ready identification; for each letter, these citations are presented in full the first time they occur and are shortened in all subsequent occurrences in the notes to that letter. Except where a work has been directly quoted, no source is given when the information is available in the *Dictionary of National Biography*, an encyclopedia, or other general reference work.

Reference to all letters is made by correspondent and date. *Post* and *Ante* references supplement but do not replace the index, which should be consulted whenever the identity of names or places is in doubt.

IMPORTANT EDITIONS OF JOHNSON'S LETTERS

1788

Letters to and from the Late Samuel Johnson, LL.D. By Hester Lynch Piozzi. Two volumes. London: 1788.

Three hundred thirty-eight letters to Hester Thrale and her family, with a few to other correspondents. For an analysis of the numerous editorial interventions, see R. W. Chapman, "Mrs. Piozzi's Omissions from Johnson's Letters to Thrales," *RES* 22, 1946, pp. 17–28.

1791

The Life of Samuel Johnson, LL.D. By James Boswell. Two volumes. London: 1791.

Boswell published for the first time three hundred forty-four letters. In subsequent editions, Edmond Malone and J. W. Croker added significantly to this corpus.

1892

Letters of Samuel Johnson, LL.D. Edited by G. B. Hill. Two volumes. Oxford: 1892.

The first scholarly edition. Hill offers texts or partial texts for six hundred eighty-seven letters; he excludes "those of his [SJ's] letters which were included by Boswell in the *Life*" (Hill I.ix).

1929

The R. B. Adam Library Relating to Dr. Samuel Johnson and His Era. Four volumes. London and New York: 1929–30.

Volume I of Adam's catalogue includes two hundred twenty-four letters.

1934

The Queeney Letters. Edited by the sixth Marquis of Lansdowne. One volume. London: 1934.

Lord Lansdowne includes thirty-two letters from Johnson to Hester Maria Thrale.

1934

Boswell's Life of Johnson. Edited by G. B. Hill, revised by L. F. Powell. Six volumes. Oxford: 1934–64.

The definitive scholarly edition of Boswell's *Life,* with authoritative annotation of the letters.

1952

The Letters of Samuel Johnson, with Mrs. Thrale's Genuine Letters to Him. Edited by R. W. Chapman. Three volumes. Oxford: 1952.

Chapman offers one thousand five hundred fifteen letters. "My edition is, in many respects, designed as a Supplement to Hill-Powell" (p. xvi).

CHRONOLOGY

1709	Is born at Lichfield, 18 Sept.
1717–25	Attends Lichfield Grammar School.
1728	Enters Pembroke College, Oxford, in October.
1729	Leaves Oxford in December.
1731	Death of his father Michael.
1732	Usher at Market Bosworth School.
1733	Resides in Birmingham; translates Lobo's *Voyage to Abyssinia.*
1735	Marries Elizabeth Porter; opens school at Edial.
1737	Leaves for London in March; begins work for Edward Cave.
1738	*London.*
1744	*An Account of the Life of Richard Savage*; *Harleian Miscellany.*
1746	Signs contract for the *Dictionary.*
1749	*Irene* produced; *The Vanity of Human Wishes.*
1750	Begins *Rambler.*
1752	Death of Elizabeth Johnson; final *Rambler.*
1755	Oxford M.A.; publication of the *Dictionary.*
1758	Begins *Idler.*
1759	Death of his mother Sarah; publication of *Rasselas.*
1760	Final *Idler.*
1762	Is granted annual pension.
1763	Meets James Boswell.
1764	Founding of The Club.
1765	Meets Henry and Hester Thrale; Dublin LL.D.; *The Dramatic Works of William Shakespeare.*
1770	*The False Alarm.*
1771	*Thoughts on the late Transactions respecting Falkland's Islands.*
1773	Hebridean tour.
1774	*The Patriot*; tour of Wales.
1775	*A Journey to the Western Islands of Scotland*; *Taxation No Tyranny*; Oxford D.C.L.; trip to Paris.

1777	Trial of Dr. Dodd; begins work on *Lives of the Poets*.
1779	First installment of *Lives*.
1781	Death of Henry Thrale; second installment of *Lives*.
1783	Founding of Essex Head Club.
1784	Final break with Hester Thrale; dies 13 Dec.

CUE TITLES AND ABBREVIATIONS

Adam Cat.	R. B. ADAM, *The R. B. Adam Library Relating to Dr. Samuel Johnson and His Era*, 4 vols., 1929–30.
Alum. Cant. I	JOHN and J. A. VENN, *Alumni Cantabrigienses*, Part I (to 1751), 4 vols., 1922–27.
Alum. Cant. II	J. A. VENN, *Alumni Cantabrigienses*, Part II (1752–1900), 6 vols., 1940–54.
Alum. Oxon. I	JOSEPH FOSTER, *Alumni Oxonienses ... 1500–1714*, 4 vols., 1891–92.
Alum. Oxon. II	JOSEPH FOSTER, *Alumni Oxonienses ... 1715–1886*, 4 vols., 1887–88.
Baker	*The Correspondence of James Boswell with David Garrick, Edmund Burke, and Edmond Malone*, ed. P. S. Baker et al., 1986.
Bibliography	W. P. COURTNEY and DAVID NICHOL SMITH, *A Bibliography of Samuel Johnson*, 1915, 1925.
Bibliography Supplement	R. W. CHAPMAN and A. T. HAZEN, *Johnsonian Bibliography: A Supplement to Courtney*, 1939.
Bloom	E. A. BLOOM, *Samuel Johnson in Grub Street*, 1957.
Burke's Correspondence	*The Correspondence of Edmund Burke*, ed. T. W. Copeland et al., 1958–70.
Chapman	*The Letters of Samuel Johnson, with Mrs. Thrale's Genuine Letters to Him*, ed. R. W. Chapman, 3 vols., 1952.
Clifford, 1952	J. L. CLIFFORD, *Hester Lynch Piozzi*, 2d ed., 1952.
Clifford, 1955	J. L. CLIFFORD, *Young Samuel Johnson*, 1955.
Clifford, 1979	J. L. CLIFFORD, *Dictionary Johnson*, 1979.
Croker	JAMES BOSWELL, *The Life of Samuel Johnson, LL.D.*, ed. J. W. Croker, rev. John Wright, 10 vols., 1868.
SJ's *Dictionary*	SAMUEL JOHNSON, *Dictionary of the English Language*, 4th ed., 1773.
DNB	*Dictionary of National Biography.*

Earlier Years	F. A. POTTLE, *James Boswell: The Earlier Years, 1740–1769*, 1966.
Fifer	*The Correspondence of James Boswell with Certain Members of The Club*, ed. C. N. Fifer, 1976.
Fleeman	SAMUEL JOHNSON, *A Journey to the Western Islands of Scotland*, ed. J. D. Fleeman, 1985.
GM	*The Gentleman's Magazine*, 1731–1907.
Greene, 1975	DONALD GREENE, *Samuel Johnson's Library*, 1975.
Hawkins	SIR JOHN HAWKINS, *The Life of Samuel Johnson, LL.D.*, 2d ed., 1787.
Hazen	A. T. HAZEN, *Samuel Johnson's Prefaces and Dedications*, 1937.
Hebrides	*Boswell's Journal of a Tour to the Hebrides with Samuel Johnson, LL.D., 1773*, ed. from the original MS by F. A. Pottle and C. H. Bennett, 1961.
Hendy	J. G. HENDY, *The History of the Early Postmarks of the British Isles*, 1905.
Hill	*Letters of Samuel Johnson, LL.D.*, ed. G. B. Hill, 1892.
Hyde, 1972	MARY HYDE, *The Impossible Friendship: Boswell and Mrs. Thrale*, 1972.
Hyde, 1977	MARY HYDE, *The Thrales of Streatham Park*, 1977.
JB	James Boswell.
Johns. Glean.	A. L. READE, *Johnsonian Gleanings*, 11 vols., 1909–52.
Johns. Misc.	*Johnsonian Miscellanies*, ed. G. B. Hill, 2 vols., 1897.
JN	*Johnsonian Newsletter.*
Later Years	FRANK BRADY, *James Boswell: The Later Years, 1769–1795*, 1984.
Life	*Boswell's Life of Johnson, Together with Boswell's Journal of a Tour to the Hebrides and Johnson's Diary of a Journey into North Wales*, ed. G. B. Hill, rev. L. F. Powell, 6 vols., 1934–50; vols. V and VI, 2d ed., 1964.
Lit. Anec.	JOHN NICHOLS, *Literary Anecdotes of the Eighteenth Century*, 9 vols., 1812–15.
Lit. Car.	F. A. POTTLE, *The Literary Career of James Boswell, Esq.*, 1929.
Lives of the Poets	*Johnson's Lives of the English Poets*, ed. G. B. Hill, 1905.

Lond. Stage	*The London Stage,* Part III (1729–47), ed. A. H. Scouten, 1961; Part IV (1747–76), ed. G. W. Stone, Jr., 1962; Part V (1776–1800), ed. C. B. Hogan, 1968.
Namier and Brooke	SIR LEWIS NAMIER and JOHN BROOKE, *The House of Commons, 1754–1790,* 3 vols., 1964.
OED	*Oxford English Dictionary.*
Piozzi, *Letters*	HESTER LYNCH PIOZZI, *Letters to and from the Late Samuel Johnson, LL.D.,* 2 vols., 1788.
Piozzi	Annotated presentation copy, given to Sir James Fellowes, of H. L. Piozzi's *Letters to and from the Late Samuel Johnson, LL.D.,* 1788 (Birthplace Museum, Lichfield).
Plomer	H. R. PLOMER et al., *Dictionary of Printers and Booksellers, 1668–1725; 1726–1775,* 2 vols., 1922, 1932.
Poems	*The Poems of Samuel Johnson,* ed. David Nichol Smith and E. L. McAdam, rev. J. D. Fleeman, 1974.
Reades	A. L. READE, *The Reades of Blackwood Hill and Dr. Johnson's Ancestry,* 1906.
RES	*Review of English Studies.*
SJ	Samuel Johnson.
Sledd and Kolb	J. H. SLEDD and G. J. KOLB, *Dr. Johnson's Dictionary,* 1955.
Thraliana	*Thraliana: The Diary of Mrs. Hester Lynch Thrale,* ed. K. C. Balderston, 1942.
TLS	*Times Literary Supplement.*
Waingrow	*The Correspondence and Other Papers of James Boswell Relating to the Making of the "Life of Johnson,"* ed. Marshall Waingrow, 1969.
Walpole's Correspondence, Yale ed.	*The Yale Edition of Horace Walpole's Correspondence,* ed. W. S. Lewis et al., 1937–83.
Wheatley and Cunningham	H. B. WHEATLEY and PETER CUNNINGHAM, *London Past and Present,* 3 vols., 1891.
Works, Yale ed.	*The Yale Edition of the Works of Samuel Johnson,* J. H. Middendorf, gen. ed., 1958–.

The Letters of

SAMUEL JOHNSON

Gregory Hickman[1]

SATURDAY 30 OCTOBER 1731

MS: Hyde Collection.

Sir: Lichfield, Oct. 30, 1731

I have so long neglected to return You thanks for the favours and Assistance I received from you at Stourbridge that I am afraid You have now done expecting it.[2] I can indeed make no apology but by assuring You that this delay, whatever was the cause of it, proceeded neither from forgetfulness, disrespect, nor ingratitude; Time has not made the Sense of the Obligation less warm, nor the thanks I return less sincere. But while I am acknowledging one Favour I must beg another, that You would excuse the om⟨issi⟩on of the Verses You desired.[3] Be pleas'd to consider that versifying against ones inclination is the most disagreable thing in the World, and that ones own disappointment is no inviting Subject, and that though the desire of gratifying You might have prevaild over my dislike of it, yet it proves upon reflection so barren that to attempt[4] to write upon it, is to undertake to build without materials.

As I am yet unemploy'd, I hope You will, if anything should offer, remember and recommend, Sir, Your humble servant,

SAM. JOHNSON

1. Gregory Hickman (1688–1748), the half-brother of SJ's cousin the Rev. Cornelius Ford, and a prominent citizen of Stourbridge, Worcestershire.

2. In the summer of 1731, Hickman had done his best to secure SJ the post of usher at the Stourbridge Grammar School, but on 6 Sept. 1731 the post went to John Hughes, a graduate of Trinity College, Oxford (Clifford, 1955, pp. 128–29).

3. "To Miss Hickman Playing on the Spinet" (*Poems*, p. 54) appears to have been addressed to Hickman's daughter Dorothy during SJ's summer visit. "It seems extraordinary if Gregory Hickman expected him to write 'Verses inspired by an Unsuccessful Application for the Post of Usher at Stourbridge School,' but that is what we gather" (*Johns. Glean.* v.66).

4. MS: "that to at-" superimposed upon "a prospect"

John Taylor[1]

THURSDAY 27 JULY 1732

MS: Hyde Collection.
ADDRESS: To Mr. Taylor, Present.
ENDORSEMENTS: 1732, 27 July 1732.

Dear Sir: Lichfield, July 27, 1732

I received a Letter last Night from Mr. Corbett,[2] who informs me of a Vacancy at Ashburne, I have no suspicion of any endeavours being wanting on Your Part to contribute to my success, and therefore do not ask for Your interest with the exactest Ceremony.[3] I have sent this Messenger with letters to Mr. Vernon,[4] and Mr. Corbett. Be pleas'd to favour me with You[r] Opinion of the means most proper to be used in this Matter, If there be[5] any reason for my coming to Ashburne, I shall readily do it. Mr. Corbett has, I suppose, given You an account of my leaving Sir ⟨Wolstan's.[6] It⟩ was really e Carcere exire.[7] I am, Dear Sir, Your humble servant, SAM. JOHNSON

1. John Taylor (1711–88), of Ashbourne, Derbyshire, a close friend of SJ since their time together at the Lichfield Grammar School. Taylor had studied law at Christ Church, Oxford, and in 1732 was practicing as an attorney in Ashbourne (Clifford, 1955, p. 134).

2. John Corbet (1710/11–59), the younger brother of Andrew Corbet (1709–41), son of a Shropshire landowner and SJ's former schoolmate. One of the Corbets' sisters was married to the rector of Market Bosworth, another to a Derbyshire squire who lived near Ashbourne (Clifford, 1955, p. 133; *Johns. Glean.* v.89).

3. William Hardestee, usher at Ashbourne Grammar School since 1713, had died the previous week (*Johns. Glean.* v.88). When the governors of the school met on 1 Aug. they elected a rival candidate, Thomas Bourne, of Leek, Staffordshire (*Johns. Glean.* v.89).

4. George Venables Vernon (1708–80), of Sudbury, Derbyshire, M.P. for Lichfield (1731–47), later first Baron Vernon (1762). Clifford describes him as "a possible influential backer" (1955, p. 134). Neither Vernon nor Corbet, however, was a governor of the school.

5. MS: "be" superimposed upon "a"

6. Sir Wolstan Dixie (*c.* 1701–67), fourth Bt., of Bosworth Park, Leicestershire. Sir Wolstan was the chief patron of Market Bosworth School, where SJ served as usher in 1732. According to JB, SJ also "officiated as a kind of domestick chaplain" to Sir Wolstan (*Life* I.84), whom John Taylor described as "an abandoned brutal rascal" (*Johns. Glean.* v.84). SJ was miserably unhappy at Market Bosworth and returned to Lichfield after a few months (Clifford, 1955, pp. 131–33).

7. *e Carcere exire*: "leaving prison."

Unidentified Correspondent

WEDNESDAY 18 SEPTEMBER 1734

MS: Hyde Collection.

Sir: [Lichfield] Septr. 18th 1734

I hope You will excuse the liberty I have taken of troubling You with twelve of my Proposals.[1] I doubt not of Your willingness to encourage any undertaking in the way of letters, and am satisfied that my success may be much promoted by Your recommendation. I am, Sir, Your most humble servant,

SAM. JOHNSON

1. "Johnson returned to Lichfield early in 1734, and in August that year he made an attempt to procure some little subsistence by his pen; for he published proposals for printing by subscription the Latin Poems of Politian. . . . The book was to contain more than thirty sheets, the price to be two shillings and sixpence at the time of subscribing, and two shillings and sixpence at the delivery of a perfect book in quires" (*Life* 1.89–90 and n. 2). The *Proposals* were issued on 5 Aug. 1734 (*Works*, Yale ed. 1.32). Though JB acquired a copy during his work on the *Life*, it was not found among the Boswell Papers (Waingrow, p. 160 n. 8). According to Sir John Hawkins, "not meeting with sufficient encouragement, Johnson dropped the design" (Hawkins, p. 27).

Edward Cave[1]

MONDAY 25 NOVEMBER 1734

MS: Hyde Collection.

ADDRESS: To Mr. Cave at St. John's Gate, London.[2]

POSTMARK: 27 NO.

ENDORSEMENTS: answer'd, Answerd Dec. 2.

1. Edward Cave (1691–1754), editor, printer, and publisher of the *Gentleman's Magazine*, which he had founded in 1731. "Although there were active rivals such as the *London Magazine*, Cave's *Gentleman's Magazine* was easily the foremost periodical of the day" (Clifford, 1955, p. 178).

2. The only remnant of the Priory of St. John of Jerusalem, the chief seat in England of the Knights Templar. Completed in 1504, the Gatehouse once formed the south entrance to the Priory. The doorway in the southwest tower led to Cave's

Sir: [Lichfield] Novr. 25th[3] 1734

As You appear no less sensible than Your Readers of the defects of your Poetical Article, You will not be displeased, if, in order to the improvement of it, I communicate to You the sentiments of a person, who will undertake on reasonable terms sometimes to fill a column.[4]

His opinion is, that the Publick would not give You a bad reception, if beside the current Wit of the Month, which a critical examination would generally reduce to a narrow Compass, You admitted not only Poems, Inscriptions etc. never printed before, which he will sometimes supply You with; but likewise short literary Dissertations in Latin or English, Critical Remarks on Authors Ancient or Modern, forgotten Poems that deserve Revival, or loose pieces, like Floyers, worth preserving.[5] By this Method your Literary Article, for so it might be call'd, will, he thinks, be better recommended to the Publick, than by low Jests, awkward Buffoonery, or the dull Scurrilities of either Party.

If such a Correspondence will be agreable to You, be pleased to inform me in two posts, what the Conditions are on which You shall expect it.[6] Your late offer gives me no reason to distrust your Generosity.[7] If You engage in any Literary projects besides this Paper, I have other designs to impart if I

office (Wheatley and Cunningham II.313–15). SJ told JB "that when he first saw St. John's Gate, the place where that deservedly popular miscellany was originally printed, he 'beheld it with reverence'" (*Life* I.111–12).

3. MS: "25th" altered from "22d"

4. The regular features of the *GM* included a section entitled "Poetical Essays," which offered several pages of original and reprinted poetry.

5. "A Letter from the late Sir John Floyer to Mr King of Bungay, Suffolk, in Recommendation of the Cold Bath" had appeared in the April issue (*GM* 1734, pp. 197–98).

6. Sir John Hawkins claims that, after receiving SJ's letter, Cave "retained him as a correspondent and a contributor to his Magazine" (Hawkins, p. 29). However, not until 1738 is there any other evidence to suggest that SJ became a regular contributor.

7. In the October issue, Cave had offered a prize of £50 for the best poem in Latin or English on "Life, Death, Judgement, Heaven, and Hell" (*GM* 1734,

could be secure from having others reap the advantage of what I should hint.

Your letter, by being directed to S. Smith[8] to be left at the Castle in Birmingham, Warwackshire, will reach Your humble Servant.[9]

---

p. 560). For SJ's comments on such prizes and their effect, see his *Life of Cave* (*GM* 1754, p. 57).

8. "S. Smith" is a pseudonym.

9. The Castle Inn, on Birmingham High Street, near the store run by SJ's uncle Andrew Jackson and the saddler's shop belonging to his uncle John Harrison (*Johns. Glean.* III.107–8).

Gilbert Repington[1]

SUNDAY 18 MAY 1735

MS: Bodleian Library.

ADDRESS: To Mr. Gilbt. Repington in Peckwater,[2] Christchurch, Oxford, by London.

POSTMARKS: LITCHFIELD, 21 MA.

ENDORSEMENT: Sam. Johnson 1735.

Sir: Lichfield, May 18th 1735

I hope You will not imagine from my Silence, that I neglected the kind offer which You[r] Brother was pleased to make, that You would take some care about my Books; I had wrote much sooner, but that I did not know till to day whither to direct.

The Books, (of which I have written a Catalogue[3] on the

1. Gilbert Repington (b. *c.* 1713), of Tamworth, near Lichfield, matriculated at Christ Church 7 Dec. 1734. His brother John (b. *c.* 1711) may have known SJ at Oxford: he matriculated at Exeter College in July 1729, and SJ left Pembroke in December (*Johns. Glean.* V.114).

2. The residential ranges of Peckwater Quadrangle, northeast of the main quadrangle, were designed by Dean Henry Aldrich of Christ Church and begun in 1705. Aldrich's three-story building, which is symmetrically divided into sets of rooms, forms three sides of the quadrangle; the library (1716–61) occupies the fourth side (*City of Oxford*, Royal Commission on Historical Monuments, 1939, p. 48).

3. MS: "Catalougue"

other side)[4] were left with Mr. Taylor,[5] from whom I had some reason to expect a regard to my Affairs. There were in the same box, which I left lock'd, some papers of a very private Nature, which I hope fell into good hands. The[6] Books are now, I hear, with Mr. Spicer of Christ[7] Church.[8] I beg You,[9] Dear Sir, that you will be pleased to collect them with what care you can, and transmit them directed to me at the Castle in Birmingham Warwickshire,[10] to which a Carrier goes weekly from Oxford.[11] I will very thankfully repay the expences of Boxes, Porters, and Letters to your Brother, or whoever else You shall think fit to receive 'em. I am sorry to give You this trouble which I hope[12] You'll excuse from a former Schoolfellow. Be pleased to answer this by the next post, for I long to know in what condition my affairs stand. If Mr. Congreve be in college pray pay my compliments[13] to him, and let him know I should think his correspondence a pleasure, and would gladly write to him, if I was inform'd what college he is of.[14] I have many other Acquaintance in the University whom I remember with Pleasure, but shall not trouble You with messages, for I shall esteem You sufficiently kind if You manage this Affair for, Dear Sir, Your humble Servant,

SAM. JOHNSON

My humble Service to Mr. Spicer.

4. The catalogue lists eighty-six items, which are described in detail by A. L. Reade (*Johns. Glean.* v.214–29).

5. *Ante* To John Taylor, 27 July 1732, n. 1. Taylor left Oxford in Sept. 1730 without taking a degree (*Johns. Glean.* v.58).

6. MS: "The" altered from "they"

7. MS: "Chhist"

8. John Spicer (b. *c.* 1714), of Co. Middlesex, matriculated at Christ Church on 20 May 1729 and took his B.A. in Mar. 1732/33. When he received his M.A. in 1735 he was still in residence.

9. MS: "of" del. before "You"

10. MS: period

11. *Ante* To Edward Cave, 25 Nov. 1734, n. 9.

12. MS: undeciphered deletion before "hope"

13. MS: "com" repeated as catchword

14. Richard Congreve (1714–82), son of John Congreve of Stretton, Staffordshire, a first cousin of the dramatist. Congreve matriculated at Christ Church in Mar. 1732/33 and took his B.A. in 1736. His elder brother Charles (1708–77) had been SJ's classmate at the Lichfield Grammar School. *Post* To Richard Congreve, 25 June 1735; 16 Oct. 1755.

Richard Congreve[1]

WEDNESDAY 25 JUNE 1735

MS: Bodleian Library.

ADDRESS: To Mr. Congreve of Ch. Church, Oxford, by London.

POSTMARKS: LITCHFIELD, 27 IV.

ENDORSEMENT: Sam. Johnson 1735.

Dear Sir: Great Haywood,[2] June 25th[3] 1735

The Excess of Ceremony with which You are pleas'd to address an old Acquaintance I should fear would have portended no great Sincerity to[4] our future Correspondence, had You not taken care by a very important kindness to obviate the omen.[5] Our former familiarity which you show in so agreeable a Light was embarrass'd with no forms, and we were content to love without complimenting each other. It was such as well became our rural Retreats, shades unpolluted by Flattery and falsehood, thickets where Interest and Artifice never lay conceal'd! To such an acquaintance I again invite you, and if in your early Life you received any pleasure from my conversation shall now expect You to repay it by a frank and unreserv'd communication of your Judgement, reflexions, and opinions. Solitude is certainly one of the greatest obstacles to pleasure and[6] improvement,[7] and as he may be[8] justly said to be alone, who has none to whom he imparts his thoughts, so he, who has a friend, though distant, with whom he converses without suspicion of being ridicul'd or betray'd, may be truly esteem'd to enjoy the advantages of Society.

It is usual for Friends that have been long separated to en-

1. *Ante* To Gilbert Repington, 18 May 1735, n. 14.

2. See below, n. 16.

3. MS: "25th" altered from "24th"

4. MS: "to" altered from "in"

5. According to A. L. Reade, it is "evident that Congreve must have given material assistance to Gilbert Repington in the despatch of the books, and that that constituted the kind act for which Johnson would not soon forget his obligation" (*Johns. Glean.* v.117–18).

6. MS: "a" superimposed upon "h"

7. "Any company, any employment whatever, he preferred to being alone" (*Life* I.144). Cf. *Post* To Hester Thrale, 21 June 1775.

8. MS: "be" superimposed upon "may"

tertain each other at their first meeting, with an account of that interval of Life which has pass'd since their last interview, a custom,[9] which I hope you will observe, but as little has happen'd to me that You can receive any pleasure from the relation of,[10] I will not trouble you with an account of time not always very agreeably spent, but instead of past disappointments shall acquaint You with my present Scheme of Life.

I am now going to furnish a House in the Country, and keep a private boarding-school for Young Gentlemen whom I shall endeavour to instruct in a method somewhat more rational than those commonly practised, which you know there is no great vanity in presuming to attempt.[11] Before I draw up my plan of Education, I shall attempt[12] to procure an account of the different ways of teaching in[13] use at the most celebrated Schools, and shall therefore hope You will favour me with the method of the Charter-house,[14] and procure me that of Westminster.[15]

It may be written in a few lines by only mentioning under each class their Exercise and Authours.

You see I ask new favours before I have thank'd You for those I have receiv'd, but however I may neglect to express my

9. MS: exclamation mark

10. SJ omits to mention his engagement and impending marriage to Elizabeth Porter. See below, n. 16.

11. SJ did not open his academy at Edial, outside of Lichfield, until late 1735 or early 1736. It attracted only a handful of pupils (Clifford, 1955, pp. 153–57). The school closed *c.* Feb. 1737. For SJ's "Scheme for the Classes of a Grammar School," see *Life* I.99–100.

12. MS: "attempt" superimposed upon undeciphered erasure

13. MS: "in" superimposed upon "at"

14. Charterhouse, Aldersgate, London, was instituted as a charitable school in 1611 for the maintenance and education of forty boys, aged ten to fourteen. The number of foundation scholars was afterwards increased to sixty (Wheatley and Cunningham I.362–65). Congreve was admitted as a scholar in July 1728 (*Johns. Glean.* x.194–95).

15. Westminster School, Dean's Yard, London, was founded in the fourteenth century as part of the great Benedictine monastery of Westminster. It was refounded by Henry VIII after the dissolution of the monastery in 1540. In the 1730s there were about 350 boys in the school (L. E. Tanner, *Westminster School,* 1934, 1951, pp. 13, 49).

gratitude, be assur'd I shall not soon forget my obligation either to Mr. Reppington, or Yourself. I am, Dear Sir, Your humble Servant,

SAM. JOHNSON

Be pleased to direct to me at Tho. Whitby's Esqr. of Great Haywood near Lichfield.[16]

16. In May–June 1735, SJ served as tutor to John Whitby (1716–51), eldest son of Thomas Whitby (?1672–1747), of Great Haywood, Staffordshire (*Johns. Glean.* v.108–13; Clifford, 1955, pp. 149–50). He left the post to marry Elizabeth Porter, 9 July 1735.

Samuel Ford[1]

MID 1735[2]

PRINTED SOURCE: *GM* 1785, p. 266.

I know not well what books to direct you to, because you have not informed me what study you will apply yourself to. I believe it will be most for your advantage to apply yourself wholly to the languages, till you go to the University. The Greek authors I think it best for you to read are these:

Cebes.[3]

Aelian.[4] Attic.

Lucian by Leeds.[5]

1. Samuel Ford (1717–93), SJ's first cousin, matriculated at Trinity College, Oxford, in 1736 and took his B.A. in 1740 from Emmanuel College, Cambridge. In 1742 he became Rector of Brampton Abbotts, Herefordshire (*Johns. Glean.* III.44). The evidence for identifying the recipient of this letter as Ford is set out by A. L. Reade in *TLS*, 18 Sept. 1924, p. 577.

2. "The directions were given by the Doctor at Lichfield (some time about his marriage) to a relative" (*GM* 1785, p. 266).

3. SJ refers to a dialogue called the *pinax* (or *Tabula*), erroneously ascribed to Cebes of Thebes, a pupil of Socrates. This dialogue was probably composed in the first century A.D. During the Renaissance it became a popular school text. SJ's *The Vision of Theodore* (1748) testifies to its influence. For summary and discussion, see *Works*, Yale ed. XVI.

4. Claudius Aelianus (*c.* 170–235), Roman rhetorician and author of the *Varia Historia*.

5. Selections from Lucian's works, 1678, ed. Edward Leedes (1627–1707), schoolmaster and philologist.

Xenophon.	
Homer.	Ionic.
Theocritus.	Doric.
Euripides.	Attic and Doric.

Thus you will be tolerably skilled in all the dialects, beginning with the Attic, to which the rest must be referred.

In the study of Latin, it is proper not to read the later authors, till you are well versed in those of the purest ages; as, Terence, Tully, Caesar, Sallust, Nepos,[6] Velleius Paterculus,[7] Virgil, Horace, Phaedrus.[8]

The greatest and most necessary task still remains, to attain a habit of expression, without which knowledge is of little use. This is necessary in Latin, and more necessary in English; and can only be acquired by a daily imitation of the best and correctest authors.

SAM. JOHNSON

6. Cornelius Nepos (*c.* 99–*c.* 24 B.C.), Roman historian, author of *De Viris Illustribus* in sixteen books.

7. Gaius Velleius Paterculus (*c.* 19 B.C.–A.D. 31), author of the *Historiæ Romanæ*, a compendium in two books.

8. Phaedrus (*c.* 15 B.C.–*c.* A.D. 50), author of beast fables based chiefly on Aesop.

Edward Cave

TUESDAY 12 JULY 1737

MS: Hyde Collection.

Greenwich, next door to the golden Heart, Church Street,[1] July 12th 1737

Sir:

Having observed in Your papers very uncommon offers of encouragement to Men of Letters,[2] I have chosen, being a Stranger in London, to communicate to You the following de-

1. SJ arrived in London *c.* 5 March 1736/37 (*Johns. Glean.* VI.58). Initially, he lived in Exeter Street, off the Strand, but in the summer "retired for some time to lodgings in Greenwich" in order to finish *Irene* (*Life* I.106).

2. *Ante* To Edward Cave, 25 Nov. 1734 and n. 7.

sign, which, I hope, if You join in it, will be of advantage to both of us.

The History of the council of Trent having been lately translated into French, and published with large Notes by Dr. Le Courayer, The Reputation of that Book is so much revived in England, that it is presumed, a new translation of it from the Italian, together with Le Courayer's Notes from the French, could not fail of a favourable Reception.

If it be answered that the History is already in English, it must be remembered, that there was the same objection against Le Courayer's Undertaking, with this disadvantage, that the French had a version by one of their best translators,[3] whereas You cannot read three Pages of the English History, without discovering that the Stile is capable of great Improvements, but whether those improvements are to be expected from this attempt, You must judge from the Specimen which, if You approve the Proposal, I shall submit to your examination.

Suppose the merit of the Versions equal, we may hope that the Addition of the Notes will turn the Ballance in our Favour, considering the Reputation of the Annotator.

Be pleas'd to favour me with a speedy Answer, if You are not willing to engage in this Scheme, and appoint me a day to wait upon You, if You are.[4] I am, Sir, Your humble Servant,

SAM. JOHNSON

3. The *Historia del Concilio Tridentino* by Paolo Sarpi (1552–1623) appeared in 1619. The first English translation, by Sir Nathaniel Brent, was published in 1620, the first French translation, by Amelot de la Houssaye, in 1683. A second French translation, by Pierre François Le Courayer, had appeared the year before this letter was written (1736), dedicated to Queen Caroline.

4. According to James Clifford, "it is reasonable to suppose" that Cave gave SJ "a vague promise of work" (Clifford, 1955, p. 176). By contrast, Thomas Kaminski speaks of "Cave's rejection" (*Early Career of SJ*, 1987, p. 9). The Sarpi project had been revived by the following summer, however, when SJ began his translation. At least six sheets were already in print when the project ground to a halt, stymied by the threats and claims of a rival translator (*Life* 1.135–36; Clifford, 1955, pp. 191–94; Kaminski, *Early Career*, pp. 69–71).

Edward Cave

c. APRIL 1738

PRINTED SOURCE: *GM* 1785, pp. 4–5.

Sir: No. 6, Castle-street,[1] Wednesday Morning

When I took the liberty of writing to you a few days ago, I did not expect a repetition of the same pleasure so soon; for a pleasure I shall always think it to converse in any manner with an ingenious and candid man; but having the inclosed poem in my hands to dispose of for the benefit of the author (of whose abilities I shall say nothing, since I send you his performance), I believed I could not procure more advantageous terms from any person than from you, who have so much distinguished yourself by your generous encouragement of poetry; and whose judgement of that art nothing but your commendation of my trifle can give me any occasion to call in question.[2] I do not doubt but you will look over this poem with another eye, and reward it in a different manner, from a mercenary bookseller, who counts the lines he is to purchase, and considers nothing but the bulk.[3] I cannot help taking notice, that, besides what the author may hope for on account of his abilities, he has likewise another claim to your regard, as he lies at present under very disadvantageous circumstances of fortune. I beg therefore that you will favour me with a letter to-morrow, that I may know what you can afford to allow him, that he may either part with it to you, or find out (which I do not expect) some other way more to his satisfaction.

I have only to add, that as I am sensible I have transcribed it very coarsely, which, after having altered it, I was obliged to do, I will, if you please to transmit the sheets from the press, correct it for you; and will take the trouble of altering any stroke of satire which you may dislike.

1. Castle Street, near Cavendish Square, where SJ continued to rent lodgings until at least 1740 (*Life* III.534).

2. SJ's first contribution to the *GM*, his ode "Ad Urbanum," appeared anonymously in the March issue (1738, p. 156).

3. SJ refers to *London*: *Post* To Edward Cave, *c.* Apr. 1738 and n. 2.

By exerting on this occasion your usual generosity, you will not only encourage learning, and relieve distress, but (though it be in comparison of the other motives of very small account) oblige in a very sensible manner, Sir, your very humble servant,

SAM. JOHNSON

Edward Cave

c. APRIL 1738

MS: Hyde Collection.

ADDRESS: To Mr. Cave at St. John's Gate.

POSTMARK: PENY POST PAYD.

Sir: Monday, No. 6 Castle Street

I am to return You thanks for the present You were so kind as to send by me,[1] and to entreat that You will be pleas'd to inform me by the Penny-post whether You resolve to print the Poem. If You please to send it me by the post with a Note to Dodsley, I will go and read the lines to him, that We may have his Consent to put his name in the Title-page.[2] As to the Printing, if it can be set immediately about, I will be so much the Authours Friend as not to content myself with meer Solicitations in his favour. I propose if[3] my calculations be near the truth to engage[4] for the reimbursement of all that You shall lose by an impression of 500 provided, as You very[5] generously propose, that the profit, if any, be set aside for the Authour's use, excepting the present You made, which, if he be a gainer, it is fit he should repay.[6] I beg that You will let one

1. SJ presumably refers to an advance.

2. Robert Dodsley (1703–64), prominent bookseller at Tully's Head, Pall Mall, published *London* on 13 May 1738. Cave was the printer.

3. MS: "if" altered from "to"

4. MS: "be" del. before "engage"

5. MS: "ve" superimposed upon "pr"

6. In the event, Dodsley purchased the whole copyright for ten guineas. According to SJ, "I might, perhaps, have accepted of less; but that Paul Whitehead had a little before got ten guineas for a poem; and I would not take less than Paul Whitehead" (*Life* I.124).

of Your Servants write an exact account of the expence of such an impression, and send it with the Poem, that I may know what I engage for. I am very sensible from your generosity on this occasion, of your regard to learning even in its unhappiest State, and cannot but think such a temper deserving of the Gratitude of those who suffer so often from a contrary Disposition.[7] I am, Sir, Your most humble Servant,

SAM. JOHNSON

I beg that You will not delay your Answer.

7. MS: comma

Edward Cave

APRIL 1738[1]

MS: Hyde Collection.

Sir:

I waited on You to take the Copy to Dodsley's, as I remember the Number of Lines which it contains it will be longer than Eugenio with the Quotations,[2] which must be subjoined at the bottom of the Page, part of the beauty of the performance (if any beauty be allow'd it) consisting in adapting Juvenals Sentiments to modern facts and Persons.[3] It will with those additions very conveniently make five Sheets.[4] And since the Expence will be no more I shall contentedly insure it, as I mention'd in my last. If it be not therefore gone to Dodsley's I[5] beg

1. Dated on the basis of the reference to *Eugenio* and a note from "J. Bland, St. John's Gate, Ap. 6th 1738" that appears on the verso.

2. *Eugenio, or, Virtuous and Happy Life*, by Thomas Beach (d. 1737), was published by Dodsley in Apr. 1737. John Nichols describes Beach as "a wine-merchant at Wrexham in Denbighshire, a man of learning, of great humanity, of an easy fortune, and much respected. . . . On the 17th of May, 1737, in less than a month after the publication of his poem, he cut his throat with such shocking resolution, that it was reported his head was almost severed from his body" (*GM* 1785, p. 5).

3. *Eugenio* contains 300 lines, *London* 263, but SJ's poem is amplified by 39 quotations from Juvenal's third satire.

4. The first edition comprised 19 folio pages.

5. MS: "it" del. before "I"

it may be sent me by the penny-post that[6] I may have it in the morning. I have compos'd a Greek Epigram to Eliza, and think She ought to be celebrated in as many different Languages[7] as Lewis le Grand.[8] Pray send me word When you will begin upon the Poem, for it is a long way to walk.[9] I would leave my Epigram but have not daylight to transcribe it. I am, Sir, Your etc.

SAM. JOHNSON

6. MS: "tonight" del. before "that"

7. MS: "different" del. before "Languages"

8. "Eliza" was the pseudonym of Elizabeth Carter (1717–1806), poet and translator. SJ's epigram, *Eἰς τὸ τῆς* 'ΕΛΙΣΣΗΣ *περὶ τῶν 'Ονείρων* Aἴνιγμα, appeared in the April issue of the *GM*, along with a Latin translation, "In Elizæ Ænigma" (*Poems*, p. 57). The epigram is an answer to a riddle by Carter that had appeared in the February issue. In the July issue SJ published another epigram in her praise, "Ad Elisam Popi Horto Lauros carpentem"; his translation, "To Eliza plucking Laurel in Mr. Pope's Gardens," appeared in the August issue (*Poems*, pp. 82–83).

9. Presumably from SJ's lodgings in Castle Street, Cavendish Square, to Cave's offices in St. John's Gate.

Edward Cave

LATE APRIL *or* EARLY MAY 1738[1]

PRINTED SOURCE: *GM* 1785, p. 5.

Sir:

I am extremely obliged by your kind letter, and will not fail to attend you to-morrow with Irene, who looks upon you as one of her best friends.[2]

I was to day with Mr. Dodsley, who declares very warmly in favour of the paper you sent him, which he desires to have a share in, it being, as he says, *a creditable thing to be concerned in.*

1. Dated with reference to the three letters that follow and the publication of *London*, 13 May 1738.

2. SJ had completed and revised his tragedy in the spring and summer of 1737. David and Peter Garrick tried unsuccessfully to interest Charles Fleetwood, the patentee of Drury Lane Theatre, in mounting a production. Cave was likewise unable to find a publisher for the play. After becoming manager of Drury Lane, David Garrick produced *Irene* in Feb. 1749. Dodsley paid SJ £100 for the copyright (*Poems*, pp. 273, 276). *Post* To Elizabeth Johnson, 31 Jan. 1740.

I knew not what answer to make till I had consulted you, nor what to demand on the Authour's part, but am very willing that, if you please, he should have a part in it, as he will undoubtedly be more diligent to disperse and promote it.[3] If you can send me word to-morrow what I shall say to him, I will settle matters, and bring the Poem with me for the press, which, as the town empties, we cannot be too quick with. I am, Sir, yours, etc.

SAM. JOHNSON

3. *Ante* To Edward Cave, *c.* Apr. 1738 and n. 2. The first edition of *London* sold out within a week, and a third was called for seven weeks later (*Poems*, p. 63).

Edward Cave

c. AUGUST 1738[1]

MS: Hyde Collection.

ADDRESS: To Mr. Cave at St. John's Gate, London.

Sir: Wednesday

I did not care to detain your Servant while I wrote an answer to your Letter, in which You seem to insinuate that I had promised more than I am ready to perform. If I have raised your Expectations by any thing that may have escap'd my memory I am sorry, and if You remind me of it shall thank you for the favour. If I made fewer alterations than usual in the[2] debates it was only because there appear'd, and still appears to me to be less need of Alteration.[3] The verses on[4] Lady Firebrace may be had when You please, for you know

1. Dated on the basis of internal evidence: the reference to the poem on Lady Firebrace (n. 5) and to work on the translation of Sarpi (n. 8).

2. MS: "th" superimposed upon "an"

3. Because of stringent prohibitions enacted by the House of Commons in Apr. 1738, parliamentary proceedings were reported by the *GM* under the transparent disguise of "Debates in the Senate of Magna Lilliputia." From June 1738 to July 1741, SJ revised the reports of William Guthrie and other assistants employed by Cave; he then wrote them himself until Mar. 1744 (Bloom, pp. 52–59; Thomas Kaminski, *Early Career of SJ*, 1987, pp. 201–3).

4. MS: "on" superimposed upon "to"

that such a subject neither deserves much thought nor requires it.[5] The Chinese Stories may be had folded down when You please to send, in which I do not recollect that You desired any alterations to be made.[6]

An answer to another Query I am very willing to write and had consulted with you about it last night, if there had been time. For I think it the most proper way of inviting such a correspondence, as may be an advantage to the Paper, not a load upon it.

As to the prize verses a backwardness to determine their degrees of merit, is nothing peculiar to me,[7] You may, if you please still have what I can say, but I shall engage with little Spirit in an affair, which I shall *hardly* end to my own Satisfaction, and *certainly* not to the satisfaction of the parties concerned.

As to Father Paul, I have not yet been just to my proposal, but have met with impediments which I hope, are now at an end, and if you find the Progress hereafter not such as You have a right to expect, You can easily stimulate a negligent Translator.[8]

5. SJ's "To Lady F——ce at Bury Assizes," six lines in praise of Bridget Bacon Firebrace's "beauteous mind, and lovely face," appeared in the *GM* for Sept. 1738 (p. 486). Lady Firebrace (1699–1782) was the second wife of Sir Cordell Firebrace, Bt., of Ipswich (*Poems*, p. 83).

6. According to John Nichols, "Du Halde's Description of China was then publishing for Mr. Cave in weekly numbers, whence Johnson was to select pieces for the embellishment of the Magazine" (*GM* 1785, p. 6). Three years before (*GM* 1735, p. 563) Cave had launched a translation of Jean Baptiste Du Halde's *Description géographique . . . de la Chine* (1735). The work, published by subscription, came out in two volumes folio (1738–41). Presumably SJ "folded down" those pages that contained the extracts he had chosen; these were published in *GM* 1742, pp. 320–23, 353–57, and 484–86.

7. In Feb. 1736 Cave had announced a competition for the best poem on "the Divine Attributes" (*GM* 1736, p. 58). Though several entries were published, beginning in Apr. 1737, no winner had been selected by Apr. 1739, when Cave informed his readers that "by Reason of the Difficulty of procuring a Decision from proper Judges . . . it was left to them [the candidates] to vote among themselves, excepting their own Poems" (*GM* 1739, p. 166).

8. *Ante* To Edward Cave, 12 July 1737 and nn. 3, 4. SJ had been receiving payments for the translation since 2 Aug. Six thousand copies of his proposal

If any, or all these have contributed to your discontent, I will endeavour to remove it. And desire you to propose the Question to which You wish for an answer. I am, Sir, Your humble Servant,

SAM. JOHNSON

---

were printed in October. For a description, see J. A.V. Chapple, "Samuel Johnson's Proposals for Printing the History of the Council of Trent," *Bull. Rylands Lib.* 44, 1963, pp. 340–69.

Edward Cave

NOVEMBER 1738[1]

PRINTED SOURCE: Chapman I.13–14.
ADDRESS: To Mr. Cave.

Sir:

I am pretty much of your Opinion, that the Commentary cannot be prosecuted with any appearance of success, for as the names of the Authours concerned are of more weight in the performance than its own intrinsick merit, the Publick will be soon satisfied with it. And I think the Examen should be push'd forward with the utmost expedition.[2] Thus, This day etc. An Examen of Mr. Pope's Essay etc. containing a succinct account of the Philosophy of Mr. Leibnitz on the System of the Fatalists, with a confutation of their Opinions, and an Illustration of the doctrine of Freewil; [with what else you think proper.]

1. Dated on the basis of the publication dates for SJ's Sarpi proposals and the advertisement for Elizabeth Carter's translation of Crousaz. See below, nn. 2–4.

2. SJ refers to two polemical works by Jean Pierre de Crousaz (1663–1750), his hostile *Examen* of Pope's *Essay on Man* and a later *Commentaire*, responding to Warburton's defense of Pope. Elizabeth Carter's translation of the *Examen* was printed by Cave in Nov. 1738; SJ's annotated translation of the *Commentaire* appeared (behind schedule) in 1739. His prediction proved accurate: "Financially the *Commentary* must have been almost as great a loss for Cave as the unfinished version of Father Sarpi" (Clifford, 1955, p. 196). For a full discussion and bibliography, see Bloom, pp. 31–36 and 276 n. 76; Thomas Kaminski, *Early Career of SJ*, 1987, pp. 76–81.

It will above all be necessary to take notice that it is a thing distinct from the Commentary.[3]

I was so far from imagining they stood still that I conceived them to have a good deal beforehand and therefore was less anxious in providing them more.[4] But if ever they stand still on my account, it must doubtless be charged to me, and whatever else shall be reasonable I shall not oppose, but beg a suspense of judgement till Morning, when I must intreat you to send me a dozen Proposals,[5] and you shall then have copy to spare. I am, Sir, Yours, impransus,[6]

SAM. JOHNSON

Pray muster up the proposals if you can, or let the Boy recall them from the Booksellers.

3. Cave's advertisement (*Daily Advertiser*, 23 Nov. 1738) reflects this advice.

4. According to John Nichols, SJ refers to the "compositors in Mr. Cave's printing-office, who appear by this letter to have then waited for copy" (*GM* 1785, p. 7).

5. *Ante* To Edward Cave, *c.* Aug. 1738, n. 8.

6. *impransus*: "without dinner": not necessarily a confession of penury, for "impransus sum" can be translated "I have not (yet) dined." As in other cases documented in the *Life*, this may well have been "no intentional fasting, but [have] happened just in the course of a literary life" (*Life* v.284). For the possibility that "impransus" is a quotation, see Arthur Sherbo, *JN* 13, 1953, p. 12.

Edward Cave

1738[1]

MS: Hyde Collection.

Dear Sir:

You may remember I have formerly talked with You about a military Dictionary. The Eldest Mr. Macbean who was with Mr. Chambers has very good Materials for such a Work which I have seen, and will do it at a very low rate.[2] I think the terms

1. Dated on the basis of SJ's conjectural borrowings from Edward Topsell. See below, n. 3.

2. Alexander Macbean (d. 1784), Scottish lexicographer and librarian, "a man of great learning" (*Life* I.187 n. 3) whom SJ employed on the *Dictionary*, *c.* 1748–54. Though no "military Dictionary" seems to have been published, Macbean did produce *A Dictionary of Ancient Geography* (1773), for which SJ wrote the preface. Pre-

of War and Navigation might be comprised with good explanations in one 8vo pica which he is willing to do for twelve shillings a Sheet, to be made up a Guinea at the second impression.

If You think on it, I will wait on You with him. I am, Sir, Your humble Servant, SAM. JOHNSON

Pray send me Topsel on Animals.[3]

sumably Macbean had been employed by or associated with Ephraim Chambers in the compilation of the *Cyclopædia* (1st ed. 1728, 2d ed. 1738). For an account of SJ's possible indebtedness to Chambers and the parallels between their respective works, see Sledd and Kolb, pp. 19–25.

3. *The Historie of Foure-Footed Beasts* (1607), by Edward Topsell, a mixture of bestiary and natural history. Arthur Sherbo conjectures plausibly that SJ consulted Topsell's *Historie* during the composition of *Marmor Norfolciense* (Apr. 1739). See *Notes and Queries* 197, 1952, pp. 123–24.

Elizabeth Johnson[1]

THURSDAY 31 JANUARY 1740

MS: Hyde Collection.

ADDRESS: To Mrs. Johnson at Mrs. Crow's in Castle Street, near Cavendish Square, London.

POSTMARK: 4 FE.

Dearest Tetty:[2] Jan. 31st 1739/40

After hearing that You[3] are in so much danger, as I apprehend from a hurt on a tendon, I shall be very uneasy till I know that You are recovered, and beg that You will omit nothing that can contribute to it, nor deny Yourself any thing that may make confinement less melancholy. You have already suffered more than I can bear to reflect upon, and I hope

1. Elizabeth Jervis Johnson (1688/89–1752), SJ's wife (m. 1735), was the daughter of William Jervis, a Warwickshire squire. In 1714/15 she married Harry Porter (d. 1734), a Birmingham mercer and woollen draper, by whom she had three children. Mrs. Johnson had been living in London since the autumn of 1737 (Clifford, 1955, p. 177).

2. "Tetty" was a common provincial diminutive of "Elizabeth."

3. MS: "so" del. before "You"

more than either of us shall suffer again.[4] One part at least I[5] have often flatterd myself we shall avoid for the future our troubles will surely never separate us more. If M⟨*five or six letters*⟩[6] does not easily succeed in his endeavours, let him not ⟨scruple⟩ to call in another Surgeon to consult with him, Y⟨ou may⟩ have two or three visits from Ranby or Shipton,[7] who is ⟨said⟩ to be the best, for a Guinea, which You need not fear to part with on so pressing an occasion, for I can send You twenty pouns more on Monday, which I have received this night;[8] I beg therefore that You will more[9] regard my happiness, than to expose Yourself to any hazards.[10] I still promise myself many happy years from your tenderness and affection, which I sometimes hope our misfortunes have not yet deprived me of. David[11] wrote to me this day on the affair of Irene,[12] who is at last become a kind of Favourite among the Players, Mr. Fletewood[13] promises to give a[14] promise in writing that it shall be the first next season, if it cannot be introduced now, and Chetwood the Prompter[15] is desirous of bargaining for

4. Presumably these sufferings included the failure of Edial Academy, in which SJ had invested much of his wife's fortune, as well as their various separations since his first trip to London, Mar. 1737.

5. MS: "We" del. before "I"

6. MS: right-hand margin mutilated

7. Both John Ranby (1703–73) and John Shipton (1680–1748) were eminent London surgeons, whose patients included various members of the Royal Family.

8. SJ and his mother Sarah had just mortgaged the family house on Market Square, Lichfield, to Theophilus Levett, who advanced the Johnsons £80 on the property. *Post* To Theophilus Levett, 1 Dec. 1743 and n. 3.

9. MS: "be" del. before "more"

10. MS: "diffi" del. before "hazards"

11. David Garrick (1717–79), actor, dramatist, and theatre manager, SJ's former pupil at Edial Academy. Garrick had ventured to London with SJ in 1737 and established a wine business in partnership with his brother Peter. Though he did not make his professional stage debut until Oct. 1741, "once he was resident in London he sought the company of actors, and he was welcomed in the green rooms of both Drury Lane and Covent Garden" (*Letters of David Garrick*, ed. D. M. Little and G. M. Kahrl, 1963, I.xxxi).

12. *Ante* To Edward Cave, Late Apr. or Early May 1738, n. 2.

13. Charles Fleetwood (d. 1747/48), patentee of Drury Lane Theatre (1734–46).

14. MS: "a" altered from "it"

15. William Rufus Chetwood (d. 1766), author of *A General History of the Stage* (1749). On the title page of the *History* he describes himself as having been for twenty years prompter at Drury Lane.

the copy, and offers fifty Guineas for the right of printing after it shall be played. I hope it will at length reward me for my perplexities.[16]

Of the time which I have spent from thee,[17] and of my dear Lucy and other affairs,[18] my heart will be at ease on Monday to give a particular account,[19] especially if a Letter should inform me that thy[20] leg is better, for I hope You do not think so unkindly of me as to imagine that I can be at rest while I believe my dear Tetty in pain.

Be assured, my dear Girl, that I have seen nobody in these rambles upon which I have been forced, that has not contribute[d] to confirm my esteem and affection for thee, though that esteem and affection only contributed to encrease my unhappiness when I reflected that the most amiable woman in the world was exposed by my means to miseries which I could not relieve. I am, My charming Love, Yours,

SAM. JOHNSON

Lucy always sends her Duty and my Mother her Service.

16. MS: "vex" del. before "perplexities"

17. Sometime in Aug. 1739, SJ left his wife in London and went first to Leicestershire in search of a schoolmaster's post, then to Lichfield and environs, where he apparently remained until the early spring of 1740. According to Clifford, "there is nothing to suggest that once the mortgage on his birthplace was settled Johnson hurried to comfort Tetty and see about his play. It may not have been until late March or early April that he finally reached the capital" (Clifford, 1955, pp. 223–24).

18. Lucy Porter (1715–86), Tetty's daughter, who helped SJ's mother in the running of the Lichfield bookshop.

19. MS: period

20. MS: "thy" written above "your" del.

Lewis Paul[1]

SATURDAY 31 JANUARY 1741

MS: Birmingham Public Library.

1. Lewis Paul (d. 1759), inventor and promoter, was a ward of the third Earl of Shaftesbury. In June 1738 he received a patent for a roller-spinning machine and set up a cotton mill at Birmingham with the financial backing of Dr. James,

Sir: St. John's Gate, Jan. 31st 1740/41

Dr. James[2] presses me with great warmth to remind You of your promise that You would exert your interest with Mr. Warren to bring their affairs to a speedy conclusion;[3] this You know, Sir, I have some right to insist upon, as Mr. Cave was in some degree diverted from attending to the arbitration by my assiduity in expediting the agreement between You, but I do not imagine many Arguments[4] necessary to prevail upon Mr. Warren to do what seems to be no less desired by Him than by the Doctor.

If he entertains any Suspicion that I shall endeavour to enforce the Doctor's arguments, I am willing, and more than barely willing to forbear all mention of the Question. He that desires only to do right can oblige nobody by acting, and must offend every man that expects favours. It is[5] perhaps for this reason that Mr. Cave seems very much inclined to resign the office of Umpire. And since I know not whom to propose in his place equally qualified and disinterested, and am yet desired to propose s⟨omeone,⟩ I believe the most eligible method of determining ⟨this⟩ vexatious affair will be that each Party should draw up in a narrow compass his own state[6] of the case and his demand upon the other, and each abate somewhat of which himself or his friends may think due to him by the Laws of rigid Justice. This will seem a tedious method, but will I hope be shortned by the desire so often expressd on each side

Thomas Warren, Edward Cave, and Elizabeth Swynfen. The mill failed a few years later (Clifford, 1955, pp. 232–33, 342 n. 10; Waingrow, p. 89 n. 25).

2. Robert James (1705–76), M.D., inventor of the famous "fever powders," had been SJ's schoolmate at Lichfield. SJ collaborated on the proposals for, wrote the dedication of, and contributed entries to James's *Medicinal Dictionary,* 1743 (Hazen, pp. 68–73).

3. Thomas Warren (d. 1767), printer and bookseller in Birmingham, had published SJ's *A Voyage to Abyssinia* in 1734 (*Works,* Yale ed. xv.xxiii–xxvi; *Johns. Glean.* v.93–94). In 1743 Warren, who contributed £1,000 to Paul's enterprise, went bankrupt as a result of his involvement in the mill (Hill I.6–7 n. 3).

4. MS: "A" superimposed upon "p"

5. MS: "It is" superimposed upon undeciphered erasure

6. MS: "s" superimposed upon "th"

of a speedy determination. If either party can make use of me in this transaction, in which there is no opportunity for malevolence or prejudice to exert themselves I shall be well satisfied[7] with the employment.

Mr. Cave who knows to whom I am writing desires me to mention his Interest, of which I need not remind You that it is complicated with yours, and therefore cannot be neglected by You without opposition to motives far stronger than the persuasions of, Sir, Your humble Servant,

SAM. JOHNSON

7. MS: "ple" partially erased before "satisfied"

Lewis Paul

TUESDAY 31 MARCH 1741

MS: Birmingham Public Library.

ADDRESS: To Mr. Paul in Birmingham.

POSTMARK: 31 MR.

At the black Boy over against
Durham Yard,[1] Strand, March 31st 1741

Sir:

The hurry of removing and some other hindrances have kept me from writing to You since You left us, nor should I have allowed myself the pleasure of doing it now, but that the Doctor has pressed me to offer You a new proposal,[2] which I know not why he do's not rather make himself, but his request whatever be the Reason of it is too small to be denied. He proposes

1. To pay You immediately or give You satisfactory security for the speedy payment of 100£.
2. To exchange general Releases with Mr. Warren.

These proposals he makes upon the Conditions formerly offerred, That the bargain for Spindles shall be vacated. The

1. Durham Yard, on the river side of the Strand, where SJ rented lodgings before moving to Bow Street (*Life* III.535). David Garrick kept his stock in the Yard during his short-lived career as a wine merchant (Wheatley and Cunningham I.543–44). The site was subsequently occupied by the Adelphi (1768).

2. *Ante* To Lewis Paul, 31 Jan. 1741.

Securities for Mr. Warrens Debts released, and the debt of[3] 65£ remitted with the addition of this new article that Mr. Warren shall give him the Books bought for the carrying on of their joint undertaking.[4] What difference this new demand may make I cannot tell nor do I intend to be understood in these proposals to express any of my own sentiments, but merely to write after a dictator.

I believe I have expressed the Doctor's meaning, but being disappointed of an interview with him cannot show him[5] this, and he generally hints his intentions somewhat obscurely.

He is very impatient for an answer, and desired[6] me to importune You for one by the return of the post. I am not willing in this affair to request any thing on my own account, for You know already that an agreement can only be made by a communication of your thoughts and a speedy agreement only by an expeditious communication.

I hope to write soon on some more agreeable Subject, for though perhaps a man cannot easily find more pleasing[7] employment than that of reconciling variances, he may certainly amuse himself better, by any other business, than that of interposing in controversies which grow every [day] more distant from accommodation, which has been hitherto my fate but I hope my endeavour will be hereafter more successful. I am, Sir, Your etc.

SAM. JOHNSON

3. MS: "for" del. before "of"

4. According to the sale catalogue of the Paul Papers, 29 July 1867, "Dr. James and Warren appear to have contracted, James to supply pills and vulnerary balsam, and Warren to publish in numbers *The Rational Farmer*, with an *Herbal*; and also the *American Traveller*, of which book Dr. James would seem to have been the author" (Hill I.8 n. 3). Since most of the Paul MSS burned in 1879, nothing more is known of "their joint undertaking."

5. MS: "it" del. before "him"

6. MS: "desired" altered from "desires"

7. MS: "pleasing" superimposed upon "useful"

John Taylor

TUESDAY 10 AUGUST 1742

MS: Berg Collection, New York Public Library.

ADDRESS: To the Revd. Dr. Taylor at Market Bosworth, Leicestershire.

POSTMARKS: 10 AV, TP.

ENDORSEMENTS: 10 June 42, Johnson 42.

Dear Sir: June[1] 10,[2] 1742

The Brevity of your last Letter gives me expectation[3] of a longer and I hope You will not disappoint me, for I am always pleased to hear of your proceedings. I cannot but somewhat wonder that Seward should give his Living for the prospects or advantages which You can offer him,[4] and should be glad to know your treaty more particularly. I think it not improper to mention that there is a slight report of an intention to Make Lord Chesterfield Lieutenant, of which, if I hear more, I will inform You farther.[5]

I propose to get Charles of Sweden ready for this winter, and shall therefore, as I imagine be much engaged for some Months with the Dramatic Writers into whom I have scarcely looked for many years.[6] Keep Irene close, You may send it back at your leisure.[7]

You have never let me know what You do about Mr. Car's

1. A mistake for "August": see postmark.

2. MS: "10" written above "20" del.

3. MS: "expectatation"

4. The Rev. Thomas Seward (1708–90), Rector of Eyam, Derbyshire, and Canon of Lichfield.

5. Sir Robert Walpole fell from power in Feb. 1742. Though he had worked vigorously to undermine Walpole's ministry, Lord Chesterfield was excluded from the new administration, headed by Lord Carteret and the Duke of Newcastle. John Taylor's patron, the third Duke of Devonshire, continued to serve as Lord-Lieutenant of Ireland until 1744, when he was succeeded by Chesterfield, who took up the post in 1745.

6. SJ's scheme for a play on "Swedish Charles" never materialized. His reading, not of "the Dramatic Writers" but of Voltaire's *Histoire de Charles XII*, is reflected in the portrait of the King that appears in *The Vanity of Human Wishes* (ll. 191–222).

7. *Ante* To Edward Cave, Late Apr. or Early May 1738, n. 2.

affair or what the Official has decided.[8] Eld is only neglected not forgotten.[9]

If the time of the Dukes government should be near expiration You must cling close and redouble your importunities,[10] though if any confidence can be placed in his Veracity, he may be expected to serve You more effectually when he is only[11] a Courtier, than while he has so much power in another Kingdom.[12]

I am well informed that a few days ago Cardinal Fleury sent to an eminent Banker for Money and receiving such a reply as the present low state of France naturally produces,[13] sent a party of the Guards to examine his Books and search his House, such is the felicity of absolute Governments, but they found the Banker no better provided than he had represented himself, and therefore broke part of his furniture and returned.[14]

It is reported that the peace between Prussia and[15] Hungary was produced wholly by the address of Carteret, who having procured a copy of Broglio's orders at the very time that they were despatched, and[16] finding them to contain instructions very inconsistent with a sincere alliance sent them immediately to the King of Prussia, who did not much regard

8. *Post* To John Taylor, 2 Jan. 1743 and n. 5.

9. Possibly John Eld (?1704–96), of Dorking, Surrey, and Seighford, Staffordshire.

10. "It is likely that Taylor hoped to receive from the Duke one of the valuable Irish deaneries or bishoprics which were so commonly given to Englishmen" (Hill I.12 n. 1).

11. MS: "not" del. before "only"

12. MS: entire paragraph scored through by Taylor

13. MS: "produces" altered from "produced"

14. André Hercule de Fleury (1653–1743), Louis XV's tutor, served as first minister from his elevation to the cardinalate in 1726 until his death. The slow improvement in the French economy that had begun under the Regency of the Duc d'Orléans and continued during the first decade of Fleury's ministry was first checked and then reversed by the War of the Austrian Succession (1740–48), during which the government was driven "to every possible expedient for filling the Treasury" (E. C. Lodge, *Sully, Colbert, and Turgot*, 1931, pp. 173–74; see also Ernest Labrousse et al., *Histoire Economique et Sociale de la France*, 1970, II.386–87).

15. MS: "and" superimposed upon "wa"

16. MS: "and" written above "sent" del.

them, till he found that he was in persuance of them exposed without assistance to the hazard, of the late [17] battle, in which it is generally believed that he [18] lost more than twice as many as the Austrians. He would then trust the French no longer.[19]

You see I am determined to write a letter, for I never was authour of so much political Intelligence before.

I am, if the relief of uneasiness can produce obligations, more obliged to You for what I imagine You have now sent Miss,[20] than for all that You have hitherto done for me.

Thurloes papers which cost here 8£ 9s 6p are intended to be reprinted in Ireland at four Guineas [21] methinks You should send orders to Faulkner to subscribe.[22] I am, Dear Sir, Your very affectionate etc.

SAM. JOHNSON

Have You begun to write out your Letters?

17. MS: "of the late" written above "and in reality" del.

18. MS: "he" altered from "his"

19. SJ summarizes a report in the *GM* (July 1742, p. 389) concerning the diplomatic intrigue between the Battle of Czaslau or Chotusitz (17 May 1742) and the signing of the Preliminaries of Breslau (11 June 1742). At Czaslau, near Prague, the Prussian army under Frederick II defeated the Austrians under Charles of Lorraine; both sides suffered heavy losses. During the battle, the French army under the command of the Maréchal de Broglie remained in Prague. According to the report in the *GM*, Broglie had been ordered not to come to the aid of the Prussians, and a copy of those orders fell into Frederick's hands, thereby exposing "the Treachery of France." Another version of the story involves a letter from Cardinal Fleury to Maria Theresa, which was shown to Frederick by a dying Austrian general (Thomas Carlyle, *History of Frederick the Great*, centenary ed., IV.352–53). Neither version mentions Lord Carteret, who had been urging the Queen and Frederick to make peace with each other in the interests of detaching the Prussians from the French. The Preliminaries ceded Silesia to Prussia in return for Frederick's withdrawal from the war (Basil Williams, *Carteret and Newcastle*, 1943, pp. 126–30).

20. *Ante* To Elizabeth Johnson, 31 Jan. 1740, n. 18.

21. "A Collection of the State Papers of John Thurloe, Esq; Secretary to Oliver Cromwell, etc. pr. 8l. 14s. in Sheets" ("Register of Books," *GM* 1742, p. 280).

22. George Faulkner (?1699–1775), Dublin printer and bookseller.

John Taylor

SUNDAY 2 JANUARY 1743

MS: Hyde Collection.

ADDRESS: To the Revd. Dr. Taylor at Market Bosworth, Leicestershire.

POSTMARK: 2 IA.

ENDORSEMENTS: 1743, Johnson 43.

Dear Sir: Janry. 2nd 1742/3

Soon after I received your last Letter, Mrs. Johnson was seized with such an illness,[1] having not been well for some time before as will easily make You excuse my neglect at answering You, I believe it is now the twelfth Week since she was taken with it, and last thursday she walked about [her] Chamber for the first time.—I never saw any body do so much that did or did not recover.

David Garric[k] sent Me Your Letter, but as I said to him You must make your own Apologies.

I know not whether it will be thought by You worth your while to write to the Duke,[2] who perhaps should know [of] your Letter, yet surely he seemed not to be s⟨*two or three words*⟩[3] you in peace, if any Method could be ⟨found⟩ of reminding him of his obligations and his ⟨*one word*⟩.

You inform [me] that You have concluded your contract with Sir Wulstan,[4] but make no mention of John Car's affair.[5]

1. The nature of this illness has not been determined. Cf. *Ante* To Elizabeth Johnson, 31 Jan. 1740; *Post* To Lucy Porter, 12 July 1749 and n. 5.

2. John Taylor's principal patron was William Cavendish (?1698–1755), third Duke of Devonshire. Cf. *Ante* To John Taylor, 10 Aug. 1742 and n. 5.

3. MS: entire paragraph heavily scored through

4. *Ante* To John Taylor, 27 July 1732, n. 6.

5. Possibly the Rev. John Carr (*c.* 1709–76), Rector of Ashby Folvile, Leicestershire, from 1749 until his death. "Tradition states, this presentation was purchased by Mr. Carr, for £1000" (John Nichols, *History of Leicestershire*, 1811, III.32–33). Given the context, it is likely that this "affair" involved the buying or selling of a living or another kind of ecclesiastical preferment.

I suppose Bosworth is now less desirable,[6] and that You will not desire an exchange for ⟨*two or three words*⟩.[7]

Mr. Stephens's proposal surely deserves no Answer,[8] he deals with You as if he was selling You a reprieve, when he is really purchasing one for himself, whoever can get what he requires may probably much more easily get a Prebend.[9]

Except Mrs. Johnson's Illness which is, I hope, now almost through and nothing very[10] ill has happened to Me, which I know You will be pleased to hear.

Pray make my Compliments to Mrs. Taylor[11]—You may Always direct immediately to me without any apprehension that I should miss it for if I change my Lodgings I will Give You notice. I am, Dear Sir, Yours etc.

SAM. JOHNSON

6. Taylor "was presented to the valuable Rectory of Market Bosworth in 1740, on the death of Mr. Beaumont Dixie" (*Lit. Anec.* IX.58). He held the living until his death.

7. MS: undeciphered deletion

8. Possibly the Rev. Robert Stephens (b. *c.* 1705), subsequently (1760–76) Rector of Eastington, Gloucestershire.

9. "In addition to the rectory of Market Bosworth he [Taylor] acquired a prebend of Westminster in 1746, the preachership of the chapel in the Broadway, Westminster in 1740, the rectory of Lawford in Essex in 1751, the perpetual curacy of St. Botolph's, Aldersgate in 1769 . . . and the rectory of St. Margaret's, Westminster in 1784" (Thomas Taylor, *Life of Dr. John Taylor*, 1910, p. 18).

10. MS: "mu" del. before "very"

11. Taylor married his first wife, Elizabeth Webb (d. 1745/46) of Croxall, Derbyshire, in 1732 (*Lit. Anec.* IX.58; *Johns. Glean.* V.81).

"*Mr. Urban*"

AUGUST 1743

PRINTED SOURCE: *GM* 1743, p. 416.

Mr. Urban:

As your Collections show how often you have owed the Ornaments of your poetical Pages, to the Correspondence of the unfortunate and ingenious Mr. *Savage*,[1] I doubt not but you

1. Richard Savage (?1697 – 1 Aug. 1743), poet and dramatist, putative son of

have so much regard to his Memory as to encourage any design that may have a tendency to the Preservation of it from Insults or Calumnies, and therefore with some Degree of Assurance intreat you to inform the Publick, that his Life will speedily be published by a Person who was favoured with his Confidence,[2] and received from himself an Account of most of the Transactions which he proposes to mention to the Time of his Retirement to *Swansey* in *Wales*.[3]

From that Period to his Death in the prison of *Bristol*, the Account will be continued from materials still less liable to Objection, his own Letters and those of his Friends; some of which will be inserted in the Work, and Abstracts of others subjoined in the Margin.[4]

It may be reasonably imagined that others may have the same Design, but as it is not credible that they can obtain the same Materials, it must be expected they will supply from Invention the want of Intelligence, and that under the Title of the Life of *Savage* they will publish only a Novel filled with romantick Adventures, and imaginary Amours.[5] You may therefore perhaps gratify the Lovers of Truth and Wit by giving me leave to inform them in your Magazine, that my Account will be published in 8vo by Mr. *Roberts* in *Warwick-lane*.[6]

Earl Rivers and the Countess of Macclesfield. His poems had been appearing in the *GM* since Aug. 1733 (Clarence Tracy, *The Artificial Bastard*, 1953, p. 119).

2. SJ first met Savage in 1737 or 1738, probably at St. John's Gate (Tracy, *The Artificial Bastard*, p. 133). By the spring of 1739 they had become intimate friends (Bloom, p. 77).

3. Savage left London in July 1739. He remained in Swansea for over a year, but then moved to Bristol, contrary to the wishes of the friends who were supporting him (Tracy, *The Artificial Bastard*, pp. 139, 144).

4. For a thorough discussion of SJ's sources and his handling of them, see *Life of Savage*, ed. Clarence Tracy, 1971, pp. xi–xvi.

5. No other contemporary biographies of Savage have been recorded.

6. The first edition appeared in Feb. 1744, "Printed for J. Roberts, in Warwick-Lane" by Edward Cave (Tracy, *Life of Savage*, pp. xxi, xxv; J. D. Fleeman, "The Making of Johnson's *Life of Savage*, 1744," *The Library* 22, 1967, p. 350). James Roberts (*c.* 1669–1754) also published SJ's *Miscellaneous Observations on the Tragedy of Macbeth* (1745).

Edward Cave

AUTUMN 1743[1]

MS: Hyde Collection.

ADDRESS: To Mr. Cave.

Sir:

I believe I am going to write a long Letter, and have therefore taken a whole Sheet of Paper. The first thing to be written about is our Historical Design.[2]

You mentioned the proposal of printing in Numbers as an alteration in the Scheme, but I believe You mistook some way or other, my meaning, I had no other view than that You might rather print too many of five Sheets than of five and thirty.

With regard to what I shall say on the manner of proceeding, I would have it understood as wholly indifferent to me, and my opinion only not my Resolution. *Emptoris sit eligere*.[3]

I think the insertion of the exact dates of the most important events in the margin or of so many events as may enable the reader to regulate the order of facts with sufficient exactness the proper medium between a Journal which has regard only to time, and a history which ranges facts according to their dependence on each other, and postpones or anticipates according to the convenience of narration. I think our work ought to partake of the spirit of History which is contrary to minute exactness, and of the regularity of a Journal which is inconsistent with Spirit. For this Reason I neither admit numbers or dates nor reject them.

I[4] am of your opinion with regard to placing most of the resolutions etc. in the Margin, and think we shall give the most complete account of Parliamentary proceedings that [can] be

1. Dated on the basis of the references to SJ's work on the *Life of Savage*. *Ante* To "Mr. Urban," Aug. 1743.

2. "Johnson was now engaged in preparing an historical account of the British Parliament" (*Life* 1.155). Nothing further is known of this project.

3. *Emptoris sit eligere*: "Let the buyer choose."

4. MS: "In" del. before "I"

contrived. The Naked Papers without an[5] Historical treatise interwoven, require some other Book to make them understood. I will date the succeeding parts with some exactness but, I think in the margin. You told me on Saturday that I had received money on this work and I find set down 13£ 2–6. reckoning the half Guinea, of last Saturday, as You hinted to me that you had many calls for Money, I would *not* press You too hard, and therefore shall desire only as I send it in two Guineas for a Sheet of Copy the rest You may pay me when it may be more convenient, and even by this[6] Sheet payment I shall for some time be very expensive.

The Life of Savage I am ready to go upon and in great Primer and Pica Notes reckon on[7] sending in half a Sheet a day,[8] but the money for that shall likewise lye by in your hands till it is done.[9]

With the debates shall I not have business enough?[10] If I had but good Pens.—Towards Mr. Savage's Life what more have You got? I would willingly have his tryal etc.[11] and know

5. MS: "Papers without an" written above "Speeches etc. without" del.

6. MS: "this" altered from "that"

7. MS: "on" written above "of" del.

8. The text of the first edition of SJ's *Life of Savage* is printed in Caslon English Roman, but set on a body or leaded so as to approximate Great Primer: the number of characters per page is therefore less than it would have been in English Roman, but more than in Great Primer. The notes are printed in pica (T. B. Reed, *A History of the Old English Letter Foundries*, 1952, pp. 27–36; James Mosley, "A Specimen of Printing Types by William Caslon 1766," *Journal of the Printing Historical Society* 16, 1981–82, pp. 24, 108, and facsimile of "Long Bodied English Roman"; information from Mr. Mark Argetsinger). SJ forecasts a measured schedule of production that is belied by his report to JB: "I wrote forty-eight of the printed octavo pages of the Life of Savage at a sitting" (*Life* v.67). J. D. Fleeman hypothesizes that, having gained access to new material, SJ hurriedly had to rewrite the second section early in 1744 ("The Making of Johnson's *Life of Savage*, 1744," *The Library* 22, 1967, pp. 346–52).

9. On 14 Dec. 1743, SJ received fifteen guineas from Cave "for compiling and writing the Life of Richd. Savage Esq." (*Life* I.165 n. 1).

10. *Ante* To Edward Cave, *c.* Aug. 1738, n. 3.

11. Either *The Proceedings at Justice Hall in the Old Bailey* (1727) or *The Old Bailey Sessions Papers* (1727) or *Select Trials for Murders . . . in the Old Bailey* (1735) (Clarence Tracy, *The Artificial Bastard*, 1953, pp. 83–84; *Life of Savage*, ed. C. Tracy, 1971, pp. xv–xvi).

whether his Defence be at Bristol,[12] and would have his Collection of Poems on account of the Preface[13]—The Plain Dealer[14]—All the Magazins that have any thing of his or relating to him. I thought my Letter would be long but it is now, ended and I am, Sir, Your etc.

SAM. JOHNSON

The Boy found me writing this, almost in the dark, when I could not quite easily read yours, I have reade the Latin—nothing in it is well.—

I had no notion of having any thing for the Inscription, I hope You don't think I kept it to extort a price.[15] I could think on Nothing till today. If You could spare me another Guinea for the Hist. I should take it very kindly tonight, but if You do not shall not think it an injury—I am almost well again—

12. "There is no evidence that, if such a document [as Savage's "defence"] ever existed, Johnson saw it" (Tracy, *Life of Savage*, p. 33 n. 29).

13. Savage's "Preface" to his *Miscellaneous Poems* (1726).

14. SJ drew on Aaron Hill's *Plain Dealer*, Nos. 28 (26 June 1724) and 73 (30 Nov. 1724) (Tracy, *Life of Savage*, p. 25 n. 22).

15. Possibly the "Epitaph on the late R——d S——e, Esq" (*GM* 1743, p. 490).

Thomas Birch[1]

THURSDAY 29 SEPTEMBER 1743

MS: British Library.

ADDRESS: To ⟨the Revd. Mr. Birch⟩.

ENDORSEMENT: 29 Sept. 1743.

Sir: Thursday, Septr. 29th 1743[2]

I hope You will excuse Me for troubling You on an occasion

1. Thomas Birch (1705–66), D.D., F.R.S., literary scholar and biographer, advisor to the staff of the *GM* and editor of the *Biographia Britannica* and the *General Dictionary*. SJ had published anonymously a Greek epigram in praise of Birch (*GM* 1738, p. 654). For an authoritative profile, see Clifford, 1955, p. 180. Birch is identified as the addressee by John Nichols (*GM* 1785, p. 7) and by JB (*Life* I.160).

2. MS: "1743" in Birch's hand

on which I know not whom else I can apply to.[3] I am at a loss for the Lives and Characters of Earl Stanhope,[4] the two Craggs[e]s,[5] and the Minister Sunderland,[6] and beg that You will inform where I may find them, and send any Pamp[h]lets etc. relating to them to Mr. Cave,[7] to be perused for a few days by, Sir, Your most humble Servant,

SAM. JOHNSON

3. SJ was working on a history of the British Parliament. *Ante* To Edward Cave, Autumn 1743, n. 2.

4. James Stanhope (1673–1721), first Earl Stanhope, one of Marlborough's most successful generals, twice Secretary of State (1714–17, 1718–21), and First Lord of the Treasury (1717–18).

5. James Craggs the Elder (1657–1721), businessman, speculator, and financier, was implicated in the scandal of the South Sea Bubble (1720). His son, James the Younger (1686–1721), was a close friend of Pope, who wrote his epitaph in Westminster Abbey ("Statesman, yet Friend to Truth! of Soul Sincere"). Craggs served as Addison's literary executor and succeeded him as Secretary of State in 1718 (Peter Smithers, *Joseph Addison*, 1954, pp. 371, 407; Pope, *Minor Poems*, ed. Norman Ault, 1954, pp. 281–83).

6. Charles Spencer (1674–1722), third Earl of Sunderland, diplomat, statesman, and bibliophile, served as Secretary of State (1706–10) and First Lord of the Treasury (1718–21). In 1721 he was forced by public pressure to resign this post to Robert Walpole, after admitting that he held fictitious stock in the South Sea Company.

7. *Ante* To Edward Cave, 25 Nov. 1734, n. 1.

Theophilus Levett[1]

THURSDAY 1 DECEMBER 1743

MS: Hyde Collection.

ADDRESS: To Mr. Levett in Lichfield.

POSTMARK: 1 DE.

At Mr. Osborne's
Bookseller in Grey's Inn,[2] Decr. 1, 1743

Sir:

I am extremely sorry that We have encroached so much upon your Forbearance with respect to the Interest, which a great

1. Theophilus Levett (1693–1746), Lichfield attorney and Town Clerk (1721–46), who had helped SJ to a post as private tutor to John Whitby (*Ante* To Richard Congreve, 25 June 1735, n. 16; *Johns. Glean.* iv.182, 190).

2. Thomas Osborne (d. 1767), publisher of the *Medicinal Dictionary*, had pur-

Perplexity of affairs hindred me from thinking of with that attention that I ought, and which I am not immediately able to remit to You, but will pay it (I think twelve pounds) in two Months.[3] I look upon this and on the future Interest of that Mortgage as my own Debt, and beg that You will be pleased to give me directions how to pay it, and not mention it to my dear Mother. If it be necessary to pay this in less time, I believe I can do it, but I take two Months for certainty, and beg an Answer whether You can allow me so much time.[4] I think myself very much obliged by Your Forbearance, and shall esteem it a great happiness to be able to serve You. I have great opportunities of dispersing any thing that You may think it proper to make publick.

I will give a Note for the Money payable at the time mentioned to any one here that You shall appoint. I am, Sir, Your most obedient and most humble Servant,

SAM. JOHNSON

---

chased the library of Lord Oxford in 1742 and employed SJ (together with William Oldys) to compile a *catalogue raisonné* of the books and pamphlets. Volumes I–II of the *Catalogus Bibliothecæ Harleianæ*, covering 15,242 works, appeared in Mar. 1743; Volumes III–IV (20,724 titles) were published in Jan. 1744. In Dec. 1743 SJ was assisting in the preparation of the *Harleian Miscellany*, a series of rare pamphlets that appeared in weekly installments, 1744–46 (Hawkins, pp. 132–49; Clifford, 1955, pp. 256–59). According to SJ, "Osborne was a man entirely destitute of shame, without sense of any disgrace but that of poverty" (*Lives of the Poets* III.187). For SJ's celebrated assault on Osborne, see *Life* I.154, 534.

3. For the Johnsons' mortgage, *Ante* To Elizabeth Johnson, 31 Jan. 1740, n. 8. Interest was fixed at 4.5 percent. For a complete text of the mortgage deed, see *Johns. Glean.* IV.8–9. The mortgage was not paid off until 27 June 1757 (*Johns. Glean.* IV.11). SJ raised the requisite twelve pounds from his friend Henry Hervey Aston (*Post* To John Levett, 17 Mar. 1752; letters to John Levett in Appendix I).

4. Levett responded favorably: *Post* To Theophilus Levett, 3 Jan. 1744.

Theophilus Levett

TUESDAY 3 JANUARY 1744

PRINTED SOURCE: Hill I.14–15.

ADDRESS: To Mr. Levett in Lichfield.

To THEOPHILUS LEVETT, 3 *January* 1744

Sir: Jan. 3, 1743/4

I am obliged to trouble you upon an affair which I have hardly time to explain, but in which I must beg that you will assist as a few words will enable you to understand it better than I do; and the Humanity and Generosity which appeared in your last letter give me no reason to doubt of your Compliance with my Request.

When I married Mrs. Johnson who was her first husband's executrix, we by the advice of his chief Creditor made a Resignation (I suppose legal) of all his affairs to Mr. Perks an Attorney of Birmingham. Soon afterwards Mr. Perks died, as was supposed, without any effects, and therefore We thought no more of the affair, but were lately accidentally informed that a Composition is offered, and then I wrote to Birmingham for Directions how to act, and received yesterday a Letter by which I am informed that the accounts are to be irrevocably settled on Thursday.[1] Having not the papers at London, there is great danger, as I apprehend, that they cannot arrive soon enough. I have however sent Miss Porter directions to open a Cabinet,[2] and bring it to you, and beg that you will find a Messenger to make the Demand in form.

Be pleased to inform Me where I may see you when you come to town, for not to have the satisfaction of waiting upon one for whom, on account of a long series of kindness to my Father and myself, I have so much Respect will be a great and uneasy Disappointment to, Sir, Your most humble Servant,

SAM. JOHNSON

1. Harry Porter (1691–1734), Elizabeth Johnson's first husband and a Birmingham mercer, died insolvent. However, by the terms of her marriage settlement his wife inherited £600; £100 of this sum was loaned to Thomas Perks, "Attorney of Birmingham." When Perks died in 1745, also insolvent, his creditors compounded with Mrs. Perks for 7*s.* 4*d.* in the pound—the "Composition" to which SJ refers. Accordingly, the Johnsons were owed £36.13.4. Their signatures do not appear on the official release, which suggests that they never received the money (*Johns. Glean.* VI.32–35, VII.87–94; *Life* I.95–96 n. 3, 530).

2. *Ante* To Elizabeth Johnson, 31 Jan. 1740, n. 18.

I had forgot to inform you that your Messenger may apply to Mr. Willm. Ward, Mercer in Birm. for directions where to go.[3]

3. William Ward took over Harry Porter's business in 1734 (*Johns. Glean.* v.106). He is named as one of Perks's creditors in the release (*Johns. Glean.* VII.88).

Thomas Longman[1]

JUNE 1746[2]

MS: Huntington Library.

ADDRESS: To Mr. Longman, Bookseller, Paternoster Row.

Sir: At the golden Anchor, near Holbourn Bars

The Contract fairly engrossed was sent to me yesterday, I suppose by Mr. Knaptons direction who is out of town.[3] I should think it a favour if You and the rest of the Gentlemen would breakfast with me that we may sign.[4] If You will appoint a day and write a note to the rest, the Bearer will take it to each of them, or if any other place be more convenient, the writings shall be brought wherever[5] You shall desire by, Sir, Your humble Servant,

SAM. JOHNSON

1. Thomas Longman (d. 1755), one of the seven partners in SJ's *Dictionary*.

2. See below, n. 4.

3. John Knapton (d. 1770), London bookseller in partnership with his brother Paul (d. 1755).

4. The contract, dated 18 June 1746, was signed by John and Paul Knapton, Thomas Longman and his nephew (also Thomas Longman, 1730–97), Charles Hitch (d. 1764), Andrew Millar (1707–68), and Robert Dodsley (1703–64), who had originally suggested the project to SJ (Hawkins, p. 345; *Life* I.182).

5. MS: "w" superimposed upon "th"

Robert Dodsley

JUNE 1746[1]

MS: Hyde Collection.

ADDRESS: To Mr. Dodsly.

1. *Ante* To Thomas Longman, June 1746 and n. 4.

Sir:

I received yesterday the agreement fairly engrossed which I have examined and find exact, I therefore wrote this morning to Mr. Knapton,[2] and find that he is gone from home and that his return is not expected till after midsummer. I conclude therefore that the writings were sent to me, that I might put an end to the treaty with the rest in his absence, I have therefore given the Bearer a note to be carried if You approve it to Mr. Longman who is named the Second in the articles, to which You may if You please add your concurrence, or send me word what Steps I shall take. I think it is by no means necessary that all the partners should sign on the same day, nor can it be done in this affair because Mr. Knapton does not return before the time at which the contract commences. His Brother directed me to apply to the Partners.[3] I am, Sir, etc.

SAM. JOHNSON

The Bonds I have not seen the Attorney should be directed to send them. I know not who he is.

2. *Ante* To Thomas Longman, June 1746, n. 3.
3. *Ante* To Thomas Longman, June 1746, nn. 3, 4.

Robert Dodsley

FRIDAY 26 DECEMBER 1746

MS: Pierpont Morgan Library.
ADDRESS: To Mr. Dodsly.

Sir: Decr. 26, 1746

That You may not have the trouble of sending to me again I have desired Mr. Stockton who writes for me to wait on You with a receipt, or I will come myself if it be desired. I am, Sir, Your most etc.

SAM. JOHNSON

James Elphinston[1]

THURSDAY 20 APRIL 1749

MS: Johnson House, London.
ADDRESS: To Mr. Elphinston.

Sir: April 20th 1749

I have for a long time intended to answer the Letter which You were pleased to send me, and know not why I have delayed it so long but that I had nothing particular either of enquiry or information to send You, and the same reason might still have the same consequence, but I[2] find in my recluse kind of Life,[3] that I am not likely to have much more to say at one time than[4] at another, and that therefore I may endanger by an appearance of neglect long continued, the loss of such an Acquaintance as I know not where to supply. I therefore write now to assure you how sensible I am of the kindness you have always expressed to me, and how much I desire the cultivation of that Benevolence which perhaps nothing but the distance[5] between us has hindred from ripening before this time into Friendship. Of myself I have very little to say, and of any body else less, let me however be allowed one thing and[6] that in my own favour that I am, Dear Sir, Your most humble Servant,

SAM. JOHNSON

1. James Elphinston (1721–1809), Scots translator and schoolmaster, the brother-in-law of SJ's friend and printer William Strahan. According to SJ, "He has a great deal of good about him; but he is also very defective in some respects. His inner part is good, but his outer part is mighty awkward" (*Life* II.171).

2. MS: "that" del. before "I"

3. After the production of *Irene* at Drury Lane, 6–20 Feb. 1749, SJ returned to full-time work on the *Dictionary* in the attic of 17 Gough Square (Clifford, 1979, pp. 7, 14, 25). *Post* To Lucy Porter, 12 July 1749, n. 1.

4. MS: "than" altered from "that"

5. MS: "di" superimposed upon "In"

6. MS: "and" superimposed upon "in"

Lucy Porter

WEDNESDAY 12 JULY 1749

MS: Current location unknown. Transcribed from photostat supplied by H. W. Liebert.

ADDRESS: To Miss Porter at Mrs. Johnson's in Lichfield.

POSTMARK: ⟨12⟩ IY.

Dear Miss: Goff Square,[1] July 12th 1749

I am extremely obliged to You for your letter which I would have answered last post but that ilness prevented me, I have been often out of order of late, and have very much neglected my affairs. You have acted very prudently with regard to Levett's affair, which will, I think, not at all embarrass me, for You may promise him that the mortgage shall be taken up at Michaelmass, or at least sometime between that and Christmas, and if he requires to have it done sooner I will endeavour it.[2] I make no doubt, by that time of either doing it myself or persuading some of my Friends to do it for me.

Please to acquaint him with it, and let me know if he be satisfied. When he once called on me, his name was mistaken and therefore I did not see him, but finding the mistake wrote to him the same day but never heard more of him, though I entreated him to let me know when to wait on him.

You frighted me, you little Gipsy, with your black wafer,[3] for I had forgot you were in mourning and was afraid your letter had brought me ill news of my mother, whose death is one of the few calamities on which I think with horrour.[4] I long to know how she dos and, how you all do. Your poor

1. "Johnson, who before this time, together with his wife, had lived in obscurity . . . had, for the purpose of carrying on this arduous work [the *Dictionary*] and being near the printers employed in it, taken a handsome house in Gough Square" (Hawkins, p. 175). Number 17, on the western side, dates from the early eighteenth century (Clifford, 1979, p. 15). The ratebooks show that SJ had leased it by Dec. 1747; he lived there until Mar. 1759 (Clifford, 1955, pp. 282, 348 n. 7).

2. *Ante* To Theophilus Levett, 1 Dec. 1743; letters to John Levett in Appendix I.

3. Lucy's uncle Joseph Porter (1688/89–1749), a London merchant, had died on 7 Apr. (*Johns. Glean.* VII.109–10).

4. Cf. *Post* To Sarah Johnson, 16 Jan. 1759; *Post* To Lucy Porter, 27 Jan. 1759.

Mamma is come home but very weak yet I hope she will grow better, else she shall go into the country.[5] She is now up stairs and knows not of my writing. I am, Dear Miss, Your most humble servant,

SAM. JOHNSON

5. Elizabeth Johnson, a "difficult hypochondriac," had lodgings in Hampstead from 1748 or earlier until her death (Clifford, 1955, p. 298). "I have, indeed, been told by Mrs. Desmoulins, who before her marriage, lived some time with Mrs. Johnson at Hampstead, that she indulged herself in country air and nice living, while her husband was drudging in the smoke of London" (*Life* 1.237–38).

Thomas Birch[1]

SATURDAY 12 MAY 1750

MS: British Library.

ADDRESS: To the Revd. Mr. Birch.

ENDORSEMENT: May 12, 1750.

Sir: Gough Square, May 12th 1750[2]

Knowing that you are now preparing to favour the publick with a new Edition of Raleigh's miscellaneous pieces,[3] I have taken the Liberty to send you a Manuscript, which fell by chance within[4] my notice. I perceive no proofs of forgery in my examination of it, and the Owner tells me that, as he has heard, the handwriting is Sir Walter's. If You should find reason to conclude it genuine, it will be a kindness to the owner, a blind person, to recommend it to the Booksellers.[5] I am, Sir, Your most humble Servant,

SAM. JOHNSON

1. *Ante* To Thomas Birch, 29 Sept. 1743, n. 1.

2. MS: "1750" in Birch's hand

3. *The Works of Sir Walter Raleigh, Kt. Political, Commercial, and Philosophical,* 2 vols. (1751).

4. MS: "withing"

5. John Nichols (*GM* 1785, p. 7) identifies the owner as the poet Anna Williams (1706–83), daughter of Zachariah Williams, the indigent Welsh inventor for whom SJ wrote *An Account of an Attempt to Ascertain the Longitude at Sea* (1755). She was operated on unsuccessfully for cataracts in 1752, and thereafter remained a part of SJ's household (Hawkins, p. 323; Clifford, 1979, pp. 92–95, 101). No further details have been recovered concerning her Raleigh manuscript.

James Elphinston

TUESDAY 25 SEPTEMBER 1750

MS: Beinecke Library. A copy in the hand of James Elphinston.[1]

Dear Sir: Septr. 25th 1750

You have as I find by every kind of evidence lost an excellent Mother; and I hope you will not think me incapable of partaking of your grief.[2] I have a Mother now Eighty-two years of age, whom therefore I must soon lose, unless it please God that she rather should mourn for me.[3] I read the letters in which you relate your Mothers death to Mrs. Strahan[4] and think I do myself honour when I tell you that I read them with tears but tears are neither to me nor to you[5] of any further[6] use, when once the tribute of nature has been paid. The business of life summons us away from useless grief, and calls us to the exercise of those virtues of which we are lamenting our deprivation. The greatest benefit which one friend can confer upon another, is to guard, and excite[7] and elevate his virtues. This your Mother will still perform, if you diligently preserve the memory of her life; and of her death; a life so far as I can learn, useful wise and Innocent;[8] and a death resigned, peaceful and holy. I cannot forbear to mention, that neither reason nor revelation denies you to hope, that you may encrease her happiness by obeying her precepts; and that she

1. MS: collated with texts in William Shaw, *Memoirs of the Life and Writings of the Late Dr. Samuel Johnson*, 1785, p. 96, and JB's *Life*, 1791, I.115

2. Rachel Honeyman Elphinston (*c.* 1680–1750), the wife of the Rev. William Elphinston, an Episcopal clergyman, died in Edinburgh on 10 Sept. (James Elphinston, *Forty Years' Correspondence*, 1791, I.7, 22).

3. Sarah Johnson died in Jan. 1759, two months before her ninetieth birthday. *Post* To Lucy Porter, 23 Jan. 1759.

4. Margaret Penelope Elphinston (1719–85), James's sister, who married William Strahan in 1738 (J. A. Cochrane, *Dr. Johnson's Printer*, 1964, pp. xiv, 5). Elphinston had sent her two letters: the first (dated 11 Sept. 1750) described their mother's death, the second (13 Sept.) her funeral (Elphinston, *Forty Years' Correspondence* I.22–25; *GM* 1809, p. 1116).

5. "neither to *you* nor to *me*" (JB)

6. "farther" (Shaw)

7. "incite" (Shaw)

8. "useful and wise; innocent" (Shaw)

may, in her present state,[9] look with pleasure, upon every act of virtue to which her instructions or example have contributed. Whether this be more than a pleasing dream, or a just opinion of seperate spirits, is indeed of no great importance to us, when we consider ourselves as acting under the eye of God: yet surely there is something pleasing in the belief, that our seperation from those whom we love is merely corporeal; and it may be a great incitment to virtuous friendship, if it can be made probable that union which[10] has received the divine approbation shall continue to eternity.

There is one expedient, by which you may in some degree continue her presence. If you write down minutely what you remember of her from your earliest years you will read it with great pleasure, and receive from it many hints of pleasing[11] recollection, when time shall remove her yet farther from you and your grief shall [be][12] matured to veneration. To this however painfull for the present I cannot but advise you, as to a source of comfort and satisfaction in the time to come for all comfort and all satisfaction is sincerly wished you by, Dear Sir, Your most obliged, most obedient, and most humble servant,

SAM. JOHNSON

9. "and that . . . state" (JB, Shaw)
10. "that that union that" (JB)
11. "soothing" (JB, Shaw)
12. "shall be" (JB, Shaw)

Charlotte Lennox[1]

LATE 1750[2]

MS: Houghton Library.

ADDRESS: To Mrs. Lenox.

ENDORSEMENT: Mr. Saml. Johnson.

1. Charlotte Ramsay Lennox (*c.* 1729/30–1804), novelist, poet, dramatist, and translator, author of *The Female Quixote* (1752), and *Shakespear Illustrated* (1753–54). After her marriage in 1747 to "a poor and shiftless Scot named Alexander Lennox, . . . Charlotte became a strolling player and a slave to the booksellers" (Clifford, 1979, p. 41). How and when she first met SJ has not been determined, but by the autumn of 1750 he was doing all he could to advance her literary career (Gae Holladay and O M Brack, Jr., "Johnson as Patron," *Greene Centennial Studies*, 1984, pp. 178–81).

2. See below, n. 5.

Madam:

I will speak to Mr. Payne[3] and to Mr. Cave, and hope to prevail with both[4] the one and the other to do as You would wish, but cannot promise, what another man will do. I shall endeavour at least to bring the whole affair to succeed.[5] What You mention I certainly told You, but I did not tell it as coming from Mr. Payne, but as my opinion, and I am inclined to believe, that they refused rather from some present want of Money than from any unwillingness to oblige You. I am, Madam, Your most humble servant,

SAM. JOHNSON

3. John Payne (d. 1787), London bookseller and accountant, later (1780) Chief Accountant of the Bank of England. A member of SJ's Ivy Lane Club, Payne published the *Rambler* (in partnership with Joseph Bouquet), part of the *Adventurer*, and the *Idler* (Clifford, 1979, p. 33; *Bibliography*, pp. 30, 39, 79).

4. MS: "bothe" with "e" del.

5. In Oct. 1750 Payne issued proposals for a subscription edition of Lennox's poems; in December he and Bouquet published her first novel, *The Life of Harriot Stuart*. Cave apparently agreed to publicize these projects by printing two of Lennox's own poems, two poems in praise of her talents, and a complimentary notice of *Harriot Stuart* (*GM* Nov. 1750, pp. 518–19; Dec. 1750, p. 575; Jan. 1751, p. 35). For fuller details and bibliography, see Duncan Isles, "The Lennox Collection," *Harvard Library Bulletin* 18, 1970, pp. 334–35.

Samuel Richardson

SATURDAY 9 MARCH 1751

MS: Pierpont Morgan Library.

Dear Sir: March 9th 1750/51

Though Clarissa wants no help from external Splendour I was glad to see her improved in her appearance but more glad to find that she was now got above all fears of prolixity, and confident enough of Success, to supply whatever had been hitherto suppressed.[1] I never indeed found a hint of any such

1. SJ refers to the fourth edition of *Clarissa*, a seven-volume octavo which was more handsomely printed than its duodecimo predecessors. Both the third and fourth editions, published simultaneously in Apr. 1751, were advertised as con-

defalcation but I fretted, for though the Story is long, every letter is short.

I wish You would add an *Index Rerum* that when the reader recollects any incident he may easily find it, which at present he cannot do unless he knows in which volume it is told;[2] for Clarissa is not a performance to be read with eagerness and laid aside for ever, but will be occasionally consulted by the busy, the aged, and the studious, and therefore I beg that this Edition by which I suppose Posterity is to abide, may want nothing that can facilitate its use. I am, Sir, Your obliged, humble Servant,

SAM. JOHNSON

---

taining "many Passages, and some Letters . . . restored from the Original Manuscripts" (T.C.D. Eaves and B. D. Kimpel, *Samuel Richardson*, 1971, pp. 314–17).

2. Richardson may be said to have responded to SJ's suggestion in two ways: by furnishing *Sir Charles Grandison* (1754) with "An Historical and Characteristical Index," and by publishing a separate "Collection of the Moral and Instructive Sentiments, Maxims, Cautions, and Reflexions, Contained in the Histories of *Pamela*, *Clarissa*, and *Sir Charles Grandison*" (1755).

John Newbery[1]

MONDAY 15 APRIL 1751

PRINTED SOURCE: Sir James Prior, *Life of Oliver Goldsmith*, 1837, I.340.

ADDRESS: To Mr. Newbery.

ENDORSEMENT: 20th April.—Received of Mr. Newbery the sum of two guineas for the use of Mr. Johnson, pr. me, Thos. Lucy.

Dear Sir: April 15, 1751

I have just now a demand upon me for more money than I

---

1. John Newbery (1713–67), bookseller in St. Paul's Churchyard, specialized in children's literature. Newbery, who published SJ's *Idler*, is portrayed in No. 19 as "that great Philosopher Jack Whirler, whose business keeps him in perpetual motion, and whose motion always eludes his business" (*Works*, Yale ed. II.60). According to Prior, "Writers of the first character sought his acquaintance and in his friendship not unfrequently found occasional alleviation of their most pressing wants" (*Goldsmith* I.340).

have by me:[2] if you could conveniently help me with two pounds, it will be a favour, to, Sir, Your most humble servant,

SAM. JOHNSON

2. At this time SJ was receiving four guineas a week for his *Rambler* essays, "but there were occasional sudden needs. . . . Were these purchases Tetty may have made?" (Clifford, 1979, p. 88). Another possibility is that these sums (*Post* To John Newbery, 29 July 1751; 24 Aug. 1751) may have been advances, not loans: SJ's "Life of Dr. Francis Cheynel" appeared in Newbery's *Student*, May–July 1751 (*Bibliography*, p. 38).

John Newbery

MONDAY 29 JULY 1751

PRINTED SOURCE: Sir James Prior, *Life of Oliver Goldsmith*, 1837, I.341.
ADDRESS: To Mr. Newbery.
ENDORSEMENT: As for preceding letter.

Sir: July 29, 1751

I beg the favour of you to send me by the bearer, a guinea, for which I will account to you on some future production. I am, Sir, Your humble servant,

SAM. JOHNSON

John Newbery

SATURDAY 24 AUGUST 1751

PRINTED SOURCE: Sir James Prior, *Life of Oliver Goldsmith*, 1837, I.341.
ENDORSEMENT: As for preceding letter.

Dear Sir: August 24, 1751

I beg the favour of you to lend me another guinea, for which I shall be glad of any opportunity to account with you, as soon as any proper thing can be thought on, or which I will repay you in a few weeks. I am, Sir, Your most humble servant,

SAM. JOHNSON

William Strahan[1]

FRIDAY 1 NOVEMBER 1751

MS: Hyde Collection.
ADDRESS: To Mr. Strahan.

Dearest Sir: Novr. 1, 1751

The message which You sent me by Mr. Stuart I do not consider as at all your own,[2] but if you were contented to be the deliverer of it to me, you must favour me so far as to return my answer, which I have written down to spare you the unpleasing office of doing it in your own words. You advise me to write, I know with very kind intentions, nor do I intend to treat your counsel with any disregard when I declare that in the present state of the matter "I shall *not* write"—otherwise than the words following—

"That my Resolution has long been, and is *not* now altered, and is now *less* likely to be altered, that I shall *not* see the Gentlemen Partners till the first volume is in the press, which they may forward or retard by dispensing or not dispensing with the last message."[3]

Be pleased to lay this my determination before them this morning, for I shall think of taking my measures accordingly to morrow morning, only this that I mean no harm, but that my citadel shall not be taken by storm while I can defend it, and that if a blockade is intended, the country is under the command of my batteries, I shall think of laying it under con-

1. William Strahan (1715–85), printer at No. 10, Little New Street (near Gough Square). Strahan not only printed the *Dictionary,* he also served as SJ's agent, banker, and paymaster (J. A. Cochrane, *Dr. Johnson's Printer,* 1964, esp. chap. 3).

2. Francis Stewart, (d. *c.* 1752), son of an Edinburgh bookseller, "an ingenious and worthy man" (*Life* 1.536), who served as one of SJ's amanuenses on the *Dictionary* and as business manager during the early years of the project (*Life* 1.187; Clifford, 1979, pp. 51–52). In Apr. 1752 Stewart was still alive, though possibly no longer working for SJ (Waingrow, pp. 166–67).

3. *Ante* To Thomas Longman, June 1746. The first volume of the *Dictionary* was not finished until Apr. 1753 (*Life* 1.255; Sledd and Kolb, p. 9).

tribution to morrow Evening.[4] I am, Sir, Your most obliged, most obedient, and most humble servant,

SAM. JOHNSON

4. The "blockade" must refer to a threat from the "Gentlemen Partners" to cut off money and supplies if copy were not immediately forthcoming: "As the patience of the proprietors was repeatedly tried and almost exhausted, by their expecting that the work would be completed within the time which Johnson had sanguinely supposed, the learned author was often goaded to dispatch" (*Life* I.287).

Lord Orrery[1]

LATE NOVEMBER 1751[2]

MS: Hyde Collection.
ENDORSEMENT: Mr. Saml. Johnson.

My Lord: Fryday morning[3]

It is, I believe, impossible for those who have the honour of your Lordship's regard to be indifferent to any thing to which You are pleased to direct their Attention. I could not forebear this morning to review what had been said concerning Virgil's Creteus,[4] and as I think the best way of examining a Conjec-

1. John Boyle (1707–62), fifth Earl of Orrery, biographer and antiquarian, friend of Swift and Pope, and author of *Remarks on the Life and Writings of Dr. Jonathan Swift* (1751).

2. Dated on the basis of evidence from an annotated, interleaved copy of the first edition of Orrery's *Remarks*, published 7 Nov. 1751 (Harvard MS: Eng. 218.14). This copy contains "A List of the Persons to whom the Earl of Orrery gave his Life of Swift"; the list includes a "Mr. Johnson." A holograph note (f. 317) responds directly to SJ's comment on *Aeneid* IX.777 (see above, no. 12 in SJ's list of "facts, and postulates"). A corrected edition of the *Remarks* appeared *c.* 10 December. For a full discussion of the evidence relating to this letter, see P. J. Korshin, "Johnson and the Earl of Orrery," in *Eighteenth-Century Studies in Honor of Donald F. Hyde*, 1970, pp. 31–33.

3. Either 15 or 22 Nov. 1751.

4. In a long digression (*Remarks*, pp. 311–21) Orrery conjectures that Virgil alludes to Horace as "amicum Cretea musis" (*Aeneid* IX.774). Orrery's theory is based on a corrupt text—"Cretea" should read "Crethea": "et Clytium Aeoliden et amicum Crethea Musis, / Crethea Musarum comitem, cui carmina semper / et citharæ cordi numerosque intendere nervis; / semper equos atque arma virum pugnasque canebat" (*Aeneid* IX.774–77). The catalogue of Turnus's victims includes "Clytius, son of Aeolus, and Cretheus, delight of the Muses—Cretheus, the

ture, is to disentangle its Complication, and consider in single Propositions, I have taken the Liberty to lay down a few facts, and postulates, of which your Lordship will be pleased to consider the ultimate Result.

1. It is known that Virgil in his Eneid interwove the History of Rome, partly by Anticipation, and perhaps partly by allusion.
2. It is probable that he descended to the commemoration of facts not historical, and of private friendship—*Genus unde tibi, Romane Cluenti,* shows that he took opportunities of gratifying single families.[5]
3. It has been believed from very early times that Homer celebrated his Friends however mean and obscure such as *Tichius* the Currier and why should not Virgil be supposed to imitate his morals as well as his Poetry.[6]
4. Such Allusions, as they are necessarily made to slight peculiarities or casual Circumstances, such as may fall in naturally with the main tenour of the Poem, must[7] be often unintelligible to Posterity and always obscure. Thus Popes Satire on Dennis

   'Tis well might Critics—
   But *Appius* reddens at each word you speak.

   This was clear enough for a few years after the publication of Dennis's Tragedy of *Appius* and Virginia, but is al-

---

Muses' comrade, whose joy was ever in song and lyre and in stringing of notes upon the chords; ever he sang of steeds and weapons, of men and battles" (trans. H. R. Fairclough, Loeb ed.). The alleged reference is to the opening of Horace's *Ode* I.xxvi: "Musis amicus tristitiam et metus / tradam protervis in mare Creticum / portare ventis, quis sub Arcto / rex gelidæ metuatur oræ, / quid Tiridaten terreat" (ll. 1–5): "Dear to the Muses, I will banish gloom and fear to the wild winds to carry o'er the Cretan Sea, all unconcerned what ruler of the frozen borders of the North is object of our fear, or what dangers frighten Tiridates" (trans. C. E. Bennett, Loeb ed.).

5. In *Aeneid* v.116–23, Virgil ascribes a Trojan origin to three Roman families: the Memmii, the Sergii, and the Cluentii.

6. In *Iliad* VII.220–21, Homer describes the great shield of Telamonian Aias, which was made by Tychius, "he that was far best of workers in hide" (trans. A. T. Murray, Loeb ed.).

7. MS: "of" del. before "must"

ready impenetrably dark to the greater number of Readers, who are equally strangers to the real and fictitious Name.[8]

5. If therefore evidence[9] can be produced as may barely turn the Balance by a[10] small weight of probability, more is not to be required. And this Probability is obtained in cases like that before us, if there be any characteristic annexed to a particular personage in a Poem which could mark out to those of the Poets time, a resemblance to some one whom that Poet might be supposed willing to commemorate.
6. We are then to suppose—that Virgil was generally understood to mean real Persons by fictitious names—and that he was generally known to be the Friend of Horace.—It then remains only to be examined whether there be any circumstance in the Character of Creteus which might determine the Romans of Augustus's time to apply to Horace rather than to any other Poet.
7. When an Eminent Man is already pointed out by his Profession, when we are prepared to expect the mention of him by knowing his alliance with the Writer, any slight additional allusion to his Works is sufficient to appropriate a passage to him, which might otherwise be indifferently applied to others.
8. Virgil introduces a Poet—thus far the passage is unlimited—He strongly expresses the species of his Poetry—numeros intendere nervis—this confines the attention, at least leads it, to the Lyric Poets, who at Rome were always few, and of whom Horace, the chief, would naturally recur.

8. " 'Twere well, might Criticks still this Freedom take; / But *Appius* reddens at each Word you speak" (Pope, *Essay on Criticism,* ll. 584–85). According to E. Audra and Aubrey Williams, "Pope applied to Dennis the name of one of the characters in his tragedy *Appius and Virginia* (Drury Lane, Feb. 5, 1709), who was as sensitive to criticism as his creator. . . . The play was withdrawn after a run of four nights, a failure which made Pope's allusion to Appius all the more stinging" (*Pastoral Poetry and An Essay on Criticism,* ed. E. Audra and Aubrey Williams, 1961, p. 306).

9. MS: "such" del. before "evidence"

10. MS: "a" altered from "an"

9. Thus far it appears that Creteus may be Horace, rather Horace than any other—if there be any allusion to the works of Horace which might still more plainly point him out, will it not follow, not only that he *may* but that he *must* be meant.

10. This allusion may be perceived in the Resemblance of *amicum Cretea Musis*, to *Musis Amicus—in mare Creticum—Musis Amicus* denominates a Poet, *Creteus Musis amicus*, points out the Poet who throw[s] his Cares *in mare Creticum.*[11]

11. It is luckily demonstrable that this Ode was written before we can believe it likely that Virgil had composed the ninth book of the Eneid, because it makes mention of *Tiridates*'s escape to Rome,[12] *quid Tiridatem terreat*—which happened in the year urbis conditæ [13] and to which Virgil is supposed to allude in the seventh Book which he was then composing.

—Seu tendere ad Indos etc.[14]

Augustus being suspected of intending to war upon the Parthians at the instigation of Tiridates.

12. To conjectures of this fanciful and capricious kind it cannot be expected that there should be no objection. The chief difficulty which can retard the reception of this arises from the last line—semper Equos atq—the poems of Horace being always either gay or moral rather than heroic. To this it may be answered

1. That introducing his Poet among heroes he was obliged to make him sing Songs of War.

2. That Horace has given many Specimens of his abilities for Martial Subjects.

11. See above, n. 4.

12. Tiridates II, an Arsacid prince of the Parthian Empire, overthrew King Phraates IV in 32 B.C. The following year, however, Phraates returned from exile. Taking his son as a hostage, Tiridates fled to Rome.

13. MS: period and comma; blank space after "conditæ" for year number, which SJ never entered

14. *seu tendere ad Indos / Auroramque sequi Parthosque resposcere signa*: "or to march

3. That Mecaenas called upon Horace to write[15] upon the Roman Wars, and that Virgil might naturally second the demand of their common patron.

4. That this is in the whole proposed only as a Conjecture a slight and uncertain Conjecture, but[16] if the last line had given us fuller evidence, it would have almost reached to certainty.

Thus, my Lord, I have detailed the evidence as it appears to me, and really think it not less strong than that which Atterbury has offered for Iapis.[17] But I am in less concern what your Lordship will think of the positions, than how You will judge of the[18] precipitant officiousness of, My Lord, Your Lordship's most obliged and most humble servant,

SAM. JOHNSON

---

on India's sons and pursue the Dawn, and reclaim their standards from the Parthian" (*Aeneid* VII.605–6, trans. H. R. Fairclough, Loeb ed.).

15. MS: "have" del. before "write"

16. MS: "and" del. before "but"

17. The title of Bishop Atterbury's "dissertation" encapsulates its argument: *Antonius Musa's Character, Represented by Virgil, in the Person of Iapis* (1740). Antonius Musa (*fl.* 23 B.C.) was Augustus's physician, Iapis ("Iapyx" in modern editions), the healer of Aeneas (*Aeneid* XII.391).

18. MS: "his"

Samuel Richardson[1]

TUESDAY 10 DECEMBER 1751

PRINTED SOURCE: Sotheby's Catalogue, 10 May 1875, Lot 83.

I thought it necessary to inform you how it happened that I seemed to give myself so little trouble about my Book when I gave you so much.[2] [He speaks of Lord Orrery's favourable

1. T.C.D. Eaves has established beyond reasonable doubt that the recipient must be Richardson, not Lord Orrery (Chapman's conjectural identification). We know from the catalogue of the Southgate sale (21–22 Jan. 1828) of a letter from SJ to Richardson, dated 10 Dec. 1751. The accuracy of this entry is confirmed by various pieces of internal evidence, analyzed in detail by Eaves; see "Dr. Johnson's Letters to Richardson," *PMLA* 75, 1960, pp. 379–80.

2. The first four volumes of the first collected edition of the *Rambler* were published in Jan. 1752 (*Bibliography*, p. 33). A comparison of ornaments indicates that

opinion of] our Charlotte's Book[3] [and mentions other matters connected with literary subjects.][4]

Richardson printed Volume IV. "Johnson extensively revised *The Rambler* for this edition and might have caused Richardson 'trouble' in many ways: for example, he could have made his revisions after Richardson's compositors had set the type from the original issues, thereby causing considerable resetting; he could have sent Richardson copy consisting partly of original issues with manuscript alterations and partly of manuscript, both doubtless difficult to set correctly; or he could have thrown the burden of proofreading on Richardson" (Eaves, "Dr. Johnson's Letters," p. 380).

3. SJ introduced Charlotte Lennox to Richardson, who read the manuscript of *The Female Quixote*, helped to persuade Andrew Millar to publish it, and printed the first edition (Mar. 1752). SJ also introduced Lennox to Lord Orrery, who helped arrange for the publication of *The Female Quixote* and then assisted in the compilation of *Shakespear Illustrated*. See Duncan Isles, "The Lennox Collection," *Harvard Library Bulletin* 18, 1970, p. 335 n. 7; 19, 1971, p. 36 n. 47.

4. Text in square brackets from Sotheby's catalogue entry.

Samuel Richardson

1751–52[1]

MS: Princeton University Library.

ADDRESS: To Mr. Richardson.

ENDORSEMENT: Mr. Johnson on some of the first of Sir Charles Grandison.

Dear Sir:

I am extremely obliged by the favour you have done me, to quarrel with what is received because one dos not receive more is not quite justifiable, yet I have almost a mind to retain these till you send me the next volume. To wish you to go on as you have begun would to many be a very kind wish, but You, sir,

1. T.C.D. Eaves argues persuasively that SJ "had been favoured with the notebooks containing the manuscript of the first part of the novel [*Grandison*] and that his letter is about these rather than the printed volumes." He therefore dates the letter to 1751–52 ("Dr. Johnson's Letters to Richardson," *PMLA* 75, 1960, p. 378). An alternative date (Apr. 1753) has been proposed by Jocelyn Harris, who believes that "Richardson's endorsement . . . referred to some of the first printed sheets, but of the narrative *only*" (*Notes and Queries* 218, 1973, p. 220).

have beyond all other men the art of improving on yourself. I know not therefore how much to wish as I know not how much to expect, but of this be certain, that much is expected from the Author of Clarissa.

James Elphinston[1]

EARLY 1752[2]

MS: Hyde Collection.

Dear Sir:

I cannot but confess the failures of my correspondence, but hope the same regard which you express for me on every other occasion will incline you to forgive me. I am often, very often, ill, and when I am well am obliged to work,[3] and indeed have never much used myself to punctuality. You are however not to make unkind inferences when I forbear to reply to your kindness, for be assured I never receive a letter from you without great pleasure, and a very warm sense of your generosity and Friendship, which I heartily blame myself for not cultivating with more care. In this as in many other cases I go wrong in opposition to conviction, for I think scarce any temporal good equally to be desired with the regard and familiarity of worthy men. I hope we shall be some time nearer to each other and have a more ready way of pouring out our hearts.

I am glad that you still find encouragement to proceed in your publication,[4] and shall beg the favour of six more volumes to add to my former six when you can with any convenience send them me.[5] Please to present a set in my name to

1. *Ante* To James Elphinston, 20 Apr. 1749, n. 1. Elphinston prints this letter in *Forty Years' Correspondence*, 1791, I.34.

2. Dated on the basis of the publication history of the Edinburgh and London editions of the *Rambler*; see below, nn. 5, 7.

3. SJ's two major projects in early 1752 were the *Dictionary* and the *Rambler*. The *Rambler* essays for February grow increasingly somber in tone (e.g. Nos. 196, 202, 203). SJ brought the series to a close on 4 Mar. (No. 208).

4. MS: "publication" superimposed upon undeciphered erasure

5. Elphinston was bringing out an edition of the *Rambler* in Edinburgh. Six

Mr. Ruddiman of whom I hear that his learning is not his highest excellence.[6]

I have transcribed the mottos and returned them I hope not too late, of which I think many very happily performed.[7] Mr. Cave has put the last in the Magazine, in which I think he did well.[8] I beg of You to write soon, and to write often and to write long letters, which I hope in time to repay you, but you must be a patient Creditor.[9] I have however this of gratitude that I think of you with regard when I do not perhaps give the proofs which I ought of being, Sir, Your most obliged and most humble servant,

SAM. JOHNSON

---

octavo volumes had appeared by Nov. 1751; each of these contains a "Version of the Mottoes" supplied by Elphinston. The final two volumes came out in July 1752 (*Poems*, p. 139). "With a laudable zeal at once for the improvement of his countrymen and the reputation of his friend, he suggested and took the charge of an edition of those Essays at Edinburgh, which followed progressively the London publication. . . . It is, unquestionably, the most accurate and beautiful edition of this work" (*Life* I.210 and n. 3).

6. Thomas Ruddiman (1674–1757), Scottish classicist and antiquarian, Keeper of the Advocates Library, Edinburgh (1730–52), author of *Rudiments of the Latin Tongue* (1714), and editor of George Buchanan's *Opera Omnia* (1715).

7. SJ refers to a composite list of mottoes (including 36 of Elphinston's translations) that appeared as part of the revised, collected edition in July 1752 (*Poems*, p. 139; *Bibliography*, p. 33; *Life* I.211 n. 2).

8. In the *GM* for Sept. 1750 (pp. 406–9), Cave had published Elphinston's translations of 30 mottoes; 10 more were to appear in the Oct. 1752 issue (pp. 468–70).

9. MS: comma

Charlotte Lennox

TUESDAY 4 FEBRUARY 1752

MS: Houghton Library.[1]

ADDRESS: To Mrs. Lennox.

ENDORSEMENT: Mr. Saml. Johnson.

Madam: Febr. 4, 1751[2]/2

I am extremely sorry to hear that your Book suffers such de-

1. MS: mutilated such that eight out of eleven lines of text are truncated along right-hand margin

2. MS: "1" superimposed upon "2"

lays, and think you unkindly treated by Mr. Richardson.[3] You see how ill we judge of our own advantages, I wish Strahan had it even now,[4] for I am afraid You will be gr⟨eatly in⟩jured by so long delay. What can be done? It is ⟨already⟩ sent to Mr. Millar,[5] and you cannot decently ma⟨ke a⟩ warm remonstrance. I wish I could help it. ⟨But⟩ if you can stay till next year the prospect of ⟨success⟩ will be better, and I will try to speak to ⟨several⟩ others for employment in the mean time, bu⟨t it is⟩ not easy to be had.[6] I am much concerned ⟨by this.⟩ I am, Madam, Your most humble servant,

SAM. JOHNSON

3. *Ante* To Samuel Richardson, 10 Dec. 1751, n. 3. Richardson's "unkind treatment" consisted of a possible delay in printing, which might have postponed the appearance of *The Female Quixote* until the following winter (Charlotte Lennox to SJ, 3 Feb. 1752, MS: Chicago Historical Society).

4. *Ante* To William Strahan, 1 Nov. 1751, n. 1.

5. *Ante* To Thomas Longman, June 1746, n. 4.

6. In her letter of 3 Feb. Lennox had requested SJ's help in finding employment as a translator.

Charlotte Lennox

THURSDAY 12 MARCH 1752

MS: Houghton Library.

ADDRESS: To Mrs. Lennox.

ENDORSEMENT: Mr. Saml. Johnson.

Madam: March 12, 1752

I am extremely obliged by your kind present, and wish it the success which it deserves.[1]

Poor Tetty Johnson's Ilness will not suffer me to think of going any whither, out of her call. She is very ill, and I am very much dejected.[2]

1. Presumably a presentation copy of *The Female Quixote* (published 13 Mar.). The book was enthusiastically reviewed in the *GM* (1752, p. 146) and in the *Covent-Garden Journal* (24 Mar. 1752); a second edition appeared on 2 July.

2. Elizabeth Johnson died on 17 Mar. *Post* To John Taylor, 18 Mar. 1752.

Mr. Millar has you in great esteem, and blames Mr. R——.[3] He says he hopes your book will eclipse Lord B——s Letters.[4] I am, Madam, Your most humble servant,

SAM. JOHNSON

3. *Ante* To Charlotte Lennox, 4 Feb. 1752 and nn. 3, 5.

4. The first public edition of Viscount Bolingbroke's *Letters on the Study and Use of History* was published by Millar on 20 Mar. 1752 (Pope had arranged for a privately printed edition in 1738). "The publication of the *Letters* set off a bitter controversy over the irreligious sentiments expressed in them; this proved damaging to Bolingbroke's reputation, but lucrative to the book-sellers. A new, corrected edition was published in the same year—and many republications of this edition, as well as foreign translations, have appeared since then" (G. H. Nadel, "New Light on Bolingbroke's *Letters on History*," *Journal of the History of Ideas* 23, 1962, p. 551).

John Levett

TUESDAY 17 MARCH 1752

MS: Hyde Collection.

ADDRESS: To——Levett Esqr. in Lichfield.

Sir: March 17th 1752

I am extremely obliged to You for the long credit and kind forbearance which I have received from You. I have sold a property principally to satisfy You, and in consequence of that Sale can now give You a Draught of one hundred pounds upon a Bookseller of credit payable on the first of May and negotiable in the mean time.[1] If You have not any evidence ⟨of the⟩ Money paid for me by Mr. Aston I know not how to ascertain it, for though I could make oath to a payment I cannot certainly tell of how much though I think of twelve pounds.[2] Would You be pleased to terminate the affair with Mr. J. Sympson?[3] I have not mentioned it to him, because I neither

1. Clifford (1979, p. 98) follows Hill (1.29) in conjecturing that this property consisted of SJ's republication rights to the *Rambler.*

2. See letters to John Levett in Appendix 1.

3. Joseph Simpson (1721–68), "a schoolfellow of Dr. Johnson's, a barrister at law, of good parts, but who fell into a dissipated course of life" (*Life* III.28). Simpson contributed one of the letters included in *Rambler* No. 107 (*Works,* Yale

would employ any one You may not desire to be employed, nor oblige You to confess any dislike. I know not indeed that any body needs to be employed, for I do not doubt your candour. I am, sir, with great respect, Your humble servant,

SAM. JOHNSON

For any Money above the hundred pounds I must beg you to accept my Note for Six Months.

---

ed. IV.207 n. 3). None of the available biographical data explains this "affair" (*Johns. Glean.* IV.155–59).

John Taylor

WEDNESDAY 18 MARCH 1752[1]

MS: Berg Collection, New York Public Library.

ADDRESS: To the Revd. Dr. Taylor.

ENDORSEMENTS: Johnson 52, 1752, 18 March 1752. About the Death of his Wife,[2] very feeling.

Dear Sir: March 18, 1752

Let me have your Company and your Instruction—Do not live away from me. My Distress is great.[3]

Pray desire Mrs. Taylor[4] to inform me what mourning I should buy for my Mother and Miss Porter, and bring a note in writing with you.

1. This is the second of two letters to Taylor, written in shock after the death of Elizabeth Johnson during the night of the 17th. The first is known only from the *Life*: "he immediately dispatched a letter to his friend, the Reverend Dr. Taylor, which, as Taylor told me, expressed grief in the strongest manner he had ever read" (I.238).

2. MS: "Mother" del. before "Wife"

3. "Johnson often said he never knew how dear she was to him, till he lost her. Her death affected him so deeply, that he grew almost insensible to the common concerns of life" (William Shaw, *Memoirs of the Life and Writings of the Late Dr. Samuel Johnson*, 1785, in *The Early Biographies of SJ*, ed. O M Brack and R. E. Kelley, 1974, p. 165). See also SJ's "Prayers Composed by Me on the Death of My Wife," *Works*, Yale ed. I.44–47.

4. Mary Tuckfield Taylor, John Taylor's second wife, "a lady of good fortune" from whom he was separated in 1763 (*Lit. Anec.* IX.58; *Life* I.472 n. 4; Thomas Taylor, *A Life of John Taylor*, 1910, pp. 23–24).

Remember me in your Prayers—for vain is the help of Man.[5] I am, Dear Sir, etc.

SAM. JOHNSON

5. "O help us against the enemy: for vain is the help of man" (Psalm 108:12).

Lord Orrery

THURSDAY 9 JULY 1752

MS: Houghton Library. A scribal copy in Orrery's letterbook.

My Lord, London, 9th July 1752

Illness is an affliction so severe as to need every alleviation that the condition of our Nature can admit, and sure there are some by which Pain may be mitigated though not appeased, and of those I should [count][1] one of the most powerfull that which your Lordship enjoys, the consciousness that all who know you wish your recovery.

πᾶσιν φιλὸ ἀνθρώποισι πάντας γὰρ φιλέεσκε—is a character applicable to your Lordship above all men whom I have ever known.[2]

I do not mean, my Lord, to except from the number of those who wish you well, even the Beings whom Idleness, Wantonness, or an opinion of their Wit incite to attack you in print, or to attempt your disturbance by private admonitions: I have lived long enough among Scriblers to know that every little Invective proceeds either from Malevolence or kindness, or love of Truth, or love of falsehood, or any other Love than the Love of Writing.[3] It would be a very severe censure of

1. MS: word omitted; "count" supplied from transcript in *Orrery Papers*, 1903, II.111.

2. "Dear to all men, for he loved them all." To pay a graceful compliment to Lord Orrery, SJ adapts two lines from the *Iliad* that describe "a man rich in substance, that was beloved of all men, for he dwelt in a home by the high-road and was wont to give entertainment to all" (VI.14–15, trans. A. T. Murray, Loeb ed.).

3. *Ante* To Lord Orrery, Late Nov. 1751 and nn. 1, 2. Four virulent pamphlet attacks on the *Remarks* appeared in Dublin in 1751–52, as well as three in London (H. Teerink, *A Bibliography of the Writings of Jonathan Swift*, ed. A. H. Scouten,

those who have attacked the *Memoirs of Swift* to say, they hated the Author without knowing him, and more severe still to say that they could know him and hate him.

I hope I shall always rejoice when I am the Occasion of good, and therefore congratulate myself upon the accident, by which I introduced Mrs. Lenox to your Lordship.[4] She tells with how much historical information you have been pleased to honour her,[5] but thinks she has not clearly explained her Plan which comprised not a complete Commentary on Shakespear, but only translations, and extracts from such Writers as he appears to have made use of.[6] I believe he read chiefly *Hall* and *Holingshead* for English History.[7]

The time of the year begins to put Mr. Faulkner into my thoughts.[8] I suppose he will visit London at his usual time. If your Lordship writes to him, may I presume to beg that you would be pleased to mention a Sett of Clark's Sermons which he promised me? [9]

We have at present no literary news: nothing is published, nor do I hear of any thing prepared for the Winter, but something undoubtedly the Winter will bring us. If it brings your

---

1963, pp. 416–17; P. J. Korshin, "The Earl of Orrery and Swift's Early Reputation," *Harvard Library Bulletin* 16, 1968, p. 171).

4. *Ante* To Samuel Richardson, 10 Dec. 1751, n. 3.

5. On 9 May 1752, Lord Orrery wrote to Charlotte Lennox, offering to "undertake any part you will assign me in your intended work" and sending her "some papers relative to Macbeth" (Duncan Isles, "The Lennox Collection," *Harvard Library Bulletin* 19, 1971, pp. 36–37). Lennox appears to have made use of this material in Volume 1 of *Shakespear Illustrated* ("The History of Macbeth," pp. 251–68). According to Duncan Isles, Orrery "may therefore also have contributed or assisted with the remaining chronicle material used in CL's discussions of *Cymbeline* . . . and of *King Lear* and the history plays" ("The Lennox Collection," p. 37 n. 51).

6. SJ's information was superfluous: on 9 May Orrery had written to Lennox, "You are entirely in the right, Madam, to translate, and not to epitomize or imitate" (Isles, "The Lennox Collection," p. 36).

7. Edward Hall (d. 1547), author of *The Union of the Noble and Illustre Famelies of Lancastre and York*; Raphael Holinshead (d. *c.* 1580), coauthor of the *Chronicles* and author of the *Historie of England*.

8. *Ante* To John Taylor, 10 Aug. 1742, n. 22.

9. The sermons of Samuel Clarke (1675–1729) were edited by his brother John and posthumously published in ten volumes (1730–31). Of all the principal

Lordship to Town, I will forgive any other disappointment, and shall make no complaints of long nights and cold days. I am, my Lord, your Lordship's etc.

SAML. JOHNSON

---

eighteenth-century homilists, "only Clarke seems to have been influential" in the making of SJ's own sermons (*Works*, Yale ed. XIV.li). Which "Sett" Faulkner had promised cannot be determined: the sale catalogue of SJ's library lists but does not describe two editions (Greene, 1975, p. 49).

John Levett

SUNDAY 26 JULY 1752

MS: Hyde Collection.

Sir: July 26, 1752

I am extremely ashamed after what I wrote last to you with so much Confidence, to have disappointed You, but I am really no otherwise than unfortunate in the affair.[1] I then told you that I had sold a property, which was exactly true, but I have not yet received a third part of the money which I expected from it; a circumstance that, after what I had written shocked me so much that I could not bear to see You, as I expected to receive the rest every day, and was willing to spare us both so disagreeable an Interview. The thing has however given me more credit, so I[2] am about to borrow the money, which I will immediately send you as soon as it comes to my hands, which cannot, unless every thing fail me, be but a few weeks, and so much for the sake of my Mother, I beg You to add to the favours already indulged to, Sir, Your most humble servant,

SAM. JOHNSON

1. *Ante* To John Levett, 17 Mar. 1752 and n. 1.
2. MS: "that" del. before "I"

Thomas Birch

SATURDAY 4 NOVEMBER 1752

MS: British Library.

ADDRESS: To the Reverend Mr. Birch.

ENDORSEMENT: 4 Nov. 1752.

Sir: Novr. 4th 1752

I beg the favour that if you have any Catalogue by you such as the Bibl. Thuaneana,[1] or any other of value, that you will lend it for a few days, to, Sir, Your most humble servant,[2]

SAM. JOHNSON

If you leave it out directed, we will call for it.

1. The *Catalogus Bibliothecæ Thuanæ* (1679), published by Joseph Quesnel, was prepared by the Parisian booksellers Jacques and Pierre Du Puy before they disposed of the library of Jacques-Auguste De Thou [or Thuanus] (1553–1617), historian, diplomat, churchman, and bibliophile (Henry Harrisse, *Le Président De Thou*, 1905, pp. 64–65 and n. 3). De Thou's *Historiarum sui Temporis* (1733) is quoted in *Rambler* No. 60 (*Works*, Yale ed. III.321). According to John Nichols, SJ "seriously entertained the thought of translating *Thuanus*" (*Life* IV.410).

2. Chapman suggests (I.47) that SJ was borrowing De Thou and other books at this time in order to extract quotations for the *Dictionary*. It seems likelier, however, that by late 1752 the process of culling was completed, and that SJ was composing the prefatory grammar and history of the language. Cf. *Post* To Thomas Birch, 20 Jan. 1753; Jan. 1754; 8 Nov. 1755.

Thomas Birch

SATURDAY 20 JANUARY 1753

MS: British Library.

ADDRESS: To the Reverend Mr. Birch.

ENDORSEMENT: 20 Janu. 1753.

Sir: Jan. 20th

I beg the favour of you to lend me Blount's[1] Censura Scrip-

1. MS: "B" superimposed upon "for"

torum,[2] I shall send my servant for it on Monday. I am, Sir, Your most humble servant,

SAM. JOHNSON

2. The *Censura celebriorum Authorum* (1690) by Sir Thomas Pope Blount (1649–97). The Blount cited in the *Dictionary* is Thomas Blount (1618–79), compiler of a legal dictionary (1670). *Ante* To Thomas Birch, 4 Nov. 1752, n. 2.

Charlotte Lennox

TUESDAY 6 MARCH 1753

MS: Houghton Library.

ADDRESS: To Mrs. Lennox, over against the King's Bakers in Berry Street, St. James's.

POSTMARK: PENY POST PAYD.

ENDORSEMENT: Mr. Saml. Johnson, March 6, 1753.

Dear Madam: March 6, 1753

I am very sorry for what happened, but cannot find that I was the cause of it, for the effect had been the same had he been out on any other occasion.[1]

The reason for which I said nothing to Mr. Lenox was no less than that I had nothing to say.[2] The Marriage is not yet solemnised or not owned, and as it would be improper for the young Gentlemen to ask a favour beforehand, it would be fit for me to propose it. To ask it I have promised you, and I will ask it in such a manner as I think most likely to succeed, for I shall sincerely rejoice if ⟨to do⟩ you any good can be within the little power of, Madam, Your most humble servant,

SAM. JOHNSON

1. Nothing further has been discovered about the incidents alluded to in this letter.

2. Presumably Alexander Lennox, the "indigent and shiftless Scot" whom Lennox had married in 1747 (Duncan Isles, "The Lennox Collection," *Harvard Library Bulletin* 18, 1970, p. 326). "The picture of him we can piece together is slight: working for Strahan the printer, a tidewaiter at the customs . . . often living apart from his wife" (M. R. Small, *Charlotte Ramsay Lennox*, 1935, p. 14).

Joseph Warton[1]

THURSDAY 8 MARCH 1753

MS: Hyde Collection.

ENDORSEMENT in JB's hand: These to be kept for Dr. Warton.

Dear Sir: March 8th 1753

I ought to have written to you before now, but I ought to do many things which I do not, nor can I indeed claim any merit from this Letter, for being desired by the Authours and Proprietor of the Adventurer,[2] to look out for another hand, my thoughts necessarily fixed upon You, whose fund of Literature will enable You to assist them with very little interruption of your Studies.

They desire you to engage to furnish one paper a month, at two Guineas a paper, which you may very easily perform.[3] We have considered that a Paper should consist of Pieces of Imagination, pictures of Life, and Disquisitions of Literature. The part which depends on the Imagination is very well supplied as You will find when you read the papers, for Descriptions of Life there is now a treaty almost made with an Authour and an Authoress,[4] and the Province of Criticism and Literature they are very desirous to assign to the Commentator on Virgil.

1. Joseph Warton (1722–1800), D.D., poet and critic, rector of Winslade, Hampshire, and later (1766–93) headmaster of Winchester College; author of *The Enthusiast* (1744) and *Odes on Various Subjects* (1746). His edition of Virgil, with accompanying critical essays and translations of the *Eclogues* and *Georgics*, appeared in 1753. According to Warton, he and SJ had "contracted close friendship" in the autumn of 1752 (Clifford, 1979, p. 111).

2. *The Adventurer* was planned by SJ and John Hawkesworth (1715–73), LL.D., miscellaneous writer, member of the Ivy Lane Club, and assistant on the *GM*, who became the new periodical's editor and principal contributor (J. L. Abbott, *John Hawkesworth*, 1982, p. 30). It appeared twice a week from 7 Nov. 1752 until 9 Mar. 1754, for a total of 140 numbers. John Payne (*Ante* To Charlotte Lennox, Late 1750, n. 3), the publisher of the *Adventurer*, paid each contributor two guineas per paper (Clifford, 1979, p. 107; *Works*, Yale ed. II.336).

3. Warton contributed 24 papers in all, beginning with the essay for 24 Apr. 1753.

4. The "Authour" is probably Samuel Richardson, who told Lady Bradshaigh

I hope this proposal will not be rejected, and that the next post will bring us your Compliance. I speak as one of the fraternity though I have no part in the paper beyond now and then a Motto,[5] but two of the Writers are my particular Friends,[6] and I hope the pleasure of seeing a third united to them, will not be denied to, Dear sir, Your most obedient and most humble servant,

SAM. JOHNSON

---

that he had been asked to contribute to the *Adventurer* "but never found Leisure to oblige the Appliers." The "Authoress" is likely to have been either Catherine Talbot (1721–70), who had contributed to the *Rambler*, or SJ's old friend and colleague Elizabeth Carter (David Fairer, "Authorship Problems in *The Adventurer*," *RES* 25, 1974, pp. 145–46).

5. SJ is being disingenuous: he had contributed the essay for 3 Mar. 1753 (No. 34), and went on to supply 29 papers in all (*Works*, Yale ed. II.336, 339).

6. One of these "particular Friends" must be John Hawkesworth; the other is probably Elizabeth Carter (Fairer, "Authorship Problems," p. 146).

William Strahan

THURSDAY 22 MARCH 1753[1]

MS: Hyde Collection.

ADDRESS: To Mr. Strahan.

Sir: March 22nd

I have inclosed the Scheme which I mentioned Yesterday, in which the work proposed is sufficiently explained.[2] The Undertaker, Mr. Bathurst is a Physician of the University of Cambridge of about eight years standing,[3] and will perform the work in such a manner as may satisfy the publick. No advice

1. Dated on the basis of SJ's reference to Bathurst as "a Physician . . . of about eight years standing": Bathurst took his B.M. from Peterhouse, Cambridge, in 1745.

2. This "Scheme" is a detailed "Proposal" for a "Geographical Dictionary," to be compiled "not merely from the Dictionaries now extant in many Languages, but from the best Surveys, Local Histories, Voyages, and particular accounts" (MS: Hyde Collection). Apparently the project never materialized.

3. Richard Bathurst (d. 1762), B.M., physician and miscellaneous writer, a

of mine will be wanting but advice will be all that I propose to contribute unless it should be thought worth while that I should write a preface, which if desired I will do and put my name to it. The terms which I am commissioned to offer are these.

1. A Guinea and half shall be paid for each sheet of the Copy.
2. The Authour will receive a Guinea and half a Week from the date of the Contract.
3. As it is certain that many books will be necessary the Authour will at the end of the work take the books furnish'd him in part of payment at prime Cost,[4] which will be a considerable reduction of the price of the Copy. Or if it seems as You thought yesterday no reduction, he will allow out of the last payment fifty pounds for the use of the Books and return them.
4. In two months after his first demand of books shall be supplied he purposes to write three sheets a week and to continue the same quantity to the end of the work unless he shall be hindered by want of Books. He dos not however expect to be always able to write according to the order of the Alphabet but as his Books shall happen to supply him, and therefore cannot send any part to the press till the whole is nearly finished.
5. He undertakes as usual the Correction. I am, sir, Your most humble servant,

SAM. JOHNSON

---

member of the Ivy Lane Club who was "greatly beloved" by SJ "for the pregnancy of his parts and the elegance of his manners" (Hawkins, p. 234). Bathurst had moved to Barbados by Jan. 1757 (Croker 1.288 n.1).

4. MS: "copy" del. before "Cost"

Samuel Richardson

TUESDAY 17 APRIL 1753

MS: Hyde Collection.

ADDRESS: To Mr. Richardson.

Dear Sir: Apr. 17

As [1] You were [2] the first that gave me any notice of this pamphlet [3] I send it you with a few little notes, which I wish you can read. It is well when Men of Learning and penetration busy themselves in these enquiries at hours of leisure.[4] But what [5] is their Idleness, is my Business. Help indeed now comes too late for me when a large part of my Book has passed the press.

I shall be glad if these strictures appear to you [6] not unwarrantable,[7] for whom should we who toil [8] in settling our language desire to please but him who is adorning it.[9] I hope your new book is printing. *Macte novâ virtute.*[10] I am, Dear Sir, most respectfully and most affectionately, your humble servant,

SAM. JOHNSON

1. MS: open quotation mark before "As"

2. MS: "were" altered from "was"

3. *An Account of the Trial of the Letter Y, Alias Y* (1753) by Richardson's friend, Thomas Edwards (see below, n. 4). "It urges a more consistent and logical spelling, one which indicates derivations, in the form of a legal argument among the various letters as to their just rights" (T.C.D. Eaves and B. D. Kimpel, *Samuel Richardson*, 1971, p. 329).

4. Thomas Edwards (1699–1757), of Turrick, Buckinghamshire, a bachelor whose enthusiasms included landscape gardening, poetry, and scholarship. His *Canons of Criticism*, an attack on Warburton's edition of Shakespeare, was published in 1748; late in 1749 Edwards sent Richardson a sonnet on *Clarissa*, which appeared anonymously in the third edition.

5. MS: "w" altered from "t"

6. MS: "you" altered from "your"

7. MS: "un" superimposed upon undeciphered erasure

8. MS: "toil" written above "tail" del.

9. Richardson forwarded this letter to Edwards, along with SJ's comments on his pamphlet, "notwithstanding the very high and undeserved compliment he makes me in it" (*Selected Letters of Samuel Richardson*, ed. John Carroll, 1964, pp. 225–27).

10. *macte novâ virtute, puer*: "'A blessing, child, on thy young valour!'" (*Aeneid* IX.641, trans. H. R. Fairclough, Loeb ed.).

Charlotte Lennox

c. MAY 1753[1]

MS: Houghton Library.

ADDRESS: To Mrs. Lenox.

Madam:

I hope you take great care to observe the Doctor's prescriptions, and take your physick regularly, for I shall soon come to enquire. I should be sorry to lose Criticism in her bloom. Your remarks are I think all very judicious, clearly expressed, and incontrovertibly certain. When Shakespeare is demolished your wings will be *full summed* and I will fly You at Milton;[2] for you are a bird of Prey, but the Bird of Jupiter.[3] I am, Madam, your most obedient servant, SAM. JOHNSON

1. Dated on the basis of SJ's references to *Shakespear Illustrated*, published 18 May 1753.

2. "inspire, / As thou art wont, my prompted song else mute, / And bear through highth or depth of nature's bounds / With prosperous wing full summed to tell of deeds / Above heroic" (*Paradise Regained* I.11–15). "Full summed," a technical term from falconry, means "wanting none of its feathers" (*The Poems of John Milton*, ed. John Carey and Alistair Fowler, 1968, p. 1078). Duncan Isles suggests that SJ may also be alluding to *Paradise Lost*: "but feathered soon and fledge / They summed their pens, and soaring the air sublime / With clang despised the ground" (VII.420–22) ("The Lennox Collection," *Harvard Library Bulletin* 19, 1971, p. 39 n. 57).

3. *Bird of Jupiter*: the eagle.

Andrew Millar

WEDNESDAY 11 JULY 1753[1]

PRINTED SOURCE: Hill I.30–31.

ADDRESS: To Mr. Millar.

Sir, July 11

You seem to have entirely mistaken Mr. Macbean's errand by objecting want of money—no money was asked—the whole af-

1. Dated with reference to the publication of Young's *Treatise on Opium* (below, n. 5) and the production schedule for SJ's *Dictionary*.

fair is that Mr. Macbean [2] and Mr. Hamilton [3] want to wager as you and I have done,[4] and so lay the money in your hand, you have therefore to put the money into Macbean's hand to be put back into yours. I have no share in the matter but that I lend Macbean the money, that is you lend on my account. You may easily see my end in it, that it will make both M— and H— push on the business, which is all that we both wish.

It is therefore my advice that it be complied with, since, as you see, there is no expense in it, but remember that I don't care, and will not have it mentioned as any obligation on me, but as done for the common interests.

When I sent back your books I returned by mistake to you a *Young upon Opium*,[5] which I had from Mrs. Strahan;[6] please to let me have it back.

Pray be so kind as to procure me the three following books—

Law's Serious Call. 8vo.[7]

Helsham's Philosophy.[8]

Present State of England—last.[9]

I am, Sir, etc.

SAM. JOHNSON

2. *Ante* To Edward Cave, 1738, n. 2.

3. Presumably Archibald Hamilton (*c.* 1719–93), Scots printer and sometime manager of William Strahan's office, who founded the *Critical Review* in 1756 (*Lit. Anec.* III.398–99).

4. Nothing further has been discovered about the circumstances of either wager. Hill speculates: "Apparently for the sake of getting the work hastened, some kind of wager had been made by the author and the publisher. . . . Macbean, who perhaps was at the head of Johnson's assistants, now wished to wager against the printer" (I.31 n. 1).

5. George Young's *A Treatise on Opium* had been published in April (*GM* 1753, p. 202).

6. *Ante* To James Elphinston, 25 Sept. 1750, n. 4.

7. William Law's *A Serious Call to a Devout and Holy Life* (1728) provided SJ with "the first occasion of my thinking in earnest of religion, after I became capable of rational enquiry" (*Life* I.68).

8. *A Course of Lectures on Natural Philosophy* by Richard Helsham (1682–1738), professor of mathematics and physics at Trinity College, Dublin, appeared posthumously in 1739. SJ owned a copy at the time of his death (Greene, 1975, p. 67).

9. Presumably the most recent edition (the thirty-seventh, 1748) of *Angliæ Notitiæ, or the Present State of England*, by Edward Chamberlayne (1616–1703). The first edition appeared in 1669.

William Strahan

SPRING *or* SUMMER 1753[1]

MS: Hyde Collection.

Sir:

I have often suspected that it is as You say, and have told Mr. Dodsley of it. It proceeds from the haste of the amanuensis to get to the end of his days work. I have desired the passages to be clipped close,[2] and then perhaps for two or three leaves it is done. But since poor Stuarts time[3] I could never get that part of the work into regularity, and perhaps never shall. I will try to take some more care but can promise nothing, when I am told there is[4] a sheet or two I order it away. You will find it sometimes close, when I make up any myself, which never happens but when I have nobody with me, I generally clip it close, but one[5] cannot always be on the watch.[6] I am, sir, your most etc.

SAM. JOHNSON

1. It is unlikely that SJ would have used the phrase "since poor Stuarts time" in a letter of 1752: Francis Stewart was alive and working for him as late as Nov. 1751 (*Ante* To William Strahan, 1 Nov. 1751 and n. 2). This letter cannot have been written later than *c.* Aug 1753–the date by which, in all probability, SJ had ceased to send MS copy of the *Dictionary* to the printer as soon as each sheet was prepared (information supplied by Professor Allen Reddick).

2. *clip*: "to curtail, to cut short"; *close*: "concise, brief, without exuberance or digression" (SJ's *Dictionary*). See below, n. 6.

3. *Ante* To William Strahan, 1 Nov. 1751, n. 2. SJ's phrase could mean either "since Francis Stewart died" or "since Stewart left the *Dictionary* project."

4. MS: "is" superimposed upon "are"

5. MS: "to" del. before "one"

6. The exact nature of the problem addressed in this letter is uncertain, though SJ is clearly discussing the preparation of MS copy for the *Dictionary.* Strahan seems to have complained that the text sent to the printing house was not written as closely or arranged as economically as it should have been. If SJ were paid a set sum for each sheet of MS copy, but the sheets were not written tightly or the quotations pasted closely, then one MS sheet would no longer equal one printed sheet and SJ would be overpaid. The term "clipped close" might also refer to the abridging of illustrative quotations, which may have sprawled beyond the stipulated limits (information supplied by Professor Allen Reddick).

Samuel Richardson

WEDNESDAY 26 SEPTEMBER 1753

MS: Huntington Library.

ADDRESS: To Mr. Richardson.

ENDORSEMENT: Mr. S. Johnson, Sept. 26, 1753.

Dear Sir: Septr. 26, 1753

I return you my sincerest thanks for the volumes of your new work;[1] but it is a kind of tyrannical kindness to give only so much at a time as makes more longed for. But that will probably be [the] effect even of the whole when You have given it.

I have no objection but to the preface in which You first mention the letters as fallen by some chance into your hands,[2] and afterwards mention your health as such that you almost despaired of going through your plan.[3] If you were to require my opinion which part should be changed, I should be inclined to the suppression of that part which seems to disclaim the composition.[4] What is modesty if it departs from truth? Of what use is the disguise by which nothing is concealed?

You must forgive this because it is meant well. And then I have another favour to ask. Mr. Martinelli, an Italian Gentleman who seems a Man of merit,[5] has on his Hands two hundred sets of a large Edition of Machiavel which he pub-

1. The first four volumes of Richardson's new novel, *The History of Sir Charles Grandison,* had gone to press in early Sept. 1753; they were published in November (T.C.D. Eaves and B. D. Kimpel, *Samuel Richardson,* 1971, p. 383).

2. "How such remarkable Collections of private Letters fell into his [the Editor's] hands, he hopes the Reader will not think it necessary to enquire" (*The History of Sir Charles Grandison,* 1754, I.iii).

3. "Here the Editor apprehended he should be obliged to stop, by reason of his precarious State of Health, and a Variety of Avocations which claimed his first Attention: But it was insisted on by several of his Friends who were well assured he had the Materials in his Power, that he should produce into public View the Character and Actions of a Man of TRUE HONOUR" (*The History of Sir Charles Grandison,* 1754, I.v).

4. In the third edition Richardson heeded this advice and dropped the sentence in question.

5. Vincenzo Martinelli (1702–85), Florentine man of letters and protégé of the

lished in Holland, and wants some Bookseller to take them from him at a low price.[6] If you think it convenient to recommend him and a Bookseller to each other, it will be a great kindness to him.

I thank you once more, dear Sir, for your Books, but cannot I prevail this time for an Index[7] such [as] I wished and shall wish to Clarissa.[8] Suppose that in one volume an accurate index was made to the three Works;—but while I am writing an objection arises—such an Index to the three, would look like the preclusion of a fourth to which I will never contribute, for if I cannot benefit mankind I hope never to injure them.[9] I am, Sir, Your most obliged and most humble Servant,

SAM. JOHNSON

P.S. I am not cool about this piracy.[10] Suppose instead of this edition you should print three or four thousand in brevier

---

Hon. Thomas Walpole, lived in England from 1748 to 1775. He was a friend of SJ, Baretti, and the Burneys.

6. Presumably *Tutte le opere di Niccolò Machiavelli*, ed. Martinelli, 1747. Despite its "Londra" imprint, the ornaments and layout of this edition strongly suggest an ascription to Jean Neaulme at The Hague (information supplied by Dr. Hugh Amory, Houghton Library).

7. Richardson responded to this and other requests by adding an index to the final volume of *Sir Charles Grandison*. "Individual remarks are restated as general principles, a reference always leading the reader back from precept to enlivening example. It is notable, however, that the Index is not an entirely mechanical extrapolation, nor is it objectively compiled" (*Sir Charles Grandison*, ed. Jocelyn Harris, 1972, p. xxxvii).

8. *Ante* To Samuel Richardson, 9 Mar. 1751, n. 1.

9. In 1755 Richardson published *A Collection of the Moral and Instructive Sentiments, Maxims, Cautions, and Reflexions, Contained in the Histories of Pamela, Clarissa, and Sir Charles Grandison*. The *Collection* is not quite an index, although the sentiments are arranged alphabetically, with volume and page numbers supplied.

10. In 1753 Richardson tried to circumvent the Irish booksellers, who operated outside English copyright laws, by making a special arrangement with George Faulkner. Faulkner had pirated the second part of *Pamela* and had served as Richardson's Irish agent for *Clarissa*. In July 1753 he promised to pay Richardson seventy guineas for the rights to *Sir Charles Grandison*, but withdrew the offer in August when he discovered that three other Irish booksellers had obtained sheets of the novel. Faulkner decided to cooperate with the pirates and advised Richardson to do the same, but Richardson would not deal with men who must

⟨8⟩vo.[11] and sell them first in the remoter parts, every printer and Bookseller in the town will help you. I will correct a volume or more, and every body will do what they can. It might be done secretly and speedily.

---

have obtained their sheets by bribing his own employees. Instead he stopped the presses, and in Sept. 1753 published *The Case of Samuel Richardson, of London, Printer; with Regard to the Invasion of his Property.* This statement summarized the actions of the pirates and named the two journeymen he suspected of betraying him (Eaves and Kimpel, *Samuel Richardson,* pp. 377–83; R. C. Cole, *Irish Booksellers and English Writers 1740–1800,* 1986, p. 72).

11. Brevier is a small type size, 20 lines of which measure 54 mm. The format of SJ's own *Lives* was brevier octavo.

Hill Boothby[1]

c. DECEMBER 1753[2]

PRINTED SOURCE: *An Account of the Life of Dr. Samuel Johnson,* ed. Richard Wright, 1805, p. 42.

Few are so busy as not to find time to do, what they delight in doing.

1. Hill Boothby (1708–56), daughter of Brooke Boothby of Ashburne Hall, Derbyshire, a pious and learned spinster whom SJ had known since 1739 (*Johns. Glean.* VI.173–74). Boothby is "the most probable candidate" for the woman SJ was considering as his second wife (*Works,* Yale ed. I.52–53).

2. Boothby's letter quoting SJ is dated 29 Dec. 1753. In it she apologizes for her delayed response to SJ's "last kind letter" (Wright, *Account,* p. 42).

Thomas Birch

JANUARY 1754

MS: British Library.

ADDRESS: To the Revd. Dr. Birch.

ENDORSEMENT: Janua. 1754.

Sir:

If you will be pleased to lend me Clarendons History for a few days,[1] it will be a favour to, Sir, Your most humble servant,

SAM. JOHNSON

1. *A History of the Rebellion* (1702–04), by Edward Hyde (1609–74), first Earl of Clarendon. In *Rambler* No. 122 SJ, who drew on Clarendon throughout the *Dictionary*, praises "the wisdom of his maxims, the justness of his reasonings, and the variety, distinctness, and strength of his characters" (*Works*, Yale ed. IV.290).

Joseph Warton

FRIDAY 8 MARCH 1754

PRINTED SOURCE: John Wooll, *Biographical Memoirs of the Late Revd. Joseph Warton*, 1806, pp. 219–20.

Dear Sir: March 8th 1754

I cannot but congratulate you upon the conclusion of a work in which you have born so great a part with so much reputation. I immediately determined that your name should be mentioned, but the paper having been some time written, Mr. Hawkesworth, I suppose, did not care to disorder its text, and therefore put your eulogy in a note.[1] He and every other man mention your papers of Criticism with great commendation, though not with greater than they deserve.[2]

But how little can we venture to exult in any intellectual powers or literary attainments, when we consider the condition of poor Collins.[3] I knew him a few years ago full of hopes

1. Hawkesworth appended to the final number of the *Adventurer* (140, 9 Mar. 1754) a footnote in praise of Warton: "The peices [*sic*] signed Z are by the Rev. Mr. Warton, whose translation of Virgil's Pastorals and Georgics would alone sufficiently distinguish him as a genius and a scholar" (1754, II.418).

2. *Ante* To Joseph Warton, 8 Mar. 1753, n. 3.

3. William Collins (1721–59), author of the *Persian Eclogues* and *Odes on Several Descriptive and Allegoric Subjects*, "a man of extensive literature and of vigorous faculties" whom SJ had known since 1744–45, when Collins was living in London and scraping by as a penurious "literary adventurer" (*Lives of the Poets* III.335–37; Richard Wendorf and Charles Ryskamp, *The Works of William Collins*, 1979, p. xvi).

and full of projects, versed in many languages, high in fancy, and strong in retention.[4] This busy and forcible mind is now under the government of those who lately would not have been able to comprehend the least and most narrow of its designs. What do you hear of him? are there hopes of his recovery?[5] or is he to pass the remainder of his life in misery and degradation? perhaps with complete consciousness of his calamity.

You have flatter'd us, dear Sir, for some time with hopes of seeing you; when you come you will find your reputation encreased, and with it the kindness of those friends who do not envy you; for success always produces either love or hatred. I enter my name among those that love, and that love you more and more in proportion as by writing more you are more known; and believe that as you continue to diffuse among us your integrity and learning, I shall be still with greater esteem and affection, Dear Sir, Your most obedient and most humble servant,

SAM. JOHNSON

Collins had been Warton's friend since 1746, when the two poets read each other's odes and resolved "to publish them immediately" (Wendorf and Ryskamp, *Collins*, p. xvi). By the time of this letter Collins had been confined for an indefinite period in MacDonald's madhouse in Chelsea.

4. Collins's projects included a "History of the Revival of Learning" and a translation of Aristotle's *Poetics* (Wendorf and Ryskamp, *Collins*, p. xvi).

5. By Sept. 1754 Collins was well enough to be living under the care of his sister in Chichester (Wendorf and Ryskamp, *Collins*, p. xxviii).

Samuel Richardson

THURSDAY 28 MARCH 1754

MS: Hyde Collection.

ENDORSEMENT: Mr. Johnson and Miss W.'s Plan. 28 March 1754.

Sir: March 28, 1754

I am desired by Miss Williams, who has waited several times upon you without finding you at home, and has been hindered by an ilness of some weeks from repeating her visits, to return you her humble thanks for your present.[1] She is likewise desirous to lay before you the inclosed plan which she has meditated a long time, and thinks herself able to execute by the help of an Amanuensis, having long since collected a great number of volumes on these subjects, which indeed she appears to me to understand better than any person that I have ever known.[2] She will however want a few of the late books. She begs that if you think her dictionary likely to shift for itself in this age of dictionaries, you will be pleased to encourage her by taking some share of the copy, and using your influence with others to take the rest, or put her in any way of making the undertaking profitable to her.

I am extremely obliged by the seventh volume.[3] You have a trick of laying yourself open to objections, in the first part of your work, and crushing them in subsequent parts. A great deal that I had to say before I read the conversation in the latter part, is now taken from me.[4] I wish however Sir Charles had not compromised in matters of religion.[5]

1. *Ante* To Thomas Birch, 12 May 1750. Williams sometimes received financial presents from friends; alternatively, Richardson's gift may have been a copy of his new novel, *The History of Sir Charles Grandison*. Williams admired the book so much that she published a poem in its praise ("Verses to Mr. Richardson on his History of Sir Charles Grandison," *GM* 1754, p. 40).

2. When she lived with her father at the Charterhouse during the 1730s, Williams assisted his fellow pensioner Stephen Gray with electrical experiments; this fact, as well as the subsequent reference to "chimistry," suggests that she was projecting a dictionary of scientific terms. This scheme does not appear to have developed further.

3. The seventh and final volume of *The History of Sir Charles Grandison* had appeared 14 Mar.

4. In the final volume of *Sir Charles Grandison*, the characters often discuss issues and events from earlier in the novel. Letters XLII and L are likely candidates for SJ's "conversation."

5. In an appendix to Volume VII, Richardson acknowledges the many objections he had received on this score: "many there are, who look upon his offered compromise with the Porretta family, in allowing the daughters of the proposed marriage to be brought up by the mother, reserving to himself the education of the sons only, as a blot in the character" ("A Concluding Note by the Editor," 1754, VII.300).

I must beg leave to introduce to your acquaintance Mr. Adams under whom I had the honour to perform exercises at Oxford, and who has lately recommended himself to the best part of Mankind by his confutation of Hume on Miracles.[6]

My Lord Corke[7] is anxious to see Mr. Falkner's letter to me,[8] I wish you would send it him, as by my desire, and when it is returned take care to keep it for my justification, for I would not have shewn it, but at his own instigation.

I cannot conclude without recommending Miss Williams's little business to you;[9] she is certainly qualified for her work, as much as any one that will ever undertake it, as she understands chimistry and many other arts with which Ladies are seldom acquainted, and I shall endeavour to put her and her helpmate into method. I can truly say that she deserves all the encouragement that can be given her, for a being more pure from any thing vicious I have never known. I am, Sir, Your most obliged and most humble servant,

SAM. JOHNSON

6. William Adams (1706–89), D.D., fellow and later (1775–89) master of Pembroke College, Oxford, first met SJ at Pembroke in 1728. Adams would have been SJ's tutor had he returned to Oxford after his one year in residence. In 1752 Adams published *An Essay on Mr. Hume's Essay on Miracles*, a response to Hume's *Essay* of 1748.

7. *Ante* To Lord Orrery, Late Nov. 1751, n. 1.

8. It is likely that George Faulkner's letter to SJ referred to the piracy of *Sir Charles Grandison* (*Ante* To Samuel Richardson, 26 Sept. 1753, n. 10).

9. SJ made a number of efforts to help Williams better herself financially. He asked Birch to forward the sale of her Raleigh manuscript (*Ante* To Thomas Birch, 12 May 1750, n. 5), encouraged Garrick to give her a benefit at Drury Lane (*Life* I.159 n. 1), and assisted in the preparation of her *Miscellanies* (1766).

Thomas Warton[1]

TUESDAY 16 JULY 1754

MS: Trinity College, Oxford.

ADDRESS: To the Rev'd. Mr. Warton of Trinity College, Oxford.

POSTMARK: 16 IY.

1. Thomas Warton (1728–90), poet and scholar, Fellow of Trinity College, Pro-

Sir: July 16, 1754

It is but an ill return for the book with which you were pleased to favour me,[2] to have delayed my thanks for it till now. I am too apt to be negligent but I can never deliberately show any disrespect to a man of your character, and I now pay you a very honest ack[n]owledgement for the advancement[3] of the literature of our native Country. You have shown to all who shall hereafter attempt the study of our ancient authours the way to success, by directing them to the perusal of the books which those authours had read. Of this method Hughes and Men much greater than Hughes seem never to have thought.[4] The Reason why the authours which are yet read of the sixteenth Century are so little understood is that they are read alone, and no help is borrowed from those who lived with them or before them. Some part of this ignorance I hope to remove by my book which now draws towards its end,[5] but which I cannot finish to my mind without visiting the libraries of Oxford which I therefore hope to see in about a fortnight.[6] I know not how long I shall stay or where I shall lodge, but

---

fessor of Poetry at Oxford (1757–67), and Poet Laureate (1785). His *Observations on The Faerie Queene of Spenser* (1754) and *History of English Poetry* (1775–81) strengthened the idea of a native English poetic tradition. Warton collaborated with his brother Joseph on several numbers of the *Adventurer*, and thereby came into contact with SJ (David Fairer, "Authorship Problems in *The Adventurer*," *RES* 25, 1974, pp. 144, 148–49).

2. SJ refers to Warton's *Observations on The Faerie Queene of Spenser.*

3. MS: "ad" superimposed upon "su"

4. John Hughes (1677–1720), poet, historian, and translator. According to SJ, Hughes's edition of Spenser (1715) was "a work for which he was well qualified as a judge of the beauties of writing, but perhaps wanted an antiquary's knowledge of the obsolete words" (*Lives of the Poets* II.162).

5. By the summer of 1754, all of the first volume and most of the second volume of the *Dictionary* had been completed (Sledd and Kolb, p. viii). SJ left room "in the first for Preface, Grammar & History none of them yet begun" (*Works,* Yale ed. I.50).

6. SJ stayed in Oxford a little less than five weeks. Warton, who acted as SJ's guide, does not mention any visits to college libraries (*Life* I.271–74). In fact SJ's time in Oxford gave him "little beyond the satisfaction of knowing that there is nothing to be done" (*Post* To William Strahan, Late July or Early Aug. 1754).

shall be sure to look for you at my arrival, and we shall easily settle the rest. I am, Dear Sir, your most obedient and most humble servant,

SAM. JOHNSON

William Strahan

LATE JULY *or* EARLY AUGUST 1754[1]

MS: Folger Shakespeare Library.

ADDRESS: To Mr. Strahan.

Sir:

I shall not be long here, but in the mean time if Miss Williams wants any money pray speak to Mr. Millar and supply her, they writ to me about some taxes which I wish you would pay.

My journey will come to very little beyond the satisfaction of knowing that there is nothing to be done, and that I leave few advantages here to those that shall come after me. I am, Sir, etc.

SAM. JOHNSON

My compliments to Mrs. Strahan.

1. G. B. Hill argues persuasively that this letter was written from Oxford in 1754, while the *Dictionary* was still in progress and Strahan and Millar were acting as SJ's bankers and paymasters (JB's *Life*, 1887, VI.xxvii–xxviii). Clifford accepts Hill's dating (1979, p. 125). According to Thomas Warton, SJ arrived in Oxford "within a fortnight" of 16 July (*Life* I.270 n. 5). Both sentences of the letter suggest strongly that SJ was writing shortly after his arrival, when he had been coldly received by the Master of Pembroke and before he had established friendly relations with Meeke, Wise, and other Oxford dons (*Life* I.271–73).

William Huggins[1]

SATURDAY 9 NOVEMBER 1754

MS: Hyde Collection.

ADDRESS: To William Huggins, Esqr., at Headly Park near Farnham.[2]

POSTMARK: 9 NO.

ENDORSEMENT: S. Johnsons Letter, Nov. 9, 54.

Sir: Novr. 9, 1754

I find that I am likely to suffer the common fate of intermedlers, and receive no thanks on either side. I can however solace myself with my good intentions without any disturbance from the event of a transaction in which nothing but my benevolence gave me any interest.[3] I supposed you desirous to recover a favourite watch, and proposed a way which is certainly the most speedy, and I believe the cheapest; if you are more affected by the provocation than the loss, and more intent on resentment than the disputed property, I have no means of pacification to offer. But your letter makes it necessary for me to tell you, that neither the loss nor the provocation is my fault. The Loss I endeavoured to repair, and should have procured restitution, or willingness in[4] restitution, had not this new expedient been found out, by which the only conviction, which I pretend to have raised, conviction of inability to defend himself, was for a time suspended, without the least knowledge or cooperation of mine. The Provocation I endeavoured to prevent, by making up the quarrel in which I was wholly on the

1. William Huggins (1696–1761), scholar of Italian literature, whose translation of Ariosto's *Orlando Furioso* appeared in 1755. During the summer of 1754, Huggins employed Giuseppe Baretti (*Post* To Robert Chambers, 21 Nov. 1754, n. 8) to help him revise the translation (*Life* IV.473–76).

2. Huggins's country house in Hampshire, where Baretti had stayed while assisting Huggins with his translation.

3. According to Baretti, his reward for helping with the Ariosto translation included a gold watch, which Huggins later claimed had been only a loan. Baretti first refused to return the watch and then pawned it. SJ was called in as "a neutral adjudicator" (J. L. Clifford, "Johnson and Foreign Visitors to London: Baretti and Others," *Eighteenth Century Studies Presented to Arthur M. Wilson*, 1972, pp. 102–3).

4. MS: "in" superimposed upon "to"

side of Mr. Croker.[5] In this attempt I failed and the feud proceeded. Mr. Baretti showed me his letter before he sent it, but he did not show it for advice, and I observed neutrality so scrupulously as not even to mend his English lest he should have it to say that I concurred with him. The second letter he did not bring till he had sent it, and when he gave it me [he] told me "You will not like it." He told the truth.

Your warm assertion of yourself to me is therefore unnecessary for I never pretended to think you in the wrong. The particular question about which I remember myself quoted, you have justly distinguished in your letter to Mr. Croker, and I have nothing to object further. Your vindication of Mr. Croker is yet less proper, for I have always maintained him to be in the right, and endeavoured to convince him how easily he might prosecute the work without the help which he regretted to have lost. Mr. Croker was indeed the man for whom I was chiefly solicitous, as he was the only man that could be much hurt. I have opposed Mr. Baretti in the whole process of this difference and in the proposal meant him no favour, nor as any favour did he acknowledge it, what I said of his condition he would resent more, than he would thank me for my interposition.

One angry paragraph seems to be the consequence of an oversight in you or me. You have read, or I have written *Hospitality* for *Hostility*, if you look on my letter you will find that *hospitality* could not or should not be the word. The laws of *Hospitality* no man ever within my knowledge charged you with breaking, the *rules of generous hostility* Mr. Croker has certainly broken if not by his application to the Sardinian Envoy,[6] which I mentioned with no great vehemence because at worst I

5. The Rev. Temple Henry Croker (?1730–?90), miscellaneous writer, worked with Huggins on the Ariosto project and may also have served as his chaplain. Croker acted as Huggins's intermediary in the affair of the watch, thereby earning Baretti's hatred (*Life* IV.475; Clifford, "Foreign Visitors," p. 102).

6. Carlo Francesco, Conte di Perrone, Sardinian envoy to England, 1749–55 (*Repertorium der diplomatischen Vertreter aller Länder*, ed. Friedrich Hausmann, 1950, II.365). Baretti had secured Perrone's protection, which was later revoked under pressure from Sir Thomas Robinson, one of the secretaries of state. Huggins's

thought it only circumstantially blameable, yet surely by his attempt on the landlord, of which I might speak more harshly, and speak truth.[7] He is however a good man who in such a quarrel dos but one thing wrong.

I will repeat it again that I have endeavoured honestly and, what is more, kindly, to moderate the violence of this dispute, if I had succeeded I should at least have spared you the impropriety of such a letter as you have been pleased to send to, Sir, Your very humble Servant,

SAM. JOHNSON

watch was eventually retrieved from the pawnbroker and returned to him (Clifford, "Foreign Visitors," p. 105).

7. "There may even have been attempts to force Baretti's landlord to allow a search of his premises" (Clifford, "Foreign Visitors," p. 103).

William Huggins

THURSDAY 14 NOVEMBER 1754

MS: Hyde Collection.

Sir: Novr. 14, 1754

I should very much blame my own negligence, if I should delay a single post to declare that I am more than satisfied, and that I shall always set the highest value on a mind so ready to receive conviction, and so candid to acknowledge it.

I was led by your letter to suspect that you had received some misinformation, but I could not conceive what might be charged upon me. I see that fiction has no limits, to show you on what allegations some will venture, I assure you that I never in my life saw either the Venetian Resident,[1] or the Landlord, nor ever sent a message to either, nor have any reason to be certain that either knows my name, or knows of my existence. I think, Sir, I may fairly claim that whatever shall be said to my disadvantage in this affair, may be judged by this Specimen. I

1. Giovanni Francesco Zon, Venetian Resident from 1754 to 1758 (*Repertorium der diplomatischen Vertreter aller Länder*, ed. Friedrich Hausmann, 1950, II.414). Zon lived in Soho Square (*Post* To Robert Chambers, 21 Nov. 1754).

hinted before that Mr. Croker has, I sincerely think without his fault, whisperers or clamourers about him, who want only to do mischief, or make themselves sport. If I had not happened to have written, what must I not have been thought?

I hope, Sir, to have now made an end of this subject, which shall no longer disturb me, and I sincerely wish that it may cease likewise to disturb you. I should be glad that every good Mind were left to the enjoyment of itself.

If you shall please to continue this correspondence upon more pleasing topicks, it will be considered as a favour by, Sir, Your most obedient and most humble servant,

SAM. JOHNSON

Robert Chambers[1]

THURSDAY 21 NOVEMBER 1754

MS: Trinity College, Oxford.

ADDRESS: To Mr. Chambers at Lincoln College, Oxford.

POSTMARK: 21 NO.

Dear Sir: Novr. 21, 1754

The Commission which I delayed to trouble you with at your departure I am now obliged to send you, and beg that you will be so kind as to carry it to Mr. *Warton* of *Trin.* to whom I should have written immediately but that I know not if he be yet come back to Oxford.

In the Catalogue of Mss. of Gr. Brit. etc.[2] Vol. 1. pag. 28 Mss. Bodl. Martyrium xv Martyrum sub Juliano auctore Theophylacto.[3]

1. Robert Chambers (1737–1803), exhibitioner of Lincoln College, Oxford; later (1766–77) Vinerian Professor of Law. Chambers left for India in 1774, where he served on the supreme court of judicature in Bengal until 1799. He was elected to The Club in 1768 and knighted in 1777.

2. SJ refers to the *Catalogi Librorum Manuscriptorum Angliæ et Hiberniæ* (Oxford, 1697) compiled by Edward Bernard (1638–96), Savilian Professor of Astronomy. SJ owned a copy at the time of his death (Greene, 1975, p. 89).

3. The actual catalogue entry reads: "Tom. 1. Part. 1. p. 28: *Martyrium* xv. Martyrum sub Juliano imp. auctore Theophylacto."

It is desired that Mr. Warton will enquire and send word what will be the cost of transcribing this manuscript.

v. 2. pag. 32 No. 1022. 58. Col. Nov.

Commentaria in Acta Apost.

Comment. in Septem Epistolas catholicas.[4]

He is desired to tell what is the age of each of these Mss. what[5] it will cost to have a transcript of the[6] two first pages of each.

The Answer is to be directed to His Excellency Mr. Zon. Venetian Resident Soho Square.[7]

If Mr. Warton be not in Oxford, you may try if you can get it done by any body else, or stay till he comes according to your own convenience. It is for an Italian Literato.

I hope, dear sir, that you do not regret the change of London for Oxford. Mr. Baretti is well,[8] and Miss Williams, and we shall all be glad to hear from you whenever you shall be so kind as to write to, sir, your most humble servant,

SAM. JOHNSON

4. "Tom. II. Part. 1. p. 32: 1022.58 Commentarius in Acta Apostolorum, & 7 Epistolas Catholicas, Græce."

5. MS: "and" del. before "what"

6. MS: "each" partially erased before "the"

7. *Ante* To William Huggins, 14 Nov. 1754, n. 1.

8. Giuseppe Baretti (1719–89), lexicographer, dramatist, and man of letters. A native of Piedmont, Baretti came to England in 1751. His work as a teacher of Italian brought him into contact with Charlotte Lennox, who introduced him to SJ.

Thomas Warton

THURSDAY 28 NOVEMBER 1754

MS: Trinity College, Oxford.

ADDRESS: To the Revd. Mr. Warton of[1] Trin. Coll., Oxford.

POSTMARK: 28 NO.

1. MS: "of" altered from "at"

Dear Sir: Nov. 28. 1754

I am extremely obliged to you and to Mr. Wise,[2] for the uncommon care which you have taken of my interest, if You can accomplish your kind design, I shall certainly take me a little habitation among You.[3]

The Books which I promised to Mr. Wise I have not yet been able to procure, but I shall send him a[4] Finnick Dictionary the only copy perhaps in England which was presented me by a learned Swede,[5] but I keep it back that it may make a set of my own Books of the new edition with which I shall accompany it more welcome.[6] You will assure him of my gratitude.

Poor dear Collins[7]—would a letter give him any pleasure; I have a mind to write.

I am glad of your hindrance in your Spenserian design, yet I would not have it delayed.[8] Three hours a day stolen from sleep and amusement will produce it, let a servitour transcribe

2. The Rev. Francis Wise (1695–1767), Radclivian Librarian (1748–67). Warton records that when Johnson visited Oxford in 1754 they both walked "three or four times, to Ellsfield, a village beautifully situated about three miles from Oxford, to see Mr. Wise . . . with whom Johnson was much pleased. . . . Here was an excellent library; particularly, a valuable collection of books in Northern literature, with which Johnson was often very busy" (*Life* I.273).

3. The "kind design" of obtaining for SJ the Degree of Master of Arts by diploma, for notable literary work done outside the University, may have originated with Warton. On 14 Dec. 1754 Wise wrote to Warton: "I have considered on what you mentioned to me at the President's, and think that it would be more apropos, and more to Mr. Johnson's good liking, if the University honours were sent to him before his book is published, that he may be able to write himself A.M. in the title page" (John Wooll, *Memoirs of Warton*, 1806, p. 228).

4. MS: "A" partially erased before "a"

5. Presumably the *Fennici Lexici Tentamen* (Stockholm, 1745) of Daniel Juslenius (1676–1752). His dictionary was a pioneering work that held its own for some eighty years (*Svensk Biografisk Lexicon*, 1973–75, XX.488–90).

6. SJ refers to the duodecimo edition of *The Adventurer* (1754), published in four volumes by John Payne (*Works*, Yale ed. II.337).

7. *Ante* To Joseph Warton, 8 Mar. 1754, nn. 3, 5.

8. Warton explains his design as that "of publishing a volume of observations on the best of Spenser's works" (*Life* I.276 n. 3). Chapman (I.58) conjecturally emends "best" to "rest."

the quotations and interleave them with references to save time. This will shorten the work and lessen the fatigue.

Can I do anything to promoting the diploma,—? I would not be wanting to cooperate with your kindness, of which whatever be the effect I shall[9] be, Dear Sir, your most obliged and most humble servant,

SAM. JOHNSON

9. MS: "shall" altered from "should"

Thomas Warton

SATURDAY 21 DECEMBER 1754

MS: Trinity College, Oxford.

ADDRESS: To the Revd. Mr Warton of Trinity, Oxon.

POSTMARK: 21 DE.

Dear Sir: Decr. 21, 1754

I am extremely sensible of the favour done me both by Mr. Wise and yourself. The Book cannot, I think, be printed in less than six weeks, nor probably so soon, and I will keep back the titlepage for such an insertion as You seem to promise me. Be pleased to let me know, what money I should send you for bearing the expence of the affair and I will take care that you may have it ready in your hand.

I had lately the favour of a Letter from your Brother with some account of poor Collins for whom I am much concerned: I have a notion that by very[1] great temperance or more properly abstinence he might yet recover.[2]

There is an Old English and Latin book of poems by Barclay called the *Ship* of *Fools*,[3] at the end of which are a number of

1. MS: "v" superimposed upon "t"

2. *Ante* To Joseph Warton, 8 Mar. 1754, n. 5.

3. Sebastian Brandt's *Das Narrenschiff* (1494), a satire on human folly, had been translated into French and Latin before Alexander Barclay (?1475–1552) published his free translation in 1509, drawing "into our mother tongue in rude language the sentences of the verses" (*Ship of Fools*, 2d ed., 1570, "The Argument"). At the time of his death, SJ owned a copy of the second edition (Greene, 1975, p. 33).

Eglogues (so he writes it from Ægloga) which are probably the first in our Language.[4] If you cannot find the book I will get Mr. Dodsly to send it you.

I shall be extremely glad to hear from you soon again to know if the affair proceeds.[5] I have mentioned it to none of my friends for fear of being laughed at for my disappointment.

You know poor Mr. Dodsly has lost his Wife,[6] I believe he is much affected. I hope he will not suffer so much as I yet suffer for the loss of mine.[7]

Οἴμι· τι δ'ὄιμι; θνῆτα γὰρ πεπόνθαμεν.[8]

I have ever since seemed to myself broken off from mankind a kind of solitary wanderer in the wild of life, without any certain direction, or fixed point of view. A gloomy gazer on a World to which I have little relation. Yet I would endeavour by the help of you and your brother to supply the want of closer union by friendship, and hope to have long the pleasure of being, Dear sir, most affectionately yours,

SAM. JOHNSON

4. "Certayne Egloges of Alexander Barclay" were published at the end of the second edition of *The Ship of Fools* (1570). The spelling *egloge* reflects a false derivation from the Greek word for "goat" (αἴξ, αἰγός), as if an eclogue were a goatherd's song.

5. *Ante* To Thomas Warton, 28 Nov. 1754, n. 3.

6. Catherine Iserloo (*c.* 1710–54), whom Robert Dodsley had married in 1732. He praised his "Kitty" in *The Muse in Livery* (1732), and suffered intensely when she died (Ralph Straus, *Robert Dodsley,* 1910, pp. 27, 126).

7. Elizabeth Johnson died on 17 Mar. 1752. *Ante* To John Taylor, 18 Mar. 1752, nn. 1, 2.

8. "Alas! but wherefore alas? Man is born to sorrow" (fragment from the lost Euripidean tragedy *Bellerophon*: *Tragicorum Græcorum Fragmenta,* ed. Augustus Nauck, 1964, No. 300, p. 449).

Joseph Warton

TUESDAY 24 DECEMBER 1754

PRINTED SOURCE: John Wooll, *Biographical Memoirs of the Late Revd. Joseph Warton,* 1806, p. 229.

Dear Sir: Dec. 24th 1754

I am sat down to answer your kind letter, though I know not whether I shall direct it so as that it may reach you; the miscarriage of it will be no great matter, as I have nothing to send but thanks, of which I owe you many, yet if a few should be lost, I shall amply find them in my own mind; and professions of respect, of which the profession will easily be renewed while the respect continues: and the same causes which first produced can hardly fail to preserve it. Pray let me know however whether my letter finds its way to you.

Poor dear Collins—Let me know whether you think it would give him pleasure if I should write to him.[1] I have often been near his state, and therefore have it in great commiseration.[2]

I sincerely wish you the usual pleasures of this joyous season, and more than the usual pleasures, those of contemplation on the great event which this festival commemorates. I am, Dear Sir, Your most affectionate, and most humble servant,

SAM. JOHNSON

1. *Ante* To Joseph Warton, 8 Mar. 1754, nn. 3, 5. Collins had been living in Oxford the previous month. Thomas Warton reported that he "saw him frequently, but he was so weak and low, that he could not bear conversation" (Richard Wendorf and Charles Ryskamp, *The Works of William Collins*, 1979, p. xxix).

2. "When I survey my past life, I discover nothing but a barren waste of time with some disorders of body, and disturbances of the mind very near to madness" (*Works*, Yale ed. I.264).

Thomas Warton

SATURDAY 1 FEBRUARY 1755

MS: Trinity College, Oxford.

Dear Sir: Febr. 1, 1755

I wrote to You some weeks ago but I believe did not direct accurately, and therefore know not whether you had my Letter. I would likewise write to your Brother but know not where to find him. I now begin to see land, after having wandered, according to Mr. Warburtons phrase, in this vast Sea of words.[1] What reception I shall meet with upon the Shore I know not, whether the sound of Bells and acclamations of the People which Ariosto talks of in his last canto[2] or a general murmur of dislike, I know not whether I shall find upon the coast, a Calypso that will court or a Polypheme that will eat me.[3] But if Polypheme comes to me have at his eyes.

I hope however the criticks will let me be at peace for though I do not much fear their skill or strength, I am a little afraid of myself, and would not willingly feel so much illwill in my bosom as literary quarrels are apt to excite.

Mr. Baretti is about a work for which he is in great want of Crescembeni,[4] which you may have again when you please.

There is nothing considerable done or doing among us here, we are not perhaps as innocent as villagers but most of us seem to be as idle. I hope however you are busy, and should be glad to know what you are doing.[5] I am, dearest Sir, your most humble servant,

SAM. JOHNSON

1. "But the English tongue, at this Juncture, deserves and demands our particular regard. . . . For we have neither Grammar nor Dictionary, neither chart nor Compass, to guide us through this wide sea of words" (William Warburton, *The Works of Shakespear*, 1747, I.xxv).

2. "Hark how the sounds of transport rend the sky! / Hark, how the thunders o'er the billows fly, / I hear the clang of bells, and trumpets loud, / Mix'd with the tumults of the shouting crowd" (*Orlando Furioso*, canto 46, stanza 2, trans. John Hoole). The lines introduce the homecoming imagined by Ariosto's narrator toward the end of his work.

3. Calypso is the Homeric nymph who takes the shipwrecked Odysseus as her lover; Polypheme is the Cyclops whom Odysseus blinds (*Odyssey* v, ix).

4. *Ante* To Robert Chambers, 21 Nov. 1754, n. 8. In 1755 Baretti published *An Introduction to the Italian Language*, in 1757 *The Italian Library*, a biographical compendium. SJ contributed to the dedications of both these works (Hazen, pp. 6, 12). The work of Giovanni Mario Crescimbeni in question here was probably the combined *Istoria della volgar poesia* and *Commentarii* (1730–31). Baretti refers to Crescimbeni's work in *The Italian Library.*

5. MS: "what you are doing what you are doing"

Samuel Richardson

MONDAY 3 FEBRUARY 1755

MS: Huntington Library.

ENDORSEMENT: Febr. 3, 1755.

Dear Sir: Febr. 3, 1755

If You have any part of the universal History yet unengaged, there [is] a Gentleman desirous of giving his assistance.[1] To recommend authours is dangerous, I have therefore sent you his Book [which] I think sets him on a level with most of those who are at present employed. I do not know him but the Gentleman to whom he dedicates informs me that he is diligent and persevering. His Patron will be answerable for any books put into his hands, and perhaps for money if any be advanced, but no request[2] of money has been made to me. I have said nothing to Mr. Millar for who should judge of an authour but You?[3] If you approve him you will therefore please to introduce him so as that no offence be given.

I am in no great haste for an Answer. You may look into the book at leisure, for I do not expect that you should catch it with the Eagerness with which the world catches at yours. I am, sir, Your most humble servant,

SAM. JOHNSON

Pray favour me with an account of the translations of Clarissa which[4] you have, I have[5] a desire to borrow some of them.[6]

1. Richardson, who owned first a sixth and then a twelfth share in the *Universal History*, was involved in the printing of the ancient part (20 vols., 1736–50) and the printing and organization of the modern part (44 vols., 1759–66). "The planning of the modern part must have been rather haphazard ... at any rate the contents of the various volumes are somewhat miscellaneous, poorly ordered and even more poorly balanced" (T.C.D. Eaves and B. D. Kimpel, *Samuel Richardson*, 1971, pp. 80, 159, 509–10). Neither the "Gentleman" nor his "Patron" has been identified.

2. MS: "such" del. before "request"

3. This sentence has been bracketed in an unidentified hand.

4. MS: "w" superimposed upon "I"

5. MS: "tr" del. before "have"

6. By 1755 *Clarissa* had been translated into French, Dutch, and German (Eaves and Kimpel, *Samuel Richardson*, pp. 318–20).

Thomas Warton

TUESDAY 4 FEBRUARY 1755

MS: Trinity College, Oxford.

ADDRESS: To the Revd. Mr. Warton of Trinity College, Oxford.

POSTMARK: 4 FE.

Dear Sir: Febr. 4, 1755

I received your letter this day with great sense of the favour that has been done me, for which I return you my most sincere thanks and entreat you to pay to Mr. Wise such returns as I ought to make for so much kindness so little deserved.

I sent Mr. Wise the Lexicon,[1] and afterwards wrote to him, but know not whether he had either the book or letter, be so good as to contrive to enquire.

But why dos my dear Mr. Warton tell me nothing of himself. Where hangs the new volume?[2] can I help? let not the past labour be lost for want of a little more, but snatch what time you can from the hall and the pupils and the coffeehouse and the parks to complete your design. I am, Dear sir, Your most obliged and most humble servant,

SAM. JOHNSON

1. *Ante* To Thomas Warton, 28 Nov. 1754, n. 2.

2. *Ante* To Thomas Warton, 28 Nov. 1754, n. 8.

Lord Chesterfield[1]

FRIDAY 7 FEBRUARY 1755[2]

MS: British Library. A copy dictated to Giuseppe Baretti by SJ, with corrections in SJ's hand.[3] Collated with the copy dictated by SJ to JB (MS: Beinecke Library, Yale University).

1. Philip Dormer Stanhope (1694–1773), fourth Earl of Chesterfield, statesman and man of letters, to whom SJ had dedicated his *Plan of a Dictionary* in 1747. For a complete account of Chesterfield's dealings with SJ, see Sledd and Kolb, pp. 85–104.

2. The second edition of JB's *Life* (1793) supplies the day of the month.

3. "This he gave to Mr. Langton; adding, that if it were to come into print, he wished it to be from that copy" (*Life* I.260).

My Lord: February 1755

I have been lately informed by the Proprietor of The World that two Papers in which my Dictionary is recommended to the Public[4] were written by your Lordship.[5] To be so distinguished is an honour which, being very little accustomed to favours from the Great, I know not well how to receive, or in what terms to acknowledge.

When upon some slight encouragment I first visited your Lordship I was overpowered like the rest of Mankind by the enchantment of your adress, and could not forbear to wish that I might boast myself[6] Le Vainqueur du Vainqueur de la Terre,[7] that I might obtain that regard for which I saw the world contending, but[8] I found my attendance so little incouraged,[9] that neither pride nor modesty would suffer me to continue it. When I had once adressed your Lordship in public, I had exhausted all the Art of pleasing which[10] a retired and uncourtly Scholar can possess. I had done all that I could, and no Man is well pleased to have his all neglected, be it ever so little.

Seven years, My lord have now past[11] since I waited in your outward[12] Rooms or was repulsed from your Door,[13] during[14] which time I have been pushing[15] on my work through difficulties of which it is useless to complain, and have

4. "I have been told that two papers in the World in which I and my labours are recommended to the Publick" (MS: Yale).

5. Chesterfield's essays had appeared in Nos. 100 (28 Nov. 1754) and 101 (5 Dec. 1754) of Robert Dodsley's *The World.*

6. "that I might be" (MS: Yale)

7. "Je chante le vainqueur des vainqueurs de la terre": the opening line of Scudéry's *Alaric,* quoted by Boileau in his *Art Poétique* (III.272).

8. "but after a short time" (MS: Yale)

9. "regarded" (MS: Yale)

10. "that" (MS: Yale)

11. "are now past" (MS: Yale)

12. "outer" (MS: Yale)

13. In this echo of Horace's *Satire* II.vi, SJ alludes ironically to the discerning and generous patronage offered Horace by Maecenas: "Septimus octavo propior iam fugerit annus, / ex quo Maecenas me coepit habere suorum / in numero": "The seventh year—nay, nearer the eighth—will soon have sped, since Maecenas began to count me among his friends" (ll. 40–42, trans. H. R. Fairclough, Loeb ed.).

14. "in" (MS: Yale)

15. "I have carried" (MS: Yale)

brought[16] it at last to the verge of Publication without one Act of assistance,[17] one word of encouragement,[18] or one smile of favour.[19] Such treatment I did not expect, for I never had a Patron before.

The Shepherd in Virgil grew at last acquainted with Love, and found him a Native of the Rocks.[20] Is not a Patron,[21] My Lord, one who looks with unconcern on a Man struggling for Life in the water and when he has reached ground encumbers him with help.[22] The notice which you have been pleased to take of my Labours,[23] had it been early, had been kind; but it has been delayed till I am indifferent and cannot enjoy it, till I am solitary and cannot impart it,[24] till I am known and do not want it.

I hope it is no very cinical asperity not to confess obligation where no benefit has been received, or to be unwilling that the Public[25] should consider me as owing that to a Patron, which Providence has enabled me to do for myself.

Having carried on my work thus far with so little obligation to[26] any favourer of Learning I shall not be disappointed[27]

16. "and brought" (MS: Yale)

17. "one word of encouragement" (MS: Yale)

18. "one act of assistance" (MS: Yale)

19. "Doctor Johnson, when he gave me this Copy of His letter desired that I would annex to it his Information to me, that whereas it is said in the Letter, that 'no assistance has been received'—he did once receive from Ld. C. the Sum of ten pounds; but as that was so inconsiderable a Sum, he thought the mention of it could not properly find place in a Letter of the kind that this was" (note in Bennet Langton's hand, MS: British Library).

20. "nunc scio, quid sit Amor. duris in cotibus illum / aut Tmaros aut Rhodope aut extremi Garamantes": "Now know I what Love is; on flinty crags Tmarus bare him—or Rhodope, or the farthest Garamantes" (*Eclogue* VIII.43–44, trans. H. R. Fairclough, Loeb ed.).

21. "Is a Patron" (MS: Yale)

22. *patron*: "commonly a wretch who supports with insolence, and is paid with flattery" (SJ's *Dictionary*). According to JB (*Life* I.264), "after experiencing the uneasiness which Lord Chesterfield's fallacious patronage made him feel," SJ substituted "patron" for "garret" in l. 160 of *The Vanity of Human Wishes* ("Toil, envy, want, the garret, and the jail").

23. "The regard now shewn me by your Lordship" (MS: Yale)

24. Elizabeth Johnson had died on 17 Mar. 1752.

25. "the world" (MS: Yale)

26. "help from" (MS: Yale)

27. "surprised" (MS: Yale)

though I should conclude it, if less be possible, with less, for I have been long wakened[28] from that Dream of hope, in which I once boasted[29] myself with so much exultation, My lord, Your Lordship's Most humble, most obedient Servant,[30]

S.J.

28. "awakened" (MS: Yale)
29. "subscribed" (MS: Yale)
30. "most humble servant" (MS: Yale)

Thomas Warton

THURSDAY 13 FEBRUARY 1755

MS: Trinity College, Oxford.

ADDRESS: To the Revd. Mr. Warton at Trinity College, Oxford.

POSTMARK: 13 FE.

Dear Sir: Febr. 13, 1755

I had a Letter last week from Mr. Wise, but have yet heard nothing from You, nor know in what state my little affair stands, of which I beg you to inform me if you can to morrow by the return of the post.[1]

Mr. Wise sends me word that he has not had the Finnick Lexicon,[2] which yet I sent some time ago and if he has it not yet must enquire after it, however do not let your letter stay for that.

Your Brother,[3] who is a better correspondent than you, and not much better, sends me word that your Pupils keep you in college, of which I am glad but do they keep you from writing too? Let them at least give you time to write to, Dear sir, your most affectionate, humble servant,

SAM. JOHNSON

1. *Ante* To Thomas Warton, 28 Nov. 1754, n. 3.
2. *Ante* To Thomas Warton, 28 Nov. 1754, n. 5.
3. *Ante* To Joseph Warton, 8 Mar. 1753, n. 1.

Thomas Warton

TUESDAY 25 FEBRUARY 1755

MS: Trinity College, Oxford.

ADDRESS: To the Revd. Mr. Warton of Trinity College, Oxford.

POSTMARK: 25 FE.

Dear Sir:

Dr. King was with me a few Minutes before your Letter,[1] this however is the first instance in which your kind intentions to me have ever been frustrated. I have now the full effect of your[2] care,[3] and benevolence, and am far from thinking it a slight honour or a small advantage, since it will put the enjoyment of your conversation more frequently in the power of, Dear sir, your most obliged and affectionate,

SAM. JOHNSON

I have enclosed a Letter to the Vicechancellor which you will read, and if you like it, seal and give him.[4]

1. William King (1685–1763), D.C.L., Principal of St. Mary's Hall, Oxford (1719–63), a scholar and satirist with strong Jacobitical leanings (*Life* I.282 n. 2; *Walpole's Correspondence*, Yale ed. XXX.89).

2. MS: "your" altered from "? you"

3. MS: "of" partially erased before "care"

4. *Post* To George Huddesford, 26 Feb. 1755.

George Huddesford[1]

WEDNESDAY 26 FEBRUARY 1755

MS: Hyde Collection.

ADDRESS: To the Revd. Dr. Huddesford.

ENDORSEMENT: Sam. Johnson, 26 Feb. 55.

Londini 4to Cal. Mart. 1755

Viro reverendo . . . Huddesford S.T.P.
Universitatis Oxoniensis Vicecancellario dignissimo S.P.D.

1. George Huddesford (*c.* 1699–1776), D.D., Vice-Chancellor of Oxford (1753–56) and President of Trinity College (1731–76).

SAM. JOHNSON.

Ingratus plane et tibi et mihi videar, nisi quanto me gaudio affecerint, quos nuper mihi honores, te, credo, auctore, decrevit Senatus academicus, literarum, quo tamen nihil levius, officio significem; ingratus etiam nisi comitatem quâ vir eximius mihi vestri testimonium amoris, in manus tradidit,[2] agnoscam et laudem. Si quid est, unde rei tam gratae accedat gratia, hoc ipso magis mihi placet, quod eo tempore in ordines academicos denuò cooptatus sim, quo tuam imminuere auctoritatem, famamque Oxoniensium laedere, omnibus modis conantur homines vafri nec tamen acuti, quibus ego, prout Viro umbratico licuit, semper restiti, semper restiturus. Qui enim, has inter rerum procellas, vel tibi vel Academiae defuerit, illum virtuti et literis, sibique et posteris defuturum existimo. Vale.

2. *Ante* To Thomas Warton, 25 Feb. 1755, n. 1.

Thomas Warton

THURSDAY 20 MARCH 1755

MS: Trinity College, Oxford.

ADDRESS: To the Revd. Mr. Warton at Trin. College, Oxford.

POSTMARK: 20 MR.

Dear Sir: March 20, 1755

After I received my diploma I wrote you a letter of thanks with a letter to the vicechancellor and sent another to Mr. Wise,[1] but have heard from nobody since, and begin to think myself forgotten. It is true I sent you a double letter, and you may fear an expensive correspondent,[2] but I would have taken it kindly if you had returned it treble, and what is a double

1. *Ante* To Thomas Warton, 28 Nov. 1754 and nn. 2, 3; *Ante* To George Huddesford, 26 Feb. 1755 and n. 1.

2. A double letter consisted of two sheets of paper, which would cost the recipient twice as much as a letter consisting of a single sheet. The cost of a double letter from London to Oxford was sixpence (Hendy, pp. 184–85).

letter to a *petty King* that having fellowship and fines—can sleep[3] without a modus in his head.[4]

Dear Mr. Warton let me hear from you, and tell me something I care not what so I hear it but from you—something I will tell you—I hope to see my Dictionary bound and lettered next week[5]—vasta mole superbus.[6] And I have a great mind to come to Oxford at Easter, but you will not invite me, shall I come uninvited or stay here where nobody perhaps would miss me if I went.[7] A hard choice but such is the world to, Dear Sir, Your most humble servant,

SAM. JOHNSON

3. MS: "and sleeps" del. above "can sleep"

4. SJ alludes to Thomas Warton's *The Progress of Discontent*: "Our pupil's hopes, tho' twice defeated, / Are with a scholarship completed. / . . . And now, intent on new designs, / Sighs for a fellowship—and fines. / . . . But the rich prize no sooner got, / Again he quarrels with his lot: / 'These fellowships are pretty things, / We live indeed like petty kings. / . . . And ev'ry night I went to bed, / Without a Modus in my head!'" (ll. 21–22, 27–28, 31–34, 127–128). A *fine* is one of the feudal dues the lord of a manor was owed by a new tenant; a *modus*, according to SJ's *Dictionary*, is "something paid as a compensation for tithes on the supposition of being a moderate equivalent."

5. The two massive folio volumes of SJ's *Dictionary* were published on 15 Apr. 1755 (*Bibliography*, p. 55).

6. *vasta mole superbus*: "proud in its prodigious bulk." Perhaps a reminiscence of *Aeneid* III.656–57, "vasta se mole moventem / pastorem Polyphemum": "the great shepherd Polyphemus, moving his mighty bulk" (trans. H. R. Fairclough, Loeb ed.).

7. After vacillating for several months, SJ eventually traveled to Oxford in late July (*Post* To Robert Chambers, 4 Aug. 1755; 7 Aug. 1755).

Thomas Warton

TUESDAY 25 MARCH 1755

MS: Trinity College, Oxford.

ADDRESS: To the Revd. Mr. Warton of Trinity College, Oxford.

POSTMARK: 25 MR.

Dear Sir: Tuesday, March 25, 1755

Though not to write when a man can write so well is an offence sufficiently heinous yet I shall pass it by. I am very glad that the Vicechancellor was pleased with my note.[1] I shall impatiently expect you at London that we may consider what to do next. I intend in the winter to open a Bibliotheque,[2] and remember that you have subscribed a Sheet a year, let us try likewise if we cannot persuade your Brother to subscribe another.[3] My Book is now coming *in luminis oras*[4] what will be its fate I know not nor[5] much think because thinking is to no purpose. It must stand the censures of *the great vulgar and the small*,[6] of those that understand it and that understand it not.[7] But in all this I suffer not alone, every writer has the same difficulties, and perhaps every writer talks of them more than he thinks.

You will be pleased to make my compliments to all my friends, and be so kind at every idle hour as to remember, Dear sir, your most humble servant,

SAM. JOHNSON

1. *Ante* To George Huddesford, 26 Feb. 1755.

2. What JB calls this "intended Review or Literary Journal" was to comprise "the Annals of Literature, foreign as well as domestick" (*Life* I.284–85). SJ's models included Jean Barbeyrac's *Bibliothèque raisonnée des Ouvrages des Savans*, 1728–53 (*Life* I.543). His project never advanced beyond the preliminary stages of planning.

3. *Ante* To Joseph Warton, 8 Mar. 1753, n. 1.

4. *nec sine te quicquam dias in luminis oras / exoritur*: "since without you nothing comes forth into the shining borders of light" (Lucretius, *De Rerum Natura* I.23, trans. W.H.D. Rouse, Loeb ed.).

5. MS: "nor" altered from "not"

6. SJ quotes from Cowley's imitation of Horace's ode, "Odi profanum vulgus" (III.1): "Hence, ye Profane; I hate ye all; / Both the Great, Vulgar, and the Small" (ll. 1–2).

7. SJ's *Dictionary*, which was extensively reviewed, provoked a wide range of critical responses. "The immediate reaction of contemporary readers was what might have been expected, with high praise from his friends, vigorous attacks by rivals or those who disagreed with his method, and divided opinions, praising some parts and condemning others" (Clifford, 1979, pp. 139–40).

Thomas Birch

SATURDAY 29 MARCH 1755

MS: British Library.

ADDRESS: To the Revd. Dr. Birch.

ENDORSEMENT: 29 March 1755.

Sir: March 29, 1755[1]

I have sent some parts of my dictionary such as were at hand for your Inspection. The favour which I beg is that if you do not like them you will say nothing.[2] I am, Sir, Your most affectionate, humble servant,

SAM. JOHNSON

1. MS: "1755" added by Birch

2. Birch responded with enthusiasm on 3 Apr. 1755, praising the *Dictionary* as "a Work long wanted, and now executed with an Industry, Accuracy and Judgement equal to the Importance of the Subject" (B.L. Add. MS: 4310, f. 309).

Charles Burney[1]

TUESDAY 8 APRIL 1755

PRINTED SOURCE: JB's *Life*, 1791, I.159.

ADDRESS: To Mr. Burney, in Lynne Regis, Norfolk.

Sir: Gough-square, Fleet-street, April 8, 1755

If you imagine that by delaying my answer I intended to shew any neglect of the notice with which you have favoured me, you will neither think justly of yourself nor of me.[2] Your civilities were offered with too much elegance not to engage attention; and I have too much pleasure in pleasing men like you, not to feel very sensibly the distinction which you have bestowed upon me.

Few consequences of my endeavours to please or to benefit mankind have delighted me more than your friendship thus

1. Charles Burney (1726–1814), MUS.D., teacher and musicologist, author of *A General History of Music* (1776–89) and member of The Club (elected 1784). In 1755 Burney was organist of St. Margaret's Church, King's Lynn. He had been following SJ's literary career since 1747, when he read and admired the *Plan of a Dictionary* (Roger Lonsdale, *Dr. Charles Burney*, 1965, p. 45). The two men met for the first time in the spring of 1758.

2. On 16 Feb. 1755 Burney had written "a long, carefully wrought, and very humble letter to Johnson, ostensibly to inquire where copies of the *Dictionary* might be obtained, but also expressing all his admiration and gratitude" (Lonsdale, *Burney*, p. 46).

voluntarily offered, which now I have it I hope to keep, because I hope to continue to deserve it.

I have no Dictionaries to dispose of for myself, but shall be glad to have you direct your friends to Mr. Dodsley,[3] because it was by his recommendation that I was employed in the work.

When you have leisure to think again upon me, let me be favoured with another letter;[4] and another yet, when you have looked into my Dictionary.[5] If you find faults, I shall endeavour to mend them; if you find none, I shall think you blinded by kind partiality: but to have made you partial in his favour, will very much gratify the ambition of, Sir, Your most obliged And most humble servant,

SAM. JOHNSON

3. Burney had collected the names of six residents of King's Lynn and environs who wished to purchase copies of the *Dictionary*.

4. "Burney took Johnson's invitation literally and replied, with almost indecent haste, on 14 April 1755" (Lonsdale, *Burney*, p. 47). According to Burney himself, SJ did not answer this second letter.

5. Burney wrote to SJ, praising the *Dictionary*, on 26 Mar. 1757. SJ did not reply until the end of the year (*Post* To Charles Burney, 24 Dec. 1757).

John Taylor

FRIDAY 11 APRIL 1755

PRINTED SOURCE: Hill I.40–41.

ADDRESS: To the Revd. Dr. Taylor.

Sir: April 11, 1755

I think your draught better than Mr. Ballard's; and the case quite clear on Mr. B——'s side; at least so far as that Dr. Wilson can have no money till the debts due out of that money which he claims are paid.[1] The law or custom of the Church must determine the rest. It seems equitable enough that he should claim that money which was received for him, and only wanted to be divided, if there were no prior claim, or debt due from it.

1. Possibly Thomas Wilson (*c.* 1704–84), D.D., Prebend of Westminster (1743) and Rector of St. Stephen's, Walbrook, whom Taylor succeeded as Rector of St. Margaret's, Westminster, in 1784 (*Post* To Hester Thrale, 13 May 1784).

What is the matter that one never sees you? I am moved, and I fancy I shall move again,[2] but how oftensoever I move, I shall be with great constancy, Your affectionate, etc.,

SAM. JOHNSON

2. What SJ means by "move" is not clear: he had just written to Charles Burney from Gough Square, his letter to Edmund Hector of 15 Apr. is sent from the same location, and he continued to rent No. 17 until 1758 (Clifford, 1979, p. 200).

Edmund Hector[1]

TUESDAY 15 APRIL 1755

MS: Beinecke Library.

ADDRESS: To Mr. Hector in Birmingham.

POSTMARK: 15 AP.

Dear Sir: Gough Square, Fleetstreet, Apr. 15, 1755

I was extremely pleased to find that you have not forgotten your old friend, who yet recollects the evenings which we have passed together at Warren's and the Swan.[2] As Nature, I suppose operates very uniformly, I believe You as well as I are come now to that part in which the gratifications and friendships of younger years operate very powerfully on the mind. Since we have again renewed our acquaintance do not let us intermit it so long again.[3]

The Books I think to send you in a strong box by the carrier, and shall be obliged if you will remit the money to my Mother who may give you a receipt in my name.[4]

1. Edmund Hector (1708–94), SJ's closest friend at the Lichfield Grammar School, moved to Birmingham in 1729, where he practiced as a surgeon until his death. According to JB, "the comfort of being near Mr. Hector, his old schoolfellow," was SJ's "chief inducement" to stay in Birmingham from 1732–34 (*Life* 1.86). For more extensive profiles of Hector and his family, see *Reades*, pp. 151–54.

2. *Ante* To Lewis Paul, 31 Jan. 1741, n. 3.

3. *Post* To Edmund Hector, 13 May 1755.

4. Presumably SJ refers to the *Dictionary*, published 15 Apr. 1755. Mrs. Johnson served as a business representative for her son in the Midlands. *Post* To Edmund Hector, 7 Oct. 1756.

I wish, come[5] of wishes what will, that my work may please you, as much as it now and then pleased me, for I did not find dictionary making so very unpleasant as it may be thought. Mr. Baske[r]vill called on me here.[6] I suppose you visit his printing house, which will I think be something very considerable.[7]—What comes of poor Warren?[8] I have not lost all my kindness for him, for when I remember you I naturally remember all our connexions, which are more pleasing to me for your sake. I am, sir, Your humble servant,

SAM. JOHNSON

5. MS: "come" superimposed upon "my work" partially erased

6. John Baskerville (1706–75), Birmingham printer and typographic designer, used the profits from a successful japanning business to set up his own press in 1750. In 1756 circulation of proposals for an edition of Virgil, to be set in type of his own design, first drew attention to Baskerville's work. In 1769 SJ presented a copy of this Virgil (1757) to Trinity College, Oxford (*Post* To Thomas Warton, 31 May 1769).

7. This "printing house" was located on Baskerville's eight-acre estate, northwest of Birmingham. It did not prove to be a financial success. In 1762 Baskerville was unable to find a buyer, and after his death his widow could not dispose of the types in England.

8. *Ante* To Lewis Paul, 31 Jan. 1741, n. 3.

Bennet Langton

TUESDAY 6 MAY 1755

MS: Hyde Collection.

ADDRESS: To Bennet Langton, Junr.,[1] Esqr., at Langton near Spilsby, Lincolnshire.[2]

POSTMARK: 6 MA.

1. Bennet Langton the younger (1737–1801), raised on the family estate in Lincolnshire, came to London in 1752, seeking an introduction to the author of the *Rambler*; he met SJ through Robert Levet (*Life* I.247–48; *Post* To Robert Chambers, 31 July 1756, n. 5). Langton tried his hand at various literary pursuits, which included an essay for *The Connoisseur*, before matriculating at Trinity College, Oxford, in 1757 (Fifer, pp. lv–lvi).

2. The Langton estate, three miles north of Spilsby, had belonged to the family since the twelfth century. Their seat consisted of a "good stone mansion" built early in the seventeenth century (John Britton, *Beauties of England and Wales*, 1807, IX.714).

Sir: May 6, 1755

It has been long observed that men do not suspect faults which[3] they do[4] not commit;[5] your own Elegance of manners and punctuality of complaisance did not suffer you to impute to me that negligence of which I was guilty, and which I have not since attoned. I received both your Letters and received them with pleasure proportionate to the esteem which so short an acquaintance strongly impressed, and which I hope to confirm by nearer knowledge, though I am afraid that gratification will be for a time witheld.

I have indeed published my Book,[6] of which I beg to know your Fathers Judgement and yours,[7] and I have now staid long enough to watch its progress into the world. It has you see, no patrons, and I think has yet had no opponents except the Criticks of the coffeehouse, whose outcries are soon dispersed into the air, and are thought on no more.[8] From this therefore I am at liberty, and think of taking the opportunity of this interval to make an excursion,[9] and why not then into Lincolnshire, or to mention a stronger attraction why not to dear Mr. Langton?[10] I will give the true reason which I know you will approve. I have a Mother more than eighty years old, who has counted the days to the publication of my book in hopes of seeing me, and to her, if I can disengage myself here, I resolve to go.[11]

3. MS: undeciphered deletion before "which"

4. MS: "do" superimposed upon partial erasure and deletion

5. MS: "commit" superimposed upon partial erasure and deletion

6. SJ refers to the *Dictionary*, published 15 Apr. 1755.

7. Bennet Langton the elder (1696–1769), Sheriff of Lincolnshire and Justice at the sessions of Louth, Spilsby, and Alford (Fifer, p. liv). Sometime in 1757 he offered SJ a parish in Lincolnshire (*Life* I.320). SJ praised the elder Langton's "considerable learning" (*Life* I.476) but criticized his intellectual isolation: "He never clarified his notions, by filtrating them through other minds" (*Life* III.47).

8. *Ante* To Thomas Warton, 25 Mar. 1755, n. 7.

9. SJ also intended to visit Thomas Warton in Oxford, Edmund Hector in Birmingham, and his mother in Lichfield. *Ante* To Thomas Warton, 20 Mar. 1755, n. 7; *Post* To Edmund Hector, 13 May 1755; *Post* To Lucy Porter, 30 Dec. 1755.

10. SJ did not visit Langton's home until 1764 (*Life* I.476).

11. SJ had not been back to Lichfield for eighteen years, and did not return until after his mother's death (Jan. 1759).

As I know, dear Sir, that to delay my visit for a reason like this will not deprive me of your esteem, I beg it may not lessen your kindness. I have very seldom received an offer of Friendship which I so earnestly desire to cultivate and mature. I shall rejoice to hear from you till I can see you, and will see you as soon as I can, for when the duty that calls me to Lichfield is discharged, my inclination will hurry me to Langton. I shall delight to hear the ocean roar or see the stars twinkle, in the company of men to whom nature does not spread her volumes or utter her voice in vain.

Do not, dear Sir, make the slowness of this letter a precedent for delay, or imagine that I approved the incivility that I have committed, for I have known you enough to love you, and sincerely to wish a further knowledge, and I assure you once more that to live in a House which contains such a Father and such a Son will be accounted a very uncommon degree of pleasure by, Dear sir, Your most obliged and most humble servant,

SAM. JOHNSON

Edmund Hector

TUESDAY 13 MAY 1755

MS: Hyde Collection.

ADDRESS: To Mr. Hector in Birmingham.

POSTMARK: 13 MA.

Dear Sir: May 13, 1755

It is no small satisfaction to me that I can yet give an old friend pleasure; since we have thus renewed our friendship let us not suffer it to be again interrupted by so long a cessation of correspondence. I shall come into the country if I can this summer, and will certainly visit him whom I have so often visited in former days.[1] Are you too come to the age in which *former days* begins to have an awful sound, and to impart an idea mixed

1. *Post* To Edmund Hector, 7 Oct. 1756, nn. 3, 7.

of pain and pleasure? These things we shall compare when we meet.

I am sorry my Books were all got from me,[2] so that your kindness is defeated, and I must entreat you to provide yourself the common way. I am, Dear sir, most affectionately yours,

SAM. JOHNSON

2. *Ante* To Edmund Hector, 15 Apr. 1755, n. 4.

Thomas Warton

TUESDAY 13 MAY 1755

MS: Trinity College, Oxford.

ADDRESS: To the Revd. Mr. Warton of Trinity College, Oxford.

POSTMARK: 13 MA.

Dear Sir: May 13, 1755

I am grieved that you should think me capable of neglecting your letters, and beg that you never will admit any such suspicion again. I purpose to come down next week, if you shall be there or any other week that shall be more agreeable to you, therefore let me know. I can stay this visit but a week but intend to make preparations for a longer stay next time, being resolved not to lose sight of the University.[1] How goes Apollonius?[2] do not let him be forgotten, somethings of this kind must be done to keep us up.[3] Pay my compliments to Mr. Wise,[4] and all my other friends. I think to com to Kettle hall.[5] I am, sir, your most affectionate, humble servant,

SAM. JOHNSON

1. *Ante* To Thomas Warton, 20 Mar. 1755 and n. 7.

2. According to Warton's own note, "A translation of Apollonius Rhodius was now intended" (*Life* 1.289 n. 1). This translation was never published.

3. That is, such learned enterprises help to preserve the standing of Oxford (which had just awarded SJ an M.A. degree).

4. *Ante* To Thomas Warton, 28 Nov. 1754, n. 2.

5. Kettell Hall, a Jacobean house on Broad Street, belonged to Oriel College. Oriel rented the building to Trinity, which used it for several decades as a college annex (*Life* 1.543–44). SJ had stayed in Kettell Hall the previous summer (Clifford, 1979, p. 123).

Thomas Warton

TUESDAY 10 JUNE 1755

MS: Trinity College, Oxford.

ADDRESS: To the Revd. Mr. Warton of Trinity College, Oxford.

POSTMARKS: [Undeciphered], 10 IV.

Dear Sir: June 10, 1755

It is strange how many things will happen to intercept every pleasure, though it [be] only that of two friends meeting together, I have promised myself every day to inform you when you might expect me at Oxford, and have not been able to fix a time. The time however is, I think, at last come and I promise myself to repose [1] in Kettle hall one [2] of the first nights of the next week.[3] I am afraid my stay with you cannot be long, but what is the inference? we must endeavour to make it cheerful. I wish your Brother could meet us,[4] that we might go and drink tea with Mr. Wyse in a body. I hope he will be at Oxford or at his nest of British and Saxon Antiquities.[5] I shall expect to see Spenser finished,[6] and many other things begun. Dodsley is gone to visit the Dutch.[7] The Dictionary sells well.[8] The rest of the world goes on as it did. I am, Dear sir, your most affectionate, humble servant,

SAM. JOHNSON

1. MS: undeciphered erasure and deletion before "repose"
2. MS: "one" superimposed upon "the"
3. *Ante* To Thomas Warton, 13 May 1755, n. 5.
4. *Ante* To Joseph Warton, 8 Mar. 1753, n. 1.
5. *Ante* To Thomas Warton, 28 Nov. 1754, n. 2.
6. Apparently Warton had already begun work on revising and expanding his *Observations on the Faerie Queene* (1754). The second edition was published in 1762.
7. Dodsley was traveling on business; nothing further is known of his trip (Ralph Straus, *Robert Dodsley*, 1910, p. 277).
8. The first edition of SJ's *Dictionary* had been published on 15 Apr. The second edition, which was published in weekly parts, began to appear on 14 June (Clifford, 1979, pp. 144, 334).

Thomas Warton

TUESDAY 24 JUNE 1755

MS: Trinity College, Oxford.

ADDRESS: To the Revd. Mr. Warton at Trinity College, Oxford.

POSTMARKS: [Undeciphered], 26 IV.

Dear Sir: June 24, 1755

To talk of coming to you and not yet to come has an air of trifling, which I would not willingly have among you, and which, I believe, you will not impute to me when I have told you that since my promise, two of our partners are dead,[1] and that I was solicited to suspend my excursion, till we could recover from our confusion.

I have not laid aside my purpose, for every day makes me more impatient of staying from you, but death, you know, hears not supplications, nor pays any regard to the convenience of mortals. I hope now to see you next week, but next week is but another name for to morrow which has been noted for promising and deceiving. I am, sir, your most humble servant,

SAM. JOHNSON

1. *Ante* To Thomas Longman, June 1746 and nn. 1, 3. Paul Knapton died on 12 June, Thomas Longman on 18 June (*GM* 1755, p. 284).

Frances Cotterell[1]

SATURDAY 19 JULY 1755

MS: Hyde Collection.

1. Frances Cotterell was the elder daughter of Admiral Charles Cotterell (d. 1754). According to JB, SJ first met Frances and her sister Charlotte in 1738, when they were living "opposite to him" in Castle Street (*Life* 1.244–45). Charlotte later maintained, however, that she and her sister did not meet SJ until "some years after his wife died" (*The French Journals of Mrs. Thrale and Doctor Johnson*, ed. Moses Tyson and Henry Guppy, 1932, p. 45).

Madam: July 19, 1755

I know not how liberally your Generosity would reward those who should do you any service, when you can so kindly acknowledge a favour which I intended only to myself. That accidentally hearing that you were in town I made haste to enjoy an interval of pleasure which I feared would be short, was the natural consequence of that self-love which is always busy in quest of happiness, of that happiness which we often miss when we think it near, and sometimes find when we imagine it lost. When I had missed you I went away disappointed, and did not know that my vexation would be so amply repaid by so kind a letter. A letter indeed can but imperfectly supply the place of its writer, at least of such a writer as Miss Cotterel, and a letter which makes me still more desire your presence is but a weak consolation under the necessity of living longer without you, with this however I must be for a time content, as much content at least[2] as discontent will suffer me, for Mr. Baretti being a single Being in this part of the world, and entirely clear from all engagements, takes the advantage of his independence and will come before me, for which if I could blame him, I should punish him, but my own heart tells me that he only does to me, what, if I could, I should do to him.

I hope Mrs. Porter[3] when she came to her favourite place, found her house dry, and her woods growing, and the breeze whistling, and the birds singing, and her own heart dancing. And for you, Madam, whose heart cannot yet dance to such musick, I know not what to hope, indeed I could hope every thing that would please you, except that perhaps the absence of higher pleasures is necessary to keep some little place vacant in your remembrance for, Madam, your most obliged, most obedient, and most humble servant,

SAM. JOHNSON

2. MS: "at least" superimposed upon undeciphered erasure

3. Mary Porter (d. 1765), the celebrated tragic actress, had retired from the stage in 1743; she lived with Frances Cotterell. In SJ's estimation, "Mrs. Porter, in the vehemence of rage, and Mrs. Clive in the sprightliness of humour, I have never seen equalled" (*Life* IV.243).

Robert Chambers[1]

MONDAY 4 AUGUST 1755[2]

MS: Hyde Collection.

ADDRESS: To Mr. Chambers.

Dear Sir: [Oxford] Monday night

Mr. Wise kept me so late that I could not come home soon enough to bid you farewel,[3] and thank you for your company and kindness. I therefore have left this note to testify my acknowledgements.

I shall be glad to see you at London, for I am, sir, affectionately yours,

SAM. JOHNSON

1. *Ante* To Robert Chambers, 21 Nov. 1754, n. 1.

2. Dated with reference to succeeding letter (To Robert Chambers, 7 Aug. 1755).

3. *Ante* To Thomas Warton, 28 Nov. 1754, n. 2.

Thomas Warton

THURSDAY 7 AUGUST 1755

MS: Trinity College, Oxford.

ADDRESS: To the Revd. Mr. Warton at Trin. College, Oxford.

POSTMARK: 7 AV.

Dear Sir: Aug. 7, 1755

I told you that among the Manuscripts are some things of Sir Thomas More. I beg you to pass an hour in looking on them, and procure a transcript of the ten or twenty first lines of each to be compared with what I have that I may know whether they are yet unpublished. The manuscripts are these.

Catalogue of Bodl. Mss.[1] page 122

1. *Ante* To Robert Chambers, 21 Nov. 1754, n. 2. Unless noted otherwise, SJ's references to the *Catalogi Librorum Manuscriptorum* (*CLM*) are correct.

F.3. Sir T. Moore

1. Fall of Angels. 2. Creation and fall of Mankind.

3. Determination of the Trinity for the Rescue[2] of Mankind.

4. Five lectures on our Saviour's passion.

5. Of the institution of the Sacrament 3. Lectures.

6. How to receive the blessed Body of our Lord sacramentally.

7. Neomenia—the new Moon.[3]

8. De tristitiâ, tædio, pavore, et oratione Christi ante captionem ejus.

Catalogue page 154

Life of Sir Thomas More qu. whether Roper's.[4]

page 363

De Resignatione magni Sigilli in manus Regis per D. Thomam Morum.

page 364[5]

Mori Defensio Moriæ[6]

If you procure the young Gentleman in the library to write out what you think fit to be written I will send to Mr. Prince the Bookseller to pay him what you shall think proper.[7]

Be pleased to make my compliments to Mr. Wise[8] and all my friends. I am, sir, your affectionate servant,

SAM. JOHNSON

2. "Restauration" (*CLM*)

3. "*Neomenia,* or concerning the time of the New Moon" (*CLM*)

4. This "Life" is the biography by William Roper (1496–1578), More's son-in-law.

5. "365" (*CLM*)

6. "Thomæ Mori Angli Apologia pro Moria Erasmi" (*CLM*)

7. Daniel Prince (d. 1796), antiquarian and bookseller (1750–96), New College Lane, Oxford.

8. *Ante* To Thomas Warton, 28 Nov. 1754, n. 2.

Robert Chambers

THURSDAY 7 AUGUST 1755

MS: Hyde Collection.

ADDRESS: To Mr. Chambers of Lincoln College, Oxford.

POSTMARK: 7 AV.

Dear Sir: Aug. 7, 1755

Being kept late by Mr. Wise,[1] I could not see you the last night but left a note in your Newton which I hope you found. I once more return you thanks for your kindness and company.

As you are soon to come to town I shall be glad if you will pay my Barber whom I forgot for a weeks shaving etc. and call at Mrs. Simpson's for a box of pills which I left behind me, and am loath to lose. I am, sir, your most humble servant,

SAM. JOHNSON

1. *Ante* To Thomas Warton, 28 Nov. 1754, n. 2.

Richard Congreve[1]

THURSDAY 16 OCTOBER 1755

MS: Bodleian Library.

ADDRESS: To the Revd. Mr. Congreve, at Leacroft near Lichfield.

POSTMARK: 16 OC.

ENDORSEMENT in an unidentified hand: from Saml. Johnson.

Dear Sir: Octr. 16, 1755

There is a kind of restoration to youth in the[2] revival of old friendships. Your letter revived many Ideas which time had not indeed obliterated but had thrown back from recollection, and hidden under later occurrences.

The occasion of your letter is very honourable to you, and is therefore in a particular manner pleasing to me. You will not expect that after so many years I should be able to give much positive evidence about the little debt that you mention. I can only say that I know not that it was ever discharged, and promise that if you pay it to my mother, I will return it, if it shall appear by any future proof to have been paid twice.

I fully persuade myself that I shall pass some of the winter months with my mother,[3] I would have come sooner but could

1. *Ante* To Gilbert Repington, 18 May 1735, n. 14; *Ante* To Richard Congreve, 25 June 1735.

2. MS: "the" superimposed upon "a"

3. *Ante* To Bennet Langton, 6 May 1755, n. 11.

not break my Shackles. It will be an additional pleasure to meet you.

Where is your Brother Charles?[4] I once received a letter from him, but I think without direction how to answer it. It is wrong in those who have been early[5] acquainted to suffer time and place to destroy that friendship, which is not easily supplied by any subsequent acquisitions. I am, Sir, your affectionate, humble servant,

SAM. JOHNSON

4. *Ante* To Gilbert Repington, 18 May 1735, n. 14.

5. MS: "early" superimposed upon "once"

Thomas Birch

SATURDAY 8 NOVEMBER 1755

MS: British Library.

ADDRESS: To the Revd. Dr. Birch.

ENDORSEMENT: 8 Nov. 1755.

Sir: Saturday, Nov. 8, 1755[1]

If you can lend me for a few days Wood's Ath. Ox. it will be a favour.[2] My servant will call for it on Monday.[3] I am, Sir, Your most humble servant,

SAM. JOHNSON

1. MS: "Nov. 8, 1755" added by Birch

2. SJ refers to *Athenæ Oxonienses* (1691–92), a biographical compendium by Anthony à Wood (1632–95). *Ante* To Thomas Birch, 4 Nov. 1752, n. 2; *Post* To Thomas Birch, 20 Mar. 1756.

3. Francis Barber (?1745–1801), SJ's Jamaican servant, was brought to England in 1750 by Richard Bathurst, the father of Dr. Richard Bathurst (*Ante* To William Strahan, 22 Mar. 1753, n. 3). Barber came to work for SJ in 1752, shortly after the death of Elizabeth Johnson. There were two interludes in his tenure with SJ: he worked for "Mr. Farren, an Apothecary in Cheapside, for about two years," beginning *c.* Oct. 1756 (Waingrow, p. 165), and served in the navy from 7 July 1758 until 8 Aug. 1760 (*Life* I.239 n. 1; *Johns. Glean.* II.5, 12–17; VIII.73–74).

Lewis Paul[1]

MONDAY 29 DECEMBER 1755

MS: Hyde Collection.

ADDRESS: To Mr. Paul.

Dear Sir: Monday, Decr. 29, 1755

I would not have you think that I forget or neglect you. I have never been out of doors since you saw me. On the day after I had been with you I was seized with a hoarseness which still continues; I had then a cough so violent that I once fainted under its convulsions. I was afraid of my Lungs. My Physician bled me yesterday and the day before,[2] first almost against his will, but the next day without any contest. I had been bled once before, so that I have lost in all 54 ounces. I live on broaths, and my cough, I thank God is much abated, so that I can sleep. You find it impossible to fix a time for coming to you, but as soon as the Physician gives me leave, if you can spare a bed, I will pass a week at your house.[3] Change of air is often of use, and, I know, you will let me live my own way. I have been pretty much dejected. I am, Sir, Your most humble servant,

SAM. JOHNSON

1. *Ante* To Lewis Paul, 31 Jan. 1741, n. 1.

2. Thomas Lawrence (1711–83), M.D., later (1767–74) President of the Royal College of Physicians, "a man of whom, in respect of his piety, learning, and skill in his profession, it may almost be said, the world was not worthy" (Hawkins, p. 401). Lawrence, who belonged to the Ivy Lane Club, tended SJ until his retirement in 1782.

3. Paul lived outside of London, "at Brook's Green near Hammersmith" (*Post* To Lewis Paul, 6 Jan. 1756).

Hill Boothby[1]

TUESDAY 30 DECEMBER 1755

MS: Hyde Collection.

1. *Ante* To Hill Boothby, *c.* Dec. 1753, n. 1.

To HILL BOOTHBY, 30 *December* 1755

Dear Madam: Dec. 30, 1755

It is again Midnight, and I am again alone. With what meditation shall I amuse this waste hour of darkness and vacuity. If I turn my thoughts upon myself what do [I] perceive but a poor helpless being reduced by a blast of wind to weakness and misery. How my present distemper was brought upon me I can give no account, but impute it to some sudden succession of cold to heat, such as in the common road of life cannot be avoided, and against which no precaution can be taken.

Of the fallaciousness of hope, and the uncertainty of Schemes every day gives some new proof, but it is[2] seldom heeded till something rather felt than seen awakens attention. This Ilness in which I have suffered some thing and feared much more, has depressed my confidence and elation, and made me consider all that I have promised myself as less certain to be attained or enjoyed. I have endeavoured to form resolutions of a better life, but I form them weakly under the consciousness of an external motive. Not that I conceive a time of Sickness a time improper for recollection and good purposes, which I believe Diseases and Calamities often sent to produce, but because no man can know how little his performance will conform to his promises, and designs are nothing in human eyes till they are realised by execution.

Continue, my Dearest, your prayers for me, that no good reso[lu]tion may be vain. You think, I believe, better of me than I deserve. I hope to be in time what I wish to be, and what I have hitherto satisfied myself too readily with only wishing.

Your Billet brought me what I much wished to have, a proof that I am still remembred by you at the hour in which I most desire it![3]

The Doctor is anxious about you.[4] He thinks you too negligent of yourself, if you will promise to be cautious, I will exchange promises, as we have already exchanged injunctions.

2. MS: "is" superimposed upon "s" 3. MS: "it" superimposed upon "to"

4. *Ante* To Lewis Paul, 29 Dec. 1755, n. 2.

However do not write to me more than you can easily bear, do not interrupt your ease to write at all.

Mr. Fitzherbert sent to day to offer me some Wine,[5] the people about me say I ought to accept it, I shall therefore be obliged to him if he will send me a Bottle.

There has gone about a report that I died today which I mention lest you should hear it and be alarmed. You see that I think my death may alarm you, which for me is to think very [highly] of earthly friendship. I believe it arose from the death of one of my neighbours.[6] You know Des Cartes's argument, "I think therefore I am."[7] It is as good a consequence "I write therefore I am alive." I might give another "I am alive therefore I love Miss Boothby," but that I hope our friendship may be of far longer duration than life. I am, Dearest Madam, with most sincere affection your most obliged, and most humble Servant,

SAM. JOHNSON

5. William Fitzherbert (1712–72), of Tissington Hall, Derbyshire, M.P. for Derby (1762–72) and cousin of Hill Boothby. When Fitzherbert's wife died in 1753, Boothby "succeeded her in the management of [his] family" (H. L. Piozzi, *Anecdotes of the Late Samuel Johnson*, 1786, p. 160). It is likely that SJ first met Fitzherbert through his father-in-law, Littleton Poyntz Meynell of Bradley Park, Derbyshire (*Life* I.82–83). According to SJ, "there was . . . no sparkle, no brilliancy in Fitzherbert; but I never knew a man who was so generally acceptable" (*Life* III.148).

6. *Post* To Lucy Porter, 30 Dec. 1755, n. 3.

7. "je pense, donc je suis" (*Discours de la methode*, 1637, IV.33). At the time of his death, SJ owned a set of Descartes's philosophical works (Greene, 1975, p. 53).

Lucy Porter

TUESDAY 30 DECEMBER 1755

MS: Hyde Collection.

Dear Madam: Decr. 30, 1755

I have been ill for about a fortnight with a cold which was extremely troublesome, and produced a cough that I one night fainted away.[1] This has pretty much hindred me, and

1. *Ante* To Lewis Paul, 29 Dec. 1755.

put my affairs a little behindhand; and my Physician tells me I must go out of London to recover.[2] All this, however, I should not have troubled you with sending an hundred miles, but for a particular reason. A report was yesterday running in the town that I was dead, the report was occasioned by my ilness and the death of my next neighbour,[3] I am afraid the story should get into the papers, and distress my dear Mother. I therefore write to tell you, that though not quite well, I am almost well,[4] that I am coming down soon,[5] that I wish you all many very many happy years, and that I am, Dear Miss, Your most obliged and most humble servant,

SAM. JOHNSON

2. *Ante* To Lewis Paul, 29 Dec. 1755, n. 2.

3. The surviving land tax assessment records indicate that this "next neighbour" might have been either Isaac Isaacs or Peter Kinsey (Guildhall Library MS: 11316/167, 11316/170; information supplied by S. Freeth, Keeper of Manuscripts, Guildhall Library).

4. In his New Year's prayer for 1756, SJ gives thanks "for my recovery from sickness" (*Works*, Yale ed. 1.59).

5. *Ante* To Bennet Langton, 6 May 1755, n. 11.

Hill Boothby

WEDNESDAY 31 DECEMBER 1755

MS: Hyde Collection.

My Sweet Angel: Dec. 31

I have read your book, I am afraid you will think without any great improvement, whether you can read my notes I know not. You ought not to be offended, I am perhaps as sincere as the writer. In all things that terminate here I shall be much guided by your influence, and should take or leave by your direction, but I cannot receive my religion from any human hand.[1] I desire however to be instructed and am far from thinking my self perfect.

1. Hill Boothby and SJ agreed to differ on theological matters. As she wrote to him on 23 July 1755: "I am desirous that, in the great and one thing necessary, you should think as I do; and I am persuaded you some time will. I will not enter

I beg you to return the book when you have looked into it. I should not have written what is in the margin, had I not had it from you, or had I not intended to show it you.

It affords me a new conviction that in these books there is little new, except new forms of expression, which may be sometimes taken even by the writer, for new doctrines.

I sincerely hope that God whom you so much desire to serve aright will bless you, and restore you to health, if he sees it best. Surely no human understanding can pray for any thing temporal otherwise than conditionally. Dear Angel do not forget me. My heart is full of tenderness.

It has pleased God to permit[2] me to be much better, which I believe will please you.

Give me leave, who have thought much on Medicine, to propose to you an easy and I think a very probable remedy for indigestion and lubricity of the bowels. Dr. Laurence has told me your case.[3] Take an ounce of dried orange peel finely powdered, divide it into scruples, and take one Scruple at a time in any manner;[4] the best way is perhaps to drink it in a glass of hot red[5] port,[6] or to eat it first and drink the wine after it. If you mix cinnamon or nutmeg with the powder it were not worse, but it will be more bulky and so more troublesome. This is a medicine not disgusting, not costly, easily tried, and if not found useful easily left off.

I would not have you offer it to the Doctor as mine. Physicians do not love intruders, yet do not take it without his leave. But do not be easily put off, for it is in my opinion very likely

---

into a controversy with you. I am sure I never can this way convince you in any part wherein we may differ" (*An Account of the Life of Dr. Samuel Johnson*, ed. Richard Wright, 1805, p. 100). Nevertheless, Boothby had sent SJ an unspecified "little book," apparently in a further attempt to bring him round to her way of thinking (Wright, *Account*, p. 130).

2. MS: "permit" superimposed upon "make" partially erased

3. *Ante* To Lewis Paul, 29 Dec. 1755, n. 2.

4. A scruple is a unit of weight equal to one twenty-fourth of an ounce. SJ habitually saved orange peel (*Life* II.330), perhaps for the same reasons he recommends it to Boothby.

5. MS: "po" del. before "red"

6. MS: period

to help you, and not likely to do you harm, do not take too much in haste, a scruple once in three hours or about five scruples a day will be sufficient to begin, or less if you find any aversion. I think using sugar with it might be bad, if Syrup, use old Syrup of Quinces, but even that I do not like. I should think better of conserve of Sloes.[7] Has the Doctor mentioned the bark? in powder you could hardly take it, perhaps you might bear the infusion?

Do not think me troublesome, I am full of care. I love you and honour you, and am very unwilling to lose you. A Dieu Je vous commende. I am, Madam, your most affectionate, humble servant,

SAM. JOHNSON

My compliments to my dear Miss.[8]

7. *sloe*: "the fruit of the blackthorn, a small wild plum" (SJ's *Dictionary*).

8. Selina Fitzherbert (d. 1823), daughter of William Fitzherbert and protégée of Hill Boothby, was a particular favorite with SJ. He presented her with books and she modeled her style on his *Rambler* essays (Wright, *Account*, pp. 87, 97).

Hill Boothby

THURSDAY 1 JANUARY 1756

MS: Beinecke Library.

ADDRESS: To Miss Boothby.

Dearest Madam: Jan. 1, 1755[1]

Though I am afraid your ilness leaves you little leisure for the reception of airy civilities, yet I cannot forbear to pay you my congratulations on the new year, and to declare my Wishes, that your years to come may be many and happy. In this wish indeed I include myself who have none but you on whom my heart reposes, yet surely I wish your good even though your situation were such,[2] as should permit you to communicate no gratifications to, Dearest dearest Madam, Your most obliged and most humble servant,

SAM. JOHNSON

1. SJ's mistake for 1756: he was still unaccustomed to the calendrical shift that had taken effect in 1752.

2. MS: "to should"

Hill Boothby

SATURDAY 3 JANUARY 1756

MS: Johnson House, London.

Dearest Madam: Jan. 3, 1755[1]

Nobody but you can recompense me for the distress which I suffered on Monday night. Having engaged Dr. Laurence to let me know, at whatever hour, the state in which he left you, I concluded when he staid for long, that he staid to see my dearest expire. I was composing myself as I could to hear what yet I hoped not to hear, when his servant brought me word that you were better. Do You continue to grow better? Let my dear little Miss inform me on a card.[2] I would not have you write, lest it should hurt you, and consequently hurt likewise, Dearest Madam, Your most affectionate and faithful servant,

SAM. JOHNSON

1. *Ante* To Hill Boothby, 1 Jan. 1756, n. 1.

2. *Ante* To Hill Boothby, 31 Dec. 1755, n. 8.

Hill Boothby

SATURDAY 3 JANUARY 1756[1]

MS: Hyde Collection.

ADDRESS: To Miss Boothby.

Dearest Dear: Saturday

I am extremely obliged to you for the kindness of your enquiry. After I had written to you Dr. Laurence came, and would have given some oil and sugar, but I took Rhenish and water, and recovered my voice. I yet cough much and sleep ill. I have been visited by another Doctor to day but I laughed at his Balsam of Peru.[2] I fasted on Tuesday Wednesday and

1. Dated with reference to SJ's letters of 3 and 8 Jan. 1756.

2. Balsam of Peru, extracted from the wood of a Central American tree, was thought "to warm the habit, to strengthen the nervous system, and attenuate viscid humours" (William Lewis, *The New Dispensatory*, 1765, p. 100).

Thursday, and felt neither hunger nor faintness. I have dined yesterday and to day, and found little refreshment. I am not much amiss, but can no more sleep than if my dearest Lady was angry at, Madam, your most humble servant,

SAM. JOHNSON

Lewis Paul

TUESDAY 6 JANUARY 1756

MS: Birmingham Public Library.

ADDRESS: To Mr. Paul at Brook's Green near Hammersmith.

POSTMARK: [Undeciphered], PENY POST PAYD.

Dear Sir: Jan. 6, 1756

I am much better but cannot yet go into the cold air. You may depend upon it, that the first excursion made by me into the Country shall be to you. I am, Sir, Your affectionate, humble servant,

SAM. JOHNSON

Hill Boothby

THURSDAY 8 JANUARY 1756

MS: Hyde Collection.

ADDRESS: To Miss Boothby.

Honoured Madam: Jan. 8, 1756

I beg of you to endeavour to live. I have returned your Law which however I earnestly entreat you to give me.[1] I am in great trouble, if you can write three words to me, be pleased to do it. I am afraid to say much, and cannot say nothing when my dearest is in danger.[2]

1. *Ante* To Andrew Millar, 11 July 1753, n. 7. In Oct. 1755, Boothby had recommended to SJ William Law's *An Appeal to all that Doubt or Disbelieve the Truths of the Gospel* as "the most clear of all his later writings" (*An Account of the Life of Dr. Samuel Johnson*, ed. Richard Wright, 1805, p. 127).

2. Hill Boothby died on 16 Jan. 1756. Giuseppe Baretti reported that when the

The Allmercifull God have mercy on You. I am, Madam, your

SAM. JOHNSON

---

news reached SJ he was "almost distracted with his grief; and that the friends about him had much ado to calm the violence of his emotion" (H. L. Piozzi, *Anecdotes of the Late Samuel Johnson,* 1786, p. 161). SJ prayed fervently "that I may improve the opportunity of instruction which thou hast afforded me, by the knowledge of her life, and by the sense of her death" (*Works,* Yale ed. 1.59–60).

Thomas Birch

FRIDAY 9 JANUARY 1756

MS: British Library.

ADDRESS: To the Revd. Dr. Birch.

ENDORSEMENT: Mr. S. Johnson, 9 Janu. 1756.

Sir: Jan. 9, 1756[1]

Having obtained from Mr. Garrick a benefit for a Gentlewoman of Learning, distressed by blindness, almost the only casualty that could have distressd her,[2] I beg leave to trouble you among my other friends with some of her tickets.[3] Your benevolence is well known and was, I believe, never exerted on a more laudable occasion. I am, Sir, Your most humble servant,

SAM. JOHNSON

1. MS: "1756" Birch's hand 2. *Post* To George Colman, 17 Jan. 1769.

3. SJ refers to Anna Williams (*Ante* To Thomas Birch, 12 May 1750, n. 5). The benefit performance, of *Merope,* took place at Drury Lane on 22 Jan. 1756. The receipts totaled £260 (*Lond. Stage,* Part IV, ii.522).

Lewis Paul

TUESDAY 13 JANUARY 1756

MS: Birmingham Public Library.

ADDRESS: To Mr. Paul at Brooks Green.

Sir: Tuesday, Jan. 13, 1755[1]

I am much confused with an accident that has happened, when your papers were brought me, I broke open the first without reading the superscription, and when I had opened it found it not to belong to me, I did not read it when I found my mistake. I see it is a very full paper, and will give you much trouble to copy again, but perhaps it will not be necessary, and you may mend the Seal—I am sorry for the mischance—You will easily believe it was[2] nothing more. If you send it me again the Child shall carry it.[3]

For bringing Mrs. Swynfen,[4] I know not well how to attempt it, I am not sure that her husband will be pleased,[5] and I think it would look too much like making myself a party instead of acting the part of a common friend, which I shall be very ready to discharge.[6] I should imagine that the best way would be to send her word when you will call on her, and, perhaps the questions on which she is to resuscitate her remembrance, and come to her at her own house. I really know not how to ask her husband to send her and I certainly will not take her without asking him. I am, sir, Your most humble servant,

SAM. JOHNSON

1. I have followed Croker, Hill, and Chapman in assigning this letter to 1756. SJ (as in his letters to Hill Boothby of this month) was still unaccustomed to the calendrical shift that had taken effect in 1752.

2. MS: "w" altered from "m"

3. *Ante* To Thomas Birch, 8 Nov. 1755, n. 3.

4. Elizabeth Desmoulins (b. 1716), daughter of Dr. Samuel Sywnfen (*c.* 1679–1736), a physician in Lichfield and Birmingham and SJ's godfather. She had served as Elizabeth Johnson's companion in the last years of Tetty's life, and was later (*c.* 1777) to join SJ's household (*Life* III.222).

5. Mr. Desmoulins, a Huguenot refugee and a writing master at the Birmingham Free Grammar School (Clifford, 1955, p. 135).

6. Mrs. Desmoulins was involved in Paul's intricate cotton-spinning schemes, by virtue of having invested £200 in his Birmingham mill (*Ante* To Lewis Paul, 31 Jan. 1741, n. 1; G. J. French, *The Life and Times of Samuel Crompton*, 1859, p. 255). Because most of his papers have been destroyed, the precise nature of Paul's financial difficulties fifteen years later cannot be determined; this and subsequent letters suggest a loss of confidence among the backers (*Post* To Lewis Paul, Late Feb. or Early Mar. 1756; 12 Mar. 1756). J. L. Clifford summarizes what can be deduced

from the surviving documents: "Paul, who had been operating a factory in Northampton, was in deep trouble, partly because of Warren's bankruptcy and James's failure to pay what he owed. Acting as go-between, Johnson tried to collect from James, to secure agreements from the others, and to interest further investors. . . . It must be admitted that the whole business is obscure, but there can be no doubt as to Johnson's active involvement" (Clifford, 1979, pp. 176–77).

Elizabeth Carter[1]

WEDNESDAY 14 JANUARY 1756

MS: Hyde Collection.

Madam: Gough Square, Jan. 14th 1756

From the liberty of writing to you if I have been hitherto detered by the fear of your understanding I am now encouraged to it by the confidence of your goodness.

I am soliciting a benefit for Miss Williams,[2] and beg that if you can by letters influence any in her favour, and who is there whom you cannot influence? you will be pleased to patronise her on this occasion. You see the time is short and as you were not in town I did not till this day, remember that you might help us, or recollect how widely and how rapidly light is diffused.

To every Joy is appended a Sorrow. The name of Miss Carter introduces the memory of Cave. Poor dear Cave I owed him much, for to him I owe that I have known you. He died, I am afraid, unexpectedly to himself, yet surely unburthened with any great crime, and for the positive duties of religion, I have yet no right to condemn him for neglect.[3] I am, with respect which I neither owe nor pay to any other, Madam, Your most obedient and most humble servant,

SAM. JOHNSON

1. *Ante* To Edward Cave, Apr. 1738, n. 8.

2. *Ante* To Thomas Birch, 9 Jan. 1756, n. 3.

3. Cave died 10 Jan. 1754. According to SJ, in the last two years of his life he had fallen into "a kind of lethargick insensibility, in which one of the last acts of reason which he exerted, was fondly to press the hand that is now writing this little narrative" (*Early Biographical Writings of Dr Johnson*, ed. J. D. Fleeman, 1973, p. 409).

Richard or William Cave

JANUARY 1756

MS: Hyde Collection.

ADDRESS: To Mr. Cave.[1]

Dear Sir:

I find this Gentleman knows more of Tickets than either You or I,[2] and I wish You would be so good as to settle with him. I fancy printed ones may serve[3] upon good strong paper, let them be dated right. There should be for Box, Pit, and Galleries. I am, Sir, Your etc.

SAM. JOHNSON

1. The likelihood is that "Mr. Cave" refers to Edward Cave's nephew Richard (d. 1766), co-printer of the *GM*, 1754–60 (*Lit. Anec.* v.58). The other possibility is Edward's younger brother William (*c.* 1695–1757) (*Lit. Anec.* v.57).

2. *Ante* To Thomas Birch, 9 Jan. 1756 and n. 3.

3. Printed tickets were less expensive than engraved ones.

John Ryland[1]

JANUARY 1756[2]

MS: Rylands Library.

ADDRESS: To Mr. Ryland.

Sir:

I have obtained a benefit play for Miss Williams,[3] which yet will not be for her benefit without the concurrence of her friends, among which she numbers you, and therefore has troubled [you] with tickets which she begs you will try to disperse among your acquaintance. We both send our compli-

1. John Ryland (?1717–98), a West India merchant of Muscovy Court, Tower Hill, London, was a member of SJ's Ivy Lane Club and a contributor to the *GM*. According to John Nichols, "perhaps no man was more acquainted with Dr. Johnson's character, or better qualified to delineate it" (*Lit. Anec.* IX.501).

2. Dated with reference to similar appeals: *Ante* To Thomas Birch, 9 Jan. 1756; *Ante* To Elizabeth Carter, 14 Jan. 1756.

3. *Ante* To Thomas Birch, 9 Jan. 1756, n. 3.

ments to Mrs. Ryland,[4] and to the young Scholar.[5] I am, Dear sir, your affectionate, humble servant,

SAM. JOHNSON

4. Honor Hawkesworth (b. *c.* 1719), the sister of SJ's friend John, married John Ryland in 1742 (J. L. Abbott, *John Hawkesworth,* 1982, pp. 4, 11, 202).

5. SJ refers to the son of John and Honor Ryland, about whom nothing more is known (information supplied by Professor J. L. Abbott). Cf. *Post* To John Ryland, 30 Oct. 1784.

Lewis Paul

LATE FEBRUARY *or* EARLY MARCH 1756[1]

MS: Birmingham Public Library.

ADDRESS: To Mr. Paul at Brooks Green, Hammersmith.[2]

POSTMARK: PENY POST PAYD.

Sir: Wednesday

I this morning found a letter which as you sent when my eye was out of order,[3] I had never read to this hour, and therefore, now I have read I make hast to tell you that if, I understand it right, that is, if Mr. Cave be your Landlord I believe I can serve you,[4] and if the difficul[t]y still continues will endeavour it. They do not I fancy, want the money, and then they may as well seize, if they must seize, for more as less, the property, I suppose, being equivalent to much more, and in no danger of being removed. I am very sorry I did not send the letter among the first things that upon recovery I was able to read, but having put it aside it had the fate of other things for which the proper time has been neglected. Let me know what I shall do, or whether any thing at all is to be done.

1. The contents of this letter demonstrate that it preceded SJ's letter to Paul of 12 Mar. 1756. See also below, n. 3.

2. MS: "Greek Book" del. after "Hammersmith"

3. SJ's prayer, "When my Eye was Restored to its Use," is dated 15 Feb. 1756 (*Works*, Yale ed. I.60). Cf. *Post* To Hester Thrale, 24 May 1773 and n. 1.

4. *Ante* To Richard or William Cave, Jan. 1756, n. 1. This "Mr. Cave" is probably William, who inherited from Edward "a competent estate" (*Lit. Anec.* v.57).

I am now thinking about Hitch.[5] I am yet inclined to believe that he will rather lend money upon Spindles, a security which he has found valid, than upon a property to be wrung by the Law from Dr. James,[6] who will not pay Miss for three box tickets which he took.[7]—It is a strange fellow—Hitch has a dislike of James. Perhaps another might think better of him, but where to find that other I know not. I can, I believe, by a third hand have Hitch sounded, but, if it had not the appearance of declining the office, I should tell you, that your own negotiation would effect more than mine. However in both these affairs I am ready to do what you would have me. I am, sir, your most humble servant,

SAM. JOHNSON

5. Charles Hitch (d. 1764), bookseller in Paternoster Row (1733–64), co-publisher of SJ's *Dictionary* and Shakespeare *Proposals* (*Bibliography*, pp. 54, 78; Plomer II.127).

6. *Ante* To Lewis Paul, 31 Jan. 1741, nn. 1, 2.

7. *Ante* To Thomas Birch, 9 Jan. 1756 and n. 3; *Ante* To Richard or William Cave, Jan. 1756.

John Hawkesworth[1]

EARLY MARCH 1756[2]

MS: Hyde Collection.

Dear Sir:

I have been looking into the Book here and there[3] and I think have had a pretty fair specimen.[4] It is written with uncommon knowledge of Mankind, which is the chief excellence of such a book. The sentences are keenly pointed, and vigorously pushed which is the second excellence. But it is too Gallick,[5]

1. *Ante* To Joseph Warton, 8 Mar. 1753, n. 2.

2. The letter (whose bottom margin is missing) was originally enclosed in a letter from Hawkesworth to Fulke Greville, dated 14 Mar. 1756 (Hill I.60–61 n. 2).

3. MS: "here and there" written above undeciphered deletion

4. *Maxims, Characters, and Reflections* by Richard Fulke Greville (*c.* 1717–1806), essayist and M.P. for Monmouth Borough (1747–54), had just been published anonymously by J. and R. Tonson.

5. "If an academy should be established for the cultivation of our stile . . . let them, instead of compiling grammars and dictionaries, endeavour, with all their

and the proper names are often ill formed or ill chosen.[6] To use a French phrase I think the good *carries it over* the bad.[7] The good is in the constituent the bad in the accidental parts.

We cannot come to morrow, but I purpose to be with you on the Saturday following, to see the spring and Mrs. Hawkesworth.[8] I am, sir, your most humble servant,

SAM. JOHNSON

Miss W—— sends her compliments.[9]

---

influence, to stop the licence of translatours, whose idleness and ignorance, if it be suffered to proceed, will reduce us to babble a dialect of *France*" (Preface to SJ's *Dictionary*, 1755). According to Greville's "Preface to the second edition," "the most common objection to the work, as it stood in the first edition, was that it abounded with French expressions. . . . To obviate this objection, many of the articles that produced it are omitted" (3d ed., 1758, p. xvii).

6. The names SJ may have had in mind include "Torismond," "Misanthes," "Craterus," and "Philinthus."

7. *Le bon l'emporte sur le mal. L'emporter sur* means "to prevail over, to outweigh."

8. Mary Hawkesworth (*c.* 1722–96), daughter of John Brown, a butcher of Bromley, Kent. After her marriage in 1744, she opened a boarding school in Bromley. The Hawkesworths lived in the Thornhill Mansion, a Tudor house on Bromley High Street, surrounded by several acres of land (J. L. Abbott, *John Hawkesworth*, 1982, pp. 12–14, 202).

9. *Ante* To Thomas Birch, 12 May 1750, n. 5.

Lewis Paul

FRIDAY 12 MARCH 1756

MS: British Library (Science Reference and Information Service).

ADDRESS: To Mr. Paul.

ENDORSEMENT: March 12, 1756. Letter from Mr. Sam. Johnson.

Sir: March 12, 1756

I am still of opinion that they will hear me at the Gate,[1] and I have no difficulty to speak to them, but though I hope I can obtain a forbearance,[2] I am confident that I shall get nothing

1. *Ante* To Edward Cave, 25 Nov. 1734, n. 2.

2. *forbearance*: "abstinence from enforcing what is due, esp. the payment of a debt" (*OED*).

more, nor would any attempt to borrow of them or sell to them have any other effect than that of disabling me from succeeding in my first request. You may easily believe that spindles are there in very little credit.

I will propose to a friend to speak to Mr. Hitch,[3] you well know it is impossible to guess what [may] be the answer when money is to be sought. If my friend refuses the errand, what shall we do? that must be considered, will you then write to him by me, as a preparative, and then see him if he gives any countenance to the affair. You are much more skilful in these transactions than I, and might much sooner find out a proper person to deal with, for my friends have not much money.

Would it be wrong if you wrote a short letter for me to show at Cave's as a kind of Credential,[4] containing only a few lines to mention the value of the stock, the certainty of the security, and your desire of my interposition, that I may not seem to thrust myself needlesly between Cave and payment, let the letter be without dejection as if the delay was a thing rather convenient than necessary to you. Cave cannot, I think, want forty pounds, nor perhaps has he twice forty to spare.

I will do my best for you in both negotiations, with Hitch my best can[5] be very little, with Cave I expect to succeed at least for so short a delay as to Midsummer,[6] and think it would [be] as well in your letter to refer payment to Michaelmass, or Christmass. If they will grant the whole of our request (for I shall make it mine too) they may more easily grant part. But once more—you know all these things better than I. I am, sir, your most humble servant,

SAM. JOHNSON

3. *Ante* To Lewis Paul, Late Feb. or Early Mar. 1756, n. 5.

4. *Ante* To Lewis Paul, Late Feb. or Early Mar. 1756, n. 4.

5. MS: "can" superimposed upon "is"

6. *Post* To Lewis Paul, 8 Oct. 1756.

Samuel Richardson

TUESDAY 16 MARCH 1756

MS: Hyde Collection.

ENDORSEMENT in Richardson's hand: March 16, 1756, Sent Six Guineas, Witness Wm. Richardson.[1]

Sir: Gough Square, March 16

I am obliged to entreat your assistance, I am now under an arrest for five pounds eighteen shillings. Mr. Strahan from whom I should have received the necessary help in this case is not at home,[2] and I am afraid of not finding Mr. Millar,[3] if you will be so good as to send me this sum, I will very gratfully repay You, and add it to all former obligations. I am, sir, Your most obedient and most humble servant,

SAM. JOHNSON

1. William Richardson (d. 1788), Samuel's nephew, worked for his uncle from 1748 to 1759 and took over the printing business in 1761 (T.C.D. Eaves and B. D. Kimpel, *Samuel Richardson*, 1971, p. 500; Plomer II.212–13).

2. *Ante* To William Strahan, 1 Nov. 1751, n. 1.

3. *Ante* To Thomas Longman, June 1746, n. 4.

Samuel Richardson

FRIDAY 19 MARCH 1756

MS: Hyde Collection.

ENDORSEMENT in Richardson's hand: Mr. S. Johnson Arrested Tuesday, 19 Febr. 1756.[1]

Dear Sir: Fryday

I return you my sincerest thanks for the favour which you were pleased to do me two nights ago.[2]

Be pleased to accept of this little book, which is all that I have published this winter.[3] The inflammation is come again

1. I accept the findings of T.C.D. Eaves and B. D. Kimpel, who conclude that Richardson's "Febr." is an error for "March" (*Samuel Richardson*, 1971, pp. 685–86).

2. *Ante* To Samuel Richardson, 16 Mar. 1756.

3. The second edition of Sir Thomas Browne's *Christian Morals* had just ap-

into my eye, so that I can write very little. I am, sir, your most obliged and most humble servant, SAM. JOHNSON

peared, with a prefatory life of Browne and "explanatory notes," both contributed by SJ (*Bibliography*, pp. 73–74).

Thomas Birch

SATURDAY 20 MARCH 1756

MS: British Library.

ADDRESS: To the Revd. Dr. Birch.

ENDORSEMENT: 20 March 1756.

20 March 1756[1]

Mr. Johnson returns Dr. Birch thanks for his book which Sickness has obliged him to keep beyond the time intended,[2] and desires his acceptance of the Life of Sir Thomas Browne, by way [of] interest for the loan.[3]

1. MS: date in Birch's hand

2. Perhaps Anthony à Wood's *Athenæ Oxonienses* (*Ante* To Thomas Birch, 8 Nov. 1755).

3. *Ante* To Samuel Richardson, 19 Mar. 1756, n. 3.

Joseph Warton

THURSDAY 15 APRIL 1756

PRINTED SOURCE: John Wooll, *Biographical Memoirs of the Late Revd. Joseph Warton*, 1806, pp. 238–39.

Dear Sir: April 15th, 1756

Though when you and your brother were in town you did not think my humble habitation worth a visit, yet I will not so far give way to sullenness as not to tell you that I have lately seen an octavo book which I suspect to be yours, though I have not yet read above ten pages.[1] That way of publishing without ac-

1. The first volume of Warton's *Essay on the Writings and Genius of Pope* appeared anonymously on 8 Apr. (Wooll, *Biographical Memoirs*, p. 237).

quainting your friends is a wicked trick. However I will not so far depend upon a mere conjecture as to charge you with a fraud which I cannot prove you to have committed.

I should be glad to hear that you are pleased with your new situation.[2] You have now a kind of royalty, and are to be answerable for your conduct to posterity. I suppose you care not now to answer a letter, except there be a lucky concurrence of a post day with a holiday. These restraints are troublesome for a time, but custom makes them easy with the help of some honour and a great deal of profit, and I doubt not but your abilities will obtain both.

For my part, I have not lately done much. I have been ill in the winter, and my eye has been inflamed,[3] but I please myself with the hopes of doing many things with which I have long pleased and deceived myself.

What becomes of poor dear Collins?[4] I wrote him a letter which he never answered. I suppose writing is very troublesome to him. That man is no common loss. The moralists all talk of the uncertainty of fortune, and the transitoriness of beauty; but it is yet more dreadful to consider that the powers of the mind are equally liable to change, that understanding may make its appearance and depart, that it may blaze and expire.[5]

Let me not be long without a letter, and I will forgive you the omission of the visit; and if you can tell me that you are now more happy than before, you will give great pleasure to, Dear Sir, Your most affectionate and most humble servant,

SAM. JOHNSON

2. In 1755 Warton had been appointed usher, or second master, at Winchester College, "with the management and advantages of a boarding house" (Wooll, *Biographical Memoirs*, p. 30).

3. *Ante* To Lewis Paul, Late Feb. or Early Mar. 1756, n. 3.

4. *Ante* To Joseph Warton, 8 Mar. 1754 and n. 3.

5. Compare Imlac's reflections on the mad astronomer: "Few can attain this man's knowledge, and few practise his virtues; but all may suffer his calamity. Of the uncertainties of our present state, the most dreadful and alarming is the uncertain continuance of reason" (*Works*, Yale ed. XVI.149).

Thomas Birch

TUESDAY 22 JUNE 1756

MS: British Library.
ADDRESS: To the Reverend Dr. Birch.
ENDORSEMENT: Mr. S. Johnson, 22 June 1756.

Sir: June 22, 1756

Being, as you will find by the proposal,[1] engaged in a work which requires the concurrence of my friends to make it of much benefit to me, I have taken the liberty of[2] recommending six receipts to your care, and do not doubt of your endeavour to dispose of them.

I have likewise a further favour to beg. I know you have been long a curious collector of books. If therefore you have any of the contemporaries or Ancestors of Shakespeare,[3] it will be of great use to lend me them for a short time;[4] my stock of those authors is yet but curta supellex.[5] I am, sir, your obliged, humble Servant,

SAM. JOHNSON

1. SJ's "Proposals For Printing, by Subscription, The Dramatick Works of William Shakespeare" were published 8 June 1756. Although the contract SJ signed on 2 June stipulated that "the work shall be published on or before Christmas 1757," the edition did not appear until 10 Oct. 1765 (*Works*, Yale ed. VII.xvi, xxiii).

2. MS: "of" altered from "to"

3. MS: "SKaKespeare"

4. SJ's "Proposals" stress the importance of examining the literary context of each play: "The editor will endeavour to read the books which the authour read, to trace his knowledge to its source, and compare his copies with their originals. . . . When therefore any obscurity arises from an allusion to some other book, the passage will be quoted" (*Works*, Yale ed. VII.56). *Ante* To Thomas Warton, 16 July 1754.

5. *curta supellex*: "poorly furnished," a tag from Persius' *Satires* (IV.52).

Charlotte Lennox

FRIDAY 30 JULY 1756

MS: Houghton Library.

Madam: July 30, 1756

The Letter which you sent me some time ago, was rather too full of wrath for the provocation. I read both the reviews, and though the Critical Reviewers, according to their plan, showed their superiority of knowledge with some ostentation, they mentioned you with great respect, and the other Reviewers though less ceremonious, said nothing that can excite or justify much resentment.[1] They have both answ[e]red the original rather than the translation. All that either has said is now forgotten except by those who have some particular motive to remember it, and therefore it will be best to leave Berci to his chance, without a vain attempt to vindicate upon principles, what was not upon any principles of judgement undertaken. The choice, if choice it might be termed, when you took the first book which was recommended to you, was unlucky. Your stile is commended which is all the part, that I would wish you to claim for by mentioning the alterations,[2] however excellent, you become answerable for that which you did not alter.[3]

I do not believe that either of the Reviews, intended you any hurt, it is certain that if they meant to hurt you they will be disappointed, and if you were not too proud already, I would tell you, that you are now got above their malice, and though you cannot expect to be always equally succes[s]ful,

1. *The Memoirs of the Countess of Berci,* "Taken from the French by the Author of the *Female Quixote,*" had been noticed by the *Critical Review* (May 1756) and the *Monthly Review* (June 1756). The writer for the *Critical Review,* who complained that *Berci* "was an old romance newly vamped up," went on to praise Lennox as translator: "the language is in general lively and spirited; and we are only sorry that it is expended upon a work, so antient and romantic" (pp. 312–13). The *Monthly Review* found the work itself wanting but the language "very passable" (p. 516).

2. Lennox combined two sources, Vital D'Audiguer's *Lysandre et Caliste* (*c.* 1616) and Madame de Tencin's *Memoires du Comte de Comminges* (1735). According to Duncan Isles, she adhered quite faithfully to Madame de Tencin, but made "major alterations" in the plot, characters, and language of D'Audiguer ("The Lennox Collection," *Harvard Library Bulletin* 19, 1971, p. 45 n. 74).

3. SJ presumably means that by defending her various changes Lennox might become vulnerable to the charge of not having altered the originals even more thoroughly.

have such a degree of reputation as will secure you from any neglect of readers or stationers.

When Mr. Lennox[4] brought me *Berci* he said *you desired me to say something about it,* which I promised without hesitation, but I did not then understand the request, nor imagined that he had any thoughts of the pamp[h]let.[5] I conceived that you wanted me to say something to Millar.[6] There is so little room in the monthly book, that I believe no mention will ever be made in it but of originals, or books of science or learning. This rule, however, I would gladly break to do you either service or pleasure.

If there be any episode or little story, more your favourite than the rest, that can be separated and will fill about four or five columns, I will press its insertion, and let it have its natural weight with the publick.[7] But I do not think it worth your while, our readers are few, and I know not when they will be more. To Sulli I am in debt.[8] If you can point me out a passage that can be refered to the present times, I will press for a place in the Gentleman's Magazine, and write an Introduction to it,[9] if I cannot get it in there I will put it in the new book,[10] but their readers are, I think, seven to one.

I have seen Mrs. Brookes, and Miss Reid, since I saw you, and I heard of you at bothe houses, yet, what much surprised me I heard no evil. I am, Madam, your most obedient and most humble servant,

SAM. JOHNSON

4. *Ante* To Charlotte Lennox, 6 Mar. 1753, n. 2.

5. SJ refers variously to the *Literary Magazine* as the "pamphlet," "the monthly book," and the "new book." He was acting editor for its first four issues (May–Aug. 1756).

6. Andrew Millar (*Ante* To Thomas Longman, June 1746, n. 4) was the publisher of *Memoirs of the Countess of Berci.*

7. No "episode or little story" ever appeared in the *Literary Magazine.*

8. SJ praises another one of Lennox's translations, the *Memoirs of Maximilian de Bethune, Duke of Sully* (1755).

9. No place was found in the *GM* for a passage from the *Memoirs.*

10. SJ's flattering review, complete with extract, appeared in the October issue of the *Literary Magazine* (Clifford, 1979, p. 338 n. 16).

Robert Chambers

SATURDAY 31 JULY 1756

MS: Hyde Collection.

ADDRESS: To Mr. Chambers at Lincoln College, Oxford.

POSTMARK: 31 IY.

Dear Sir: July 31, 1756

Your Life came indeed too late for the month, but we suffered no inconvenience from the delay, because we had more materials than room.[1] I have sent it already to the press, unread, for the next month, and am much obliged to you for doing it. I will contrive to find you more work. If you could send us any performances from Oxford they would be of great advantage to us.[2] I wish you could add something to the printed accounts of any events that happen among you. I shall take care to send you the monthly number[3] gratis, if you contribute to it. But you must not tell that I have any thing in it.[4] For though it is known conjecturally I would not have it made certain.

Your friends Mr. Levett[5] and Miss Williams[6] are both well, and I believe nothing has happened here in which you can be much interested. You have little to do with war or trade, and if your curiosity outgoes your interest, and inclines you to

1. *Ante* To Charlotte Lennox, 30 July 1756, n. 5. Chambers's contribution may have been the anonymous "Life of Ben Jonson" that appeared in the fourth number of the *Literary Magazine*, 15 July–15 Aug. 1756, pp. 169–71 (H. W. Liebert, "'The Choice of Life': A Poem Addressed to Dr. Samuel Johnson," privately printed for The Johnsonians, 1969, p. 2).

2. By the end of the summer SJ had been supplanted as editor, which perhaps explains why no such "performances" appeared in the *Literary Magazine*.

3. MS: "monthly month"

4. SJ had been responsible for almost half of the first issue (May 1756), and remained the *Magazine*'s principal contributor through August (Clifford, 1979, pp. 167, 170).

5. Robert Levet (1705–82), "an obscure practiser in physick amongst the lower people" (*Life* I.243) whom SJ had known since 1746 and whom he was to eulogize in his poem "On the Death of Dr. Robert Levet." For "many years" before 1763, "Mr. Levet had an apartment in his house, or his chambers, and waited upon him every morning" (*Life* I.243).

6. *Ante* To Thomas Birch, 12 May 1750, n. 5.

know what little concerns you, intelligence will reach you as soon as me, who have scarcely any information but from the publick papers.

I think much on my friends, and shall take pleasure to hear of your operations at Lincoln College, when I am unconcerned about the marches and countermarches in America,[7] therefore pray write sometimes to, Dear sir, your affectionate servant,

SAM. JOHNSON

7. Although the Seven Years' War did not officially begin until June 1756, the French and the English had been skirmishing for over a year in the region of Lakes Ontario and Champlain and down the Ohio and Mississippi rivers (Basil Williams, *The Whig Supremacy*, 2d ed., 1962, pp. 347–49).

John Taylor

SATURDAY 31 JULY 1756

MS: Berg Collection, New York Public Library.

ADDRESS: To the Revd. Dr Taylor at Market Bosworth, Leicestershire.

POSTMARK: 31 IY.

ENDORSEMENTS: Johnson 1756, 31 July 56—very fine.

Dear Sir: July 31, 1756

I promised to write to you, and write now rather to keep my promise than that I have any thing to say, that might not be delayed till we meet. I know not how it happens, but I fancy that I write letters with more difficulty than some other people, who write nothing but letters, at least I find myself very unwilling to take up a pen only to tell my friends that I am well, and indeed I never did exchange letters regularly but with dear Miss Boothby.[1]

However let us now begin, and try who can continue punctuality longest. There is this use in the most useless letter, that it shows one not to be forgotten, and they may at least in the

1. *Ante* To Hill Boothby, *c.* Dec. 1753, n. 1.

begining of friendship, or in great length of absence keep memory from languishing, but our friendship has been too long to want such helps, and I hope our absence will be too short to make them necessary.

My Life admits of so little variety, that I have nothing to relate, you who are married, and a magistrate may have many events to tell both foreign and domestick. But I hope you will have nothing to tell of unhappiness to yourself.

I was glad of your prospect of reconciliation with ⟨Mouseley⟩ which is, I hope, now completed, to have one's neighbour one's enemy is uncomfortable in the country where good neighbourhood is all the pleasure that is to be had.[2] Therefore now you are on good terms with your Neighbors[3] do not differ about trifles. I am, Dear sir, Your most affectionate servant,

SAM. JOHNSON

My compliments to your Lady.[4]

2. *Post* To John Taylor, 18 Nov. 1756.

3. MS: "Neighbors" written above "country" del.

4. *Ante* To John Taylor, 18 Mar. 1752, n. 3.

Unidentified Correspondent

TUESDAY 28 SEPTEMBER 1756

MS: Houghton Library.

Dear Sir: Sept. 28, 1756

My good friend Mr. Vaillant[1] has communicated to me your kind intention of contributing to the success of my Edition of Shakespeare.[2] I have sent you a dozen of receipts signed. Mr. Vaillant can give you proposals.

I shall consider your concurrence in this design as a very

1. Paul Vaillant (*c.* 1715–1802), bookseller in the Strand; later (1759) Sheriff of London (Plomer II.250).

2. *Ante* To Thomas Birch, 22 June 1756 and n. 1.

valuable addition to the little interest that I have hitherto been able to form. I am, sir, your most humble servant,

SAM. JOHNSON

Lewis Paul

WEDNESDAY 29 SEPTEMBER 1756

MS: Hyde Collection.

ADDRESS: To Mr. Paul.

ENDORSEMENT: Sepr. 25, 1756. Letter from Mr. Sam. Johnson.

Sir: Sept. 29, 1756

I would not have it thought that if I sometimes trangress the rules of civility, I would violate the laws of friendship. If I had heard any thing from the gate I would have informed you,[1] and I will send to them lest they should neglect to transmit any accounts that they receive. I have been many times hindred from coming to you, but if by coming I could have been of any considerable use, I would not have been hindred. They are so cold at the gate both to the landlord and to you, that if I could think of any body else to apply to, I would trouble them no more. I am thinking of Dicey.[2] I am, sir, your humble servant,

SAM. JOHNSON

1. *Ante* To Edward Cave, 25 Nov. 1734, n. 2; *Ante* To Lewis Paul, Late Feb. or Early Mar. 1756 and n. 3.

2. Presumably SJ refers to Cluer Dicey, printer and bookseller in Bow Churchyard and Aldermary Churchyard, 1736–80 (Plomer II.73; Ian Maxted, *The London Book Trades, 1775–1800,* 1977, p. 65).

Edmund Hector

THURSDAY 7 OCTOBER 1756

MS: Hyde Collection.

ADDRESS: To Mr. Hector in Birmingham.

POSTMARKS: 7 OC, RJ.

Dear Sir: Octr. 7, 1756

After a long intermission of our correspondence you took some time ago a very kind method of informing me that there was no intermission of our friendship,[1] yet I know not why, after the interchange of a letter or two, we have fallen again into our former Silence.[2] I remember that when we were nearer each other we were more diligent in our correspondence, perhaps only because we were both younger, and more ready to employ ourselves in things not of absolute necessity. In early life every new action or practice is a kind of experiment, which when it has been tried, one is naturally less eager to try again. Friendship is indeed one of those few states of which it is reasonable to wish the continuance through life, but the form and exercise of friendship varies, and we grow to [be] content to show kindness on important occasions, without squandering our ardour in superfluities of empty civility.[3]

It is not in mere civility that I write now to you but to inform you that I have undertaken a new Edition of Shakespeare, and that the profits of it are to arise from a Subscription. I therefore solicite the interest of all my friends, and believe myself sure of yours without Solicitation.[4] The proposals[5] and receipts may be had from my Mother to whom I beg you to send for as many as you can dispose of, and to remit to her money which you or your acquaintance shall collect.[6] Be so kind as to mention my undertaking to any other friends that I may have in your part of the kingdom, the activity of a few solicitors may produce great advantages to me.

I have been thinking every month of coming down into the

1. *Ante* To Edmund Hector, 15 Apr. 1755 and n. 4; 13 May 1755.

2. *Ante* To Edmund Hector, 15 Apr. 1755; 13 May 1755.

3. "There is a kind of restoration to youth in the revival of old friendships" (*Ante* To Richard Congreve, 16 Oct. 1755); "a friendship of twenty years is interwoven with the texture of life" (*Post* To Hester Thrale, 13 Nov. 1783). SJ desired to number Hector among his few lifelong friends (*Post* To Edmund Hector, 11 Nov. 1756).

4. *Post* To Edmund Hector, 11 Nov. 1756.

5. *Ante* To Thomas Birch, 22 June 1756, n. 1.

6. *Ante* To Edmund Hector, 15 Apr. 1755, n. 4.

country,[7] but every Month has brought its hinderances. From that kind of melancholy indisposition which I had when we lived together at Birmingham,[8] I have never been free, but have always had it operating against my health and my Life[9] with more or less violence. I hope however to see all my friends, all that are remaining, in no very long time, and particularly you whom I always think on with great tenderness. I am, Sir, your most affectionate servant,

SAM. JOHNSON

7. *Ante* To Edmund Hector, 13 May 1755. SJ did not visit Hector until the summer of 1770 (*Post* To Hester Thrale, Early July 1770).

8. *Ante* To Edmund Hector, 15 Apr. 1755, n. 1. Hector had helped SJ to combat this "indisposition" and complete his translation of Lobo (*Life* 1.87). Hector reported to JB that he "was afraid of Dr. Johnson's head" during SJ's stay in Birmingham (Waingrow, p. 90).

9. MS: "Li" superimposed upon "ha"

Lewis Paul

AUTUMN 1756

MS: Birmingham Public Library.
ADDRESS: To Mr. Paul.

Sir:

I am astonished at what you tell me. I cannot well come out to night, but will wait on you on Monday Evening. I have been very busy, but have now some leisure. I repeat again that I am astonished. Henry is just now out of town but I could send to him,[1] if there was any likelihood of advantage from it. I am certain it is not done with his privity, for, he has no interest in it, and he is too wise to do ill without interest. I am, sir, your humble servant,

SAM. JOHNSON

I am ready to do on this occasion any thing that can be done.

1. David Henry (1710–92), Scots bookseller and Edward Cave's brother-in-law, became co-printer of the *GM* (along with Richard Cave) in 1754.

Lewis Paul

FRIDAY 8 OCTOBER 1756

MS: Birmingham Public Library.

ADDRESS: To Mr. Paul.

ENDORSEMENT: Letter from Mr. Johnson.

Sir: Octr. 8, 1756

You think it hard by this time that you cannot have a letter.

I engaged Mr. Newberry who sent me on Monday night the note enclosed, and appeared to think the matter well settled[1]—On Tuesday I wrote to Mr. Henry but soon heard he was out of town[2]—I knew not what to do—I then had recourse to young Mr. Cave who very civilly went about the business,[3] and came to me yesterday in the evening with this account.

Mr. Cave seized and has a man in possession.[4]

He made a sale and sold only a fire-shovel for four shillings.

The goods were appraised at about eight pounds.

Mr. Cave will stay three weeks without any further motion in the business, but will still keep his possession.

He expects that you should pay the expence of the Seizure, how much it is I could not be informed.

He will stay to Christmas upon Security. He is willing to continue you tenant, or will sell the mill to any that shall work or buy the Machine. He values his mill at a thousand pounds.

He did not come up about this business, but another.

Mr. Bowker,[5] as young Mr. Cave thinks, is at Northampton.

1. *Ante* To John Newbery, 15 Apr. 1751, n. 1.

2. *Ante* To Lewis Paul, Autumn 1756, n. 1.

3. "Young Mr. Cave" must refer to Richard (*Ante* To Richard or William Cave, Jan. 1756, n. 1).

4. "Mr. Cave" must refer to William, Richard's uncle (*Ante* To Richard or William Cave, Jan. 1756, n. 1).

5. "Mr. Bowker" was the cotton manufacturer "with whom Paul had now [post-1743] connected himself" (G. J. French, *Life and Times of Samuel Crompton*, 1859, p. 265). Nothing further is known of their business dealings.

These, Sir, are the particulars that I have gathered. I am, Sir, your very humble servant,

SAM. JOHNSON

Lewis Paul

AUTUMN 1756

MS: Birmingham Public Library.

ADDRESS: To Mr. Paul.

Sir:

I am no less surprised than yourself at the treatment which you have met with, and agree with you that Mr. Cave must impute to himself part of the discontent that He shall suffer till the Spindles are produced.

If I have any opportunity of dispelling the gloom that overcasts him at present, I shall endeavour it both for his sake and yours, but [it] is [1] to little purpose that remonstrances are offered to voluntary inattention, or to obstinate prejudice. Cuxon in one place and Garlick in the other, leave no room for the unpleasing reasonings of, your humble servant,

SAM. JOHNSON

1. MS: "is" altered from "it"

Lewis Paul

AUTUMN 1756

MS: Birmingham Public Library.

ADDRESS: To Mr. Paul.

ENDORSEMENT: Letter from Mr. Johnson.

Sir: Wednesday

You will think I forget you, but my Boy is run away, and I know not whom to send.[1] Besides nothing seemed to require

1. *Ante* To Thomas Birch, 8 Nov. 1755, n. 3. Barber himself told JB that he left SJ "about 1757" (Waingrow, p. 165). *Post* To Charlotte Lennox, 10 Mar. 1757.

much expedition for Mr. Cave has left London almost a fortnight. They intimate at the Gate some desire to know your determination.[2] I will be with you in a day or two. I am, Sir, your humble servant,

SAM. JOHNSON

2. *Ante* To Edward Cave, 25 Nov. 1734, n. 2; *Ante* To Lewis Paul, Late Feb. or Early Mar. 1756 and n. 3.

Edmund Hector

THURSDAY 11 NOVEMBER 1756

MS: Hyde Collection.

ADDRESS: To Mr. Hector in Birmingham.

POSTMARK: 11 NO.

Dear Sir: Nov. 11, 1756

I was very much gratified by your last letter, do not let us again intermit our correspondence. What changes time makes in the mind. A letter from an old friend raises in me emotions very different from those which I felt when we used to talk to one another formerly by every post or carrier.[1] As we come forward into life we naturally turn back now and then upon the past. I now think more upon my Schooldays than I did when I had just broken loose from a Master. Happy is he that can look back upon the past with pleasure. Of those happy Beings have you known many? I long to sit with you for a few days in some retreat, and compare the which[2] experience has given us with those which we once formed from conjecture. Shall we like each other when we meet, as we liked once? let neither form too great expectations and there will be less danger of disappointment.

I sincerely thank you for the readiness with which you undertake my subscription.[3] I hope all my old friends will be per-

1. *Ante* To Edmund Hector, 7 Oct. 1756.

2. MS: word or words omitted before "which"

3. *Ante* To Edmund Hector, 7 Oct. 1756.

suaded to help me. As you receive three or four Guineas send them to my Mother, She may want them.

I should be glad to hear of any of our common friends, with whom we sometimes spent our time at Birmingham,[4] for every body whose memory stands in my mind connected with yours has some claim to the kindness of, Dear Sir, your most affectionate,

SAM. JOHNSON

4. *Ante* To Edmund Hector, 15 Apr. 1755, n. 1.; 7 Oct. 1756, n. 8.

John Taylor

THURSDAY 18 NOVEMBER 1756

MS: Berg Collection, New York Public Library.

ADDRESS: To the Revd. Dr. Taylor at Market Bosworth, Leicestershire.

POSTMARK: 18 NO.

ENDORSEMENTS: Johnson 1736, 10 Novr. 1756. One of the best Letters in the World.

Dear Sir: Novr. 18, 1756

You have no great title to a very speedy answer yet I did not intend to have delayed so long.[1] I am now in doubt whether you are not come to town, if you are double postage is a proper fine.[2]

There is one honest reason why those things are most subject to delays which we most desire to do. What we think of importance we wish to do well, to do any thing well, requires time, and what requires time commonly finds us too idle or too busy to undertake it. To be idle is not the best excuse, though if a man studies his own reformation it is the best reason he can allege to himself, both because it is commonly true, and because it contains no fallacy, for every man that thinks he is idle condemns himself and has[3] therefore a

1. SJ had last written to Taylor on 31 July 1756.

2. SJ's letter fills two sheets, and thus was charged double (8*d.* instead of 4*d.*). See Hendy, p. 185.

3. MS: "has" superimposed upon "ma"

chance to endeavour amendment, but the busy mortal has often his own commendation, even when his very business is the consequence of Idleness, when he engages himself in trifles only to put the thoughts of more important duties out of his mind, or to gain an excuse to his own heart for omitting them.

I am glad however that while you forgot me you were gaining upon the affections of other people. It is in your power to be very useful as a neighbor, a magistrate, and a Clergyman, and he that is useful, must conduct his life very imprudently not to be beloved. If Mousley makes advances I would wish you not to reject them. You once esteemed him and the quarrel between you arose from misinformation, and ought to be forgotten.[4]

When you come to town let us contrive to see one another more frequently at least once a week. We have both lived long enough to bury many friends, and have therefore learned to set a value on those who are left. Neither of[5] us now can find many whom he has known so long as we have known each other. Do not let us lose our intimacy at a time when we ought rather to think of encreasing it. We both stand almost single in the world. I have no brother,[6] and with your sister[7] you have little corespondence.[8] But if you will take my advice, you will make some overtures of reconciliation to her. If you have been to blame, you know it is your duty first to seek a renewal of kindness, if she has been faulty, you have an opportunity to exercise the virtue of forgiveness. You must consider that of

4. *Ante* To John Taylor, 31 July 1756.

5. MS: "of" superimposed upon "now"

6. Nathaniel Johnson (1712–37) was buried 5 Mar. 1737 at St. Michael's Church, Lichfield, three days after SJ left for London with Garrick. The only surviving letter from Nathaniel, written to his mother sometime after SJ's marriage in 1735, suggests strained relations between the brothers (*Johns. Glean.* VI.58–60; I.1).

7. Elizabeth Taylor, wife of an apothecary named "Galliff or Getcliffe" (Thomas Taylor, *Life of Dr. John Taylor,* 1910, p. 7).

8. The text following this sentence and ending with "influence over her" has been deleted and then recopied above in Taylor's hand.

her faults and follies no very great part is her own. Much has been the consequence of her education, and part may be imputed to the neglect with which you have sometime treated her. Had you endeavoured to gain her kindness and her confidence you would have had more influence over her. I hope that, before I shall see you, she will have had a visit or a letter from you. The longer you delay the more you will sometime repent. When I am musing alone, I feel a pang for every moment that any human being has by my peevishness or obstinacy spent in uneasiness. I know not how I have fallen upon this, I had no thought of it, when I began the letter, ⟨yet⟩ am glad that I have written it. I am, Dearest Sir, Your most affectionate,

SAM. JOHNSON

Unidentified Correspondent

NOVEMBER 1756

MS: Pierpont Morgan Library.

Sir: Thursday, Nov. 1756[1]

I am sorry that I should have given any pain, but know not how I could have helped it. The Poem I have long been desirous to return, but having lost or mislaid the letter know not whither to send it. If at the first or second time of calling you had thought it proper to have left only two lines, you might have saved all the rest of your trouble.

To give opinions of manuscripts is to me never pleasing, nor do I think an authour just to himself who rests in any opinion but that of the publick.[2] Something however I will say. I think too much of the work past in digression. The paragraphs are

1. MS: month and year added in unidentified hand

2. "About things on which the public thinks long it commonly attains to think right" (*Lives of the Poets* II.132); "I rejoice to concur with the common reader; for by the common sense of readers uncorrupted with literary prejudices, after all the refinements of subtilty and the dogmatism of learning, must be finally decided all claim to poetical honours" (*Lives of the Poets* III.441).

too long, and the sense too much deduced from line to line so as to require more attention than readers are willing to bestow. The authour may improve his work perhaps with no great difficulty by breaking it into shorter paragraphs. He seems too much to have studied Thompson,[3] a man of genius, but not very skilful in the art of composition, to whom however much will be forgiven as an original, that will not be forgiven to an imitator, or a successor.[4]

I must again repeat, that I wish this had been said sooner, and that the trouble which you complain of had been spared. The season of publication is now only begining so that no time has been lost. I am, sir, your very humble servant,

SAM. JOHNSON

3. James Thomson (1700–48), author of *The Seasons* and *The Castle of Indolence*.

4. "As a writer he is entitled to one praise of the highest kind: his mode of thinking and of expressing his thoughts is original. . . . The great defect of *The Seasons* is want of method; but for this I know not that there was any remedy" (*Lives of the Poets* III.298–99).

Charlotte Lennox

THURSDAY 10 MARCH 1757[1]

MS: Houghton Library.

ADDRESS: To Mrs. Lenox at Mr. Cooper's in Gerard Street, Soho.

POSTMARK: PENY POST PAYD.

ENDORSEMENT: Mr. Johnson.

Madam: March 10

I saw last week at Mr. Dodsly's a Book, called Histoire des Conjurations par P. Tertre which I told him was a good book,[2] so far as could be judged by the title, for him to publish, and for you to translate. He seemed not to dislike the proposal, but

1. Dated on the basis of SJ's reference to Lennox's *Maintenon*; see below, n. 3.

2. *Histoire des Conjurations, Conspirations et Révolutions Célèbres* (1754–60). The first eight volumes are by Père F.-J. Duport du Tertre (1715–59), the last two by J.-L. Ripault Desormeaux (Duncan Isles, "The Lennox Collection," *Harvard Library Bulletin* 19, 1971, p. 49 n. 91).

had not then all the volumes, I think he had only the Second. Now you have ended Maintenon you may perhaps think on it.[3] I never saw it before, and saw little of it then but fancy it likely to succeed.[4] Mr. Dodsly will lend you his volume if you send for it. I am, Madam, your most humble servant,

SAM. JOHNSON

I have no servant,[5] and write therefore by the post.

3. Lennox's *Memoirs for the History of Madame de Maintenon* appeared 12 Mar. 1757.

4. No English translation of the *Histoire* is known to have been published.

5. *Ante* To Thomas Birch, 8 Nov. 1755, n. 3; *Ante* To Lewis Paul, Autumn 1756 ("Wednesday") and n. 1.

Charles O'Conor[1]

SATURDAY 9 APRIL 1757

MS: Huntington Library. A copy in an unidentified hand.

ADDRESS: To Charles O'Conor, Esq.

Sir: London, April 9, 1757[2]

I have lately by the favor of Mr. Faulkner,[3] seen your account of Ireland, and cannot forbear to solicit a prosecution of your design.[4] Sir William Temple complains that Ireland is less known than any other country, as to it's ancient state.[5] The

1. Charles O'Conor (1710–91), Irish antiquary and historian, author of *Dissertations on the Ancient History of Ireland* (1753) and a member of the Royal Irish Academy. "Possessed . . . of abilities which must command pre-eminence, he was debarred of every benefit which such qualities and circumstances could procure, by being a Roman Catholick" (*GM* 1791, p. 776).

2. MS: "1755"

3. *Ante* To Samuel Richardson, 28 Mar. 1754, n. 8.

4. In the preface to the revised edition of his *Dissertations* (1766), O'Conor paid extensive tribute to SJ: "Far from joining in the current Prejudice against the present Subject, or oppressing the writer who undertook it, with Censure . . . he approved of an Endeavor to revive . . . the antient Language and Literature of a Sister Isle" (p. iv).

5. "I have . . . often observed with wonder, that we should know less of Ireland, than of any other country in Europe" (*An Introduction to the History of England*, 1695, p. 32).

natives have had little leisure, and little encouragement for enquiry; and strangers not knowing the language, have had no ability.

I have long wished that the Irish Literature were cultivated. Ireland is known by tradition to have been once the seat of piety, and learning; and surely it would be very acceptable to all those who are curious either in the original of nations, or the affinities of Languages, to be further informed of the revolutions of a people so ancient, and once so illustrious.

What relation there is between the Welch, and Irish languages, or between the language of Ireland, and that of Biscay, deserves enquiry.[6] Of these provincial, and unextended tongues, it seldom happens that more than one, are understood by any one man; and therefore, it seldom happens that a fair comparison can be made. I hope you will continue to cultivate this kind of learning, which has lain too long neglected, and which if it be suffered to remain in oblivion for another century, may perhaps never be retrieved. As I wish well to all useful undertakings, I would not forbear to let you know how much you deserve, in my opinion, from all lovers of study, and how much pleasure your work has given to, Sir, Your most obliged and most humble Servant,

SAM. JOHNSON

6. Welsh, Breton, and Irish all descend from Common Celtic, which was spoken in Central Europe and the Rhineland toward the end of the Bronze Age. Common Celtic split into two main branches, Goidelic (Irish and Scots Gaelic) and Brythonic (Welsh, Cornish, and Breton).

Edmund Hector

SATURDAY 16 APRIL 1757

MS: Bodleian Library.

ADDRESS: To Mr. Hector in Birmingham.

POSTMARK: 1⟨6⟩ AP.

Dear Sir: London, Apr. 16, 1757

My Mother informs me that you have lately remitted her some money for the receipts.[1] I am very sensibly touched by your kindness. The Subscription though it does not quite equal perhaps my utmost hope, for when was hope not disappointed? yet goes on tolerably, and the undertaking will I think be some addition to my fortune, whatever it may be to my reputation.[2]

I rather take it unkindly that you do not from time to time let me hear from you. I am now grown very solicitous about my old Friends, with whom I passed the hours of youth and cheerfulness, and am glad of any opportunity to revive the memory of past pleasures. I therefore tear open a letter with great eagerness when I know the hand in[3] which it is superscribed. You[r] letters are always so welcome, that you need not encrease their value by making them scarce. I am, Sir, your most affectionate Friend,

SAM. JOHNSON

1. *Ante* To Edmund Hector, 7 Oct. 1756; 11 Nov. 1756.

2. Under the terms of his contract with Tonson, SJ was to receive 250 free sets to sell at two guineas apiece. If more than 250 people subscribed, he was entitled to additional sets at the cost of one guinea per set (*Life* 1.545). Almost 1,000 subscriptions had been collected by the time the edition appeared in 1765.

3. MS: "i" superimposed upon "b"

John Levett

TUESDAY 21 JUNE 1757

MS: Hyde Collection.

ADDRESS: To John Levet, Esqr., in Lichfield.

POSTMARK: 21 IV.

Sir: June[1] 21, 1757

It is not many weeks past the time that I promised you to pay

1. MS: "July"

the mortgage and I shall be obliged to you not to take advantage of so small a lapse.[2]

The account, I think, stands thus.

for Principal and Interest	*146*
Of which Mr. Aston [3] paid--*	12
I paid John Asbridge by your bill which I have by me	14
By Miss Porter	20
	46

I have this day sent my Mother a Bank note of 100£. so that you may easily settle the affair,[4] which I am sorry [to] have so long and so uneasily protracted.[5]

The money paid by Mr. Aston was I am very confident three years interest, but if I was to declare upon oath, I would not go to the utmost. Ten pounds I could swear to. I suppose you do not think I would cheat you of ten or twelve pounds, nor do I believe you would require them unjustly of me.[6]

Be so kind as to spare my Mother all the trouble you can, and the twelve pounds shall make no difference between us. I am, Sir, Your very humble servant,

SAM. JOHNSON

*Of this you know I have at present no proof, but I believe it may be got, from some Banker's books. I have set this down to my mother ⟨certainly⟩ 10.

2. At the beginning of June, Levett had threatened foreclosure (note from Lucy Porter to unidentified correspondent, 7 June 1757, MS: Hyde Collection).

3. See letters to John Levett in Appendix I.

4. On 8 June SJ had arranged to borrow £100 from Jacob Tonson, "probably as an advance on the Shakespeare edition" (Clifford, 1979, pp. 188–89).

5. *Ante* To Theophilus Levett, 1 Dec. 1743 and n. 3; *Ante* To John Levett, 17 Mar. 1752; letters to John Levett in Appendix I.

6. "On 27 June 1757, Levett acknowledged payment in full of all principal money and interest due" (*Johns. Glean.* IV.9).

Thomas Warton

TUESDAY 21 JUNE 1757

MS: Trinity College, Oxford.

ADDRESS: To the Reverend Mr. Warton, Professor of Poetry in Oxford.

Dear Sir: June 21, 1757

Dr. Marsili of Padua, a learned Gentleman, and good Latin Poet, has a mind to see Oxford.[1] I have given him a Letter to Dr. Huddesford,[2] and shall be glad if you will introduce him, and show him any thing in Oxford.

I am printing my new Edition of Shakespeare.[3]

I long to see you all, but cannot conveniently come yet. You might write to me now and then, if you were good for any thing. But honores mutant mores.[4] Professors forget their friends. I will certainly complain to Miss Jones.[5] I am, sir, your most humble servant,

SAM. JOHNSON

Please to make my compliments to Mr. Wise.[6]

1. Giovanni Marsili (1727–95), poet, translator, and professor of botany at the University of Padua, was a friend of Giuseppe Baretti (Norbert Jonard, *Giuseppe Baretti*, 1963, pp. 72, 174; Baretti, *La Frustra Letteraria*, ed. Luigi Piccioni, 1932, I.265).

2. *Ante* To George Huddesford, 26 Feb. 1755, n. 1.

3. *Ante* To Thomas Birch, 22 June 1756, n. 1.

4. Polydorus Vergilius, *Proverbium libellus*, 1498, sig. f.6.

5. Mary Jones (*fl.* 1740–61), author of *Miscellanies in Prose and Verse* (1750), also contributed to *Poems by Eminent Ladies* (1755). According to Thomas Warton, "Miss Jones lived at Oxford, and was often of our parties. She was a very ingenious poetess . . . and on the whole was a most sensible, agreeable, and amiable woman. She was sister of the Rev. Oliver Jones, Chantor of Christ Church Cathedral at Oxford, and Johnson used to call her the *chantress*" (Fifer, p. 233).

6. *Ante* To Thomas Warton, 28 Nov. 1754, n. 2.

Unidentified Correspondent[1]

THURSDAY 27 OCTOBER 1757

PRINTED SOURCE: *European Magazine*, Dec. 1816, p. 488.

1. A covering note to the editor of the *European Magazine* reports "that circumstances have placed in my possession a few Letters—of our great Moralist and

Dear Sir: Oct. 27, 1757[2]

I have been thinking and talking with Mr. Allen[3] about some literary business for an inhabitant of Oxford. Many schemes might be plausibly proposed, but at present these may be sufficient.

1. An Ecclesiastical Hist. of England.—In this there are great materials, which must be compressed into a narrow compass. This book must not exceed 4 vols. 8vo.
2. A Hist. of the Reformation (not of England only but) of Europe.—This must not exceed the same bulk, and will be full of events, and very entertaining.
3. The Life of Richard the First.
4. The Life of Edward the Confessor.

All these are works for which the requisite materials may be found at Oxford, and any of these well executed would be well received.

I impart these designs to you in confidence that what you do not make use of yourself shall revert to me, uncommunicated to any other. The schemes of a writer are his property, and his revenue, and therefore they must not be made common. I am, Sir, Your most humble Servant,

SAM. JOHNSON

Lexicographer JOHNSON, and of Dr. PERCY" (Dec. 1816, p. 488). This note, which does not specify a recipient for the letter, is signed "J. W."—perhaps a younger member of the Warton family. According to Croker, however, "This letter was found by Mr. Peter Cunningham, in the papers of Allen, the printer, and was intended, no doubt, for Thomas Warton, though perhaps, from some change of opinion, not forwarded to him" (JB's *Life*, ed. J. W. Croker, 1848, p. 108). It seems probable that the letter preserved among Allen's papers was a draft or a copy. Thomas Warton remains the likeliest recipient.

2. Date from Croker, *Life*, p. 108.

3. Edmund Allen (1726–84), printer in Bolt Court, "a worthy obliging man" and SJ's "very old acquaintance" (*Life* III.269).

Charles Burney

SATURDAY 24 DECEMBER 1757

MS: Texas Christian University Library.

ADDRESS: To Mr. Burney at Lynn, Norfolk.

ENDORSEMENT: From Johnson, Decr. 24, 1757, No. 2.

Sir: Gough Square, Dec. 24, 1757

That I may show myself sensible of your favours, and not commit the same fault a second time I make haste to answer the letter which I received this morning. The truth is, the other likewise was received,[1] and I wrote[2] an answer, but being desirous to transmit you some proposals and receipts, I waited till I could find a convenient conveyance, and day was passed after day, till other things drove it from my thoughts, yet not so, but that I remember with great pleasure your commendation of my dictionary.[3] Your praise was welcome not only because I believe it was sincere, but because praise has been very scarce. A man of your candour will be surprised when I tell you that among all my acquaintance there were only two who upon the publication of my book did not endeavour to depress me with threats of censure[4] from the publick, or with objections learned from those who had learned them from my own preface.[5] Yours is the only letter of goodwill that I have yet received, though indeed I am promised something of that sort from Sweden.[6]

1. Burney had written to SJ on 26 Mar. 1757, enclosing the names of six subscribers to his edition of Shakespeare (Roger Lonsdale, *Dr. Charles Burney*, 1965, pp. 49–50).

2. MS: "wr" superimposed upon "had"

3. Burney had praised the *Dictionary* as "a Work, I believe, not yet equaled in any Language, . . . a Repository and, I had almost said, Universal Register of whatever is sublime and beautiful in english Literature" (Lonsdale, *Burney*, p. 50).

4. MS: "censure" superimposed upon "abuse"

5. One of these two friends was definitely Thomas Birch (*Ante* To Thomas Birch, 29 Mar. 1755, n. 2). The other may have been Bennet Langton (*Ante* To Bennet Langton, 6 May 1755 and n. 7).

6. SJ's correspondent may have been the "learned Swede" who had presented him with a copy of the "Finnick Dictionary." *Ante* To Thomas Warton, 28 Nov. 1754 and n. 5.

How my new Edition will be received I know not, the subscription has not been very successful. I shall publish about March.[7]

If you can direct me how to send proposals I should wish that they were in such hands.

I remember, sir, in some of the first letters with which you favoured me, you mentioned your Lady.[8] May I enquire after her? In return for the favours which you have shown me, it is not much to tell you that I wish you and her all that can conduce to your happiness. I am, sir, your most obliged and most humble servant,

SAM. JOHNSON

7. *Ante* To Thomas Birch, 22 June 1756, n. 1.

8. Esther Sleepe Burney (?1723–62), Charles Burney's first wife (m. 1749) and the mother of Frances (Lonsdale, *Burney*, pp. 22, 515).

Jacob Tonson[1]

FRIDAY 10 FEBRUARY 1758

MS: Birthplace Museum, Lichfield.

ADDRESS: To Jacob Tonson, Esqr.

Sir, Febr. 10, 1758

An accident has happened to me which Mr. Strahan will tell you, and from which I must beg to be extricated by your assistance. The affair is about forty pounds.[2] I think it necessary to assure you that no other such vexation can happen to me for I have no other of any consequence but to my friends. I am, sir, your most humble servant,

SAM. JOHNSON

1. Jacob Tonson (d. 1767), bookseller in the Strand, the principal publisher of SJ's edition of Shakespeare. SJ described him as "a man who is to be praised as often as he is named" (*Lives of the Poets* I.160).

2. Tonson loaned SJ the money immediately, as a promissory note dated 10 Feb. attests (MS: Birthplace Museum).

Charles Burney

WEDNESDAY 8 MARCH 1758

MS: Berg Collection, New York Public Library.

ENDORSEMENTS: From S. Johnson, Mar. 8, 1758. From Dr. Johnson, March 8th 1758.

Sir: London, March 8, 1758

Your kindness is so great, and my claim to any particular regard from you so little that I am at a loss how to express my sense of your favours, but I am indeed much pleased to be thus distinguished by you.[1]

I am ashamed to tell you that my Shakespeare will not be out so soon as I promised my subscribers; but I did not promise them more than I promised myself. It will however be published before summer.[2]

I have sent you a bundle of proposals, which I think, do not profess more than I have hitherto performed. I have printed many of the plays and have hitherto left very few passages unexplained; where I am quite at a loss, I confess my ignorance, which is seldom done by commentators.[3]

I have likewise inclosed twelve receipts, not that I mean to impose upon you the trouble of pushing them with more importunity than may seem proper, but that you may[4] rather have more than fewer than you shall want. The proposals you

1. According to JB, "This letter was an answer to one in which was enclosed a draft for the payment of some subscriptions to his Shakspeare" (*Life* I.327 n. 2).

2. "If 'before summer' means by the beginning of summer . . . this confident statement signifies that Johnson believed that the next two and one-half months were enough to enable him to write his preface and tend to anything else that still remained undone. It must mean also that by this time he had corrected page-proof—necessarily including footnotes—of the bulk of the plays, and that what was left to do was mainly the printer's job" (B. H. Bronson, *Works*, Yale ed. VII.xx).

3. "Not a single passage in the whole work has appeared to me corrupt, which I have not attempted to restore; or obscure, which I have not endeavoured to illustrate. In many I have failed like others, and from many, after all my efforts, I have retreated, and confessed the repulse. I have not passed over, with affected superiority, what is equally difficult to the reader and to myself, but where I could not instruct him, have owned my ignorance" (*Works*, Yale ed. VII.110–11).

4. MS: "may" altered from "more"

will disseminate as there shall be opportunity. I once printed them at length in the Chronicle, and some of my friends (I believe Mr. Murphy who formerly wrote the Gray's Inn Journal)[5] introduced them with a splendid encomium.[6]

Since the life of Brown,[7] I have been a little engaged from time to time in the *Literary Magazine*,[8] but not very lately.[9] I have not the collection by me, and therefore cannot draw out a catalogue of my own parts, but will do it, and send it.[10] Do not buy them, for I will gather all those that have any thing of mine in them, and send them to Mrs. Burney,[11] as a small token of gratitude for the regard which she is pleased to bestow upon me. I am, sir, your most obliged and most humble servant,

SAM. JOHNSON

5. Arthur Murphy (1727–1805), actor, journalist, and playwright, met SJ in 1754 when he went to Gough Square to apologize for having translated back into English a French version of *Rambler* No. 190 (*Life* 1.356). Murphy's weekly periodical, the *Gray's Inn Journal*, appeared for two years, Oct. 1752–Oct. 1754. SJ reviewed it in the first number of the *Literary Magazine* (*Bibliography*, p. 76).

6. "We embrace the Opportunity of informing all Persons of Taste, that an Edition of the Works of our great dramatic Genius is now preparing for the Public by one of the best Critics of this Age . . . who has approved himself, in various Branches of Writing, an English Classic of the first Magnitude. . . . We know him to be possessed of a Genius to which we may apply what was said of Caesar, 'The Alps and Pyreneans sink before him'" (*London Chronicle*, 12–14 Apr. 1757, pp. 358–59).

7. *Ante* To Samuel Richardson, 19 Mar. 1756, n. 3.

8. *Ante* To Robert Chambers, 31 July 1756, n. 4.

9. SJ ceased to contribute to the *Literary Magazine* after May 1757 (Clifford, 1979, p. 185).

10. Such a catalogue has not been recovered.

11. *Ante* To Charles Burney, 24 Dec. 1757, n. 8.

Robert Chambers

SATURDAY 8 APRIL 1758

MS: Hyde Collection.

ADDRESS: To Mr. Chambers of Lincoln College, Oxford.

POSTMARK: ⟨8⟩ AP.

FRANK: J. Philipps.[1]

1. Sir John Philipps (?1701–64), sixth Bt., of Picton Castle, Pembrokeshire, M.P.

Dear Sir: Apr. 8, 1758

I have only time to tell you that I have little interest, but that I wish you success.[2] You will read[3] the inclosed papers and do with them as you please.[4] I am, sir, your most humble servant,

SAM. JOHNSON

for Carmarthen (1741–47), Petersfield (1754–61), and Pembrokeshire (1761–64). He and his wife gave Anna Williams a yearly allowance (*Life* v.276, 550; *Post* To Robert Chambers, 31 Dec. 1760).

2. "In the spring of 1758 the Vinerian statutes were being prepared, and the appointment of Scholars, Fellows, and a Professor of the Common Law contemplated. Chambers, not yet twenty-one, seems to have written Johnson asking his opinion of a career leading to the professorship, and Johnson's help in securing a scholarship" (E. L. McAdam, *Dr. Johnson and the English Law,* 1951, pp. 65–66). *Post* To Robert Chambers, 14 Apr. 1758; 1 June 1758.

3. MS: "send" del. before "read"

4. These "papers" were letters of recommendation. *Post* To Robert Chambers, 14 Apr. 1758.

Robert Chambers

FRIDAY 14 APRIL 1758

MS: Hyde Collection.

ADDRESS: To Mr. Chambers of Lincoln College.

Dear Sir: Apr. 14, 1758

I long to hear how you go on in your solicitation, and what hopes you have of success.[1] Of what value do you expect any of these new benefactions to be.[2] The great fault of our constitution is that we have many little things which may support idleness, but scarcely any thing great enough to kindle ambition. So that very few men stay in the houses who are qualified to live elsewhere. A professorship of the common law is at least

1. *Ante* To Robert Chambers, 8 Apr. 1758 and n. 2.

2. The "benefactions" were those of Charles Viner (1678–1756), who left the unsold sets of his *Abridgment of Law and Equity* and his residuary estate to found a professorship at Oxford, "that young gentlemen who shall be students there and shall intend to apply themselves to the study of the common laws of England, may be instructed and enabled to pursue their studies to their best advantage" (E. L. McAdam, *Dr. Johnson and the English Law,* 1951, p. 4).

decent, but I do not expect it to be of much use; it will not be worth the acceptance of any practical Lawyer, and a mere speculatist will have no authority.[3] However I am glad it is thought on.

I have sent you a parcel of receipts, as a fund out of which any body that wants them may be supplied.[4] Set down the numbers of those which you give to others.

Let me know which of my letters you delivered, and how they were received. I have no pretensions to much regard from those to whom I wrote, having never done any thing for them. However let me hear what they said to you. I am, sir, your most affectionate and most humble servant,

SAM. JOHNSON

3. SJ's forecast proved unduly pessimistic: the first Vinerian Professor was William (later Sir William) Blackstone, and he was succeeded in 1766 by Chambers himself.

4. *Post* To Thomas Warton, 14 Apr. 1758 and n. 3.

Thomas Warton

FRIDAY 14 APRIL 1758

MS: Trinity College, Oxford.

ADDRESS: To the Reverend Mr. Warton, Professor of Poetry in Oxford.

Dear Sir: Apr. 14, 1758

Your notes upon my poet were very acceptable to me, I beg that you will be so kind as to continue your searches. It will be reputable to my work, and suitable to your professorship to have something of yours in the notes. You have given no directions about your name, I shall therefore put it. I wish your Brother would take the same trouble. A commentary must arise from the fortuitous discoveries of many men, in devious walks of literature. Some of your remarks are on plays already printed, but I purpose to add an appendix of notes, so that nothing comes too late.[1]

1. The appendix to SJ's edition of Shakespeare (vol. VIII) incorporates "the

You[2] give yourself too much uneasiness, dear sir about the loss of the papers.[3] The loss is nothing, if nobody has found them, nor even then perhaps if the numbers be known. You are not the only Friend that has[4] had the same mischance. You may repair your want out of a stock which [is] deposited with Mr. Allen of Magdalen Hall,[5] or out of a parcel which I have just sent to Mr. Chambers for the use of any body that will be so kind as to want them. Mr. Langtons are well,[6] and Miss Roberts,[7] whom I have at last brought to speak upon the information which you gave me, that she had something to say. I am, Dear Sir, Your most humble Servant,

SAM. JOHNSON

observations of many of his friends," including those of Thomas but not of Joseph Warton (*Bibliography*, p. 107).

2. MS: "Your" with "r" partially erased

3. According to Warton, these papers were receipts for SJ's edition of Shakespeare (*Life* I.336 n. 1).

4. MS: "has" altered from "had"

5. Possibly Hollyer Allen (*c.* 1730), of Odiham, Hampshire, who took his B.A. from Magdalen Hall in 1753 (*Alum. Oxon.* II.i.17).

6. *Ante* To Bennet Langton, 6 May 1755, nn. 1, 7.

7. ?Judy Roberts (*fl.*1758–63), the niece of Bennet Langton the elder (*Life* I.430; Fifer, p. 309 n. 6).

Thomas Warton

THURSDAY 1 JUNE 1758

MS: Trinity College, Oxford.

ADDRESS: To the Revd. Mr. Warton.

Dear Sir: June 1, 1758

You will receive this by Mr. Baretti, a Gentleman particularly intitled to the notice and kindness of the Professor of Poesy.[1] He has time but for a short stay, and will be glad to have it filled up with as much as he can hear and see.

In recommending another to your favour, I ought not to omit thanks for the kindness which you have shown to myself.

1. *Ante* To Thomas Warton, 1 Feb. 1755, n. 4.

Have you any more notes on Shakespeare?[2] I shall be very glad of them.

I see your Pupil sometimes,[3] his mind is as exalted as his stature.[4] I am half afraid of him, but he is no less amiable than formidable. He will, if the forwardness of his Spring be not blasted, be a credit to you and to the University.

He brings some of my plays with him which he has my permission to show you, on condition that you both hide them from every body else. I am, Dear Sir, your most obedient and most humble servant,

SAM. JOHNSON

2. *Ante* To Thomas Warton, 14 Apr. 1758 and n. 1.

3. *Post* To Bennet Langton, 27 June 1758, n. 1.

4. "The earth does not bear a worthier man than Bennet Langton" (*Life* III.161). Langton's remarkable height was almost as much a subject of comment as his admirable character: he is described as resembling a May-pole and a stork (*Life* V.33 n. 3; Fifer, p. lxxv).

Robert Chambers

THURSDAY 1 JUNE 1758

MS: Hyde Collection.

ADDRESS: To Mr. Chambers in Lincoln College.

Dear Sir: June 1, 1758

I am extremely glad that you are likely to succeed.[1] The honour is not less that you have one of the scholarships without opposition, for you have it only because your character makes opposition hopeless. Nothing remains but that you consider how much will be expected from one that begins so well, and that you take care not to break the promise you have made.[2]

Mr. Newberry left a packet for you on your table which you forgot to mention.[3]

I need not recommend Mr. Baretti to you he is now taking a

1. *Ante* To Robert Chambers, 8 Apr. 1758 and n. 2.

2. *Ante* To Robert Chambers, 14 Apr. 1758, n. 3.

3. *Ante* To John Newbery, 15 Apr. 1751, n. 1.

ramble through part of England, and I hope will be well used, wherever he comes. I am, Dear sir, Your most affectionate and most humble servant,

SAM. JOHNSON

Mr. Wise wrote me an answer with high commendations of you.[4]

4. *Ante* To Thomas Warton, 28 Nov. 1754, n. 2. It is likely that SJ had addressed one of his letters of recommendation to Wise.

Bennet Langton

TUESDAY 27 JUNE 1758

MS: Hyde Collection.

ADDRESS: To Bennet Langton, Esqr., of Trinity College, Oxon.

POSTMARK: 29 IV.

Dear Sir: June 27, 1758

Though I might have expected to hear from you upon your entrance into a new state of life at a new place,[1] yet recollecting, not without some degree of shame, that I owe you a letter upon an old account, I think it my part to write first. This indeed I do not only from complaisance but from interest, for living on in the old way I am very glad of a correspondent so capable as yourself to diversify the hours. You have at present too many novelties about you to need any help from me to drive along your time.

I know not any thing more pleasant or more instructive than to compare experience with expectation, or to register from time to time the difference between Idea and Reality.[2] It is by this kind of observation that we grow daily less liable to be disappointed. You, who are very capable of anticipating futurity, and raising phantoms before your own eyes must often

1. Langton had matriculated 7 July 1757 at Trinity College, Oxford.

2. "The use of travelling is to regulate imagination by reality, and instead of thinking how things may be, to see them as they are" (*Post* To Hester Thrale, 21 Sept. 1773).

have imaged to yourself an academical life, and have conceived what would be the manners, the views, and the conversation of men devoted to letters, how they would chuse their companions, how they would direct their Studies, and how they would regulate their lives. Let me know what you expected and what you have found. At least record it to yourself before custom has reconciled you to the scenes before you, and the disparity of your discoveries to your hopes has vanished from your mind. It is a rule never to be forgotten, that whatever strikes strongly should be described while the first impression remains fresh upon the mind.

I love, dear sir, to think on you, and therefore should willingly write more to you but that the post will not now give me leave to do more than send my compliments to Mr. Warton, and tell you that I am, Dear sir, most affectionately your very humble servant,

SAM. JOHNSON

Bennet Langton

THURSDAY 21 SEPTEMBER 1758

MS: Hyde Collection.

ADDRESS: To Bennet Langton, Esqr., at Trinity College, Oxon. [*Readdressed in an unidentified hand*] at Langton, Near Spilsby, Lincolnshire.

POSTMARKS: 21 SE, [Undeciphered].

Dear Sir: London, Septr. 21, 1758

I should be sorry to think that what engrosses the attention of my friend should have no part of mine. Your mind is now full of the fate of Dury,[1] but his fate is past, and nothing remains

1. Major-General Alexander Dury was killed in early Sept. 1758 while attempting to embark at St. Cas, where the British land forces had retreated after a failed expedition against St. Malo. Dury's wife was the sister of Bennet Langton's mother. Langton sent a copy of this letter to his widowed aunt via a common friend, to whom he wrote: "the more I think of Her Situation the more Reason I see for pitying her. . . . Her Misfortune is as great as the General was amiable in His Conduct" (Langton's covering letter, quoted in Sotheby's Catalogue, 18 Dec. 1986, Lot No. 24, p. 30).

but to try what reflection will suggest to mitigate the horrors of a violent ⟨death which is⟩[2] more formidable at the first glance than ⟨on⟩ a nearer and more steady view. A violent de⟨ath is⟩ never very painful, the only danger is lest it should be unprovided. But if a man can be supposed to make no provision for death in war, what can be the state that would have awakened him to the care of futurity; when would that man have prepared himself to die, who went to seek death without preparation?

What then can be the reason why we lament more him that dies of a wound than that dies of a fever? A Man that languishes with disease, ends his life with more pain, but with less virtue, he leaves no example[3] to his friends, nor bequeathes any[4] honour to his descendants.

The only reason why we lament a soldier's death is that we think he might have lived longer, yet this cause of grief is common to many other kinds of death which are not so passionately bewailed. The truth is that every death is violent which is the effect of[5] accident, every death which is not gradually brought on by the miseries of age, or[6] when life is extinguished for any other reason ⟨than⟩ that it is burnt out. He that dies before six⟨ty of⟩ a cold or consumption dies in reality by a violent ⟨death⟩ yet his end is borne with patience, only because the ⟨c⟩ause of his untimely[7] end is silent and invisible. Let us endeavour to see things as they are, and then enquire whether we ought to complain. Whether to see life as it is will give us much consolation I know not, but the[8] consolation which is drawn from truth, if any there be, is solid and durable, that which may be derived from errour must be like its original fallacious and fugitive. I am, Dear dear Sir, Your most humble Servant,

SAM. JOHNSON

2. MS: mutilated, probably by removal of seal
3. MS: "am" supplied below "ex-" in another hand
4. MS: "a" superimposed upon "h"
5. MS: "of of"
6. MS: "or" written above undeciphered deletion
7. MS: "untimely" superimposed upon "short life" del.
8. MS: "the" superimposed upon "con"

William Drummond[1]

SUNDAY 1 OCTOBER 1758

PRINTED SOURCE: James Elphinston, *Forty Years' Correspondence*, 1791, I.58–59.[2]

ADDRESS: William Drummond, ov Callandar, Esquire.

Sir, London, Oct. 1, 1758

An old intimacy widh Mr. *Elphinston*,[3] and a littel acquaintance widh yoor son,[4] hav prevailed upon me to' doo dhat, to' hwich I hav no right; to' obtrude my opinnion ov dhe skeme, hwich yoo hav formed for hiz edducacion.

Ov two' methods ov Edducacion, boath rezonabel, and boath in manny instances succesfool; I shood always think dhat better, to' hwich dhe pupil guivs dhe prefference. Attension wil not always be fixed in compliance widh our own choice, and much les wil it obey dhe advice ov anoddher. Dhe Itallian phraze, by hwich dhey expres dhe utmoast felicity ov picture, iz, dhat it waz don widh fondnes.[5] He dhat in hiz studdies follows dhe choice, even ov him hoos judgement he revverences moast, wil bring to' dhe work but half hiz mind; he wil apply hiz understanding, but not hiz affeccions; and may labor at hiz task, but wil scarcely lov it.

I find yoor yong gentelman not much plezed widh dhe prospect ov spending dhe next three years under a private master,[6]

1. William Drummond (*c.* 1708–74), of Callendar, Perthshire, a bookseller in Edinburgh. Drummond was "a gentleman of good family, but small estate, who took arms for the house of Stuart in 1745; and during his concealment in London till the act of general pardon came out, obtained the acquaintance of Dr. Johnson, who justly esteemed him as a very worthy man" (*Life* II.26–27).

2. Elphinston's phonetic spelling has been retained.

3. *Ante* To James Elphinston, 20 Apr. 1749, n. 1.

4. Alexander Monro Drummond (*c.* 1741–82), a friend of James Elphinston, went on to study medicine at the University of Edinburgh and to serve as physician to Sir William Hamilton's first wife in Naples (*Diary of Silas Neville*, ed. Basil Cozens-Hardy, 1950, p. 198; *Walpole's Correspondence*, Yale ed. XXIV.199 and n. 2). Drummond had been on a trip to London; he left *c.* 2 Oct. 1758 to return to Scotland (Elphinston, *Forty Years' Correspondence* I.62–65).

5. "con amore"

6. A certain "Mr. Menyies" of Coupar, "now propozed yoor sons master for three years" (Elphinston, *Forty Years' Correspondence* I.56, 63).

and dezirous raddher ov partaking dhe pubblic instruccions ov dhe professors ov Eddinburrough: and indeed, I doo not see hwat can be hoped at Coopar in Fife, equal to' dhe advantages ov a pubblic ospital, and pubblic lectures; widh dhe conversacion ov manny ingenious men, emmulously cultivating dhe same studdies.[7]

It iz verry daingerous to' cros dhe stream ov curiossity; or, by oppoziscion and disappointments, hwich yong men (hoo hav not experienced graiter evils) often feel widh much sensibillity, to' repres dhe ardor ov improovment; hwich, if wonce extinguished, iz seldom kindeled a seccond time.[8]

Havving said dhus much widhout anny previous invitacion or permission, I think myself obleged to' entreat yoor pardon; and hope dhat yoo wil not suspect anny unbenevvolent motive to' hav braught dhis trubbel upon yoo from, Sir, your moast umbel servant,

SAM. JOHNSON

7. Elphinston also wrote to William Drummond on 1 Oct., urging him to send his son to study at Edinburgh: "Yoo fear, no dout, dhe temptacions ov a capital; but hware iz dhe village widhout dhem? . . . Yoor son iz now more sedate, dhan yoo can wel imadgine; and may be az much under inspeccion at Eddinburrough, az at Coopar" (Elphinston, *Forty Years' Correspondence* 1.56–57).

8. Despite SJ's and Elphinston's joint entreaties, Drummond apprenticed his son to Menyies (Elphinston, *Forty Years' Correspondence* 1.63).

Anna Maria Smart[1]

LATE 1758[2]

PRINTED SOURCE: Christopher Smart, *Poems,* 1791, I.xxi–xxii.

Madam,

To enumerate the causes that have hindered me from answer-

1. Anna Maria Carnan (1732–1809), the stepdaughter of the bookseller John Newbery, had married the poet Christopher Smart in 1752 (Arthur Sherbo, *Christopher Smart,* 1967, p. 86). In 1757 Smart was admitted to St. Luke's Hospital for the Insane, and Mrs. Smart went to work to help support her two small daughters.

2. Arthur Sherbo has conclusively dated this letter to the end of 1758 (*JN* 24, 1964, pp. 10–11; Sherbo, *Smart,* pp. 126–27).

ing your letter would be of no use; be assured that disrespect had no part in the delay. I have been always glad to hear of you, and have not neglected to enquire after you. I am not surprised to hear that you are not much delighted with Ireland.[3] To one that has passed so many years in the pleasures and opulence of London, there are few places that can give much delight; but we can never unite all conveniences in any sphere; and must only consider which has the most good in the whole, or more properly which has the least evil. You have gone at the worst time; the splendor of Dublin is only to be seen in a parliament winter;[4] and even then matters will be but little mended. I think, Madam, you may look upon your expedition as a proper preparative to the voyage which we have often talked of. Dublin, though a place much worse than London, is not so bad as Iceland.[5] You will now be hardened to all from the sight of poverty, and will be qualified to lead us forward, when we shrink at rueful spectacles of smoaky cottages and ragged inhabitants. One advantage is also to be gained from the sight of poor countries; we learn to know the comforts of our own. I wish, however, it was in my power to make Ireland please you better;[6] and whatever is in my power you may always command. I shall be glad to hear from you the history of your management; whether you have a house or a shop, and what companions you have found; let me know every good and every evil that befalls you. I must insist that you don't use me as I have used you, for we must not copy the faults of our friends: for my part I intend to mend mine, and for the future to tell you more frequently that I am, etc.

SAM. JOHNSON

3. At some time in late 1758 "Anna Maria Smart had gone to Dublin, leaving her children with her mother and stepfather. There she opened a shop and sold, among other things, Dr. James's powders" (Sherbo, *Smart*, pp. 126–27).

4. The Irish Parliament, which met every other year, did not sit in the winter of 1758.

5. For many years SJ considered visiting Iceland (*Life* I.242, III.455).

6. By Jan. 1762 Anna Maria Smart had returned to England in order to manage her stepfather's newspaper, the *Reading Mercury* (Sherbo, *Smart*, pp. 122–23).

Bennet Langton

TUESDAY 9 JANUARY 1759

MS: Hyde Collection.

ADDRESS: To Bennet Langton, Esqr., at Langton, Lincolnshire [*added in an unidentified hand*] near Alford.

POSTMARK: 9 IA.

ENDORSEMENT in an unidentified hand: Return'd being Missent to Lincoln.

Dearest Sir: Jan. 9, 1759[1]

I must have indeed slept very fast not to ⟨have⟩ been awakened by your letters. None of your suspicions are true, I am not much richer than when you left me, and what is worse, my omission of an answer to your first letter will prove that I am not much wiser. But I go on as I formerly did, designing to be some time or other both rich and wise, and yet cultivate neither mind nor fortune. Do you take notice of my example, and learn the danger of delay. When I was as you are now, towering in ⟨the⟩ confidence of twenty one little did I suspect that I should be a⟨t⟩ forty nine what I now am.

But you do not seem to need my admonitions. You are busy in acquiring and in communicating knowledge, and while you are studying enjoy the end of Study, by making others wiser and happier. I was much pleased with the tale that you told me of being tutor[2] to your Sisters.[3] I who have no Sisters nor brothers,[4] look with some degree of innocent envy on those who may be said to be born to friends, and cannot see without wonder how rarely that native union is afterwards regarded. It sometimes indeed happens that some supervenient cause of discord may overpower this original amity, but it seems to me more frequently thrown away with levity or lost by negligence, than destroyed by injury or violence. We tell the Ladies that

1. MS: "1758"

2. MS: initial "t" of "tutor" superimposed upon "y"

3. Langton's three surviving sisters were Elizabeth (d. 1790), Diana (*c.* 1742–1809), and Juliet (*c.* 1757–91) (Fifer, p. liv).

4. *Ante* To John Taylor, 18 Nov. 1756 and n. 6.

good Wives make good husbands, I believe it is a more certain position that good Brothers make good Sisters.

I am satisfied with your stay at home, as Juvenal with his friend's retirement to Cumae. I know that your absence is best though it be not best for me.

> Quamvis digressu veteris confusus amici,
> Laudo tamen vacuis quod sedem figere Cumis
> Destinet, atq. unum civem donare Sibyllae.[5]

Langton is a good *Cumæ*, but who must be Sibylla? Mrs. Langton is as wise as Sibyl and as good, and will live, if my wishes can prolong life, till she shall in time be as old[6] but she differs in this that She has not scattered her precepts in the wind[7], at least not those which she bestowed upon You.

The two Wartons just looked into the town and were taken to see *Cleone*[8] where David says they were starved for want of company to keep them warm. David and Doddy have had a new quarrel, and I think cannot conveniently quarrel any more.[9] Cleone was well acted by all the characters, but Bellamy left nothing to be desired.[10] I went the first night and sup-

5. "Though put out by the departure of my old friend, I commend his purpose to fix his home at Cumæ, and to present one citizen to the Sibyl" (Juvenal, *Satires* III.1–3, trans. G. G. Ramsay, Loeb ed.). Juvenal's contrast between Cumæ and Rome is recast in *London*, ll. 2–8.

6. Diana Turnor (*c.*1712–93), daughter of Edmund Turnor of Stoke Rochford, Lincolnshire (Fifer, p. liv).

7. Aeneas, praying for the aged Sibyl's guidance, begs that she prophesy intelligibly: "Foliis tantum ne carmina manda, / Ne turbata volent rapidis ludibria ventis; / ipsa canas oro": "Only trust not thy verses to leaves, lest they fly in disorder, the sport of rushing winds / chant them thyself I pray" (*Aeneid* VI.74–76, trans. H. R. Fairclough, Loeb ed.).

8. Robert Dodsley's *Cleone* was first performed on 2 Dec. 1758 at Covent Garden (*Lond. Stage*, Part IV, ii.699).

9. Garrick had declined to produce Dodsley's *Cleone*, calling it "cruel, bloody, and unnatural" (Thomas Davies, *Memoirs of the Life of David Garrick*, 1808, I.251).

10. On opening night at Covent Garden, George Anne Bellamy (?1731–88), who played the title role and spoke the epilogue, heard SJ exclaim aloud from the pit, "I will write a copy of verses upon her myself." Bellamy then knew that her "success was insured" (G. A. Bellamy, *An Apology for the Life of George Anne Bellamy*, 1785, III.77–78, 79–80).

ported it as publickly as I might, for Doddy, you know, is my patron, and I would not desert him.[11] The play was very well received.[12] Doddy after the danger was over went every night to the Stage side, and cry'd at the distress of poor Cleone.[13]

I have left off housekeeping [14] and therefore made presents of the game which you were pleased to send me.[15] The Pheasant I gave to Mr. Richardson, the Bustard [16] to Dr. Lawrence,[17] and the pot [18] I placed with Miss Williams, to be eaten by myself.[19] She desires that her compliments, and good wishes may be accepted by the Family, and I make the same request for myself.

Mr. Reynolds has within these few days raised his price to twenty guineas a head,[20] and Miss is much employed in Miniatures.[21] I know not any body ⟨else⟩ whose prosperity has encreased since you left them.

Murphy is to have his Orphan of China acted next month, and is therefore, I suppose, happy.[22] I wish I could tell you of

11. At a private reading of *Cleone*, SJ urged Langton to "go into the slaughter-house again, Lanky. But I am afraid there is more blood than brains." He did, however, praise the play's "power of language" and its "pathetic effect" (*Life* IV.20).

12. *Cleone* was performed on twelve nights during the period 2 Dec.–16 Dec. 1758 (*Lond. Stage*, Part IV, iv.699–701).

13. Charles Churchill records these tears in "The Journey": "Let Them [the Muses] with Glover o'er Medea doze; / Let Them with Dodsley wail Cleona's woes, / Whilst He, fine feeling creature, all in tears, / Melts as they melt, and weeps with weeping Peers" (*Poetical Works*, ed. Douglas Grant, 1956, ll. 103–6).

14. *Post* To Lucy Porter, 23 Mar. 1759, n. 1.

15. MS: defective; "send me" supplied in an unidentified hand, possibly JB's

16. MS: defective; "Bustard" supplied in an unidentified hand, possibly JB's

17. *Ante* To Lewis Paul, 29 Dec. 1755, n. 2.

18. *pot*: "sausage" (*OED*).

19. Anna Williams moved to Bolt-Court in Fleet Street when SJ gave up his house in Gough Square. SJ often took tea with her there (*Life* I.350 n. 3, 421).

20. Since 1756–57, Sir Joshua Reynolds's price for a "head," a portrait measuring approximately 30″ x 25″, had been fifteen guineas (Ellis Waterhouse, *Reynolds*, 1973, pp. 39–41).

21. Frances Reynolds (1729–1807) accompanied her older brother to London in 1753 to serve as his housekeeper, a position she occupied until 1777. Sir Joshua discouraged her from painting full portraits, preferring that she undertake the more delicate art of watercolors (Richard Wendorf and Charles Ryskamp, "A Blue-Stocking Friendship," *Princeton University Library Chronicle* 41, 1980, p. 188).

22. Arthur Murphy's *Orphan of China* was not produced until 21 Apr. 1759

any great good to which I was approaching, but at present my prospects do not much delight me, however I am always pleased when I find that you, dear Sir, remember Your affectionate, humble servant,

SAM. JOHNSON

(*Lond. Stage,* Part IV, iv.722). In his biography of Garrick, Murphy attributed the delay to a "disagreeable controversy" with the actor-manager (*Life of David Garrick,* 1801, I.330).

Sarah Johnson

SATURDAY 13 JANUARY 1759

MS: William Salt Library, Stafford. A copy in the hand of Edmond Malone.

ADDRESS: To Mrs. Johnson, in Lichfield.

ENDORSEMENT in an unidentified hand: Pray, acknowledge the receipt of this by return of the post, without fail.

Honoured Madam, Jan. 13, 1758[1]

The account which Miss gives me of your health, pierces my heart.[2] God comfort, and preserve you, and save you, for the sake of Jesus Christ.

I would have Miss read to you from time to time the Passion of our Saviour, and sometimes the sentences in the Communion Service, beginning—*Come unto me, all ye that travel and are heavy laden, and I will give you rest.*[3]

I have just now read a physical book, which inclines me to think that a strong infusion of the bark would do you good. Do, dear Mother, try it.

Pray send me your blessing, and forgive all that I have done

1. "Written by mistake for 1759, as the subsequent letters shew" (Malone's note).

2. *Ante* To Elizabeth Johnson, 31 Jan. 1740, n. 18.

3. "Hear what comfortable words our Saviour Christ saith unto all that truly turn to him: 'Come unto me all that travail and are heavy laden, and I will refresh you'" ("The Order of the Ministration of the Holy Communion," *Book of Common Prayer*). SJ has substituted the King James Version's "give you rest" (Mt. 11:28) for the *BCP*'s "refresh you."

amiss to you. And whatever you would have done, and what debts you would have paid first, or any thing else that you would direct, let Miss put it down; I shall endeavour to obey you.

I have got twelve guineas to send you,[4] but unhappily am at a loss how to send it to-night. If I cannot send it to-night, it will come by the next post.

Pray, do not omit anything mentioned in this letter. God bless you for ever and ever. I am, your dutiful Son,

SAM. JOHNSON

4. "I find in his Diary a note of the payment to Mr. Allen, the printer, of six guineas, which he had borrowed of him, and sent to his dying mother" (Hawkins, p. 366).

Lucy Porter

TUESDAY 16 JANUARY 1759

MS: Hyde Collection.

ADDRESS: To Miss Porter at Mrs. Johnson's in Lichfield.

POSTMARK: 16 IA.

ENDORSEMENT: Jany. 16, 1759.

My Dear Miss: Jan. 16, 1759[1]

I think myself obliged to you beyond all expression of gratitude for your care of my dear Mother, God grant it may not be without success. Tell Kitty that I shall never forget her tenderness for her mistress.[2] Whatever you can do, continue to do. My heart is very full.

I hope you received twelve guineas on Monday.[3] I found a way of sending them by means of the post-master after I had

1. MS: "8" del. before "9"

2. Catherine Chambers (1708–67), Sarah Johnson's maid, "came to live with my Mother about 1724, and has been but little parted from us since" (*Works*, Yale ed. I.116). Chambers was "evidently not a mere servant, and may have been a connexion of Mrs. Johnson" (*Reades*, p. 242).

3. *Ante* To Sarah Johnson, 13 Jan. 1759 and n. 4.

written my letter, and hope they came safe. I[4] will send you more in a few days.

God bless you all. I am, My dear, Your most obliged and most humble servant,

SAM. JOHNSON

Over the leaf is a letter to my Mother.

4. MS: "I" altered from "it"

Sarah Johnson

TUESDAY 16 JANUARY 1759

MS: Hyde Collection.[1]

Dear honoured Mother: Jan. 16, 1759

Your weakness afflicts me beyond what I am willing to communicate to you. I do not think you ought to fear death, but I know not how to bear the thought of loosing you. Endeavour to do all you [can] for yourself, eat as much as you can.

I pray often for you, do you pray for me. I have nothing to add to my last letter. I am, Dear dear Mother, your dutiful son,

SAM. JOHNSON

1. See postscript, *Ante* To Lucy Porter, 16 Jan. 1759.

Sarah Johnson

THURSDAY 18 JANUARY 1759

MS: William Salt Library, Stafford. A copy in the hand of Edmond Malone.

ADDRESS: To Mrs. Johnson, in Lichfield.

Dear honoured Mother, Jan. 18, 1759

I fear you are too ill for long letters; therefore I will only tell you, you have from me all the regard that can possibly subsist in the heart. I pray God to bless you for evermore, for Jesus Christs sake. Amen.

Let Miss write to me every post, however short. I am, dear Mother, your dutiful Son,

SAM. JOHNSON

Lucy Porter

SATURDAY 20 JANUARY 1759

MS: William Salt Library, Stafford. A copy in the hand of Edmond Malone.

ADDRESS: To Miss Porter at Mrs. Johnson's in Lichfield.

Dear Miss: Jan. 20, 1759

I will, if it be possible, come down to you. God grant I may yet [see] my dear mother breathing and sensible.[1] Do not tell, lest I disappoint her. If I miss to write next post, I am on the road. I am, my dearest Miss, your most humble Servant,

SAM. JOHNSON

1. "Sarah Johnson probably died on Sunday, January 21, or possibly on Saturday, the twentieth" (Clifford, 1979, p. 342 n. 7).

Sarah Johnson

SATURDAY 20 JANUARY 1759

MS: JB's *Life*, ed. Malone, 1804, 1.309.[1]

Dear honoured Mother, Jan. 20, 1759

Neither your condition nor your character make it fit for me to say much. You have been the best mother, and I believe the best woman in the world. I thank you for your indulgence to me, and beg forgiveness of all that I have done ill, and all that I have omitted to do well.[2] God grant you his Holy Spirit, and

1. "This letter was written on the second leaf of the preceding, addressed to Miss Porter" (Malone's note).

2. "We have left undone those things which we ought to have done, And we have done those things which we ought not to have done" (General Confession, "The Order for Morning Prayer," *Book of Common Prayer*).

receive you to everlasting happiness, for Jesus Christ's sake. Amen. Lord Jesus receive your spirit. Amen. I am, dear, dear Mother, your dutiful Son, SAM. JOHNSON

William Strahan[1]

SATURDAY 20 JANUARY 1759

MS: Houghton Library.

Sir: Jan. 20, 1759

When I was with you last night I told you of a thing which I was preparing for the press. The title will be The choice of Life or The History of——Prince of Abissinia.[2]

It will make about two volumes like little Pompadour[3] that is about one middling volume.[4] The bargain which I made with Mr. Johnston[5] was seventy five[6] pounds (or guineas) a volume, and twenty five pounds for the second Edition. I will sell this either at that price or for sixty,[7] the first edition of which he shall himself fix the number, and the property then to revert to me, or for forty pounds, and share the profit that is retain half the copy.[8] I shall have occasion for thirty pounds

1. *Ante* To William Strahan, 1 Nov. 1751, n. 1. Strahan was also the printer of *Rasselas* (G. J. Kolb, "*Rasselas*: Purchase Price, Proprietors, and Printings," *Studies in Bibliography* 15, 1962, pp. 257–58).

2. SJ's *Rasselas* was published 20 Apr. 1759 as *The Prince of Abissinia. A Tale* (Clifford, 1979, p. 212).

3. MS: "little Pompadour" superimposed upon undeciphered erasure

4. G. J. Kolb hypothesizes that SJ is referring to *The History of the Marchioness de Pompadour* (1758), his translation of Mademoiselle de Fauques' *Histoire* (?1758). The evidence is fully set out in "Johnson's 'Little Pompadour': A Textual Crux and a Hypothesis," in *Restoration and Eighteenth-Century Literature*, ed. Carroll Camden, 1963, pp. 131–42. Both the *History* and *Rasselas* were published in two duodecimo volumes.

5. William Johnston (*fl.* 1748–74), prominent London bookseller and eventual partner (along with Strahan and Robert Dodsley) in *Rasselas* (Kolb, "*Rasselas*," p. 257).

6. MS: "five" superimposed upon "pounds" partially erased

7. MS: "sixty" written above "fifty five pounds" del.

8. As G. J. Kolb points out, SJ here sets out "three alternative, and comparable, sets of terms, which appear to be about equally satisfactory to him." The first is to

on Monday night when I shall deliver the book which I must entreat you upon such delivery to procure me.[9] I would have it offered to Mr. Johnston, but have no doubt of selling it, on [10] some of the terms mentioned.

I will not print my name, but expect it to be known.[11] I am, Dear sir, your most humble servant, SAM. JOHNSON

Get me the money if you can.[12]

---

ask "seventy five pounds (or guineas) a volume" for the first edition and twenty-five pounds for the second. The second alternative is to ask sixty pounds for the first edition and then to have exclusive ownership of the copyright. The third "reduces further the amount of cash . . . for Johnson but guarantees to him half the profit . . . on the sale of (presumably) the second edition" ("Johnson's 'Little Pompadour,'" p. 127). In the event, SJ received £100 for the first edition and £25 for the second (*Bibliography*, p. 85).

9. SJ "told Sir Joshua Reynolds that he composed it in the evenings of one week," and that he "sent it to the press in portions as it was written" (*Life* I.341). The presumption is that he required immediate payment because of his mother's illness (*Post* To Lucy Porter, 23 Jan. 1759; *Works*, Yale ed. XVI.xx–xxiii).

10. MS: "on" superimposed upon "at"

11. Though *Rasselas* appeared without SJ's name on the title page, he was indeed widely recognized as the author (Clifford, 1979, pp. 213–15).

12. *Post* To Lucy Porter, 23 Jan. 1759; 27 Jan. 1759.

Lucy Porter

TUESDAY 23 JANUARY 1759

PRINTED SOURCE: JB's *Life*, ed. Malone, 1804, I.310.
ADDRESS: To Miss Porter in Lichfield.

Jan. 23, 1759

You will conceive my sorrow for the loss of my mother, of the best mother. If she were to live again, surely I should behave better to her. But she is happy, and what is past is nothing to her; and for me, since I cannot repair my faults to her, I hope repentance will efface them.[1] I return you and all those that

1. SJ's prayer of this date, the day of his mother's burial, echoes and expands these sentiments: "Forgive me whatever I have done unkindly to my Mother, and

have been good to her my sincerest thanks, and pray God to repay you all with infinite advantage. Write to me, and comfort me, dear child. I shall be glad likewise, if Kitty will write to me.[2] I shall send a bill of twenty pounds in a few days, which I thought to have brought to my mother;[3] but God suffered it not. I have not power or composure to say much more. God bless you, and bless us all. I am, dear Miss, Your affectionate humble Servant,

SAM. JOHNSON

---

whatever I have omitted to do kindly. Make me to remember her good precepts, and good example, and to reform my life according to thy holy word, that I may lose no more opportunities of good; I am sorrowful, O Lord, let not my sorrow be without fruit" (*Works,* Yale ed. I.66).

2. *Ante* To Lucy Porter, 16 Jan. 1759, n. 2.

3. *Ante* To William Strahan, 20 Jan. 1759.

Lucy Porter

THURSDAY 25 JANUARY 1759

MS: Pierpont Morgan Library.[1]

Jan. 25, 1759

You will forgive me if I am not yet so composed as to give any directions about any thing—But You are wiser and better than I and I shall be pleased with all that you shall do. It is not of any use for me now to come down,[2] nor can I bear the place, if you want any directions Mr. Howard will advise you.[3] The twenty pounds I could not get a bill for to night but will send it on Saturday. I am, My dear, Your affectionate servant,

SAM. JOHNSON

1. The cover and the beginning of the letter are missing.

2. MS: "d" superimposed upon "to"

3. Charles Howard (1707–71), a proctor in the Ecclesiastical Court of Lichfield and SJ's friend from boyhood (*Johns. Glean.* IV.112; Clifford, 1955, p. 152).

Lucy Porter

SATURDAY 27 JANUARY 1759

MS: Hyde Collection.

ADDRESS: To Mrs. Lucy Porter in Lichfield.

POSTMARK: 27 IA.

Dear Madam: Jan. 27, 1759

I have sent you a note of twenty pounds with which I [would] have done what you suppose my dear Mother would[1] have directed. I repose wholly on your prudence and can send ten pounds more when you please.[2]

I am not able to determine any thing. My grief makes me afraid to be alone. Write to me dear Child.

I should think it best that you staid in the house, and that Kitty carried on the trade.[3] She has been very good, and is my old friend. Tell me what you would have done. God bless you. I am, My dearest, your affectionate servant,

SAM. JOHNSON

1. MS: "whould" 2. *Ante* To William Strahan, 20 Jan. 1759.

3. SJ refers to the book business that Mrs. Johnson had been running since her husband's death in 1731 (Clifford, 1955, p. 130). *Post* To Lucy Porter, 6 Feb. 1759.

Lucy Porter

TUESDAY 6 FEBRUARY 1759

MS: Hyde Collection.

ADDRESS: To Mrs. Lucy Porter in Lichfield.

POSTMARK: 6 FE.

Dear Miss: Febr. 6, 1759

I had no reason to forbear writing but that it makes my heart heavy, and I had nothing particular to say which might not be delayed to the next post, but had no thoughts of ceasing to correspond with my dear Lucy, the only person now left in the world with whom I think myself connected. There needed not my dear Mother's desire, for every heart must lean to somebody, and I have nobody but you, in whom I put all my little affairs with too much confidence to desire you to keep receipts as you prudently proposed.

If you and Kitty will keep the house, I think I shall like it best. Kitty may carry on the trade for her self, keeping her own stock apart, and laying aside any money that she receives for any of the goods which her dear good Mistress has left behind her. I do not see, if this scheme be followed, any need of appraising the books. My Mothers debts, dear Mother! I suppose I may pay with little difficulty, and the little trade may go silently forward. I fancy Kitty can do nothing better, and I shall not want to put her out of a house where she has lived so long and with so much virtue.[1] I am very sorry that she is ill, and earnestly hope that she will soon recover; let her know that I have the highest[2] value for her, and would do any thing for her advantage. Let her think of this proposal. I do not see any likelier method by which she may pass the remaining part of her life in quietness and competence.

You must have what part of the house you please while you are inclined to stay in it, but I flatter myself with hopes that you and I shall sometime pass our days together.[3] I am very solitary and comfortless, but will not invite you to come hither till I can have hope of making you live here so as not to dislike your situation. Pray my dearest, write to me as often as you can. I am, Dear Madam, your affectionate humble servant,

SAM. JOHNSON

1. *Ante* To Lucy Porter, 16 Jan. 1759, n. 2. It is probable that Catherine Chambers continued to live in the Lichfield house until her death in 1767. A. L. Reade suggests that, in addition to selling books, she may also have taken in lodgers (*Reades*, p. 242).

2. MS: initial "h" superimposed upon "m"

3. Such hopes were never realized. In 1763 Lucy Porter inherited £10,000 from her brother, a captain in the Navy, and used the sum to build "a stately house" (*Life* II.462), into which she moved in 1766 (*Reades*, p. 242). SJ visited her there, but she never came to London (*Life* II.462).

Lucy Porter

THURSDAY 15 FEBRUARY 1759

PRINTED SOURCE: Hill 1.85.

My Dear Miss, London, Feb. 15, 1759

I am very much pleased to find that your opinion concurs with mine.[1] I think all that you propose is right and beg that you would manage every thing your own way, for I do not doubt but I shall like all that you do.

Kitty shall be paid first, and I will send her down money to pay the London debts afterwards, for as I have had no connexion with the trade, it is not worth while to appear in it now.[2] Kitty may close her mistress's account and begin her own. The stock she shall have as you mention. I hope she continues to recover.

I am very much grieved at my Mother's death, and do not love to think nor to write about it. I wish you all kinds of good, and hope sometime to see you. I am, dear Miss, Your affectionate servant, SAM. JOHNSON

1. *Ante* To Lucy Porter, 6 Feb. 1759.

2. *Ante* To Lucy Porter, 27 Jan. 1759; 6 Feb. 1759.

Lucy Porter

THURSDAY 1 MARCH 1759

MS: Hyde Collection.

Dear Madam: March 1, 1759[1]

I thought your last letter long in coming, and did not require or expect such an inventory of little things as you have sent me, I could have taken your word for a matter of much greater value. I am glad that Kitty is better, let her be paid first, as my dear dear Mother ordered, and then let me know

1. MS: "1758"

at once the sum necessary to discharge her other debts, and I will send it you very soon.

I beg, my dear, that you would act for me without the least scruple, for I can repose my self very confidently upon your prudence, and hope we shall never have reason to love each other less. I shall take it very kindly, if you make it a rule to write to me once at least every week, for I am now very desolate, and am loath to be universally forgotten. I am, Dear Sweet, your affectionate servant,

SAM. JOHNSON

Lucy Porter

FRIDAY 23 MARCH 1759

MS: Birthplace Museum, Lichfield.

ADDRESS: To Mrs. Lucy Porter in Lichfield.

POSTMARK: 24 MR.

Dear Madam: March 23, 1759

I beg your pardon for having so long omitted to write. One thing or other has put me off. I have this day moved my things, and you are now to direct to me at Staple Inn London.[1] I hope, my dear, you are well, and Kitty mends, I wish her success in her trade. I am going to publish a little story book, which I will send you when it is out.[2] Write to me, my dearest girl, for I am always glad to hear from you. I am, my dear, Your humble servant,

SAM. JOHNSON

1. Though SJ had given up his lease on the Gough Square house in Sept. 1758, he "may have worked out some kind of an agreement . . . which would allow him to stay on for a while in one room, keeping his belongings there" (Clifford, 1979, p. 201). From late Mar. until mid-June 1759 he rented lodgings in Staple Inn, Holborn, one of the inns of chancery belonging to Gray's Inn (Wheatley and Cunningham II.259; Clifford, 1979, p. 211).

2. *Ante* To William Strahan, 20 Jan. 1759 and n. 2.

Lucy Porter

THURSDAY 10 MAY 1759

PRINTED SOURCE: JB's *Life*, ed. Croker, 1831, I.342.

Dear Madam: 10th May, 1759

I am almost ashamed to tell you that all your letters came safe, and that I have been always very well, but hindered, I hardly know how, from writing. I sent, last week, some of my works, one for you, one for your aunt Hunter,[1] who was with my poor dear mother when she died, one for Mr. Howard,[2] and one for Kitty.

I beg you, my dear, to write often to me, and tell me how you like my little book.[3]

I am, dear love, Your affectionate humble servant,

SAM. JOHNSON

1. Lucy Porter Howard (1690–1768), Elizabeth Johnson's sister-in-law and the widow of SJ's former schoolmaster, the Rev. John Hunter (*Reades*, p. 243).

2. *Ante* To Lucy Porter, 25 Jan. 1759, n. 3.

3. *Ante* To William Strahan, 20 Jan. 1759 and n. 2.

Elizabeth Montagu[1]

SATURDAY 9 JUNE 1759

MS: Beinecke Library.[2]

Madam: June 9th 1759

I am desired by Mrs. Williams to sign receipts with her name for the subscribers which you have been pleased to procure,

1. Elizabeth Robinson Montagu (1720–1800), author, letter-writer, and prominent Bluestocking, whose Mayfair *conversazioni* provided a center for London intellectual and artistic life. Although SJ maintained that Montagu's *Essay on the Writings and Genius of Shakespear* (1769) contained "not one sentence of true criticism," he acknowledged her "a very extraordinary woman; she has a constant stream of conversation, and it is always impregnated; it always has meaning" (*Life* II.88, IV.275).

2. Catalogued as part of the C. B. Tinker Collection, but now missing.

and to return her humble thanks for your favour, which was conferred with all the grace that Elegance can add to Beneficence.[3] I am your most obedient and most humble servant,

SAM. JOHNSON

3. SJ had published proposals for Anna Williams' *Miscellanies in Prose and Verse* in 1750, but the collection did not appear until 1766 (Hazen, p. 213).

Unidentified Correspondent

JULY 1759[1]

PRINTED SOURCE: *GM* 1785, p. 288.

[Oxford]

. . . is now making tea for me. I have been in my gown ever since I came here.[2] It was at my first coming quite new and handsome.[3] I have swum thrice, which I had disused for many years. I have proposed to Vansittart climbing over the wall, but he has refused me.[4] And I have clapped my hands till they are sore, at Dr. King's speech.[5]

1. Dated on the basis of the reference to "Dr. King's speech" (see below, n. 5) and SJ's statement to Lucy Porter that he had been "for seven weeks at Oxford" (*Post* To Lucy Porter, 9 Aug. 1759).

2. "Lord Stowell informs me that he [SJ] prided himself in being, during his visits to Oxford, accurately academic in all points; and he wore his [M.A.] gown almost *ostentatiously*" (JB's *Life*, ed. J. W. Croker, 1832, I.151 n. 1).

3. SJ had arrived at Oxford in mid-June (*Post* To Lucy Porter, 9 Aug. 1759).

4. Robert Vansittart (1728–89), D.C.L., fellow of All Souls' College, later (1767–89) Regius Professor of Civil Law at Oxford. Vansittart was also a member of the notorious Monks of Medmenham Abbey. SJ had known him for at least seven years; it is likely that they met through Joseph and Thomas Warton (Clifford, 1979, p. 111).

5. *Ante* To Thomas Warton, 25 Feb. 1755, n. 1. King spoke on 7 July 1759, during the installation of the seventh Earl of Westmorland as Chancellor of Oxford (*Life* I.348 n. 2).

Lucy Porter

THURSDAY 9 AUGUST 1759

MS: British Library (Charnwood Collection).

ADDRESS: To Miss Lucy Porter in Lichfield.

POSTMARK: [Undeciphered].

Dear Madam: Aug. 9, 1759

I beg pardon for having been so long without writing. I have been for seven weeks at Oxford, and was very well used among them,[1] but I have no great pleasure in any place. Please to let me know what money is necessary to pay what yet remains of my dear Mother's debts,[2] for I expect to receive some in a short time.[3] Be so kind as to write to me often though I should sometimes omit it, for I have no greater pleasure than to hear from you. My respects to Kitty. I am, My Dear, Your obliged, humble Servant, SAM. JOHNSON

1. *Ante* To Unidentified Correspondent, July 1759.

2. *Ante* To Lucy Porter, 6 Feb. 1759.

3. This may have been payment from John Newbery for SJ's contributions to *The World Displayed; or, a Curious Collection of Voyages and Travels* (*Bibliography*, p. 98; Clifford, 1979, p. 225).

George Hay[1]

FRIDAY 9 NOVEMBER 1759

MS: Hyde Collection.

Sir: Gray's Inn,[2] November the 9th 1759

I should not have easily prevailed upon myself to trouble a

1. George Hay (1715–78), D.C.L., M.P. for Stockbridge (1754–56), Calne (1757–61), Sandwich (1761–68), and Newcastle-under-Lyme (1768–78), served as one of the Lords of the Admiralty, 1756–65; he was knighted in 1773 (Namier and Brooke II.599–600). Hay was a friend of John Wilkes, who had applied to him in March (at the request of Tobias Smollett) for the release of Francis Barber (*Johns. Glean.* II.12–13).

2. SJ rented lodgings in Gray's Inn, High Holborn, for approximately one year, from Aug. 1759 to Aug. 1760, when he moved to Inner Temple Lane.

Person in your high station with a request, had I not observed that Men have commonly benevolence in proportion to their capacities, and that the most extensive minds are most open to Solicitation.

I had a Negro Boy named Francis Barber, given me by a Friend whom I much respect, and treated by me for some years with great tenderness.[3] Being disgusted[4] in the house he ran away to Sea, and was in the Summer on board the Ship stationed at Yarmouth to protect the fishery.[5]

It [would] be a great pleasure, and some convenience to me, if the Lords of the Admiralty would be pleased to discharge him, which as he is no seaman, may be done with little injury to the King's Service.[6]

You were pleased, Sir, to order his discharge in the Spring at the request of Mr. Wilkes,[7] but I left London about that time and received no advantage from your favour.[8] I therefore presume to entreat that you will repeat your order, and inform me how to cooperate with it so that it may [be] made effectual.

I shall take the liberty of waiting at the Admiralty next Tuesday for your Answer. I hope my request is not such as it is necessary to refuse, and what it is not necessary to refuse, I doubt not but your humanity will dispose you to grant, even to one that can[9] make no higher pretensions to your favour, than, Sir, Your most obedient and most humble Servant,

SAM. JOHNSON

3. *Ante* To Thomas Birch, 8 Nov. 1755, n. 3.

4. *disgust*: "to strike with dislike; to offend" (SJ's *Dictionary*).

5. Barber served on H.M.S. *Stag* from Dec. 1758 until Aug. 1760 (*Johns. Glean.* II.13–14).

6. Barber is described in the Muster Books as "L.M." (for "Landman"). He was discharged by Admiralty order on 8 Aug. 1760 (*Johns. Glean.* II.14).

7. See above, n. 1. SJ approached Smollett, who in turn wrote to Wilkes, 16 Mar. 1759: "You know what manner of animosity the said Johnson has against you; and I dare say you desire no other opportunity of resenting it than that of laying him under an obligation. He was humble enough to desire my assistance on this occasion, though he and I were never cater-cousins" (*Johns. Glean.* II.12).

8. SJ was in Oxford from mid-June until early August (*Ante* To Lucy Porter, 9 Aug. 1759).

9. MS: "c" superimposed upon "t"

Elizabeth Montagu

MONDAY 17 DECEMBER 1759

MS: V. Tritton, Parham Park.

Madam, Gray's Inn, Decr. 17, 1759

Goodness so conspicuous as yours will be often solicited, and perhaps sometimes solicited by those who have little pretension to your favour. It is now my turn to introduce a petitioner, but such as I have reason to believe you will think worthy of your notice. Mrs. Ogle, who kept the Musick room in Soho Square, a woman who struggles with great industry for the support of eight children, hopes by a benefit concert to set herself free from a few debts which she cannot otherwise discharge.[1] She has, I know not why, so high an opinion of me, as to believe, that you will pay less regard to her application than to mine. You know, Madam, I am sure you know, how hard it is to deny, and therefore would not wonder at my compliance, though I were to suppress a motive which you know not, the vanity of being supposed to be of any importance with Mrs. Montague. But though I may be willing to see the world deceived for my advantage, I am not deceived myself[2] for I know that Mrs. Ogle will owe whatever favours she shall receive from the patronage which we humbly entreat on this occasion, much more to your compassion for honesty in distress, than to the request of, Madam, Your most obedient and most humble servant,

SAM. JOHNSON

1. Mrs. Ogle was the widow of an oboist and impresario who presented concerts at the Great Room in Dean Street, Soho. Mr. Ogle had died sometime after Jan. 1755 (*A Biographical Dictionary of Actors, Actresses, Musicians, Dancers, Managers, and Other Stage Personnel in London, 1660–1800*, ed. P. H. Highfill et al., 1987, XI.97).

2. MS: "m" superimposed upon "f"

Robert Chambers

MONDAY 23 JUNE 1760

MS: Hyde Collection.

ADDRESS: To Mr. Chambers in Lincoln College.

Dear Sir: June 23, 1760

The Gentleman who brings this is [a] very learned and celebrated Mathematician of Italy. I am sorry that he visits Oxford in the vacation, but am the less sorry since you are there, whose civility and knowledge will supply the place of many other friends to whom I might have recommended him. I am, Dear sir, your most obliged servant, SAM. JOHNSON

Thomas Percy[1]

SATURDAY 4 OCTOBER 1760

MS: University of Rochester Library.

ADDRESS: To the Revd. Mr. Percy at Easton Mauduit, Northamptonshire, by Castle Ashby bag.[2]

POSTMARK: 4 OC.

Dear Sir: Oct. 4, 1760

That I have neglected so long to write to you is a reason why I should neglect no longer. I will not trouble you with apologies, but tell you, what I can tell with great truth, that I am very sorry for all appearance of disrespect, and hope to avoid it for the future, and shall think it a favour to hear that you forgive me.

Your friend[3] called on me with Mr. Dodsly's offer which I

1. Thomas Percy (1729–1811), antiquarian and clergyman, rector of Easton Maudit, Northamptonshire (1753–82), later Dean of Carlisle (1778) and Bishop of Dromore (1782). SJ, who had known Percy since 1756 (*Life* 1.48 n. 2) praised him for "extension of mind" and "accuracy of enquiry" (*Post* To JB, 23 Apr. 1778). Percy was elected to The Club in 1768.

2. Castle Ashby, the seat of the Earls of Northampton, is approximately two miles from Easton Maudit.

3. B. H. Davis identifies this friend as Thomas Apperley, "who had carried

think moderately good, that is, not so good as might be hoped, nor so bad as might be feared.[4] I think he might afford to advance you for the copy two pounds a sheet to be reckoned to the expences, which when the profits come to be divided will amount only to one pound given to you only that you will have the immediate use of two pounds. I will explain this by a calculation, both[5] ways. Suppose a volume to consist of twelve sheets, the expence of printing and publishing to be three pounds ten shillings a sheet and the profit as set down in each case

	12 Sheets	12 Sheets	
Paper print etc.	42–0–0	42–0–0	Paper etc.
Editor	24–0–0	00 0–0	To Editor
	68–0–0		
Sold for	91–0–0	91–0–0	Sold for
Profit	23–0–0	49–0–0	profit
to each	12–10–0	24–10–0	to each

Thus in one case you get 24 pound or 2 pound a Sheet in the other 36 or three pounds a Sheet and an earlier use of the money. Another point is to be considered, whether you bargain for the first edition only or for all future editions. If you are to share only in the first, your bargain ought to be the better. But upon the whole, I would not have you reject the offer as it is, for I know not who will make a better.[6] I will in

messages earlier from Percy to Johnson" (Davis, *Thomas Percy*, 1989, p. 75). *Post* To Thomas Apperley, 17 Mar. 1768, n. 1.

4. Percy had offered his *Reliques of Ancient English Poetry* to Robert and James Dodsley; his terms were 100 guineas for three volumes (*Correspondence of Thomas Percy and William Shenstone*, ed. Cleanth Brooks, 1977, pp. 79, 97; *Post* To Thomas Percy, 29 Nov. 1760). On 27 Nov. 1760 Percy wrote to Shenstone: "Mr. Dodsley and I have broke off all treaty on the Subject of the Old Ballads: James Dodsley is generous enough and offered me terms that would have repaid my Labour: but his brother (who if you remember had never much opinion of the work) has I suppose persuaded him to desist: for the other has receded from his own offers" (Brooks, *Correspondence*, pp. 79–80). By 22 May 1761 Robert Dodsley had changed his mind and accepted Percy's terms; the *Reliques* were published in 1765.

5. MS: "bothe" with "e" del.

6. See above, n. 4.

another letter tell[7] you what may occur to me for the improvement of the work, and once more beg you to forgive, and procure Mrs. Percy's forgiveness for,[8] Dear Sir, your most humble servant,

SAM. JOHNSON

7. MS: "tell" superimposed upon "cou"

8. In 1759 Percy had married Anne Gutteridge (1731–1806), daughter of Barton Gutteridge of Desborough, Northamptonshire.

Bennet Langton

SATURDAY 18 OCTOBER 1760

MS: Hyde Collection.

ADDRESS: To Bennet Langton, junr., Esqr., at Langton near Spilsby, Leicestershire.

POSTMARK: ⟨18⟩ OC.

Dear Sir: Octr. 18, 1760

You that travel about the world have more materials for letters than I who stay at home, and should therefore write with frequency proportionate to your opportunities.[1] I should be glad to have all England surveyed by you, if you would impart your observations in narratives as agreeable as your last; Knowledge is always to [be] wished to those who can communicate it well. While you have [been] riding and running, and seeing the tombs of the learned, and the camps of the valiant, I have only staid at home, and intended to do great things which I have not done. Beau[2] went away to Cheshire,[3] and has not yet found his way back. Chambers passed the vacation at Oxford.[4]

1. Langton traveled after matriculating at Oxford in 1757—first in England, and then, accompanied by Topham Beauclerk, on the Continent. He returned to England in Mar. 1763.

2. Topham Beauclerk (1739–80), only son of Lord Sidney Beauclerk and the great-grandson of Charles II and Nell Gwynne, matriculated in 1757 at Trinity College, Oxford, where he met Langton and, through him, SJ. The "gay, dissipated Beauclerk" (*Life* 1.249), one of the original members of The Club (1760), "could take more liberty with him [SJ], than any body with whom I ever saw him" (*Life* 1.249).

3. Possibly to Cholmondeley Castle, the seat of the Earls of Cholmondeley.

4. *Ante* To Robert Chambers, 21 Nov. 1754, n. 1.

I am very sincerely solicitous for the preservation or recovery of Mr. Langton's sight, and am glad that the Chirurgeon at Coventry gives him so much hope. Mr. Sharpe is of opinion that the tedious maturation of the cataract is a vulgar errour, and that it may be removed as soon as it is[5] formed.[6] This notion deserves to be considered, I doubt whether it be universally true, but if it be true in some cases, and those cases can be distinguished, it may save a long and uncomfortable delay.

Of dear Mrs. Langton you give me no account which is the less friendly, as you know how highly I think of her, and how much I interest myself in her health.[7] I suppose you told her of my opinion, and likewise suppose it was not followed; however I still believe it to be right.

Let me hear from you again, wherever you are,[8] or whatever you are doing, whether you wander or sit still plant trees or make Rusticks,[9] play with your Sisters,[10] or muse alone, and in return I will tell you the success of Sheridan—who at this instant is playing Cato, and[11] has already plaid Richard twice.[12]

5. MS: "is" superimposed upon "n"

6. Samuel Sharp (?1700–78), F.R.S., prominent surgeon, the author of *Letters from Italy* (1766). In two articles on cataracts, Sharp described a new surgical technique for removal of cataracts, but did not specify when the procedure should be performed (*Philosophical Transactions of the Royal Society* 48, 1753, pp. 161–63, 322–31).

7. *Ante* To Bennet Langton, 9 Jan. 1759; *Post* To Hester Thrale, 29 Sept. 1777.

8. MS: "are" traced over, possibly in JB's hand

9. According to JB, the "Rustics" was an unpublished collection of essays written by Langton at "about this time" (*Life* I.358 n. 1).

10. *Ante* To Bennet Langton, 9 Jan. 1759, n. 3.

11. MS: "and and"

12. Thomas Sheridan the younger (1719–88), actor and rhetorician, son of Swift's friend Thomas the elder, and father of the playwright Richard Brinsley. Sheridan's theatrical career began while he was still an undergraduate at Trinity College, Dublin; he went on to become manager of the city's Theatre Royal. Though widely considered one of the foremost tragedians of the age, Sheridan himself emphasized his career as teacher of rhetoric: "Acting is a poor thing in the present state of the stage. For my own part, I engaged in it merely as a step to something greater, a just notion of eloquence" (*Boswell's London Journal*, ed. F. A. Pottle, 1950, pp. 136–37).

He had more company the second than the first night, and will make I believe a good figure in the whole, though his faults seem to be very many, some of natural deficience, and some of laborious affectation. He has, I think no power of[13] assuming either that Dignity or Elegance which some men who have little of either in common life, can exhibit on the stage. His voice when strained is unpleasing, and when low is not always heard. He seems to think too much on the audience, and turns his face too often to the Galleries.

However I wish him well, among other reasons because I like his wife.[14]

Make haste to write to, Dear Sir, your most affectionate servant,

SAM. JOHNSON

13. MS: "of of"

14. Frances Chamberlaine (1724–66), novelist and dramatist, married Thomas Sheridan in 1747. SJ admired Mrs. Sheridan's novel, *Memoirs of Miss Sidney Bidulph* (1761), and praised her as a "sensible, ingenious, unassuming, yet communicative" companion (*Life* 1.389–90).

Thomas Percy

SATURDAY 29 NOVEMBER 1760

MS: Victoria and Albert Museum.

ADDRESS: To the Revd. Mr. Percy.

Dear Sir: Nov. 29, 1760

I went this morning to Mr. Millar, and found him very well disposed to your project.[1] I told him the price of 3 vols. was an hundred guineas, to which[2] he made no objection. I said nothing of advancing any money for he was in great haste, and I did not at once recollect it. There is only one thing which I dislike. He wants the Sheets that are in my hands to show to I know not whom, so that there is yet some danger. If we had not had this Specimen I think we should have immediately

1. *Ante* To Thomas Percy, 4 Oct. 1760 and n. 4.

2. MS: "w" superimposed upon "th"

bargained. Perhaps after all the bargain is made.[3] You will know from his own Letter, which he promised me to write to night, and which, if he writes it, will make this Superfluous. But, this business being of moment I would not appear to neglect it. Make all compliments to Mrs. Percy,[4] for, Sir, your most humble Servant,

SAM. JOHNSON

3. On 22 May 1761 Percy wrote to William Shenstone: "And now, Sir, let me inform you, that the work is at length to come out of Mr. Dodsley's shop:—He has thought better of the scheme, and has come up to my terms: which Mr. Millar would indeed have done as to money, but he wanted to lay me under some difficulties about the execution that prevented us from coming to an agreement" (*Correspondence of Thomas Percy and William Shenstone*, ed. Cleanth Brooks, 1977, p. 97).

4. *Ante* To Thomas Percy, 4 Oct. 1760, n. 8.

Robert Chambers

WEDNESDAY 31 DECEMBER 1760

MS: Hyde Collection.

ADDRESS: To Mr. Chambers of Lincoln College, Oxford.

POSTMARK: 1 IA.

Dear Sir: Decr. 31, 1760

The Newspapers inform us that we are in danger of losing Sir John Philips,[1] and that he is now ill of a mortified leg at Oxford.[2] He is the chief friend of Miss Williams, who is very solicitous about him and begs that you will enquire[3] about his condition as minutely as you can, and favour us with the best account you can get.[4] I wish [you] many happy years, for I am, Dearest Sir, your most affectionate, humble servant,

SAM. JOHNSON

Miss Williams sends her compliments and good wishes.

1. *Ante* To Robert Chambers, 8 Apr. 1758, n. 1.

2. "Sir John Philips, Member of Parliament for Petersfield, lies dangerously ill of a mortification in his leg, at Oxford" (*London Chronicle*, 25–27 Dec. 1760, p. 622).

3. MS: "en" superimposed upon "q"

4. "Sir John Phillips, Bart. who has been ill of a fever in Oxford, is now out of all danger" (*Daily Register*, 31 Dec. 1760, p. 1214).

Lucy Porter

TUESDAY 13 JANUARY 1761

MS: A.D.H. Pennant.

ADDRESS: To Miss Lucy Porter in Lichfield.

POSTMARK: 13 IA.

Dearest Madam: Inner Temple lane, Jan. 13, 1761

I ought to have begun the new year with repairing the omissions of the last, and to have told you sooner what I can always tell you with truth, that I wish you long life, and happiness always encreasing, till it shall end at last in the happiness of heaven.

I hope, my dear, you are well; I am at present pretty much disordered by a cold and cough, I have just been blooded, and hope I shall be better.

Pray give my love to Kitty.[1] I should be glad to hear that she goes on well. I am, my dearest dear, your most affectionate Servant,

SAM. JOHNSON

1. *Ante* To Lucy Porter, 16 Jan. 1759, n. 2.

Giuseppe Baretti

WEDNESDAY 10 JUNE 1761

PRINTED SOURCE: *European Magazine* 11, 1787, pp. 385–87.

London, June 10, 1761

You reproach me very often with parsimony of writing: but you may discover by the extent of my paper, that I design to recompense rarity by length. A short letter to a distant friend is, in my opinion, an insult like that of a slight bow or cursory salutation;—a proof of unwillingness to do much, even where there is a necessity of doing something. Yet it must be remembered, that he who continues the same course of life in the same place, will have little to tell. One week and one year are very like another. The silent changes made by time are not always perceived; and if they are not perceived, cannot be recounted. I have risen and lain down, talked and mused, while you have roved over a considerable part of Europe: yet I have not envied my Baretti any of his pleasures, though perhaps I have envied others his company; and I am glad to have other nations made acquainted with the character of the English, by a traveller who has so nicely inspected our manners, and so successfully studied our literature. I received your kind letter from Falmouth, in which you gave me notice of your departure for Lisbon; and another from Lisbon, in which you told me, that you were to leave Portugal in a few days.[1] To either of these how could any answer be returned? I have had a third from Turin, complaining that I have not answered the former.[2] Your English stile still continues in its purity and vigour. With vigour your genius will supply it; but its purity must be continued by close attention. To use two languages familiarly, and without contaminating one by the other, is very difficult; and to use more than two, is hardly to be hoped. The praises which some have received for their multiplicity of languages, may be sufficient to excite industry, but can hardly generate confidence.

I know not whether I can heartily rejoice at the kind reception which you have found, or at the popularity to which you are exalted. I am willing that your merit should be distinguished; but cannot wish that your affections may be gained. I would have you happy wherever you are: yet I would have you wish to return to England.[3] If ever you visit us again, you will find the kindness of your friends undiminished. To tell you how many enquiries are made after you would be tedious,

1. Baretti left London 13 Aug. 1760 and sailed to Lisbon, arriving 31 Aug. He left for Spain 17 Sept. (Giuseppe Baretti, *Lettere familiari*, ed. Luigi Piccioni, 1941, pp. xiv, 91, 190).

2. Baretti landed in Genoa 18 Nov. 1761 and traveled straight to Turin (Lacy Collison-Morley, *Giuseppe Baretti*, 1909, p. 129).

3. Baretti did not revisit England until Nov. 1766 (Norbert Jonard, *Giuseppe Baretti*, 1963, p. 267).

or if not tedious, would be vain; because you may be told in a very few words, that all who knew you, wish you well; and all that you embraced at your departure, will caress you at your return: therefore do not let Italian academicians nor Italian ladies drive us from your thoughts. You may find among us what you will leave behind, soft smiles and easy sonnets. Yet I shall not wonder if all our invitations should be rejected: for there is a pleasure in being considerable at home, which is not easily resisted.

By conducting Mr. Southwell to Venice, you fulfilled, I know, the original contract:[4] yet I would wish you not wholly to lose him from your notice, but to recommend him to such acquaintance as may best secure him from suffering by his own follies, and to take such general care both of his safety and his interest as may come within your power. His relations will thank you for any such gratuitous attention: at least they will not blame you for any evil that may happen, whether they thank you or not for any good.

You know that we have a new King and a new Parliament.[5] Of the new Parliament Fitzherbert is a member.[6] We were so weary of our old King, that we are much pleased with his successor; of whom we are so much inclined to hope great things, that most of us begin already to believe them. The young man is hitherto blameless; but it would be unreasonable to expect much from the immaturity of juvenile years, and the ignorance of princely education. He has been long in the hands of the Scots, and has already favoured them more than the Eng-

4. It is probable that SJ had arranged for Baretti to act as tutor and guide to Edward Southwell, of the Southwell family of Wisbech Castle, Cambridgeshire (A. T. Mackenzie, "Two Letters from Giuseppe Baretti to SJ," *PMLA* 86, 1971, p. 218; *Correspondence of Thomas Gray*, ed. Paget Toynbee and Leonard Whibley, 1971, II.470–71 n. 2).

5. George III (1738–1820) succeeded his grandfather 25 Oct. 1760. He opened the first Parliament of his reign 18 Nov. 1760 (Stanley Ayling, *George the Third*, 1972, pp. 63, 70).

6. The Duke of Newcastle procured for William Fitzherbert a seat at Bramber, "which he vacated a year later to stand for Derby, where he was returned unopposed" (Namier and Brooke II.429).

lish will contentedly endure.[7] But perhaps he scarcely knows whom he has distinguished, or whom he has disgusted.

The Artists have instituted a yearly exhibition of pictures and statues, in imitation, as I am told, of foreign Academies. This year was the second exhibition.[8] They please themselves much with the multitude of spectators, and imagine that the English school will rise in reputation. Reynolds is without a rival, and continues to add thousands to thousands, which he deserves, among other excellencies, by retaining his kindness for Baretti.[9] This exhibition has filled the heads of the Artists and lovers of art. Surely life, if it be not long, is tedious, since we are forced to call in the assistance of so many trifles to rid us of our time, of that time which never can return.

I know my Baretti will not be satisfied with a letter in which I give him no account of myself: yet what account shall I give him? I have not, since the day of our separation, suffered or done any thing considerable. The only change in my way of life is, that I have frequented the theatre more than in former seasons. But I have gone thither only to escape from myself. We have had many new farces, and the comedy called The Jealous Wife, which, though not written with much genius, was yet so well adapted to the stage, and so well exhibited by the actors, that it was crowded for near twenty nights.[10] I am

7. Lord Bute, the King's former tutor, had been highly influential in forming the new Administration. He was to become First Lord of the Treasury in 1762 (Ayling, *George the Third*, p. 92).

8. "A public exhibition of pictures by living painters was opened on the 21st of April, 1760, at a large room in the Strand, belonging to the Society for the Encouragement of Arts, Manufactures, and Commerce" (C. R. Leslie and Tom Taylor, *Life and Times of Sir Joshua Reynolds*, 1865, I.179–81). A similar exhibition was held in May 1761 at the Society of Artists' Rooms. Repeated on an annual basis, these exhibitions led to the formation of the Royal Academy in 1768 (Leslie and Taylor, *Reynolds*, I.180).

9. Reynolds's annual income in the early 1760s reached £6,000 (Leslie and Taylor, *Reynolds*, I.183; *Post* To Giuseppe Baretti, 20 July 1762).

10. George Colman's *The Jealous Wife* opened at Drury Lane 12 Feb. 1761, and ran for twenty performances that season (*Lond. Stage*, Part IV, II.843–70). "Until the end of the eighteenth century it was performed almost every year, and for more than a century it remained a stock piece in theatrical repertoire" (E. R. Page, *George Colman the Elder*, 1935, p. 58).

digressing from myself to the play-house; but a barren plan must be filled with episodes. Of myself I have nothing to say, but that I have hitherto lived without the concurrence of my own judgment; yet I continue to flatter myself, that, when you return, you will find me mended. I do not wonder that, where the monastick life is permitted, every order finds votaries, and every monastery inhabitants. Men will submit to any rule, by which they may be exempted from the tyranny of caprice and of chance. They are glad to supply by external authority their own want of constancy and resolution, and court the government of others, when long experience has convinced them of their own inability to govern themselves. If I were to visit Italy, my curiosity would be more attracted by convents than by palaces; though I am afraid that I should find expectation in both places equally disappointed, and life in both places supported with impatience, and quitted with reluctance. That it must be so soon quitted, is a powerful remedy against impatience; but what shall free us from reluctance? Those who have endeavoured to teach us to die well, have taught few to die willingly; yet I cannot but hope that a good life might end at last in a contented death.

You see to what a train of thought I am drawn by the mention of myself. Let me now turn my attention upon you. I hope you take care to keep an exact journal, and to register all occurrences and observations; for your friends here expect such a book of travels as has not been often seen.[11] You have given us good specimens in your letters from Lisbon. I wish you had staid longer in Spain, for no country is less known to the rest of Europe; but the quickness of your discernment must make amends for the celerity of your motions. He that knows which way to direct his view, sees much in a little time.

Write to me very often, and I will not neglect to write to you;[12] and I may perhaps in time get something to write: at

11. Baretti's epistolary travel narrative, *Lettere familiari*, appeared in 1762, his *Journey from London to Genoa* in 1770. *Post* To Hester Thrale, 20 July 1770 and n. 6.

12. *Post* To Giuseppe Baretti, 20 July 1762.

Lichfield July 27. 1732

Dear Sir

I received a Letter last Night from Mr Corbett, who inform'd me of a Vacancy at Ashburne, I have no suspicion of any endeavours being wanting on Your Part to contribute to my success, and therefore do not ask for Your interest with the usual Ceremony. I have sent this Messenger with Letters to Mr Vernon, and Mr Corbett. Be pleased to favour me with Your Opinion of the means most proper to be used in this Matter. If there be any occasion for my coming to Ashburne, I shall readily do it. Mr Corbett has, I suppose, given You an account of my leaving Sir Wolstan Dixey & Carcere Scale.

TO JOHN TAYLOR, 27 JULY 1732

(Hyde Collection)

Dearest Tetty

After hearing that ~~so~~ you are in so much danger, as I apprehend from a hurt on a tendon, I shall be very uneasy till I know that you are recovered, and beg that you will omit nothing that can contribute to it, nor deny yourself any thing that may make confinement less melancholy. You have already suffered more than I can bear to reflect upon, and I hope more than either of us shall suffer again. One part at least ~~We~~ I have often flattered myself we shall avoid for the future our troubles will surely never separate us more. If M[illegible] does not easily succeed in his endeavours, let him not so call in another Surgeon to consult with him, y[illegible] have two or three visits from Ranby or Shipton, who is to be the best, for a Guinea, which you need not fear to part with on so pressing an occasion, for I can send you twenty pound more on Monday, which I have received this night; I beg therefore that you will ~~be~~ more regard my happiness, than to expose yourself to any ~~diffi~~ hazards. I still promise myself many happy years from your tenderness and affection, which I sometimes hope our misfortunes have not yet deprived me of. David wrote to me this

TO ELIZABETH JOHNSON, 31 JANUARY 1740

the only extant letter from Johnson to his wife (Hyde Collection)

Mar 9. 1750-51.

Dear Sir

Though Clarissa wants no help from external Splendour I was glad to see her improved in her appearance but more glad to find that she was now got above all fears of prolixity, and confident enough of Success, to supply whatever had been hitherto suppressed. I never indeed found a hint of any such defalcation but I fretted for though the Story is long, every letter is short.

I wish you would add an Index Rerum that when the reader recollects any incident he may easily find it, which at present he cannot do unless he knows in which volume it is told; for Clarissa is not a performance to be read with eagerness and laid aside for ever, but will be occasionally consulted by the busy, the aged, and the studious, and therefore I beg that this Edition by which I suppose Posterity is to abide, may want nothing that can facilitate its use.

I am Sir Your obliged, humble Servant

March 9th 1750/51. Sam: Johnson.

busy

TO SAMUEL RICHARDSON, 9 MARCH 1751

(The Pierpont Morgan Library)

2 ✻ (2) Decr 1757

Sir

That I may shew myself sensible of your
favours, and not commit the same fault a second time
I make haste to answer the letter which I received this morning. The truth is, the other likewise
was received, and I wrote an answer, but being
desirous to transmit you some proposals and receipts, I waited till I could find a convenient
conveyance, and day was passed after day, till
other things drove it from my thoughts, yet
not so, but that I remember with great pleasure your commendation of my dictionary. Your
praise was welcome not only because I believe
it was sincere, but because praise has been very
scarce. A man of your candour will be surprised when I tell you that among all my acquain-

TO CHARLES BURNEY, 24 DECEMBER 1757

(Special Collections, Mary Couts Burnett Library, Texas Christian University)

least, you will know by my letters, whatever else they may have or want, that I continue to be, Your most affectionate friend,

SAM. JOHNSON

Thomas Percy

SATURDAY 12 SEPTEMBER 1761

MS: Hyde Collection.

ADDRESS: To the Revd. Mr. Percy at Easton Mauduit, Northamptonshire, by Castle Ashby bag.

POSTMARK: 12 SE.

Dear Sir: Septr. 12, 1761

The kindness of your invitation would tempt one to leave pomp and tumult behind, and hasten to your retreat, however as I cannot perhaps see another coronation so conveniently as this,[1] and I may see many young Percies,[2] I beg your pardon for staying till this great ceremony is over after which I purpose to pass some time with you,[3] though I cannot flatter myself that I can even then long enjoy the pleasure which your company always gives me, and which is likewise expected from that of Mrs. Percy,[4] by, sir, your most affectionate,

SAM. JOHNSON

1. The coronation of George III took place in Westminster Abbey on 22 Sept. 1761. SJ was interested enough in the occasion to contribute to John Gwynn's pamphlet *Thoughts on the Coronation* (*Bibliography*, pp. 100, 144). Donald Greene argues that SJ was responsible for "the whole of the actual text" (*Works*, Yale ed. x.291).

2. Thomas and Anne Percy had six children, only two of whom survived to adulthood. *Post* To Thomas Percy, 27 Nov. 1770 and nn. 1, 2.

3. SJ visited Percy in the summer of 1764, when he stayed for almost two months (*Post* To Thomas Percy, 23 June 1764).

4. *Ante* To Thomas Percy, 4 Oct. 1760, n. 8.

George Staunton[1]

TUESDAY 1 JUNE 1762

MS: Osborn Collection, Beinecke Library.[2]

ADDRESS: To Dr. Staunton at Captain Forests in Princess Street, Bristol.

POSTMARK: 1 IV.

ENDORSEMENT: June 1st 1762, Letter from Saml. Johnston.

Dear Sir: June 1, 1762

I make haste to answer your kind letter in hope of hearing again from you before you leave us. I cannot but regret that a Man of your qualifications should find it necessary to seek an Establishment in Guadaloupe, which if a peace should restore to the French I shall think it some alleviation of the loss, that it must restore likewise Dr. Staunton to the English.[3]

It is a melancholy consideration that so much of our time is necessarily to be spent upon the care of living, and that we can seldom obtain ease in one respect but by resigning it in another; yet I suppose we are by this dispensation not less happy in the whole than if the spontaneous bounty of nature poured all that we want into our hands: a few ⟨if they⟩ were thus left to themselves would perhaps spend ⟨their⟩ time in laudable persuits, but the greater part would prey upon the quiet of each other, or for want of[4] other objects would prey upon themselves.

This however is our condition, which we must improve and solace as we can, and though we cannot choose always our place of residence, we may in every place find rational amuse-

1. George Leonard Staunton (1737–1801), M.D., lived in London from Oct. 1759 until his departure for Guadaloupe in 1762. Staunton practiced as a physician in the West Indies, returning to England in 1770. From 1781 to 1784 he undertook various diplomatic missions in India. In 1785 he was created a baronet, in 1787 elected F.R.S.

2. The original MS is badly mutilated. Lacunae have been filled in from the transcript prepared for JB and used as copy for the *Life* (MS: Beinecke Library).

3. The British had captured Guadaloupe in 1759; it was restored to France under the terms of the Peace of Paris in 1763.

4. MS: "of" superimposed upon "ot"

ments, and possess in every place the comforts of piety and a pure conscience.

In America there is little to be observed except natural curiosities. The new world must have many vegetables and animals with which Philosophers are but little acquainted. I hope you[5] will furnish yourself with some books of natural history, and some glasses and other instruments of observation. Trust as little as ⟨you can⟩ to report, examine all that you can by your own ⟨senses.⟩ I do not doubt but you will be able to add much ⟨to⟩ knowledge, and perhaps to medicine. Wild nations ⟨trust⟩ to simples, and perhaps the Peruvian Bark is the only specifick which those extensive regions may ⟨afford us.⟩[6]

Wherever you are, and whatever be your fortune be certain, dear Sir, that you carry with you my kind wishes, and that whether you return hither or stay in the other hemisphere, to hear that you are happy will give pleasure to, Sir, your most affectionate, humble servant,

SAM. JOHNSON

5. MS: "your" with "r" del.

6. The bark of the cinchona tree, native to the Andes, is the source of quinine.

Unidentified Correspondent

TUESDAY 8 JUNE 1762

MS: Beinecke Library. The transcript prepared for JB and used as copy for the *Life*.

Madam: June 8, 1762

I hope You will believe that my delay in answering Your letter could proceed only from my unwillingness to destroy any hope that You had formed. Hope is itself a species of happiness, and perhaps the chief happiness which this world affords, but like all other pleasures immoderately enjoyed, the excesses of hope must be expiated by pain, and expectations improperly indulged must end in disappointment. If it be asked, what is the improper expectation which it is dangerous to indulge, experience will quickly answer, that it is such expectation, dictated not by reason but by desire; expectation raised not by the common occurrences of life but by the wants of the Expectant; an Expectation that requires the common course of things to be changed, and the general rules of Action to be broken.

When You made Your request to me, You should have considered, Madam, what You were asking.[1] You ask me to solicit a great Man to whom I never spoke,[2] for a Young Person whom I had never seen, upon a supposition which I had no means of knowing to be true. There is no reason why amongst all the great, I should chuse to supplicate the Archbishop, nor why among all the possible objects of his bounty, the Archbishop should chuse Your Son. I know, Madam, how unwillingly conviction is admitted, when interest opposes it; but surely, Madam, You must allow that there is no reason why that should be done by me which any other man may do with equal reason, and which indeed no man can do properly without some very particular Relation both to the Archbishop and to You. If I could help You in this exigence by any proper means, it would give me pleasure, but this proposal is so very remote from all usual methods, that I cannot comply with it but at the risque of such answer and suspicions, as I believe You do not wish me to undergo.

I have seen Your Son this morning, he seems a pretty Youth, and will perhaps find some better friend than I can procure him, but though he should at last miss the University he may still be wise, useful, and happy. I am, Madam, Your most humble Servant,

SAM. JOHNSON

1. According to JB, "a lady" had "solicited him to obtain the Archbishop of Canterbury's patronage to have her son sent to the University" (*Life* I.368).

2. Thomas Secker (1693–1768), D.D., Archbishop of Canterbury (1758–68). SJ "expressed a great opinion of Abp. Secker but said he pretended to no great knowledge of books" (*Life* IV.524).

Giuseppe Baretti

TUESDAY 20 JULY 1762

PRINTED SOURCE: *European Magazine* 13, 1788, p. 147.[1]
ADDRESS: To Mr. Joseph Baretti, At Milan.

Sir: London, July 20, 1762

However justly you may accuse me for want of punctuality in correspondence, I am not so far lost in negligence, as to omit the opportunity of writing to you, which Mr. Beauclerk's passage through Milan affords me.[2]

I suppose you received the Idlers, and I intend that you shall soon receive Shakespeare, that you may explain his works to the ladies of Italy, and tell them the story of the editor, among the other strange narratives with which your long residence in this unknown region has supplied you.

As you have now been long away, I suppose your curiosity may pant for some news of your old friends. Miss Williams and I live much as we did. Miss Cotterel still continues to cling to Mrs. Porter,[3] and Charlotte is now big of the fourth child.[4] Mr. Reynolds gets six thousands a year.[5] Levet is lately married, not without much suspicion that he has been wretchedly cheated in his match.[6] Mr. Chambers is gone this day, for the

1. Giuseppe Baretti sent copies of this and a second letter (21 Dec. 1762) to the *European Magazine*, hoping to prove that SJ "did not make quite so light of his old friend" as H. L. Piozzi's *Letters* (1788) might have led readers to believe (Clifford, 1952, pp. 322–25).

2. Beauclerk left for the Continent the following month, on his way to Naples (Fifer, p. lvii). *Post* To Giuseppe Baretti, 21 Dec. 1762.

3. Frances Cotterell lived with the actress Mary Porter. *Ante* To Frances Cotterell, 19 July 1755, nn. 1, 3. Baretti claimed to have introduced SJ to one of the Cotterell sisters (Hill 1.43 n. 1).

4. *Ante* To Frances Cotterell, 19 July 1755. Charlotte Cotterell (d. 1796) was the wife of the Rev. John Lewis (*c.* 1717–83), Dean of Ossory (1755–83).

5. In 1762 Reynolds had close to 150 sitters (listed in Charles Leslie and Tom Taylor, *Life and Times of Sir Joshua Reynolds*, 1865, 1.218). During this period of his career he charged twenty guineas for a head, fifty guineas for a half-length, and one hundred guineas for a full-length portrait (Ellis Waterhouse, *Reynolds*, 1973, pp. 39–41).

6. *Ante* To Robert Chambers, 31 July 1756, n. 5. Robert Levet "married, when

first time, the circuit with the Judges.[7] Mr. Richardson is dead of an apoplexy,[8] and his second daughter has married a merchant.[9]

My vanity, or my kindness, makes me flatter myself, that you would rather hear of me than of those whom I have mentioned; but of myself I have very little which I care to tell. Last winter I went down to my native town, where I found the streets much narrower and shorter than I thought I had left them, inhabited by a new race of people, to whom I was very little known. My play-fellows were grown old, and forced me to suspect, that I was no longer young. My only remaining friend has changed his principles, and was become the tool of the predominant faction.[10] My daughter-in-law, from whom I expected most, and whom I met with sincere benevolence, has lost the beauty and gaiety of youth, without having gained much of the wisdom of age.[11] I wandered about for five days, and took the first convenient opportunity of returning to a place, where, if there is not much happiness, there is at least such a diversity of good and evil, that slight vexations do not fix upon the heart.

I think in a few weeks to try another excursion;[12] though to what end? Let me know, my Baretti, what has been the result of your return to your own country: whether time has made any alteration for the better, and whether, when the first raptures of salutation were over, you did not find your thoughts confessed their disappointment.

---

he was near sixty, a woman of the town" (*GM* 1785, I.101). The marriage ended in separation after Levet's wife incurred debts in his name, left him, and was acquitted of a charge of pickpocketing. Levet was living with SJ again by 1763 (*Life* I.417).

7. *Ante* To Robert Chambers, 21 Nov. 1754, n. 1.

8. Richardson suffered a stroke on 28 June and died on 4 July 1761 (T.C.D. Eaves and B. D. Kimpel, *Samuel Richardson*, 1971, p. 517).

9. Martha Richardson (1736–85) married the widower Edward Bridgen (d. 1787) on 24 Apr. 1762 (Eaves and Kimpel, *Richardson*, p. 482 n. 47).

10. Donald Greene proposes John Levett as "the unidentified renegade" (*The Politics of SJ*, 1960, p. 297).

11. "Miss Lucy is more kind and civil than I expected . . . though a little discoloured by hoary virginity" (*Post* To Hester Thrale, 20 July 1767).

12. SJ visited Devonshire with Reynolds from 16 Aug. to 26 Sept. 1762.

Moral sentences appear ostentatious and tumid, when they have no greater occasions than the journey of a wit to his own town: yet such pleasures and such pains make up the general mass of life; and as nothing is little to him that feels it with great sensibility, a mind able to see common incidents in their real state, is disposed by very common incidents to very serious contemplations. Let us trust that a time will come, when the present moment shall be no longer irksome; when we shall not borrow all our happiness from hope, which at last is to end in disappointment.

I beg that you will show Mr. Beauclerk all the civilities which you have in your power; for he has always been kind to me.

I have lately seen Mr. Stratico, Professor of Padua,[13] who has told me of your quarrel with an Abbot of the Celestine order; but had not the particulars very ready in his memory. When you write to Mr. Marsili, let him know that I remember him with kindness.

May you, my Baretti, be very happy at Milan, or some other place nearer to, Sir, Your most affectionate, humble servant,

SAM. JOHNSON

13. Simone Stratico (1733–1824), F.R.S., mathematician and engineer, succeeded to the chair of medicine at the University of Padua at the age of twenty-five. Stratico traveled to England in 1761 with the Venetian embassy that marked the accession of George III. He stayed on for several years to pursue his mathematical studies.

Lord Bute[1]

TUESDAY 20 JULY 1762

MS: V. Tritton, Parham Park.

My Lord, July 20, 1762

When the bills[2] were yesterday delivered to me by Mr. Wed-

1. John Stuart (1713–92), third Earl of Bute, Prime Minister (1762–63).

2. "The expression 'bills' was a general term at the time for notes, cheques, and warrants, and no doubt covered some kind of Treasury warrant" (*Life* 1.376 n. 2).

derburne,[3] I was informed by him of the future favours which his Majesty has by your Lordship's recommendation been induced to intend for me.[4]

Bounty always receives part of its value from the manner in which it is bestowed; your Lordship's kindness includes every circumstance that can gratify delicacy, or enforce obligation. You have confered your favours on a Man who has neither alliance[5] nor interest, who has not merited them by services, nor courted them by officiousness; you have spared him the shame of solicitation, and the anxiety of suspense.[6]

What has been thus elegantly given, will, I hope, not be reproachfully enjoyed; I shall endeavour to give[7] your Lordship the only recompense, which generosity desires, the gratification of finding that your benefits are not improperly bestowed. I am, My Lord, Your Lordship's most obliged, most obedient, and most humble Servant, SAM. JOHNSON

3. Alexander Wedderburn (1733–1805), Scots lawyer and politician, M.P. for Ayr Burghs (1761–68), later Solicitor-General (1771–78) and Lord Chancellor (1793–1801); created first Baron Loughborough (1780) and first Earl of Rosslyn (1801). Wedderburn's sister was married to Bute's favorite, Sir Henry Erskine; Wedderburn himself was a close associate of the Prime Minister (Namier and Brooke III.618).

4. SJ had been awarded a pension of £300 per annum.

5. MS: "alliance" altered from "alliances"

6. "He [SJ] expressed his sense of his Majesty's bounty, and thought himself the more highly honoured, as the favour was not bestowed on him for having dipped his pen in faction. 'No, Sir,' said Lord Bute, 'it is not offered to you for having dipped your pen in faction, nor with a *design* that you ever should'" (Arthur Murphy, "Essay on Johnson's Life and Genius," *Johns. Misc.* I.418).

7. MS: "give" superimposed upon "? wis"

Lucy Porter

SATURDAY 24 JULY 1762

MS: Rylands Library.

ADDRESS: To Miss Porter in Lichfield.

POSTMARK: 24 IY.

Dear Madam: July 24, 1762

If I write but seldom to you, it is because it seldom happens that I have any thing to tell you that can give you pleasure, but last Monday I was sent for by the chief Minister the Earl of Bute, who told me that the King had empowered him to do something for me, and let me know that a[1] pension was granted me of three hundred a year.[2] Be so kind as to tell Kitty.[3] I am, Dearest Madam, your most affectionate,

SAM. JOHNSON

1. MS: "he" del. before "a" 2. *Ante* To Lord Bute, 20 July 1762.

3. *Ante* To Lucy Porter, 16 Jan. 1759, n. 2.

Henry Bright[1]

TUESDAY 12 OCTOBER 1762

MS: Hyde Collection.[2]

Sir: Inner Temple Lane, Oct. 12, 1762

I address myself to you by the advice of Mr. Warton, the Professor of Poetry, whom I lately consulted about the Education of a young Gentleman,[3] whose peculiarity of circumstances requires something *uncommon* in the *method of teaching* and in the *Skill of the teacher.*

My young Friend after having been some years employed in a Shop, is seized with a very strong inclination for Scholarship, and is desirous of studying the learned languages, and of going to the University as soon as he can be qualified for academical Lectures.[4] I think there is reason to hope that the

1. The Rev. Henry Bright (1724–1803), Headmaster of Abingdon Grammar School, Berkshire, later tutored Henry Thrale's nephew, Ralph Plumbe, and his daughter Queeney (*Post* To Henry Bright, 9 Jan. 1770; Hyde, 1977, p. 43).

2. MS: defective along right-hand margin; see below, n. 5

3. George Strahan (1744–1824), the second son of SJ's printer, William Strahan; later Vicar of St. Mary's, Islington (1773–1824), and editor of SJ's *Prayers and Meditations*.

4. George Strahan had been apprenticed by his father to a bookseller. He

maturity of his understanding and the strength of his resolution, may enable him to make up the time which he has lost, by the help of ample and candid information, and my request to you is that you will be pleased to inform me whether you are willing to take into your house a Pupil to be instructed out of the School by such comprehensive and compendious methods as your Learning and Experience may supply.

I can recommend the young Gentleman as one of uncommon purity of Manners, and Gentleness of temper, and believe that if you undertake to instruct him, you will be satisfied with his proficiency, and pleased with his company.

If you do not reject this proposal as inconvenient or impracticable, you will favour me with notice of the terms[5] which you shall expect, that my friends may consider it, and take their resolution. I am, Sir, Your most humble Servant,

SAM. JOHNSON

---

began his studies under Bright in 1763, and within eighteen months had advanced far enough to enter University College, Oxford, as a Scholar of the House (*Post* To William Strahan, 24 Oct. 1764). Three years later he became a Fellow of University College (J. A. Cochrane, *Dr. Johnson's Printer,* 1964, pp. 153–55).

5. MS: lacuna; "terms" supplied in another hand

Robert Chambers

FRIDAY 22 OCTOBER 1762

MS: Hyde Collection.

ADDRESS: To Mr. Chambers at University College, Oxford.

POSTMARK: 22 OC.

Dear Sir: Oct. 22, 1762

I thank you for transmitting my letter,[1] to which I have had an answer reasonable enough as to the conditions, but written in so unscholarlike a manner, that I must entreat the favour of you to make some enquiry into his abilities by such means as

1. *Ante* To Henry Bright, 12 Oct. 1762.

may not hurt him. I suppose it very possible that a Schoolmaster sufficiently skilful and learned, may for want of use be no great writer of English letters, but having at present nothing or but little to put in ballance against his deficiencies, I am in doubt what to determine. You will by taking ⟨this⟩ affair a little to heart, do what will be considered as [a] very important kindness to, Sir, Your most humble servant,

SAM. JOHNSON

Miss Williams sends her compliments.

Topham Beauclerk

c. OCTOBER 1762[1]

PRINTED SOURCE: JB's *Life*, 1793, I.215.

[Mr. Langton recollects the following passage in a letter from Dr. Johnson to Mr. Beauclerk:] The Havannah is taken;[2]—a conquest too dearly obtained; for, Bathurst died before it.[3] "*Vix Priamus tanti totaque Troja fuit.*"[4]

1. Dated on the basis of SJ's reference to the conquest of Havana; see below, n. 2.

2. On 12 Aug. 1762 the Spanish surrendered Havana to the English army and navy under the command of the third Earl of Albemarle. The news reached London on the evening of 29 Sept., and was published in the *London Gazette Extraordinary* the following day. On 3 Oct. Horace Walpole reported to Sir Horace Mann: "Here is the Havannah. Here it is, following despair, and accompanied by glory, riches, and twelve ships of the line; not all in person, for four are destroyed. The booty—that is an undignified term, I should say, the plunder, or the spoils, which is a more classic word for such heroes as we are, amounts to at least a million and half" (*Walpole's Correspondence*, Yale ed. XXII.82 and n. 1).

3. *Ante* To William Strahan, 22 Mar. 1753 and n. 3.

4. In the first of Ovid's *Heroides*, Penelope writes to Ulysses: "Troia iacet certe, Danais invisa puellis; / vix Priamus tanti totaque Troia fuit": "Troy, to be sure, is fallen, hated of the daughters of Greece; but scarcely were Priam and all Troy worth the price to me" (ll. 3–4, trans. Grant Showerman, Loeb ed.).

Lord Bute

WEDNESDAY 3 NOVEMBER 1762

MS: Huntington Library.

My Lord: Temple Lane, November 3, 1762

That generosity by which I was recommended to the favour of his Majesty, will not be offended at a solicitation necessary to make that favour permanent and effectual.[1]

The pension appointed to be paid me at Michaelmas I have not received, and know not where or from whom I am to ask it. I beg therefore that your Lordship will be pleased to supply Mr. Wedderburne with such directions as may be necessary, which I believe his friendship will make him think it no trouble to convey to me.

To interrupt your Lordship at a time like this with such petty difficulties is improper and unseasonable,[2] but your knowledge of the world has long since taught you, that every man's affairs, however little, are important to himself. Every Man hopes that he shall escape neglect, and with reason may every man, whose vices do not preclude his claim, expect favour from that beneficence which has been extended to, My Lord, Your Lordship's most obliged and most humble Servant,

SAM. JOHNSON

1. *Ante* To Lord Bute, 20 July 1762.

2. The preliminaries of the Peace of Paris, which ended the Seven Years' War, were signed on 3 Nov.

Giuseppe Baretti

TUESDAY 21 DECEMBER 1762[1]

PRINTED SOURCE: *European Magazine* 13, 1788, pp. 148–50.[2]

ADDRESS: Al Sign. Giuseppe Baretti, Milano.

1. Written in response to a letter from Baretti dated 21 July 1762. For a complete transcript, see A. T. McKenzie, "Two Letters from Giuseppe Baretti to SJ," *PMLA* 86, 1971, pp. 218–24.

2. *Ante* To Giuseppe Baretti, 20 July 1762, n. 1. See also J. C. Riely, "Johnson to Baretti," *Library Chronicle* 36, 1970, pp. 115–17.

Sir, Dec. 21, 1762

You are not to suppose, with all your conviction of my idleness, that I have passed all this time without writing to my Baretti. I gave a letter to Mr. Beauclerk, who, in my opinion, and in his own, was hastening to Naples for the recovery of his health; but he has stopped at Paris, and I know not when he will proceed. Langton is with him.[3]

I will not trouble you with speculations about peace and war.[4] The good or ill success of battles and embassies extends itself to a very small part of domestic life: we all have good and evil, which we feel more sensibly than our petty part of public miscarriage or prosperity. I am sorry for your disappointment,[5] with which you seem more touched than I should expect a man of your resolution and experience to have been, did I not know that general truths are seldom applied to particular occasions; and that the fallacy of our self-love extends itself as wide as our interest or affections. Every man believes that mistresses are unfaithful, and patrons capricious; but he excepts his own mistress and his own patron. We have all learned that greatness is negligent and contemptuous, and that in Courts life is often languished away in ungratified expectation; but he that approaches greatness, or glitters in a Court, imagines that destiny has at last exempted him from the common lot.

Do not let such evils overwhelm you as thousands have suffered and thousands have surmounted; but turn your thoughts with vigour to some other plan of life, and keep always in your mind, that, with due submission to Providence, a man of genius has been seldom ruined but by himself. Your patron's weakness or insensibility will finally do you little hurt,

3. *Ante* To Bennet Langton, 18 Oct. 1760, n. 1.

4. *Ante* To Lord Bute, 3 Nov. 1762, n. 2.

5. In his letter to SJ of 21 July 1762, Baretti had told the "iniquitous story" of the unfulfilled promises of patronage from Karl Joseph (1716–82), Graf von Firmian, Governor of Lombardy (McKenzie, "Two Letters," pp. 219–20; *Repertorium der diplomatischen Vertreter aller Länder*, ed. Friedrich Hausmann, 1950, II.71, 258).

if he is not assisted by your own passions. Of your love I know not the propriety, nor can estimate the power; but in love, as in every other passion, of which hope is the essence, we ought always to remember the uncertainty of events.[6] There is indeed nothing that so much seduces reason from her vigilance, as the thought of passing life with an amiable woman; and if all would happen that a lover fancies, I know not what other terrestrial happiness would deserve pursuit. But love and marriage are different states. Those who are to suffer the evils together, and to suffer often for the sake of one another, soon lose that tenderness of look and that benevolence of mind which arose from the participation of unmingled pleasure and successive amusement. A woman we are sure will not be always fair; we are not sure she will always be virtuous; and man cannot retain through life that respect and assiduity by which he pleases for a day or for a month. I do not however pretend to have discovered that life has any thing more to be desired than a prudent and virtuous marriage; therefore know not what counsel to give you.

If you can quit your imagination of love and greatness, and leave your hopes of preferment and bridal raptures to try once more the fortune of literature and industry, the way through France is now open. We flatter ourselves that we shall cultivate with great diligence the arts of peace; and every man will be welcome among us who can teach us any thing we do not know. For your part, you will find all your old friends willing to receive you.

Reynolds still continues to encrease in reputation and in riches. Miss Williams, who very much loves you, goes on in the old way. Miss Cotterel is still with Mrs Porter. Miss Charlotte is married to Dean Lewis, and has three children. Mr. Levet has married a street-walker.[7] But the gazette of my narration must

6. Baretti had conceived a "hopeless and unruly passion" for Rosina, the young daughter of Don Remigio Fuentes, one of his closest friends (McKenzie, "Two Letters," pp. 220, 223 n. 15; Norbert Jonard, *Giuseppe Baretti*, 1963, p. 142).

7. These items of news are repeated from SJ's earlier letter to Baretti of 20 July 1762.

now arrive to tell you, that Bathurst went physician to the army, and died at the Havannah.[8]

I know not whether I have not sent you word that Huggins[9] and Richardson are both dead.[10] When we see our enemies and friends gliding away before us, let us not forget that we are subject to the general law of mortality, and shall soon be where our doom will be fixed for ever. I pray God to bless you, and am, Sir, Your most affectionate, humble servant. Write soon.

SAM. JOHNSON

8. *Ante* To William Strahan, 22 Mar. 1753 and n. 3; *Ante* To Topham Beauclerk, *c.* Oct. 1762 and n. 2

9. *Ante* To William Huggins, 9 Nov. 1754, n. 1.

10. *Ante* To Giuseppe Baretti, 20 July 1762, n. 8.

Frances Reynolds[1]

TUESDAY 21 DECEMBER 1762

MS: Hyde Collection. A copy in the hand of Frances Reynolds.

Dear Madam: Decr. 21, 1762

If Mr. Mudge should make the offer you mention, I shall certainly comply with it, but I cannot offer myself unasked.[2] I am much pleased to find myself so much esteemed by a man whom I so much esteem.

Mr. Tolcher is here; full of life, full of talk, and full of enter-

1. *Ante* To Bennet Langton, 9 Jan. 1759, n. 21. SJ's letter was written in the aftermath of his trip to Devon with Joshua Reynolds (16 Aug.–26 Sept. 1762), during the course of which the travelers stayed in Torrington with Frances and her two sisters, Elizabeth and Mary (J. L. Clifford, "Johnson's Trip to Devon in 1762," *Eighteenth-Century Studies in Honor of D. F. Hyde*, 1970, p. 12).

2. SJ was about to become the godfather of William Mudge (1762–1820), son of John Mudge (1721–93), "the celebrated surgeon" and former schoolmate of Joshua Reynolds (*Life* 1.378). Reynolds and SJ had stayed with Mudge and his wife Jane during their three weeks in Portsmouth (Clifford, "Johnson's Trip," pp. 16–17).

prise.[3] To see brisk young fellows of seventy four, is very pleasing to those who begin to suspect themselves of growing old.

You may tell at Torrington that whatever they may think, I have not forgot Mrs. Johnsons widow[4] nor school, Mr. Johnsons salmon, nor Dr. Morisons Idlers.[5] For the widow I shall apply very soon to the Bishop of Bristol who is now sick.[6] The salmon I cannot yet learn any hope of making into a profitable scheme,[7] for where I have enquired which was where I think the information very faithful I was told that dried salmon may be bought in London for a penny a pound; but I shall not yet drop the search.

For the school, a Sister of Miss Carwarthen's[8] has offered herself to Miss Williams, who sent her to Mr. Reynolds, where the business seems to have stoped. Miss Williams thinks her well qualified and I am told she is a woman of elegant manners and of a Lady-like appearance. Mr. Reynolds must be written to, for as she knows more of him than of me, she will probably choose rather to treat with him.

Dr. Morrison's Books shall be sent to him with my sincere acknowledgements of all his civilities.

I am going for a few Days or weeks to Oxford, that I may free myself from a cough, which is sometimes very violent;

3. Henry Tolcher, Alderman of Portsmouth, had helped to entertain SJ during his visit (Clifford, "Johnson's Trip," p. 19; *Johns. Misc.* II.419).

4. Elizabeth Johnson (1721–*c.* 1797), the eldest sister of Joshua and Frances Reynolds and the wife of William Johnson (*c.* 1722–95), merchant and mayor of Torrington (R. S. Gower, *Joshua Reynolds*, 1902, p. 3; Clifford, "Johnson's Trip," p. 12; information from Dr. John Edgcumbe). According to Frances Reynolds's note on this passage, Mrs. Johnson had enlisted SJ's aid in trying "to procure a pension" for the widow of a clergyman.

5. The Rev. Thomas Morrison (1705–78), Rector of Langtree, near Great Torrington, and author of *A Pindarick Ode on Painting Addressed to Joshua Reynolds, Esq.* (1767).

6. Thomas Newton (1704–82), D.D., Bishop of Bristol (1761–82), author of *Dissertation on the Prophecies* (1754–58), and SJ's former schoolmate at Lichfield Grammar School.

7. The scheme was that of William Johnson, "a bustling, ambitious man" (Clifford, "Johnson's Trip," p. 12).

8. Possibly the sister of Penelope Carwardine (?1730–?1800), painter of miniatures and friend of both Joshua and Frances Reynolds.

however if you design me the favour of any more letters, do not let the uncertainty of my Abode hinder you, for they will be sent after me, and be very gladly received by, Madam, Your most obliged, Humble servant,

SAM. JOHNSON

Miss Williams sends her compliments.

George Strahan[1]

SATURDAY 19 FEBRUARY 1763

MS: Berg Collection, New York Public Library.

ADDRESS: To Mr. Strahan at the Reverend Mr. Bright's in Abingdon, Berkshire.[2]

POSTMARK: 19 FE.

Dear George: Febr. 19th

I am glad that you have found the benefit of confidence and hope you will never want a friend to whom you may safely disclose any painful secret. The state of your mind you had not so conceal'd but that it was suspected at home, which I mention that if any hint should be given you, it may not be imputed to me, who have told nothing, but to yourself, who had told more than you intended.

I hope you read more of Nepos[3] or of some other Book than you construe to Mr. Bright. The more books you look into for your entertainment with the greater variety of stile you will make yourself acquainted. Turner I do not know,[4] but think[5] that if Clark be better you should change it,[6] for I shall never be willing that you should trouble yourself with

1. *Ante* To Henry Bright, 12 Oct. 1762 and n. 3.

2. *Ante* To Henry Bright, 12 Oct. 1762 and n. 1.

3. *Ante* To Samuel Ford, Mid 1735, n. 6.

4. Presumably *Exercises to the Accidence* (1707), a popular school text by William Turner (*c.* 1658–1726), Master of Stamford Grammar School (1693–1723).

5. MS: "th" superimposed upon "ho"

6. Presumably *A New Grammar of the Latin Tongue* (1733) by John Clarke (1687–1734), schoolmaster and classicist.

more than one book, to learn the government of words. What book that one shall be Mr. Bright must determine. Be but diligent in reading and writing, and doubt not of the success.

Be pleased to make my compliments to Miss Page and the Gentlemen. I am, Dear sir, yours affectionately,

SAM. JOHNSON

Robert Chambers

TUESDAY 15 MARCH 1763

MS: Hyde Collection.

ADDRESS in SJ's hand: To Robert Chambers, Esqre., of University College, Oxford.

POSTMARK: ⟨15⟩ MR.

FRANK: Free Harborough.[1]

Dear Sir: March 15, 1763

If you will be so kind as to send me a speedy answer to the question inclosed,[2] you will do a favour to a very ingenious Gentleman, who has some interest in it, and to whom it be very[3] pleasing to me, to procure any gratification.

Be pleased to make my compliments to the Gentlemen of your College. Langton is come home.[4] I am, Sir, Your most humble servant,

SAM. JOHNSON

1. Bennet Sherard (1709–70), third Earl of Harborough. Lord Harborough's first wife was the sister of Lord Verney, Edmund Burke's patron; this chain of association may explain the link with SJ.

2. The note enclosed with SJ's letter asks whether "some Gentleman resident in Oxford" would determine whether the Rev. Thomas Warter of Christ Church "has yet proceeded to take his degree of B.D." According to *Alum. Oxon.* (II.iv.1505), Warter, who took his B.A. in 1749 and his M.A. in 1752, never received a B.D.

3. MS: undeciphered deletion before "very"

4. *Ante* To Giuseppe Baretti, 21 Dec. 1762.

George Strahan

SATURDAY 26 MARCH 1763

MS: Hyde Collection.

ADDRESS: To Mr. Strahan at the Revd. Mr. Bright's in Abingdon, Berks.

POSTMARK: 26 MA.

Dear Sir: March 26, 1763

You did not very soon answer my Letter,[1] and therefore cannot complain that I make no great haste to answer yours. I am well enough satisfied with the proficience that you make, and hope that you will not relax the vigour of your diligence. I hope you begin now to see that all is possible which was proposed. Learning is a wide field, but six years spent in close application are a long time, and I am still of opinion that if you continue to consider knowledge as the most pleasing and valuable of all acquisitions, and do not suffer your course to be interrupted, you may[2] take your degree not only without deficiency, but with great distinction.

You must still continue to write Latin. This is the most difficult part, indeed the only part that is very difficult of your undertaking. If you can exemplify the rules of Syntax, I know not whether it will be worth while to trouble yourself with any more translation, you will more encrease your number of words, and advance your skill in phraseology, by making first a short theme or two every day, and when[3] you have learned prosody a stated number of verses. It will be pleasing to go from reading to composition and from composition to reading. But do not be very solicitous about method, any method will do if there be but diligence. Let me know if you please once a week what you are doing. I am, Dear George, your humble servant,

SAM. JOHNSON

1. *Ante* To George Strahan, 19 Feb. 1763.

2. MS: "may" altered from "make"

3. MS: "w" superimposed upon "a"

Lucy Porter

TUESDAY 12 APRIL 1763

PRINTED SOURCE: JB's *Life*, ed. Croker, 1831, I.372–73.
ADDRESS: To Mrs. Lucy Porter, in Lichfield.

My Dear: 12th April 1763

The newspaper has informed me of the death of Captain Porter.[1] I know not what to say to you, condolent or consolatory, beyond the common considerations which I suppose you have proposed to others, and know how to apply to yourself. In all afflictions the first relief is to be asked of God.

I wish to be informed in what condition your brother's death has left your fortune;[2] if he has bequeathed you competence or plenty, I shall sincerely rejoice; if you are in any distress or difficulty, I will endeavour to make what I have, or what I can get, sufficient for us both. I am, madam, yours affectionately,

SAM. JOHNSON

1. Jervis Henry Porter (1718–63), R.N., Lucy's brother, was the captain of H.M.S. *Hercules* at the time of his death, 31 Mar. 1763 (*Johns. Glean.* IV.94; *Reades*, p. 237).

2. *Ante* To Lucy Porter, 6 Feb. 1759, n. 3.

George Strahan

SATURDAY 16 APRIL 1763

MS: Hyde Collection.

Dear Sir: Apr. 16, 1763

Your account of your proficiency is more nearly [1] equal, I find, to my expectation than to your own. You are angry that a theme on which you took so much pains was at last a kind of English Latin; what could you expect more? If at the end of seven years you write good Latin, you will excel most of your

1. MS: "ne" superimposed upon "equa"

contemporaries. Scribendo disces scribere,[2] it is only by writing ill that you can attain to write well. Be but diligent and constant, and make no doubt of success.

I will allow you but six[3] weeks for Tully's Offices.[4] Walkers Particles I would not have you trouble yourself to learn at all by heart,[5] but look in it from time to time and observe his notes and remarks, and see how they are exemplified. The translation from Clark's history will improve you,[6] and I would have you continue it to the end of the book.

I hope you read by the way at loose hours other books though you do not mention them, for no time is to be lost, and what can be done with a master is but a small part of the whole. I would have you now and then try at some English verses. When you find that you have mistaken any thing review the passage carefully and settle it in your mind.

Be pleased to make my compliments, and those of Miss Williams to all our friends. I am, Dear sir, yours most affectionately,

SAM. JOHNSON

2. *Scribendo disces scribere*: "You will learn to write by writing."

3. MS: "five" del. before "six"

4. Cicero's *De officiis*.

5. *A Treatise of English Particles* (1673) by William Walker (1623–84).

6. SJ may be referring to the edition of Eutropius' *Historiæ Romanæ* by John Clarke (*Ante* To George Strahan, 19 Feb. 1763, n. 6.), first published in 1722, or to Clarke's edition of Sallust's *Bellum Catilinarium* (1734).

George Grenville[1]

SATURDAY 2 JULY 1763

MS: Loren Rothschild.

ENDORSEMENT: Pd. July 2 to Mr. C. Loyd to pay it to the Bearer.

Sir: July 2, 1763

Be pleased to pay to the Bearer seventy five pounds being the

1. George Grenville (1712–70), M.P. for Buckingham (1741–70), First Lord of the Treasury (1763–65) in succession to Lord Bute (Namier and Brooke II.537–40). SJ's request for payment is included in the *Grenville Papers*, ed. W. J. Smith, 1852, II.68.

quarterly payment of a pension granted by his Majesty,[2] and due on the 24th day of June last, to, Sir, your most humble Servant,

SAM. JOHNSON

2. *Ante* To Lord Bute, 20 July 1762.

Lucy Porter

TUESDAY 5 JULY 1763

MS: Hyde Collection.

ADDRESS: To Miss Lucy Porter in Lichfield.

POSTMARK: 5 IY.

My Dearest Dear: July 5, 1763

I am extremely glad that so much Prudence and Virtue as yours is at last rewarded with so large a fortune,[1] and doubt not but that the excellence which you have shown in circumstances of difficulty, will continue the same in the convenience of wealth.

I have not written to you sooner having nothing to say which you would not easily suppose, nothing but that I love you, and wish you happy, of which you may be always assured whether I write or not.

I have had an inflammation in my eyes, but it is much better, and will[2] be, I hope, soon quite well.

Be so good as to let me know, whether you design to stay at Lichfield this summer, if you do, I purpose to come down.[3] I shall bring Frank with me,[4] so that Kitty must contrive to make two beds,[5] or get a servant's bed at the three Crowns,[6] which

1. *Ante* To Lucy Porter, 12 Apr. 1763 and n. 1; 6 Feb. 1759, n. 3.

2. MS: comma after "will"

3. *Post* To Lucy Porter, 12 July 1763.

4. *Ante* To Thomas Birch, 8 Nov. 1755, n. 3.

5. *Ante* To Lucy Porter, 16 Jan. 1759, n. 2.

6. The inn in Breadmarket Street, Lichfield, next door to SJ's house: "not one of the great inns, but a good old fashioned one" (*Life* II.461).

may be as well. As I suppose she may want sheets and tablelinen and such things I have sent ten pounds which she may lay out in conveniences. I will pay her for our board what you think proper; I think a guinea a week for me and the boy.

Be pleased to give my love to Kitty. I am, my dearest Love, your most humble servant, SAM. JOHNSON

Lucy Porter

TUESDAY 12 JULY 1763

MS: Hyde Collection.

ADDRESS: To Mrs. Lucy Porter in Lichfield.

POSTMARK: 12 IY.

My Dearest Love: July 12, 1763

I had forgot my debt to poor Kitty; pray let her have the note, and do what you can for her, for she has been always very good. I will help her to a little more money if she wants it, and will write. I intend that she shall have the use of the house as long as she and I live.[1]

That there should not be room for me at the[2] house is some disappointment to me, but the matter is not very great. I am sorry you have had your head filled with building for many reasons.[3]

It was not necessary to settle immediately for Life at any one place, you might have staid and seen more of the world.

You will not have your work done, as you do not understand it, but at twice the value.

You might have hired a house at half the interest of the money for which you build it. If your house cost you a thousand pounds.[4] You might hire the palace for twenty

1. *Ante* To Lucy Porter, 6 Feb. 1759, n. 1.

2. MS: "t" superimposed upon "L"

3. *Ante* To Lucy Porter, 6 Feb. 1759, n. 3.

4. According to JB, Lucy Porter spent "about a third" of her legacy of £10,000 on her new house and garden (*Life* II.462).

pounds[5] and make forty of your thousand pounds, so in twenty years you would have save[d] four hundred[6] pounds, and still have had your thousand. I am, Dear dear, Your etc.

SAM. JOHNSON

5. The Bishop's Palace at Lichfield, built in 1687–88 by one of Sir Christopher Wren's masons, was not occupied by a bishop until 1867. It had been rented for thirty years by SJ's friend Gilbert Walmesley (1680–1751), Registrar of the Ecclesiastical Court (*Johns. Glean.* III.171; Nikolaus Pevsner, *Staffordshire*, 1974, p. 188).

6. MS: "forty"

George Strahan

THURSDAY 14 JULY 1763

MS: Berg Collection, New York Public Library.

ADDRESS: To Mr. Strahan at the Reverend Mr. Bright's in Abingdon, Berks.

POSTMARKS: ⟨14⟩ IY, R·J.[1]

Dear George: Thursday, July 14, 1763

To give pain ought always to be painful, and I am sorry that I have been the occasion of any uneasiness to you, to whom I hope never to [do] any thing but for your benefit or your pleasure. Your uneasiness was without any reason on your part, as you had written with sufficient frequency to me, and I had only neglected to answer then, because as nothing new had been proposed to your study no new direction or incitement could be offered you. But if it had happened that you had omitted what you did not omit, and that I had for an hour, or a week, or a much longer time thought myself put out of your mind by something to which presence gave that prevalence, which presence will sometimes give, even where there is the most prudence and experience, you are not to imagine that my friendship is light enough to be blown away by the first cross blast, or that my regard or kindness hangs by so slender[2] a hair, as to be broken off by the unfelt weight of a petty of-

1. The initial mark of Richard Jones, a letter receiver in the Temple, London (Hendy, p. 59).

2. MS: "slender" superimposed upon "slig"

fence.[3] I love you, and hope to love you long. You have hitherto done nothing to diminish my goodwill, and though you had done much more than you have supposed imputed to you my goodwill would not have been diminished.

I write thus largely on this suspicion which you have suffered to enter your mind, because in youth we are apt to be too rigorous in our expectations, and to suppose that the duties of life are to be performed with unfailing exactness and regularity, but in our progress through life we are forced to abate much of our demands, and to take friends such as we can find them, not as we would make them.

These concessions every wise man is more ready to make to others as he knows that he shall often want them for himself; and when he remembers how often he fails in the observance or cultivation of his best friends, is willing to suppose that his friends may in their turn neglect him without any intention to offend him.

When therefore it shall happen, as happen it will, that you or I have disappointed the expectations of the other, you are not to suppose that you have ⟨lost me⟩ or that I intended to lose you, nothing will ⟨remain but⟩ to repair the fault, and to go on as if it never had been committed. I am, sir, your affectionate servant,

SAM. JOHNSON

3. MS: "offence" superimposed upon "sin" partially erased

John Taylor

SATURDAY 13 AUGUST 1763

MS: Berg Collection, New York Public Library.

ADDRESS: To the Reverend Dr. Taylor in Ashbourn, Derbyshire.

POSTMARK: ?17 AV.

ENDORSEMENTS: Johnson 63, 1763, 13 May 1763.

Dear Sir: August 13, 1763

You may be confident that what I can do for you either by help or counsel in this perplexity shall not be wanting, and I take it as a proof of friendship that you have recourse to me in this strange revolution of your domestick life.[1]

I do not wonder that the commotion of your mind made it difficult for you to give me a particular account, but while my knowledge is only general, my advice must be general too.

Your first care must be of your self and your own quiet. Do not let this vexation take possession of your thoughts, or sink too deeply into your heart. To have an unsuitable or unhappy marriage happens every day to multitudes, and you must endeavour to bear it like your fellow sufferers by diversion at one time and reflection at another. The happiness of conjugal life cannot be ascertained or secured either by sense or by virtue, and therefore its miseries may be numbered among those evils which we cannot prevent and must only labour to endure with patience, and palliate with judgement. If your condition is known I should [think] it best to come from the place, that you may not be a gazing Stock to idle people who have nobody but you to talk of. You may live privately in[2] a thousand places till the novelty of the transaction is worn away. I shall be glad to contribute to your peace by any amusement in my power.

With respect to the Lady I so little understand her paper that I know not what to propose. Did she go with[3] a male or female companion? With what money do you believe her provided? To whom do you imagine she will recur for shelter? What is the abuse of her person which she mentions? What is [the] danger which she resolves never again to incur? The tale of Hannah I suppose to be false, not that if it be true it will justify her violence and precipitation, but it will give her cause great superiority in the publick opinion and in the courts of

1. Earlier in the month John Taylor's second wife, Mary Tuckfield Taylor, left him and went to live with her sister Elizabeth. A pair of Chancery suits reveals certain details of their estrangement (MSS: P.R.O. C12, 1009/39; C12, 1230/77; C12, 2083/21; C12, 2365/13; C12, 393/62). According to Mrs. Taylor, she had "for some time ... frequently received very personal Ill Usage" from her husband. "She frequently made great Complaints on that Account and declared to him that she should be Obliged for her Comfort and Safety to leave him" (MS: P.R.O. C12, 2365/13, 30 Nov. 1770).

2. MS: "for" del. before "in"

3. MS: "with with"

Justice, and it will be better for you to endure hard conditions than[4] bring your character into a judicial disquisition.[5]

I know you never lived very well together but I suppose that an outrage like this must have been preceded by some uncommon degree[6] of discord from which you might have prognosticated some odd design, or that some preparations for this excursion must have been made of which the recollection may give you some direction what to conjecture, and how to proceed.

You know that I have never advised you to any thing tyrannical or violent, and in the present case it is of great importance to keep yourself in the right, and not injure your own right by any intemperance[7] of resentments or eagerness of reprisal. For the present I think it prudent to forbear all pursuit, and all open enquiry, to wear an appearance of complete indifference, and calmly wait the effects of time, of necessity, and of shame. I suppose she cannot live long without your money, and the confession of her want will probably humble her. Whether you will inform her brother I must leave to your discretion who know his character and the terms on which you have lived. If you write to him, write like a man ill-treated but neither dejected nor enraged.

I do not know what more I can say without more knowledge of the case, only I repeat my advice that you keep yourself cheerful, and add that I would contribute[8] nothing to the publication of your own misfortune. I wondered to see the note transcribed by a hand which I did not know. I am, Dear sir, your most affectionate,

SAM. JOHNSON

4. MS: "that"

5. There is no mention of "the tale of Hannah" in the Chancery suits. Hannah was a household servant with whom it was alleged that Taylor was having an affair. *Post* To John Taylor, 3 Sept. 1763; 29 Sept. 1763.

6. MS: "degree" altered from "degrees"

7. MS: "intermperance"

8. MS: "would have contribute"

John Taylor

THURSDAY 18 AUGUST 1763

MS: Berg Collection, New York Public Library.

ADDRESS: To the Reverend Dr. Taylor in Ashbourne, Derbyshire.

POSTMARK: 18 AV.

ENDORSEMENTS: Johnson 63, 1763, 18 Augt. 1763. Very good.

Dear Sir: August 18, 1763

I have endeavoured to consider your affair according to the knowledge which the papers that you have sent me, could afford, and will very freely tell you what occurs to me.

Who Mr. Woodcock is I know not,[1] but unless his character in[2] the world, or some particular relation to your self entitle him to uncommon respect, you seem to treat him with too much deference by soliciting his interest and condescending to plead your cause before him, and imploring him to settle those terms of separation which you have a right to prescribe. You are in my opinion to consider yourself as a man injured and instead of making defence to expect submission. If you desert yourself who can support you? You needed not have confessed so much weakness as is made appear by the tale of the halfcrown and the pocket picked by your wife's companion. However nothing is done that can much hurt you.

You enquire what the fugitive Lady has in her power. She has, I think, nothing in her power but to return home and mend her behaviour. To obtain a separate maintenance she must prove either cruelty to her person or infidelity to her bed, and I suppose neither charge can be supported.[3] Nature has given women so much power that the Law has very wisely given them little.

1. "Mr. Woodcock" is identified in the records of the Chancery suits as Taylor's "sollicitor and agent." A. L. Reade conjectures that he may have been Elborough Woodcock (d. 1794), register of affidavits in the Court of Chancery (*Johns. Glean.* IX.228).

2. MS: "in" superimposed upon "or"

3. In May 1764 a deed of separation was executed, in which John Taylor agreed to pay his wife maintenance of £160 per annum (MS: P.R.O. C12, 2365/13).

The Letter for Mr. Tuckfield I think you do not want, it is[4] his part to write to you, who are illtreated by his sister.[5] You owe him, I think no obligations, but have been accustomed to act among your wife's relations with a character of inferiority which I would advise you to take this opportunity of throwing off for ever. Fix yourself in the resolution of exacting reparation for the wrong that you suffer, and think no longer that you are to be first insulted and then to recompense by submission the trouble of insulting you.

If a separate alimony should come to be stipulated I do not see why you should by an absurd generosity pay your wife for disobedience and elopement, what allowance will be proper I cannot tell, but would have you consult our old friend Mr. Howard.[6] His profession has acquainted him with matrimonial law, and he is in himself a cool and wise man. I would not have him come to Ashbourne nor you go to Lichfield; meet at Tutbury or some other obscure and commodious place and talk the case at large with him, not merely as a proctor but as a Friend.[7]

Your declaration to Mr. Woodcock that you[8] desired nothing to be a secret was manly and right; persist in that strain of talking, receive nothing, as from favour or from friendship; whatever you grant, you are to grant as by compassion, whatever you keep, you[9] are to keep by right. With Mr. Tuckfield you have no business, till he bring his sister in his hand, and desires you to receive her.

I do not mean by all this to exclude all possibility of accommodation; if there is any hope of living happily or decently, cohabitation is the most reputable for both.

Your first care must be to procure to yourself such diversions as may preserve you from melancholy and depression of

4. MS: "is" altered from "his"

5. SJ refers to John Tuckfield (*c.* 1719–67), of Little Fulford, Devon, Mary Taylor's half-brother, M.P. for Exeter (1747–67) (Namier and Brooke III.565; MS: P.R.O. C12, 2083/21).

6. *Ante* To Lucy Porter, 25 Jan. 1759, n. 3.

7. Tutbury, Staffordshire, on the River Dove four miles northwest of Burton-on-Trent. Tutbury is approximately halfway between Lichfield and Ashbourne.

8. MS: "your"

9. MS: "your"

mind, which is a greater evil than a disobedient wife. Do not give way to grief, nor nurse vexation in solitude, consider that your case is not uncommon, and that many live very happily who have like you succeeded ill in their ⟨n⟩uption[10] connexion.

I cannot but[11] think that it would be prudent to remove from the clamours, questions, hints, and looks of the people about you, but of this you can judge better than, Dear sir, your affectionate,

SAM. JOHNSON

10. MS: "⟨n⟩uption" possibly a mistake for "nuptial"

11. MS: "but" superimposed upon "yet"

John Taylor

THURSDAY 25 AUGUST 1763

MS: Pembroke College, Oxford.

ADDRESS: To the Reverend Dr. Taylor in Ashbourne, Derbyshire.

POSTMARK: 25 AV.

ENDORSEMENTS: 25 Augt. 63, Johnson 63.

Dear Sir: August 25, 1763

Having with some impatience reckoned upon hearing from you these two last posts, and been disappointed I can form to myself no reason for the omission but your perturbation of mind, or disorder of body arising from it, and therefore I once more advise removal from Ashbourne as the proper remedy both for the cause and the effect.

You perhaps ask whither should I go? anywhither where your case is not known, and where your presence will cause neither looks nor whispers. Where you are the necessary subject of common talk, you will not easily be at rest.

If you cannot conveniently write to me yourself let somebody write for you to, Dear Sir, Your most affectionate,

SAM. JOHNSON

Thomas Percy

SATURDAY 3 SEPTEMBER 1763

MS: Fitzwilliam Museum.

ENDORSEMENT: NB. Mr. Johnson's intended Visit was not performed till the following year 1764.

Dear Sir: Temple Lane, Sept. 3, 1763

Considering the tumults and the distress of the court[1] you will not wonder that you have heard nothing of Mr. Lye's affair.[2] I have never seen Lord Bute since we talked together.[3] But I do not despair, I wait for calmer times and will then try the fate of our petition.[4]

Miss Williams and I have at last determined to enjoy the pleasure of your company and Mrs. Percy's in your own fields

1. Lord Bute had resigned as prime minister on 8 Apr. 1763. After "wranglings, accusations and counter-accusations and every kind of nastiness," he was succeeded by a precarious coalition ministry—a triumvirate composed of George Grenville, Lord Halifax, and Lord Egremont (Stanley Ayling, *George the Third*, 1972, pp. 103–4). Grenville "knew that he was regarded merely as a stopgap, and that through the summer of 1763 intricate parleys were being conducted and bargains struck among his rivals and enemies" (p. 105). Grenville's ministry lasted until the summer of 1765, when it was succeeded by Lord Rockingham's coalition.

2. The Rev. Edward Lye (1694–1767), F.S.A., "the first Etymologist of the Age," was rector of Yardley Hastings, Northamptonshire, and Percy's "near Neighbour and intimate Friend" (*Correspondence of Thomas Percy and William Shenstone*, ed. Cleanth Brooks, 1977, p. 10). Lye, who had published Junius' *Etymologicum Anglicanum* in 1743, was working on a *Dictionarium Saxonico-et Gothico-Latinum*. About thirty sheets had been printed by the time of his death, and the rest of the work was seen through the press in 1772 by the Rev. Owen Manning (*Lit. Anec.* IX.753).

3. *Ante* To Lucy Porter, 24 July 1762. Though Bute was no longer prime minister, he was still widely considered the King's most influential adviser. However, "it is significant that the letters, hitherto so full and frequent, from George to his Dear Friend, appear almost to cease from September, 1763" (Ayling, *George the Third*, p. 109).

4. This "petition" may have been a plan to obtain a pension for Lye, who "had almost relinquished the design [his *Dictionarium*] from a dread of the labour and the expense" (*Lit. Anec.* IX.752). No pension was forthcoming, but the project was kept afloat by a subscription, to which Dr. Thomas Secker, the Archbishop of Canterbury, contributed £50 (*Lit. Anec.* X.752–53). *Post* To Edward Lye, 17 Aug. 1765.

and groves, if you will favour us[5] with notice at what time and by what way we may most conveniently approach you.[6] I purpose to bring Shakespeare with me, and strike a stroke at him with your kind help.[7] Be pleased to get together all observations that you have made upon his works.[8]

If I can do any thing for you here before I come to you, you will be pleased to command, Dear Sir, your most humble servant,

SAM. JOHNSON

5. MS: "us" superimposed upon "yo"

6. *Post* To Thomas Percy, 23 June 1764.

7. During his stay in Northamptonshire the following summer, SJ corrected proofs of his *Othello* (*Works*, Yale ed. VII.xxiii).

8. The Appendix to SJ's *Shakespeare* (1765, vol. VIII) includes notes by Percy on *Henry IV, King Lear, Romeo and Juliet,* and *Othello.*

John Taylor

SATURDAY 3 SEPTEMBER 1763

MS: Berg Collection, New York Public Library.

ADDRESS: To the Revd. Dr. Taylor in Ashbourn, Derbyshire.

POSTMARK: 3 SE.

ENDORSEMENTS: Johnson 63, 3d. Septr. 1763.

Dear Sir: Sept. 3, 1763

Mr. Woodcock, whatever may be his general character seems to have yielded on this occasion a very easy admission to very strong prejudices. He believes every thing against you and nothing in your favour. I am therefore glad that his resolution of neutrality so vehemently declared, has set you free from the obligation of a promise made with more frankness than prudence to refer yourself to his decision. Your letters to him are written with great propriety, with coolness and with spirit and seem to have raised his anger only by disappointing his expectations of being considered as your protector, and being solicited for favour and countenance. His attempts to intimidate you are childish and indecent; what have you to dread from the Law? The Law will give Mrs. Taylor no more than her due and you do not desire to give her less.

I wish you had used the words *pretended* friendship and would have [you] avoid on all occasions to declare whether if she should offer to return, you will or will not receive her. I do not see that you have any thing more than to sit still, and expect the motions of the Lady and her friends. If you think it necessary to retain Council, I suppose you will have recourse to Dr. Smalbrook,[1] and some able Man of the common Law or chancery, but though you may retain them provisionally, you need do nothing more; for I am not of opinion that the Lady's friends will suffer her cause to be brought into the Courts.

I do not wonder that Mr. Woodcock is somewhat incredulous when you tell him[2] that you do not know your own income; pray take care to get information, and either grow wiser or conceal your weakness. I could hardly believe you myself when I heard[3] that a wrong letter had been sent to Woodcock by your servant who made the packet. You are the first man who being able to read and write had packets of domestik quarrels made by a servant. Idleness[4] in such degrees must end in slavery, and I think you may less disgracefully be governed by your Lady than by Mr. Flint.[5] It is a maxim that no man ever was enslaved by influence while he was fit to be free.

I cannot but think that Mr. Woodcock has reason on his side when he advises the dismission of Hannah. Why should you not dismiss her. It is more injury to her reputation to keep her than to send her away, and the loss of her place you may recompense by a present or some small annuity conveyed to her. But this I would have you do not in compliance with solicitation or advice, but as a justification of yourself to the world; the world has always a right to be regarded.

1. Richard Smalbroke (*c.* 1716–1805), D.C.L., an advocate in Doctors' Commons and Chancellor of the diocese of Lichfield (*Johns. Glean.* VI.116).

2. MS: "h" superimposed upon "th"

3. MS: "h" superimposed upon "s"

4. MS: "Id" altered from "If"

5. Thomas Flint (1724–87), Taylor's secretary and general clerk (*Johns. Glean.* IX.25, 41).

In affairs of this kind it is necessary to converse with some intelligent man, and by considering the question in all states to provide means of obviating every charge. It will surely be right to spend a day with Howard. Do not on this occasion either want money or spare it.

You seem to be so well pleased to be where you are that I shall not now press your removal, but do not believe that every one who[6] rails at your wife, wishes well to you. A small country town is not the place in which one would chuse to quarrel with a wife, every human being in such places is a spy. I am, dear Sir, yours affectionately, SAM. JOHNSON

6. MS: "who" superimposed upon "tha"

George Strahan

TUESDAY 20 SEPTEMBER 1763

MSS: Berg Collection, New York Public Library; Houghton Library.[1]

ADDRESS: To Mr. Strahan at the Reverend Mr. Bright's in Abingdon, Berks.

POSTMARK: 20 SE.

Dear Sir: Septr. 20, 1763

I should have answered your last letter sooner if I could have given you any valuable or useful directions, but I know not any way by[2] which the composition of Latin verses can be much facilitated. Of the grammatical part which comprises the knowledge of the measure of the foot, and quantity of the syllables, your grammar will teach you all that can be taught, and even of that you can hardly teach any thing by rule but the measure of the foot. The quantity of syllables even of those for which rules are given, is commonly learned by practice,

1. The MS has been mutilated, presumably by a collector of autographs. The majority of the letter is in the Berg Collection; a fragment comprising part of the complimentary close, the date, and the signature (with three lines of text on the recto, "retained by observation . . . readiness in") is in the Houghton.

2. MS: "by" altered from "th"

and retained by observation. For the poetical part, which comprises variety of expression, propriety[3] of terms dexterity in selecting commodious words, and readiness in changing[4] their order, it will all be produced by frequent essays, and resolute perseverance. The less help you have the sooner you will be able to go forward without help.

I suppose you are now ready for another authour. I would not have you dwell longer upon one book, than till your familiarity with its stile makes it easy[5] to you; every new book will for a time be difficult. Make it a rule to write something in Latin every day, and let me know what you are now doing, and what your scheme is to do next.

Be pleased to give my compliments to Mr. Bright Mr. Stevenson and Miss Page. I am, Dear sir, your affectionate servant,

SAM. JOHNSON

3. MS: "and" del. before "propriety"
4. MS: undeciphered deletion before "changing"
5. MS: "easy" del. before "easy"

John Taylor

THURSDAY 29 SEPTEMBER 1763

MS: Berg Collection, New York Public Library.

ADDRESS: To the Reverend Dr. Taylor in Ashbourn, Derbyshire.

POSTMARK: 29 SE.

ENDORSEMENTS: Johnson 63, 29 Septr. 1763.

Dear Sir: Septr. 29, 1763

The alterations which you made in the letter, though I cannot think that they much mended it, yet did no harm, and perhaps the letter may have the effect of reducing the Lady and her friends to terms truly moderate and reasonable by showing what slight account you make of menaces and terror. I no more desire than you to bring the cause before the Courts, and if they who are on the Lady's side can prove nothing, they have in reality no such design. It is not likely that even if they had proof of incontinency they would desire to produce it, or make any other use of it, than to terrify you into their own Conditions.

Of the letter which you sent me I can form no judgement till you let me know how it came into your hands. If the servant who received it produced it voluntarily, I suspect that it was written on purpose to be shown you, if you discovered it by accident, it may be supposed to be written that it might be shown to others. I do not see that it deserves or requires any notice on either supposition.

You suspect your housekeeper at Ashbourn of treachery, and I doubt not but that the Lady has been [careful to] leave friends and spies behind her. But let your servant be treacherous as you suppose, it is your own fault if she has any thing to betray. Do your own business, and keep your own secrets, and you may bid defiance to servants and to treachery.

Your conduct with regard to Hannah, has, I think, been exactly right, it will be fit to keep her in sight for some months, and let her have directions to show herself as much as she can.

Your ill health proceeds immediately from the perturbation of your mind. Any incident which makes a man the talk and spectacle of the world without any addition to his honour is naturally vexatious, but talk and looks are all the evils which this domestick revolution has brought upon you. I know that you and your wife lived unquietly together, I find that provocations were greater than I had known and do not see what you have to regret but that you did not separate in a very short time after you were united. You know, however, that I was always cautious when I touched on your differences, that I never advised extremities, and that I commonly softened rather than instigated resentment. What passes in private can be known only to those between whom it passes, and they who [are] ignorant of the cause and progress of connubial differences, as all must be, but the parties themselves, cannot without rashness give any counsel concerning them. Your determination against cohabitation with the Lady I shall therefore pass over, with only this hint,[1] that you must keep it to yourself, for as by elopement she makes herself liable to the charge of violating the marriage contract, it will be prudent to keep her in the criminal state, by leaving her in appearance a possibility of return, which preserves your superiority in the contest, without taking from you the power of limiting her future authority, and prescribing your own conditions.

I cannot but think that by short journeys, and variety of scenes you may dissipate your vexation, and restore your health, which will certainly be impaired by living where every thing seen or heard impresses your misfortunes on your mind. I am, Dear Sir, Your most etc. etc. SAM. JOHNSON

1. MS: "di" del. before "hint"

James Boswell

THURSDAY 8 DECEMBER 1763

MS: Beinecke Library. The transcript (in the hand of Margaret Boswell) used as copy for the *Life*.

ADDRESS in JB's hand: A Mr. Mr. Boswell, à la Cour de l'Empereur, Utrecht.[1]

Dear Sir: London, Dec. 8, 1763

You are not to think yourself forgotten or criminally neglected that you have had yet no letter from me—I love to see my friends to hear from them to talk to them and to talk of them, but it is not without a considerable effort of resolution that I prevail upon myself to write. I would not however gratify my own indolence by the omission of any important duty or any office of real kindness.

To tell you that I am or am not well, that I have or have not been in the country, that I drank your health in the Room in

1. JB lived in Utrecht from Sept. 1763 to June 1764, studying civil law at the University in preparation for a career as an advocate. He rented a set of rooms at an inn called the "Keizershof" or "Cour de l'Empereur," on the Cathedral Square (*Earlier Years*, p. 124).

which we sat last together and that your acquaintance continue to speak of you with their former kindness topicks with which those[2] letters are commonly filled which are written only for the sake of writing I seldom shall think worth communication but if I can have it in my power to calm any harrassing disquiet to excite any virtuous desire to rectify any important opinion or fortify any generous resolution you need not doubt but I shall at least wish to prefer the pleasure of gratifying a friend much less esteemed than yourself before the gloomy calm of idle Vacancy. Whether I shall easily arrive at an exact punctuality of correspondance I cannot tell. I shall at present expect that you will receive this in return for two which I have had from you. The first indeed gave me an account so hopeless of the state of your mind that it hardly admitted or deserved an answer; by[3] the second I was much better pleased[4] and the pleasure will still be increased by such a narrative of the progress of your studys as may evince the continuence of an equal and rational application of your mind to some usefull enquiry.

You will perhaps wish to ask what Study I would recommend. I shall not speak of Theology because it ought not to be considered as a question whether you shall endevour to know the will of God.

I shall therefore consider only such Studies as we are at liberty to pursue or to neglect, and of these I know not how you will make a better choice than by studying the civil Law as your father advises[5] and the Ancient languages as you had determined for yourself; at[6] least resolve while you remain in any setled residence to spend a certain number of hours every day amongst your Books. The dissipation of thought of which you

2. MS: "these"

3. MS: "answer by"

4. "I wrote to Johnson a plaintive and desponding letter, to which he paid no regard. Afterwards, when I had acquired a firmer tone of mind, I wrote him a second letter, expressing much anxiety to hear from him" (*Life* 1.473). JB's first letter was sent *c.* 15 Aug. 1763, the second on 7 Oct. (*Earlier Years*, p. 491; *Boswell in Holland*, ed. F. A. Pottle, 1952, p. 43).

5. Alexander Boswell (1707–82), Lord Auchinleck, a judge of the Scots Court of Session and the High Court of Justiciary (*Earlier Years*, pp. 9–10).

6. MS: "yourself at"

complain is nothing more than the Vacillation of a mind suspended between different motives and changing its direction as any motive gains or loses Strength. If you can but kindle in your mind any strong desire, if you can but keep predominant any Wish for some particular excellence or attainment the Gusts of imagination will break away without any effect upon your conduct and commonly without any traces left upon the Memory.

There lurks perhaps in every human heart a desire of distinction which inclines every Man first to hope and then to believe that Nature has given him something peculiar to himself. This vanity makes one mind nurse aversions and another actuate desires till they rise by art much above their original state of power and as affectation in time improves to habit, they at last tyrannise over him who at first encouraged them only for Show. Every desire is a Viper in the Bosom who while he was chill was harmless but when warmth gave him strength exerted it in poison. You know a gentleman who when first he set his foot into the gay World as he prepared himself to whirl in the Vortex of pleasure imagined a total indifference and universal negligence to be the most agreable concomitants of Youth and the strongest indication of any airy temper and a quick apprehension. Vacant to every object and sensible of every impulse he thought that all appearance of diligence would deduct something from the reputation of Genius and hoped that he should appear to attain amidst all the ease of carelessness and all the tumult of diversion that knowledge and those accomplishments which Mortals of the common fabrick obtain only by mute abstraction and solitary drudgery. He tried this scheme of life awhile was made weary of it by his sence and his Virtue; he then wished to return to his Studies and finding long habits of idleness and pleasure harder to be cured than he expected [7] still willing to retain his claim to some extraordinary prerogitives resolved the common consequences of irregularity into an unalterable decree of destiny

7. MS: "expected" superimposed upon "imagined" partially erased

and concluded that Nature had originally formed him incapable of rational employment.

Let all such fancys illusive and destructive be banished henceforward from your thoughts forever. Resolve and keep your resolution. Chuse and pursue your choice. If you spend this day in Study you will find yourself still more able to study tomorrow. Not that you are to expect that you shall at once obtain a compleat Victory. Depravity is not very easily overcome. Resolution[8] will sometimes relax and diligence will sometimes be interrupted. But let no accidental surprize or deviation whether short or long dispose you to despondency. Consider these failings as incident to all Mankind, begin again where you left off and endevour to avoid the Seducements that prevailed over you before.

This my Dear Boswell is advice which perhaps has been often given you, and given you without effect, but this advice if you will not take from others you must take from your own reflections, if you purpose to do the dutys of the station to which the Bounty of providence has called you.[9]

Let me have a long letter from you as soon as you can.[10] I hope you continue your journal and enrich it with many observations upon the country in which you reside. It will be a favour if you can get me any books in the Frisick Language[11] and can enquire how the poor are maintained in the Seven Provinces.[12] I am, Dear Sir, your most affectionate servant,

SAM. JOHNSON

8. MS: "overcome resolution"

9. During his time in Holland, JB was "by heroic effort modest, studious, frugal, reserved, and chaste" (*Earlier Years*, p. 130).

10. JB composed a "noble" reply on 20–21 Dec. (Pottle, *Holland*, pp. 95–97).

11. After making "all possible enquiry," JB reported that "of the old Frisick there are no remains, except some ancient laws" (*Life* 1.475). As a sample of "the modern Frisick, or what is spoken by the boors at this day," he procured for SJ "*Gisbert Japix's Rymelerie*, which is the only book they have" (*Life* 1.475–76).

12. "I am sorry to observe, that neither in my own minutes, nor in my letters to Johnson which have been preserved by him, can I find any information how the poor are maintained in the Seven Provinces" (*Life* 1.475). The Seven Provinces are the northern provinces of the Netherlands, which composed the Dutch Republic: Holland, Friesland, Groningen, Drenthe, Utrecht, Gelderland, and Overijssel.

Lucy Porter

TUESDAY 10 JANUARY 1764

PRINTED SOURCE: JB's *Life*, ed. Croker, 1831, I.498–99.

My Dear: London, 10 Jan. 1764

I was in hopes that you would have written to me before this time, to tell me that your house was finished, and that you were happy in it.[1] I am sure I wish you happy.

By the carrier of this week you will receive a box, in which I have put some books, most of which were your poor dear mamma's, and a diamond ring, which I hope you will wear as my new year's gift. If you receive it with as much kindness as I send it, you will not slight it; you will be very fond of it.

Pray give my service to Kitty, who, I hope, keeps pretty well.[2] I know not now when I shall come down; I believe it will not be very soon.[3] But I shall be glad to hear of you from time to time.

I wish you, my dearest, many happy years; take what care you can of your health. I am, my dear, Your affectionate humble servant,

SAM. JOHNSON

1. *Ante* To Lucy Porter, 12 July 1763.

2. *Ante* To Lucy Porter, 16 Jan. 1759, n. 2.

3. SJ next visited Lichfield during the final illness of Catherine Chambers, May–Oct. 1767.

John Taylor

TUESDAY 22 MAY 1764

MS: Berg Collection, New York Public Library.

ADDRESS: To the Reverend Dr. Taylor in Ashbourn, Derbyshire.

POSTMARK: 22 MA.

ENDORSEMENTS: 22 May 64, 22 May 1764.

Dear Sir: May 22d 1764

I congratulate you upon the happy end of so vexatious an affair, the happyest that could be next to Reformation and Reconcilement.[1] You see how easily seeming difficulties are surmounted.

That your mind should be harried, and your spirits weakened it is no wonder; your whole care now should be to settle and repair them. To this end I would have you make use of all diversions, sports of the field abroad, improvements of your estate or little schemes of building, and pleasing books at home or if you cannot compose yourself to read, a continual succession of easy company. Be sure never to be unemployed, go not to bed till you sleep, and rise as soon as you wake, and give up no hours to musing and retrospect. Be always busy.

You will hardly be quite at rest till you have talked yourself out to some friend or other, and I think you and I might contrive some retreat for part of the summer where we might spend some time quietly together, the world knowing nothing of the matter.

I hear you talk of letting your house at Westminster.[2] Why should you let it? Do not shew your self either intimidated or ashamed but come and face mankind like one that expects not censure but praise. You will now find that you have money enough, come and spend a little upon popular hospitality. Your low[3] spirits have given you bad counsel, you shall not give your wife, nor your wife's friends, whose power you now find to be nothing, the triumph of driving you out of life. If you betray yourself who can support you? All this I shall be glad to dilate with you in a personal interview at some proper place where we may enjoy a few days in private. I am, Dear Sir, yours affectionately,

SAM. JOHNSON

1. *Ante* To John Taylor, 18 Aug. 1763, n. 3; 13 Aug. 1763, n. 1. The vexation did not end with the separation agreement, however, for later in the year Taylor issued a bill of complaint against his brother-in-law, claiming that he was still owed £2,500 of his wife's fortune. In 1770 Taylor went to court again, in an attempt to gain part of Mary Taylor's inheritance from her brother. No judgements in either suit have been uncovered.

2. Taylor lived at 20 Dean's Yard, 1760–88 (information supplied by Dr. Richard Mortimer, Keeper of the Muniments, Westminster Abbey).

3. MS: "dej" del. before "low"

Thomas Percy

SATURDAY 23 JUNE 1764

MS: Hyde Collection.

ADDRESS: To the Reverend Mr. Percy.

Dear Sir: London, June 23, 1764

I should not think our visit an event so important as to require any previous Notification, but that Mrs. Williams tells me, such was your desire. We purpose to set out on Monday morning in the Berlin in which we could not get places last week,[1] and hope to have the honour in the evening of telling You and Mrs. Percy[2] that we are Your humble servants.[3]

SAM. JOHNSON

1. *berlin*: "a coach of a particular form" (SJ's *Dictionary*). On their return journey, 18 Aug. 1764, SJ and Anna Williams took a chaise (defined in the *Dictionary* as "a carriage of pleasure drawn by one horse") to Newport Pagnell, and the berlin from Newport to London (*Life* I.554; B. H. Davis, "Johnson's Visit to Percy," in *Johnson After Two Hundred Years*, ed. P. J. Korshin, 1986, p. 35).

2. *Ante* To Thomas Percy, 4 Oct. 1760, n. 8.

3. According to Percy's diary, SJ and Anna Williams arrived on schedule, the evening of 25 June (*Life* I.553).

Joshua Reynolds

c. FRIDAY 10 AUGUST 1764

MS: Hyde Collection.

ADDRESS: To Joshua Reynolds, Esq., in Leicester Fields, London.

POSTMARK: 1⟨1⟩ AV.

At the Revd. Mr. Percy's at Easton Maudit,
Dear Sir: Northamptonshire (by Castle Ashby), August 19th[1] 1764

I did not hear of your sickness till I heard likewise of your

1. SJ misdated the letter: the evidence of the postmark is confirmed by Percy's diary, which records that SJ returned to London on 18 Aug. (*Life* I.554). It seems improbable that SJ would have sent the letter had he been on the verge of departure. I have therefore assigned a conjectural date early within the possible period (*c.* 9–18 Aug.).

recovery, and therefore escaped that part of your pain, which every Man must feel to whom you are known as you are known to me.[2]

Having had no particular account of your disorder, I know not in what state it has left you. If the amusement of my company can exhilarate the languor of a slow recovery, I will not delay a day to come to you, for I know not how I can so effectually promote my own pleasure as by pleasing you, or my own interest as by preserving you, in whom if I should lose you, I should lose almost the only Man whom I call a Friend.

Pray let me[3] hear of you[4] from yourself or from dear Miss Reynolds.[5] Make my compliments to Mr. Mudge.[6] I am, Dear Sir, your most affectionate and most humble servant,

SAM. JOHNSON

2. "In the summer of this year [1764] a violent and very dangerous illness attacked Mr. Reynolds. . . . His illness, however, was but of short duration" (James Northcote, *Life of Sir Joshua Reynolds*, 1818, pp. 135–36). Ellis Waterhouse describes this illness as "probably a slight stroke" (*Reynolds*, 1973, p. 44).

3. MS: undeciphered deletion before "me"

4. MS: "you" superimposed upon "m"

5. *Ante* To Frances Reynolds, 21 Dec. 1762, n. 1.

6. *Ante* To Frances Reynolds, 21 Dec. 1762, n. 2.

William Strahan

WEDNESDAY 24 OCTOBER 1764

MS: Hyde Collection.

ADDRESS: To Mr. Strahan, Printer, in New Street, Shoelane, London.

POSTMARKS: OXFORD, 25 OC.

Sir: [Oxford] Oct. 24, 1764

I think I have pretty well disposed of my young friend George, who if you approve of it, will be entered next Monday a Commoner of University College, and will be chosen next day a Scholar of the House.[1] The Scholarship is a trifle, but it gives

1. Strahan was duly elected at the end of the month.

him a right, upon a vacancy to a Fellowship of more than sixty pounds a year if he resides, and I suppose of more than forty if he takes a Curacy or small living.[2] The College is almost filled with my friends, and he will be well treated.[3] The Master is informed of the particular state of his education,[4] and thinks, what I think too, that for Greek he must get some private assistance, which a servitour of the College is very well qualified and will be very willing to afford him on very easy terms.[5]

I must desire your opinion of this scheme by the next post, for the opportunity will be lost if we do not[6] now seize it, the Scholarships being necessarily filled up on Tuesday.

I depend on your proposed allowance of a hundred a year, which must the first year be a little enlarged because there are some extraordinary expences,[7] as

Caution (which is allowed in his last quarter)	7–0–0[8]
Thirds. (he that enters upon a room pays two thirds of the furniture that[9] he finds and receives from his Successor two thirds of what he pays. So that if he pays 20£ he receives 13–6–8) this perhaps may be	12–0–0
Fees at entrance matriculation etc. perhaps	2–0–0

2. *Ante* To Henry Bright, 12 Oct. 1762, nn. 3, 4.

3. SJ's friends in University College included Robert Chambers, the Rev. John Coulson (1719–88), and Nathan Wetherell (see below, n. 4).

4. Nathan Wetherell (1726–1807), D.D., had been elected Master of University College earlier that year (*Alum. Oxon.* II.iv.1530).

5. *servitor*: "one of the lowest order in the university" (SJ's *Dictionary*). Undergraduates were divided into five categories or "orders": gentleman commoners, who paid double fees; commoners, "who paid their way entirely"; scholars, "the recipients of special grants"; battelers, "who paid lower fees and in return were expected to fetch their own meals and generally look after themselves"; and servitors, who performed "certain menial tasks for the commoners and scholars" (Clifford, 1955, p. 109). SJ himself had been a commoner.

6. MS: "not not"

7. MS: period after "expences"

8. "Caution money" functioned as a security deposit, which the student forfeited if College accounts were not settled within a given period. SJ was required to pay the same amount to the bursar of Pembroke College when he entered in 1728 (*Life* I.58 n. 2).

9. MS: "that" altered from "the"

	21–0–0
His gown (I think — — —	2–10–0
	23–10–0

If You send us a Bill for about thirty pounds we shall set out commodiously enough. You should fit him out with cloaths and Linen, and let him start fair, and it is the opinion of those whom I consult, that with your hundred a year, and the petty Scholarship, he may live with great ease to himself, and Credit to you. Let me hear as soon as is possible.

In your affair with the university, I shall not be consulted, but I hear nothing urged against your proposal.[10] I am, sir, your humble servant,

SAM. JOHNSON

My compliments to Mrs. Strahan.

10. It seems likely that Strahan was hoping to purchase from the Clarendon Press the lease which would have entitled him to print Bibles and prayer books. This lease, held by Mark Baskett, came due on 25 Mar. 1765. After a prolonged dispute, it was acquired in Dec. 1765 by Messrs. Wright and Gill, of Abchurch Lane, London (Plomer II.18, 273).

Frances Reynolds

SATURDAY 27 OCTOBER 1764

MS: Hyde Collection.

ADDRESS: To Miss Reynolds in Leicester Fields, London.

POSTMARKS: OXFORD, 29 OC, 30 OC.

ENDORSEMENT: Dr. Johnson I believe about 64.

My Dearest Dear: [Oxford] Oct. 27

Your letter has scarcely come soon enough to make an answer possible. I wish we could talk over the affair. I cannot go now. I must finish my book.[1] I do not know Mr. Collier.[2] I have not

1. SJ's edition of Shakespeare was published on 10 Oct. 1765 (*Works*, Yale ed. VII.xxiii).

2. Frances Reynolds glosses this sentence in her copy of the letter: "Capt. Col-

money before hand sufficient. How long have you known Collier that you should put yourself into his hands. I once told you, that Ladies were timorous and yet not cautious.

If I might tell[3] my thoughts to one with whom they never had any weight. I should think it best to go through France. The expence is not great. I do not much like obligations, nor think the grossness of a Ship very suitable to a Lady. Do not go till I see you. I will see you as soon as I can. I am, My Dearest, most zealously yours,

SAM. JOHNSON

You quite disturb me with this sudden folly.

---

lier, since Sir George, proposed at that time, to sail to the Mediterraine *with his Lady*" (MS: Hyde Collection). George Collier (1738–95), R.N., was captain of H.M.S. *Edgar*, 1763–66. He was knighted in 1775, and rose to the rank of vice-admiral (1794), as well as being elected M.P. for Honiton (1784–90) (Namier and Brooke II.239).

3. MS: "till"

David Garrick

SATURDAY 18 May 1765

MS: Berg Collection, New York Public Library.
ADDRESS: To David Garrick, Esq.

Dear Sir: May 18, 1765

I know that great regard will be had to your opinion of an Edition of Shakespeare.[1] I desire therefore to secure an honest prejudice in my favour by securing your suffrage,[2] and that this prejudice may really be honest, I wish you would name

1. *Ante* To Frances Reynolds, 27 Oct. 1764, n. 1. SJ himself did not share this "great regard." According to Edmond Malone, he told Garrick, "I much doubt if you ever examined one of his plays from the first scene to the last" (*Life* v.244 n. 2).

2. On 31 May Garrick wrote to SJ: "My brother greatly astonished me this morning by asking me, 'if I was a subscriber to your Shakspeare?' I told him yes, that I was one of the first, and as soon as I had heard of your intention; and that I gave you, at the same time, some other names, among which were the Duke of Devonshire, Mr. Beighton, etc." (*Letters of David Garrick*, ed. D. M. Little and G. M. Kahrl, 1963, II.460). However, SJ later complained to JB that "Garrick got me no subscriptions" (*Hebrides*, p. 207).

such plays as you would see, and they shall be sent you by, sir, your most humble servant,

SAM. JOHNSON

George Strahan

SATURDAY 25 MAY 1765

PRINTED SOURCE: JB's *Life*, ed. Croker, 1831, I.502.

ADDRESS: To Mr. G. Strahan, Univer. Coll. Ox.

Dear Sir: 25 May 1765

That I have answered neither of your letters you must not impute to any declension of good will, but merely to the want of something to say. I suppose you pursue your studies diligently, and diligence will seldom fail of success. Do not tire yourself so much with Greek one day as to be afraid of looking on it the next; but give it a certain portion of time, suppose four hours, and pass the rest of the day in Latin or English. I would have you learn French, and take in a literary journal once a month, which will accustom you to various subjects, and inform you what learning is going forward in the world. Do not omit to mingle some lighter books with those of more importance; that which is read *remisso animo*[1] is often of great use, and takes great hold of the remembrance. However, take what course you will, if you be diligent you will be a scholar. I am, dear sir, yours affectionately,

SAM. JOHNSON

1. *remisso animo*: "in a relaxed spirit."

John Taylor

MONDAY 15 JULY 1765

MS: Berg Collection, New York Public Library.

ADDRESS: To the Reverend Dr. Taylor in Ashbourn, Derbyshire.

POSTMARK: 16 IY.

ENDORSEMENTS: Johnson 1765, 15 July 65.

Dear Sir: Temple, July 15, 1765

It is so long since I heard from you that I know not well whither to write. With all your building and feasting you might have found an hour in some wet day for the remembrance of your old friend.[1] I should have thought that since you have led a life so festive and gay, you would have i⟨nvited⟩ me to partake of your hospitality. I do not ⟨know⟩ but I may come invited or uninvited, and stay a few days with you in august or september, unless you send me a prohibition, or let me know that I shall be insupportably burthensome. Let me know your thoughts on this matter, because I design to go to some place or other,[2] and would be [unwilling] to produce any inconvenience for my own gratification.

Let me know how you go on in the world, and what entertainment may be expected in your new room by, Dear sir, Your most affectionate servant,

SAM. JOHNSON

1. Taylor was adding a large octagonal drawing room to his house, "stuccoed and gilded" in the Adam style (*Life* III.498–99; Thomas Taylor, *Life of John Taylor*, 1910, p. 19).

2. SJ did not travel to Derbyshire that summer. In the autumn, according to H. L. Piozzi, he "followed" the Thrales to Brighton, "whence we were gone before his arrival" (*Johns. Misc.* I.233).

Hester Thrale[1]

TUESDAY 13 AUGUST 1765

MS: Hyde Collection.

ADDRESS: To Mrs. Thrale in Brighthelmston.

POSTMARK: 13 AV.

Madam: London, Aug. 13, 1765

If you have really so good an opinion of me as You express, it

1. SJ had been introduced to Hester Lynch Thrale (1741–1821) and her husband Henry (1728–81) by Arthur Murphy, who brought him to dinner at the Thrales' house in Southwark on 9 Jan. 1765 (*Thraliana* I.158–59).

will not be necessary to inform you how unwillingly I miss the opportunity of coming to Brighthelmston in Mr. Thrale's company,[2] or since I cannot do what I wish first, how eagerly I shall catch the second degree of pleasure by coming to You and Him, as soon as I can dismiss my work from my hands.[3]

I am afraid to make promises even to myself, but I hope that the week after the next, will be the end of my present business. When business is done what remains but pleasure?[4] and where should pleasure be sought but under Mrs. Thrale's influence?

Do not blame me for a delay by which I must suffer so much, and by which I suffer alone. If you cannot think I am good, pray think I am mending, and that in time I may deserve to be, Dear Madam, your most obedient and most humble servant,

SAM. JOHNSON

2. Hester Thrale, pregnant with her second child, "never had a Day's Health during the whole Gestation" (Hyde, 1977, p. 22). "It was probably because of her ill health that the family went to Brighton late in the summer" (Clifford, 1952, p. 58).

3. *Ante* To John Taylor, 15 July 1765, n. 2. It is probable that the Thrales hurried back to Southwark in mid-September because of Hester's impending confinement and Henry's candidacy for Parliament (Clifford, 1952, pp. 58–59).

4. MS: comma before question mark

Edward Lye

SATURDAY 17 AUGUST 1765

PRINTED SOURCE: Hill I.121–22.

Dear Sir: Aug. 17, 1765

I think you may be encouraged by the liberality of the Archbishop to hope for more Patrons of your undertaking, and therefore advise you to open your Subscription.[1] The method may perhaps be not at first to advertise but to send your proposal with a letter to such of the Bishops and others as you

1. *Ante* To Thomas Percy, 3 Sept. 1763, nn. 2, 4.

hope to find favourers of literature, sending at the same time to all your inferiour[?] friends, particularly to our Club.[2] When you see how far your personal interest will carry you, an estimate may be easily made of the probability of success, and the measures will be easily adjusted. I would have the whole price paid at once, which all will readily comply with, and much trouble will be saved. In contracting with your printer, oblige him to a certain number of Sheets weekly. If you print at London, you will like Mr. Allen the printer better than most others.[3] He is a Northamptonshire Man. Go on boldly, I doubt not your Success.

Please to make Mrs. Calvert the compliments of Mrs. Williams, and of, Dear Sir, Your most humble Servant,

SAM. JOHNSON

We have Gothick types at London.

2. The Literary Club had been founded in 1764, at the instigation of Sir Joshua Reynolds. There were originally ten members; in 1768 the membership was expanded to twelve (*Life* 1.477–78; Fifer, p. lxxx). Of these, five (SJ, Reynolds, Langton, Goldsmith, and Percy) subscribed to Lye's *Dictionarium* ("Names of the Subscribers").

3. *Ante* To Unidentified Correspondent, 27 Oct. 1757, n. 3. Allen did print the *Dictionarium* (1772).

David Garrick

SPRING OR SUMMER 1765

MS: Folger Shakespeare Library.

Thursday

Mr. Johnson has been so hindred that he could wait on Mr. Garrick only once (last fryday in the afternoon) he will call as soon as he can.

Mr. Johnson begs to have the plays back if they are done with.[1]

1. *Ante* To David Garrick, 18 May 1765.

David Garrick

c. SATURDAY 14 SEPTEMBER 1765[1]

MS: Hyde Collection.

Mr. Johnson congratulates Mr. Garrick on his recommencement.[2]

If any receipts are lost they shall be replaced.[3] If Mr. Garrick remembers that he subscribed, it is quite sufficient.

Compliments to Mrs. Garrick.[4]

1. See below, n. 2.

2. The Drury Lane season of 1765–66, which marked Garrick's return to the stage after a two-year absence on the Continent, began on 14 Sept. with *The Beggar's Opera* (*Lond. Stage*, Part IV, iv.1125, 1128).

3. *Ante* To David Garrick, 18 May 1765, n. 2.

4. Eva Maria Veigel (1724–1822), a former dancer whom Garrick had married in 1749 (*Letters of David Garrick*, ed. D. M. Little and G. M. Kahrl, 1963, I.97 n. 4).

Edward Lye

THURSDAY 26 SEPTEMBER 1765

MS: Hyde Collection.

ADDRESS: To the Reverend Mr. Lye at Yardley, near Castle Ashby, Northamptonshire.

POSTMARK: ⟨26⟩ SE.

Johnson's Court,
Fleetstreet,[1] Sept. 26, 1765

Dear Sir:

I see little to change in your proposals, only for *writing demy* I would read as more generally intelligible, *writing paper* and I would stop at *a sufficient number of subscribers*. What is added being, in my opinion, rather deficient in dignity.[2]

1. SJ lived at No. 7, Johnson's Court, from 1765 to 1776. He occupied "a good house . . . in which he had accommodated Miss Williams with an apartment on the ground floor, while Mr. Levett occupied his post in the garret" (*Life* II.5).

2. Lye published three versions of his "Proposals for Printing by Subscription Dictionarium Saxonico-Gothico-Latinum." These are dated 1766, 20 June 1767, and 1 Sept. 1767. None of them refers to "writing demy," "writing paper," or "a sufficient number of subscribers."

The success of your subscription I do not doubt,[3] and wish you were closely engaged at the press. Two sheets of Saxon letters will not be sufficient. There ought always to be one sheet printing, another in your hands for correction, and a third composing. There ought to be more, but this is the least and if at Oxford they will not do this, you must not print at Oxford; for your Edition will be retarded beyond measure.[4] They must get four sheets of letter at least, which will cost very little, there being few peculiar characters.

Stipulate with the printer to give you a certain number of sheets weekly, you ought not to have less than three, and you will not easily have more.

Mrs. Williams sends her best compliments to You and to Mrs. Calvert, and begs that you will return her thanks to Mrs. Percy for her letter, in the contents of which she takes great interest.

The Hare will come safe if it be directed to, sir, your most humble servant,

SAM. JOHNSON

3. The list of subscribers that appears at the beginning of Lye's *Dictionarium* includes 164 individuals and institutions.

4. *Ante* To Edward Lye, 17 Aug. 1765; *Ante* To Thomas Percy, 3 Sept. 1763, nn. 2, 4.

John Taylor

TUESDAY 1 OCTOBER 1765

MS: Haverford College Library.

ADDRESS: To the Reverend Dr. Taylor in Ashbourne, Derbyshire.

POSTMARK: 1 OC.

ENDORSEMENTS: Johnson 1765, 2d. Octr. 65.

Johnson's Court,
Fleetstreet, Oct. 1,[1] 1765

Dear Sir:

You need be no longer in pain, for I received your letter, but though when I wrote to you I expected to have had it soon in

1. MS: "2"

my power to come to you,[2] yet, as it often happens, one thing or ⟨other⟩ has obstructed my purpose. My Shakespeare is now out of my hands,[3] and I do not see what can hinder me any longer. When I find that I can come I will write to you, for I suppose you will meet me at Derby. I think it time that we should see one another, and spend a little of our short life together.[4] I am, Dear Sir, Yours affectionately,

SAM. JOHNSON

2. *Ante* To John Taylor, 15 July 1765.

3. *Ante* To Frances Reynolds, 27 Oct. 1764, n. 1.

4. SJ did not visit Ashbourne until the summer of 1770 (*Post* To Hester Thrale, 20 July 1770).

Jacob Tonson[1]

WEDNESDAY 9 OCTOBER 1765

MS: Birthplace Museum, Lichfield.

ADDRESS: To Jacob Tonson, Esq.

Johnson's Court,
Fleetstreet, Oct. 9, 1765

Sir:

Among those that will call for Shakespeare there are a few (perhaps twenty) that have receipts for two Guineas, and have therefore nothing to pay. The Guinea which You should receive must therefore be charged to my account.[2] I hope to meet you to night at Mr. Steevens's,[3] but we shall not perhaps

1. *Ante* To Jacob Tonson, 10 Feb. 1758, n. 1.

2. According to the terms of his agreement with Tonson, SJ was entitled to acquire and dispose of extra copies of the edition (above and beyond his 250 free sets), "paying to the said Jacob Tonson one Guinea for each Sett in sheets" (*Life* I.545). Having received the full price of two guineas, SJ therefore owed Tonson one guinea per set, for a total debt of "perhaps twenty" guineas.

3. George Steevens (1736–1800) had left Cambridge in 1756, without taking a degree, to begin a career as reviewer and editor. In 1773 he revised SJ's Shakespeare and later assisted him with the *Lives of the Poets*. Steevens, who was elected to The Club in 1774, "passed many a social hour with him [SJ] during their long acquaintance, which commenced when they both lived in the Temple" (*Life* IV.324). "A very pleasant tête-à-tête companion," he lived on the edge of Hampstead Heath (*Lit. Anec.* II.662; *Johns. Misc.* II.328 n. 2).

talk there of business, I therefore write now to remove what might be otherwise a little difficulty, and to assure you that your civility during this transaction is very sincerely acknowledged by, sir, your most humble servant,

SAM. JOHNSON

Joseph Warton

WEDNESDAY 9 OCTOBER 1765

PRINTED SOURCE: John Wooll, *Biographical Memoirs of the Late Revd. Joseph Warton,* 1806, pp. 309–10.

Dear Sir: Oct. 9th 1765

Mrs. Warton [1] uses me hardly in supposing that I could forget so much kindness and civility as she showed me at Winchester.[2] I remember likewise our conversation about St. Cross.[3] The desire of seeing her again will be one of the motives that will bring me to Hampshire.

I have taken care of your book;[4] being so far from doubting your subscription, that I think you have subscrib'd twice: you once paid your guinea into my own hand in the garret in Gough Square.[5] When you light on your receipt, throw it on the fire; if you find a second receipt, you may have a second book.

To tell the truth, as I felt no solicitude about this work, I

1. Mary Daman (d. 1772), Warton's first wife, whom he married in 1747/48 (Wooll, *Biographical Memoirs*, pp. 14, 51).

2. SJ and Sir Joshua Reynolds spent the day in Winchester on their way to Devon, Aug. 1762 (Clifford, 1979, p. 279).

3. St. Cross, a medieval almshouse on the outskirts of Winchester, was founded in 1136 by Henry of Blois in order to provide board and lodging for thirteen poor men. In 1777 SJ tried to get a place at St. Cross for his "old acquaintance," the aged and infirm Isaac De Groot (*Post* To Bennet Langton, 29 June 1777).

4. *Ante* To Frances Reynolds, 27 Oct. 1764, n. 1.

5. This incident must have occurred between June 1756, when SJ signed the publication agreement with Tonson, and September 1758, when Thomas Bodward took possession of most of the house. During this period SJ used the garret, formerly the *Dictionary* workroom, as his library (Clifford, 1979, pp. 199–201).

receive no great comfort from its conclusion; but yet am well enough pleased that the publick has no farther claim upon me.—I wish you would write more frequently to, Dear Sir, Your affectionate humble servant,

SAM. JOHNSON

Charles Burney

WEDNESDAY 16 OCTOBER 1765

PRINTED SOURCE: JB's *Life*, 1791, I.271, collated with excerpt in Sotheby's Catalogue, 5 May 1930, Lot No. 155, p. 26.

ADDRESS: To Charles Burney, Esq., in Poland-street.

Sir: Oct. 16, 1765

I am sorry that your kindness to me has brought upon you so much trouble, though you have taken care to abate that sorrow, by the pleasure which I receive from your approbation.[1] I defend my criticism in the same manner with you. We must confess the faults of our favourite,[2] to gain credit to our praise of his excellencies. He that claims, either in himself or for another, the honours of perfection, will surely injure the reputation which he designs to assist.[3]

Be pleased to make my compliments to your family.[4] I am, Sir, Your most obliged and most humble servant,

SAM. JOHNSON

1. "Mr. Burney having occasion to write to Johnson for some receipts for subscriptions to his Shakespeare, which Johnson had omitted to deliver when the money was paid, he availed himself of that opportunity of thanking Johnson for the great pleasure which he had received from the perusal of his Preface to Shakespeare" (*Life* I.499).

2. "favourites" (Sotheby's catalogue)

3. "Shakespeare with his excellencies has likewise faults, and faults sufficient to obscure and overwhelm any other merit. I shall shew them in the proportion in which they appear to me, without envious malignity or superstitious veneration" (*Works*, Yale ed. VII.71).

4. Burney's wife Esther had died in 1762, leaving him with six children (Roger Lonsdale, *Dr. Charles Burney*, 1965, p. 56).

Thomas Leland[1]

THURSDAY 17 OCTOBER 1765

MS: Trinity College, Dublin. A copy, perhaps in the hand of Leland's son John (L. F. Powell).

London, Johnsons
court, Fleetstreet, Octr. 17, 1765

Sir,

Among the names subscribed to the degree which I have had the honour of receiving from the University of Dublin,[2] I find none of which I have any personal knowledge but those of Doctr. Andrews[3] and yourself.[4]

Men are to be estimated by those who know them not, only as they are represented by those who know them, and therefore I flatter myself that I owe much of the pleasure which this distinction gives me, to your concurrence with Dr. Andrews in recommending me to that learned Society.

Having desired the Provost to return my general thanks to the University, I beg that you, Sir, will accept my particular and immediate acknowledgements. I am, Sir, your most obedient and most humble Servant,

SAM. JOHNSON

1. Thomas Leland (1722–85), D.D., Fellow of Trinity College, Dublin (1746–81), and author of the *History of the Life and Reign of Philip, King of Macedon* (1758) and the *History of Ireland* (1773). SJ may have known Leland through their common friend Edmund Burke.

2. The degree was that of LL.D. For the text of the diploma, dated 8 July 1765, see *Life* I.489.

3. Francis Andrews (*c.* 1718–74), LL.D., Provost of Trinity College, Dublin, and Professor of Modern History (*Alumni Dublinenses*, ed. G. D. Burtchaell and T. U. Sadleir, 1924, p. 13).

4. MS: "yourselfs"

Jacob Tonson

SATURDAY 19 OCTOBER 1765

MS: Birthplace Museum, Lichfield.

ADDRESS: To Jacob Tonson, Esq.

Johnson's Court,
Sir: Fleetstreet, Oct. 19, 1765

I have lately heard, and heard so often that I can hardly any longer refuse credit, that my Edition is sold stiched by the Booksellers (I am afraid at your own Shop) for forty shillings that is for four shillings under the Subscription.[1] The Subscription was settled with your consent; and your consent alone implied a promise that you would not undersel me. This promise was likewise verbally made by you in my room in Gough Square, when we treated about the Edition. This is the worse, as the demand for the Book has been such, as left yet no temptation to lower the price.[2]

If your Servants have acted without orders, it is time that some direction should be given. If it be done with your knowledge, it is an action which I have a right to resent.[3] But I would willingly think it negligence or mistake. I am, sir, your most humble servant,

SAM. JOHNSON

1. SJ's "four" is a mistake for "two": the subscription price of his Shakespeare was two guineas (42 shillings) per unbound set.

2. The first impression, of 1,000 copies, was sold out within the month. A reprint followed immediately (*Works*, Yale ed. VII.xxiii–iv; *Bibliography*, p. 107; *Bibliography Supplement*, p. 147).

3. According to Philip Gaskell, eighteenth-century retailers "would occasionally offer a discount" on their advertised prices (*A New Introduction to Bibliography*, 1972, p. 179). Whether the discount in this instance was authorized or unauthorized cannot be determined.

Charles Jenkinson[1]

SATURDAY 26 OCTOBER 1765

MS: British Library.

1. Charles Jenkinson (1729–1808), M.P. for Cockermouth (1761–66), Appleby (1767–72), Harwich (1772–74), Hastings (1774–80), and Saltash (1780–86). Jenkinson had been private secretary to Lord Bute and a secretary to the Treasury during George Grenville's ministry. From 1765 to 1772 he served as auditor to the Princess Dowager. Jenkinson rose to become Secretary at War under Lord North (1778–82); in 1796 he was created Earl of Liverpool (Namier and Brooke II.674–78).

Sir: Oct. 26, 1765

You will find all your papers carefully preserved, and uncommunicated to any human Being.[2] I once hoped to have made better use of them, but shall be much delighted to see them employed for the same purpose by a Man so much more versed in publick affairs.[3]

I intended, Sir, to have applied to you for the Intelligence which your kindness has given me without application.

If my Edition pleases you, and such as You it will really produce that additional reputation on which you are pleased to congratulate me. To gain and to preserve the esteem of such men will always be the ambition of, Sir, Your most obliged, most obedient, and most humble Servant,

SAM. JOHNSON

2. On 25 Oct. Jenkinson had written to SJ: "About 2 Years ago I put into your Hands some Papers concerning the late Negotiations for the Peace. If you have no further Use for them I should be obliged to you if you would return them to Me" (B.L. Add. MS: 38305, f. 19).

3. In the autumn of 1765 SJ was beginning to serve, in succession to Edmund Burke, as "fact-gatherer" for W. G. ("Single-Speech") Hamilton (1729–96), M.P. for Pontefract (E. L. McAdam, *Dr. Johnson and the English Law*, 1951, p. 55). Discussing this letter, McAdam surmises: "It is possible that Johnson had already performed one service for Hamilton via Burke. . . . Nothing is known of any use to which Johnson put the papers, but it is just the sort of information which Hamilton constantly sought" (p. 55). Despite his use of the past tense ("once hoped"), SJ may even have been "looking forward to the possibility of an eventual seat in Parliament" (*Works*, Yale ed. I.97).

Edmund Hector

SATURDAY 7 DECEMBER 1765

MS: Hyde Collection.

ADDRESS: To Mr. Hector in Birmingham.

POSTMARK: 7 DE.

Dear Sir: Decr. 7,[1] 1765

I am very glad of a letter from you upon any occasion, but

1. MS: "8"

could wish that when you had despatched business, you would give a little more to friendship, and tell me something of your self.

The Books must be had by sending to Mr. Tonson the receipts and second payment which belongs to him.[2] Any Bookseller will do it, or any Correspondent here. It would be extremely inconvenient, and uncustomary for me to charge myself with the distribution.

I never refuse any subscriber a new receipt when he has lost that which he had. You have three by which you may supply the three deficiencies. When the former receipts are found they must be destroyed.

If Mr. Taylor be my old Friend, make my kindest compliments.[3]

My heart is much set upon seeing you all again, and I hope to visit you in the Spring or Summer,[4] but many of my hopes have been disappointed. I have no correspondence in the country, and know not what is doing. What is become of Mr. Warren?[5] His Friend Paul has been long dead.[6] And to go backwarder, What was the fate of poor George Boylston?[7]

A few years ago I just saluted Birmingham, but had no time to see any friend, for I came[8] in after midnight with a Friend, and went away in the morning.[9] When I come again I shall surely make a longer stay; but in the mean time should think it an act of kindness in you to let me know something of the present state of things, and to revive the pleasure which your

2. *Ante* To Jacob Tonson, 9 Oct. 1765 and n. 2.

3. John Taylor (1711–75), a Birmingham merchant who made a fortune in the gilding and japanning trade. Hector had introduced SJ to Taylor *c.* 1732 (*Life* 1.86 and n. 3; Clifford, 1955, p. 135).

4. SJ passed through Birmingham in 1767, on his way from Lichfield to Oxford, but did not stop to see Hector (*Post* To Edmund Hector, 3 Nov. 1767).

5. *Ante* To Lewis Paul, 31 Jan. 1741, n. 3.

6. *Ante* To Lewis Paul, 31 Jan. 1741, n. 1.

7. George Boylston of Lichfield, Hector's first cousin (*Johns. Glean.* III.71; *Reades*, p. 152).

8. MS: "wen" del. before "came"

9. Presumably SJ refers to his brief trip to Lichfield in the winter of 1761–62 (*Ante* To Giuseppe Baretti, 20 July 1762).

company has formerly given to, Dear Sir, your affectionate and most humble Servant,

SAM. JOHNSON

James Boswell

TUESDAY 14 JANUARY 1766

MS: Beinecke Library. The transcript (in the hand of Alexander Boswell) used as copy for the *Life*.

ADDRESS:[1] A Mr. Mr. Boswell, chez Mr. Waters, Banquier, à Paris.[2]

Johnsons Court,
Fleet Street, Jan. 14, 1766

Dear Sir,

Apologies are seldom of any use. We will delay till your arrival the reasons good or bad which have made me such a sparing and ungrateful correspondent. Be assured for the present that nothing has lessened either the esteem or love with which I dismissed you at Harwich.[3] Both have been encreased by all that I have been told of you by yourself or others, and when you return, you will return to an unaltered and I hope unalterable friend.[4]

All that you have to fear from me, is the vexation of disappointing me. No man loves to frustrate expectations which have been formed in his favour; and the pleasure which I promise myself from your journals and remarks is so great that perhaps no degree of attention or discernment will be sufficient to afford it.

Come home however and take your chance. I long to see

1. The address, missing in the MS, is supplied from *Life*, 1791, I.273.

2. JB's Grand Tour ended with two and a half weeks in Paris (12–31 Jan. 1766). His mailing address was c/o the banker John Waters.

3. JB left for Holland on 6 Aug. 1763. "My revered friend walked down with me to the beach, where we embraced and parted with tenderness, and engaged to correspond by letters" (*Life* I.472).

4. JB arrived in London on 12 Feb. 1766. "Immediately to Johnson; received you with open arms. You kneeled, and asked blessing. . . . He hugged you to him like a sack, and grumbled, 'I hope we shall pass many years of regard' " (*Boswell on the Grand Tour: Italy, Corsica, and France*, ed. Frank Brady and F. A. Pottle, 1955, p. 281).

you and to hear you, and hope that we shall not be so long separated again. Come home and expect such a welcome as is due to him whom a wise and noble curiosity has led where perhaps no native of this Country ever was before.[5]

I have no news to tell you that can deserve your notice, nor would I willingly lessen the pleasure that any novelty may give you at your return. I am afraid we shall find it difficult to keep among us a mind which has been so long feasted with variety. But let us try what esteem and kindness can effect.

As your Father's liberality has indulged you with so long a ramble, I doubt not but you will think his sickness, or even his desire to see you, a sufficient reason for hastening your return.[6] The longer we live and the more we think, the higher value we learn to put on the friendship and tenderness of Parents and of friends. Parents we can have but once, and he promises himself too much, who enters life with the expectation of finding many friends. Upon some motive I hope that you will be here soon, and am willing to think that it will be an inducement to your return that it is sincerely desired by, Dear Sir, Your affectionate humble Servant,

SAM. JOHNSON

5. JB sailed to Corsica in Oct. 1765 and traveled to the center of the island, where he spent a week with General Pasquale Paoli, the leader of the rebels. "The Corsican state was almost unknown, and although the British had traded with the island for many years, apparently no British gentleman had ever penetrated the interior" (Brady and Pottle, *Grand Tour*, p. 145). In early Nov. 1765 JB wrote to SJ "from the palace of Pascal Paoli, sacred to wisdom and liberty. . . . I gave him a sketch of the great things I had seen in Corsica, and promised him a more ample relation" (p. 194).

6. Lord Auchinleck had written to JB on 1 Oct. 1765, urging his son's speedy return and emphasizing his "great distress with a stoppage of urine, that has forced us to come in to Edinburgh for the aid of physicians" (Brady and Pottle, *Grand Tour*, p. 215). However, JB would have lingered in Paris had not his mother died on 11 Jan. 1766 (*Earlier Years*, pp. 273–74).

Lucy Porter

TUESDAY 14 JANUARY 1766

MS: Hyde Collection.

ADDRESS: To Mrs. Lucy Porter in Lichfield.

POSTMARK: 14 IA.

Johnson's Court,
Fleetstreet, Jan. 14, 1766

Dear Madam:

The reason why I did not answer your letters was that I can please myself with no answer. I was loath that Kitty should leave the house, till I had seen it once more,[1] and yet for some reasons I cannot well come during the session of Parliament.[2] I am unwilling to sell it, yet hardly know why.[3] If it can be let, it should be repaired,[4] and I purpose to let Kitty have part of the rent while we both live, and wish that you would get it surveyed, and let me know how much money will be necessary to fit it for a Tenant. I would not have you stay longer than is convenient,[5] and I thank you for your care of Kitty.

Do not take my omission amiss. I am sorry for it, but know not what to say, you must act by your own prudence, and I shall be pleased. Write to me again, I do not design to neglect you any more. It is [a] great pleasure to me to hear from you, but this whole affair is painful to me. I wish you, my Dear, many happy years. Give my respects to Kitty. I am, Dear Madam, your most affectionate, humble servant,

SAM. JOHNSON

1. *Ante* To Lucy Porter, 6 Feb. 1759, n. 1.

2. *Ante* To Charles Jenkinson, 26 Oct. 1765, n. 3.

3. SJ still owned the house at the time of his death. It was sold in 1785 for £235 (*Johns. Glean.* IV.20; *Life* IV.440).

4. *Post* To Lucy Porter, 13 Nov. 1766.

5. *Ante* To Lucy Porter, 6 Feb. 1759, n. 3.

Bennet Langton

SATURDAY 8 MARCH 1766

MS: Hyde Collection.

ADDRESS: To Bennet Langton, Esq., Junr., at Langton, near Spilsby, Lincolnshire.

POSTMARK: 8 MR.

Johnson's Court,
Dear Sir: Fleetstreet, March 8,[1] 1766

What your friends have done, that from your departure till now, nothing has been heard of you, none of us are able to inform the rest, but as we are all neglected alike, no one thinks himself entitled to the privilege of complaint.

I should have known nothing of you or of Langton, from the time that dear Miss Langton left us,[2] had not I met Mr. Simpson of Lincoln one day in the street,[3] by whom I was informed that Mr. Langton,[4] your Mamma,[5] and yourself had been all ill, but that you were all recovered.

That sickness should suspend your correspondence I did not wonder, but hoped that it would be renewed at your recovery.

Since you will not inform us where you are, or how you live, I know [not] whether you desire to know any thing of us. However I will tell you, that the Club subsists, but we have less of Burke's company since he has been engaged in publick business, in which he has gained more reputation than perhaps any man at his appearance ever gained before.[6] He made two speeches in the house for repealing the Stamp-act, which were publickly commended by Mr. Pit, and have filled the town with wonder.[7]

1. MS: "9"

2. SJ refers to Elizabeth Langton, Bennet's eldest sister. *Ante* To Bennet Langton, 9 Jan. 1759, n. 3.

3. The Rev. Thomas Sympson (1726–86), Priest Vicar of Lincoln Cathedral.

4. *Ante* To Bennet Langton, 6 May 1755, n. 7.

5. *Ante* To Bennet Langton, 9 Jan. 1759, n. 6.

6. Edmund Burke, who had become M.P. for Wendover on 23 Dec. 1765, was "an almost instantaneous success in the House" (Namier and Brooke II.145–47).

7. By the end of 1765, the Stamp Act "had brought forth defiance and disturbance in America on a large scale, and occasioned a boycott of imported goods so

Burke is a great man by Nature, and is expected soon to attain civil greatness. I am grown greater too, for I have maintained the newspapers these many weeks,[8] and what is greater still, I have risen every morning since Newyears day at about eight,[9] when I was up I have indeed done but little, yet it is no slight advancement to obtain for so many hours more the consciousness of being.

I wish you were in my new study, I am now writing the first letter in it. I think it looks very pretty about me.[10]

Dyer is constant at the Club,[11] Hawkins is remiss.[12] I am not over diligent. Dr. Nugent,[13] Dr. Goldsmith and Mr. Reynolds are very constant. Mr. Lye is printing his Saxon and Gothick dictionary⟨;⟩ all the club subscribes.[14]

---

damaging to British mercantile and manufacturing interests that a powerful lobby for repeal soon sprang up at home to reinforce the urgency of dealing with the threat of rebellion across the Atlantic" (Stanley Ayling, *George the Third,* 1972, p. 136). Burke, who had written against the Act in the *Annual Register* for 1765, joined in the Rockingham Whigs' campaign for repeal. Formal debate began in the House of Commons on 14 Jan. 1766; Burke spoke on 17 Jan. (his maiden speech) and again on 27 Jan. Garrick praised his "Virgin Eloquence" and Pitt called him "a very able advocate" (*Letters of David Garrick,* ed. D. M. Little and G. M. Kahrl, 1963, II.490; C. B. Cone, *Burke and the Nature of Politics,* 1957, pp. 88–93). The Act was repealed on 18 Mar.

8. SJ's edition of Shakespeare (published 10 Oct. 1765) had touched off a long series of letters in the *St. James's Chronicle* concerning textual cruxes. These letters began as early as 6 Nov. 1765 and continued for at least three years.

9. SJ's New Year's list for 1766 included the resolution "To rise early." On 3 Mar. he noted, "I have never, I thank God, since Newyears day deviated from the practice of rising" (*Works,* Yale ed. I.99, 103).

10. Sir John Hawkins describes this "new study" as "an upper room, which had the advantages of a good light and free air" (Hawkins, p. 452). In a prayer dated 7 Mar. 1766, "Entring N[ovum] M[useum]," SJ gives thanks for the "new conveniences for study" (*Works,* Yale ed. I.103).

11. Samuel Dyer (1725–72), classical scholar and translator, "a man of profound and general erudition" who had also belonged to SJ's Ivy Lane Club (*Life* IV.11 and n. 1; Clifford, 1979, pp. 35–37).

12. Sir John Hawkins (1719–89), magistrate and musicologist, "a very *unclubable* man" who withdrew from the group after a dispute with Burke (*Life* I.479–80 and n. 1).

13. Christopher Nugent (d. 1775), M.D., F.R.S., one of the original members of The Club and Burke's father-in-law.

14. *Ante* To Edward Lye, 17 Aug. 1765 and n. 2.

You will pay my compliments to all my Linco[l]nshire friends. I am, Dear Sir, most affectionately yours,

SAM. JOHNSON

Bennet Langton

SATURDAY 10 MAY 1766

MS: Hyde Collection.

ADDRESS: To Bennet Langton, junior, Esqr., at Langton, near Spilsby, Lincolnshire.

POSTMARK: 10 MA.

Johnson's Court,
Fleetstreet, May 10, 1766

Dear Sir:

In supposing that I should be more than commonly affected by the [death] of Peregrine Langton you were not mistaken;[1] he was one of those whom I loved at once by instinct and by reason. I have seldom indulged more hope of any thing than of being able to improve our acquaintance to friendship. Many a time have I placed myself again at Langton, and imagined the pleasure with which I should walk to Partney in a summer morning.[2] But this is no longer possible. We must now endeavour to preserve what is left us, his example of Piety, and economy. I hope you make what enquiries you can, and write down what is told you.[3] The little things which distinguish domestick characters are soon forgotten, if you delay to enquire you will have no information, if you neglect to write, information will be vain.[4]

1. Peregrine Langton (1703–66), Bennet's uncle. SJ had met him during his stay at Langton, Jan.–Feb. 1764.

2. Partney, Lincolnshire, a village on the road from Spilsby to Louth, approximately two miles from Langton; "the place of residence of Mr. Peregrine Langton" (JB's note).

3. Bennet Langton's enquiries resulted in a detailed account of his uncle's domestic and financial planning; JB printed this account as a long footnote to the *Life* (II.17–19 n. 9).

4. "If a life be delayed till interest and envy are at an end, we may hope for impartiality, but must expect little intelligence; for the incidents which give excellence to biography are of a volatile and evanescent kind, such as soon escape the

His art of life certainly deserves to be known and studied. He lived in plenty and elegance upon an income which to ma[n]y would appear indigent and to most, scanty.[5] How he lived therefore every man has an interest in knowing.[6] His death, I hope, was peaceful, it was surely happy.

I wish I had written sooner, lest writing now I should renew your grief, but I would not forbear saying what I have now said.

This loss is, I hope, the only misfortune of a family to whom no misfortune at all should happen, if my wishes could avert it. Let me know how you all go on. Has Mr. Langton got him the little horse that I recommended? It would do him good to ride about his estate in fine weather.

Be pleased to make my compliments to Mrs. Langton, and to dear Miss Langton, and Miss Di. and Miss Juliet,[7] and to every body else.

The Club holds very well together. Monday is my night.[8] I continue to rise tolerably well,[9] and read more than I did. I hope something will yet come on it. I am, Sir, your most affectionate servant,

SAM. JOHNSON

---

memory, and are rarely transmitted by tradition" (*Rambler* No. 60, *Works*, Yale ed. III.322–23).

5. According to his nephew's account (see above, n. 3), Peregrine Langton lived on "an annuity for life of two hundred pounds *per annum*" (*Life* II.17–18 n. 9).

6. "I have often thought that there has rarely passed a life of which a judicious and faithful narrative would not be useful. . . . The business of the biographer is often to pass slightly over those performances and incidents, which produce vulgar greatness, to lead the thoughts into domestick privacies, and display the minute details of daily life, where exterior appendages are cast aside, and men excel each other only by prudence and by virtue" (*Rambler* No. 60, *Works*, Yale ed. III.320–21).

7. *Ante* To Bennet Langton, 9 Jan. 1759, n. 3.

8. "Of his being in the Chair of The Literary Club, which at this time met once a week in the evening" (JB's note).

9. *Ante* To Bennet Langton, 8 Mar. 1766 and n. 9.

William Jessop[1]

SATURDAY 28 JUNE 1766

MS: British Library.

ADDRESS: To the Reverend Mr. Jessop in Lismore in the County of Waterford, Ireland.

POSTMARK: 28 IV.

ENDORSEMENT: Johnson.

Johnson's Court
in Fleetstreet, June 28th 1766

Sir:

If your letter had been less ceremonious it would not have pleased me less. I read poor Grierson's paper with a very tender remembrance both of his learning and his humour.[2]

What you propose to offer to the world is really wanting in our language, and as I have no reason to doubt your ability to supply the deficiency, I shall be willing to do any thing that can be reasonably required.[3] You will therefore, if you do not change your mind, contrive to transmit your book to, Sir, Your most obedient servant,

SAM. JOHNSON

1. The Rev. William Jessop (*c.* 1728–1816), one of the vicars choral of the cathedral of Lismore and prebendary of Mora and Clashmore. Jessop had attended Trinity College, Dublin, along with George Grierson (Henry Cotton, *Fasti Ecclesiæ Hibernicæ*, 1848–60, I.204; *Alumni Dublinenses*, ed. G. D. Burtchaell and T. U. Sadleir, 1924, p. 440).

2. George Grierson (*c.* 1728–55), government printer at Dublin, was also an accomplished philologist. According to William Maxwell (1732–1818), D.D., who was introduced to SJ in 1754 by Grierson, "Dr. Johnson highly respected his abilities, and often observed, that he possessed more extensive knowledge than any man of his years he had ever known" (*Life* II.117).

3. It is possible that Jessop hoped to publish a book based on materials left by Grierson. There is no record, however, of such a work.

William Drummond[1]

WEDNESDAY 13 AUGUST 1766

MS: Beinecke Library. The transcript (in the hand of Margaret Boswell) used as copy for the *Life*.

ADDRESS in JB's hand: To Mr. William Drummond.

1. *Ante* To William Drummond, 1 Oct. 1758, n. 1.

To WILLIAM DRUMMOND, 13 *August* 1766

Johnsons Court,
Sir: Fleet Street, Aug. 13, 1766

I did not expect to hear that it could be in an assembly convened for the propagation of Christian knowledge a question whether any nation uninstructed in religion should receive instruction or whether that instruction should be imparted to them by a translation of the Holy Books into their own language.[2] If obedience to the will of God be necessary to happiness and knowledge of his Will be necessary to obedience I know not how he that withholds this knowledge or delays it can be said to love his neighbour as himself. He that voluntarily continues ignorance is guilty of all the crimes which ignorance produces: as to him that should extinguish the tapers of a light-House might justly be imputed the calamities of Shipwreck. Christianity is the highest perfection of humanity and as no Man is good but as he wishes the good of others no man can be good in the highest degree who wishes not to others the largest measure of the greatest good. To omit for a year or for a day the most efficacious method of advancing Christianity in compliance with any purposes that terminate on this side of the grave is a crime of which I know not the World has yet had an example except in the practice of the Planters of America a Race of Mortals whom I suppose no other Man wishes to resemble.[3]

The Papists have indeed denied to the laity the Use of the bible but this prohibition in few places now very rigorously enforced is defended by Arguments which have for their foundation the care of Souls. To[4] obscure upon motives

2. "Some of the members of the society in Scotland for propagating Christian knowledge, had opposed the scheme of translating the holy scriptures into the Erse or Gaelick language, from political considerations of the disadvantage of keeping up the distinction between the Highlanders and the other inhabitants of North-Britain" (*Life* II.27).

3. "Johnson's deepest rancor against exploiters of native populations seems to have been directed against . . . English sugar planters of the West Indies" (Donald Greene, *The Politics of Samuel Johnson*, 1960, p. 270). See *Life* III.200 for SJ's toast "to the next insurrection of the negroes in the West Indies."

4. MS: "Souls to"

merely political the light of Revelation is a practice reserved for the reformed and surely the blackest midnight of Popery is meridian sunshine to such a reformation. I am not very willing that any Language should be totally extinguished, the similitude and derivation of languages afford the most indubitable proof of the traduction of nations and the geneology of mankind. They[5] add often physical certainty to historical evidence and often supply the only Evidence of ancient migrations and the Revolution of ages which left no written monuments behind them.

Every mans opinions at least his desires are a little influenced by his favourite Studies. My zeal for Languages may seem perhaps rather over-heated even to those by whom I desired to be well esteemed. To those who have nothing in their thoughts but trade or Policy present power or present Money I should not think it necessary to defend my opinions but with Men of letters I would not unwillingly compound by wishing the continuance of every Language however narrow in its extent or however incommodious for common purposes till it is reposited in some Version of a known book that it may be always hereafter examined and compared with other languages and then permitting its disuse. For this purpose the translation of the Bible is most to be desired. It is not certain that the same Method will not preserve the Highland language for the purposes of learning and abolish it from daily use. When the Highlanders read the Bible they will naturally wish to have its obscurities cleared and to know the history collatoral or appendant. Knowledge always desires increase. It[6] is like fire which must first be kindled by some external agent but which will afterwards propogate itself. When they once desire to learn they will naturally have recourse to the nearest language by which that desire can be gratified and one will tell another that if he would attain knowledge he must learn English.[7]

This speculation may perhaps be thought more subtle than

5. MS: "mankind they" 6. MS: "increase it"

7. "Of the Earse language, as I understand nothing, I cannot say more than I

the [grossness][8] of real life will easily admit. Let it however be remembered that the efficacy of ignorance has been long tried and has not produced the consequence expected. Let knowledge therefore take its turn and let the patrons of privation stand awhile aside and admit the operation of positive principles.

You will be pleased Sir to assure the worthy Man who is employed in the new translation that he has my wishes for his success, and if here or at Oxford I can be of any Use that I shall think it more than honour to promote his undertaking.[9] I am sorry that I delayed so long to write. I am, Sir, your most humble servant,

SAM. JOHNSON

---

have been told. It is the rude speech of a barbarous people, who had few thoughts to express, and were content, as they conceived grossly, to be grossly understood" (*Works*, Yale ed. IX.114).

8. MS: erasure; "grossness" supplied from text in *Life*

9. The first translation of the New Testament into Scots Gaelic was undertaken by the Rev. James Stuart (1700–1789), Minister of Killin, Perthshire. It was published in Edinburgh in 1767.

James Boswell

THURSDAY 21 AUGUST 1766

MS: Beinecke Library. The transcript (in the hand of Margaret Boswell) used as copy for the *Life*.
ADDRESS in JB's hand: To James Boswell, Esq.

Dear Sir: London, August 21, 1766

The reception of your Thesis put me in mind of my debt to you.[1] Why did you dedicate it to a man whom I know you do

1. In order to be admitted to the Faculty of Advocates, JB had to present and defend a Latin thesis on one of the titles of the Pandects. "The thesis was on Tit. x, Lib. XXXIII of the Pandects, *De supellectile legata* (Legacies of Household Furniture) and was not a work of deep research" (*Earlier Years*, p. 291). JB successfully defended it and "passed advocate" on 26 July 1766. He sent the thesis to SJ in an attempt to "move his indolence" (*Life* II.20).

not much love.[2] I will punish you for it, by telling you that your Latin wants correction.[3] In the beginning *Spei alteræ* not to urge that it should be *primæ* is not grammatical *alteræ* should be *alteri*. In the next line you seem to use *genus* absolutely for what we call *family* that is for *illustrious extraction* I doubt without authority. *Homines nullius originis* for *Nullis orti majoribus* or *Nullo loco nati* is I am affraid barbarous.[4]—Ruddiman is dead.[5]

I have now vexed you enough and will try to please you. Your resolution to obey your father I sincerely approve but do not accustom yourself to enchain your volatility by vows. They[6] will sometime leave a thorn in your mind which you will perhaps never be able to extract or eject. Take this warning it is of great importance.

The study of the Law is what you very justly term it, copious and generous,[7] and in adding your name to its Proffessors you have done exactly what I always wished when I wished you best. I hope that you will continue to pursue it vigorously and constantly. You gain at least what is no small advantage security from those troublesome and wearysome discontents which are always obtruding themselves upon a mind vacant unemployed and undetermined.

You ought to think it no small inducement to dilligence and perseverance that they will please your father. We all live upon the hope of pleasing some body and the pleasure of pleasing

2. All but the first three words of this sentence are suppressed in the *Life*. The dedicatee was John Stuart (1744–1814), Viscount Mountstuart, eldest son of the third Earl of Bute, later fourth Earl and first Marquess of Bute. JB had traveled with Mountstuart in Italy, June–July 1765, and hoped to profit from his political influence (*Earlier Years*, pp. 224–33).

3. "This censure of my Latin relates to the Dedication, which was as follows" (*Life* II.20 n. 4).

4. In a letter dated 6 Nov. 1766, JB defended the purity of his Latin at great length. F. A. Pottle characterizes this defense as "sophistical on some points," but adds that it "clearly proved Johnson captious on others" (*Earlier Years*, p. 291).

5. *Ante* To James Elphinston, Early 1752, n. 6. Because "Ruddiman is dead," he cannot be appealed to on matters of Latin grammar and usage.

6. MS: "vows they"

7. "This alludes to the first sentence of the *Prooemium* of my Thesis. '*Jurisprudentiæ studio nullum uberius, nullum generosius*' " (*Life* II.21 n. 3).

ought to be greatest and at last always will be greatest when our endeavours are exerted in consequence of our duty.

Life is not long and too much of it must not pass in idle deliberation how it shall be spent; deliberation[8] which those who begin it by prudence and continue it with subtilty must after long expence of thought conclude by chance.[9] To prefer one future mode of life to another upon just reasons requires faculties which it has not pleased our Creator to give us.

If therefore the Proffession you have chosen has some unexpected inconveniencies console yourself by refflecting that no Profession is without them and that all the importunities and perplexities of Business are softness and Luxury compared with the incessant cravings of Vacancy and the unsatisfactory expedients of idleness.

Hæc sunt quæ nostra potui te voce monere;
Vade, age.[10]

As to your History of Corsica you have no materials which others have not or may not have.[11] You[12] have somehow or other warmed your imagination. I wish there were some cure like the Lover's leap for all heads of which some single Idea has obtained an unreasonable and irregular possession. Mind your own affairs and leave the Corsicans to theirs.[13] I am, Dear Sir, Your most humble servant,

SAM. JOHNSON

8. MS: "spent deliberation"

9. "'Very few,' said the poet, 'live by choice. Every man is placed in his present condition by causes which acted without his foresight, and with which he did not always willingly co-operate'" (*Works*, Yale ed. XVI.67).

10. "*hæc sunt, quæ nostra liceat te voce moneri. / Vade age*": "This it is whereof by my voice thou mayest be warned. Now go thy way" (*Aeneid* III.461–62, trans. H. R. Fairclough, Loeb ed.).

11. Since JB's return to Scotland in Mar. 1766, he had begun to read and take notes for his *Account of Corsica* (1768), part of an extended personal campaign to make England intervene on the side of the Corsican nationalists.

12. MS: "have you"

13. *Post* To JB, 23 Mar. 1768 and n. 2.

David Garrick

FRIDAY 10 OCTOBER 1766

MS: Houghton Library.

ENDORSEMENT: Johnson about a 100 pounds.

Dear Sir: Oct. 10, 1766

I return you tha[n]ks for the present of the Dictionary, and will take [care] to return your other books.

I have had it long in my mind to tell you that there is an hundred pounds of yours in Mr. Tonson's hands, if you have not yet received it. I know not whether any other paper than what I gave you be necessary. If there is anything more to be done, I am ready to do it.[1]

Please to make my compliments to Mrs. Garrick. I am, Sir, your obliged etc. SAM. JOHNSON

1. This transaction cannot be explained with certainty. It is possible that SJ was repaying a debt to Garrick by authorizing his publisher Jacob Tonson to deduct the sum in question from the amount owed SJ for *Dictionary* sales. We know that SJ had a standing account with Tonson, whom he may well have used as an unofficial private banker (*Ante* To Jacob Tonson, 9 Oct. 1765; cf. *Ante* To William Strahan, Late July or Early Aug. 1754 and n. 1).

Lucy Porter

THURSDAY 13 NOVEMBER 1766

MS: Houghton Library.

ADDRESS: To Mrs. Lucy Porter in Lichfield.

POSTMARK: 13 NO.

ENDORSEMENT: 1766.

Dear Madam: Nov. 13, 1766

Soon after I had received your letter I went to Oxford, and did not return till last Saturday.[1] I do not very clearly under-

1. SJ had spent a month at Oxford, helping Robert Chambers with the first four of his Vinerian lectures (*Works*, Yale ed. I.111; *Post* To Robert Chambers, 11 Dec. 1766, n. 1).

stand what need there is of my coming to Lichfield. It is now too late in the year to repair the poor old house,[2] if the reparation can be delayed. Nor can I very easily discover what I can do towards it when I come more than pay the money which it shall cost.[3] The days are now grown short, and a long Journey will be uncomfortable, and I think it better to delay doing whatever is to be done till Spring. I will come down, however, if you desire it.[4]

I am sorry to have no better account of poor Kitty's health. I hope she will be better. Pray give my love to her, and desire her not to forget my request.[5]

I should take it kindly if you would now and then write to me, and give me an account of your own health, and let me know how you go on in your new house.[6] I am, Dear Madam, your most affectionate, humble servant,

SAM. JOHNSON

2. *Ante* To Lucy Porter, 14 Jan. 1766. SJ's birthplace was built in 1707–8 by his father (*Johns. Glean.* IV.16).

3. MS: comma

4. SJ did not travel to Lichfield until the following May, when he "came down" to attend the dying Catherine Chambers.

5. *Ante* To Lucy Porter, 14 Jan. 1766; *Post* To Thomas Lawrence, 17 June 1767 and n. 5.

6. *Ante* To Lucy Porter, 6 Feb. 1759, n. 3.

Robert Chambers

WEDNESDAY 19 NOVEMBER 1766

MS: Hyde Collection.

ADDRESS: To Robert Chambers, Esq.

Dear Sir: Wednesday Morning, Nov. 19, 1766

I have been twice to see you and missed you.[1] I have now a little favour to ask. I beg to be informed, if you know or can enquire what are the reasons for which Dr. Blackstone thinks

1. When he was not at Oxford, Chambers occupied rooms in King's Bench Walk, Inner Temple.

the late embargo to [2] be not [3] legal, as I hear he does.[4] It always seemed legal to me.[5] But I judge upon mere principles without much knowledge of laws or facts.

Absurdum est cui plus licet, ei minus non licere.[6] I am, sir, etc.

SAM. JOHNSON

2. MS: "no" del. before "to" 3. MS: "not" written above "not" del.

4. In Nov. 1766, SJ appears to have been composing, for the use of W. G. Hamilton, his "Considerations on Corn," the background to which is summarized by Donald Greene: "In 1766 there was a shortage of grain, the price had risen high, and there was much public turbulence as a result. In September, during the Parliamentary recess, the Chatham government, in an attempt to relieve the situation, had by order-in-council proclaimed an embargo on the export of grain. A confused mass of legislation for the control of the grain trade was in force, and it was a nice legal question whether the King-in-Council had the authority to impose the embargo" (*The Politics of SJ*, 1960, p. 198).

5. SJ's impression of Blackstone's opinion was mistaken: "In the editions of the *Commentaries* published after this event, Blackstone flatly affirms the legality of the embargo, and cites the relevant statutes" (E. L. McAdam, *Dr. Johnson and the English Law*, 1951, p. 57).

6. *Absurdum est cui plus licet, ei minus non licere*: "It would be absurd if the right to more does not include a right to less" (translation supplied by Professor Peter White).

Robert Chambers

THURSDAY 11 DECEMBER 1766

MS: Hyde Collection.

ADDRESS: To Robert Chambers, Esq., at University College, Oxford.

POSTMARK: 11 DE.

ENDORSEMENT: Mr. Johnson, Decr. 11, 1766.

Dear Sir: Decr. 11, 1766

I suppose you are dining and supping, and lying in bed. Come up to town, and lock yourself up from all but me, and I doubt not but Lectures will be produced. You must not miss another term.[1]

1. In May 1766 Chambers had been elected the second Vinerian Professor of Law at Oxford, in succession to William Blackstone. The professorship carried with it the obligation to deliver 60 lectures each year; a fine of £2 was levied for

If you could get me any information about the East Indian affairs, you may promise that if it is used at all, it shall be used in favour of the Company.[2] Come up and work, and I will try to help you. You asked me what amends you could make me. You shall always be my friend. I am, Dear, your affectionate, humble servant,

SAM. JOHNSON

---

every omission. However, "Chambers panicked and produced no lectures for the scheduled start of his course in the fall. In the midst of this crisis, Johnson generously came to his rescue and inaugurated a collaboration that would continue fitfully for at least three years" (*A Course of Lectures on the English Law,* ed. T. M. Curley, 1986, p. 19). This collaboration, which was kept a strict secret, was known only to Hester Thrale (E. L. McAdam, *Dr. Johnson and the English Law,* 1951, p. 69; *Post* To Hester Thrale, 14 Dec. 1768).

2. The Chatham administration, which had come to power in July 1766, was threatening a parliamentary investigation into the affairs of the East India Company. "Their purpose in so doing was to challenge the Company in its enjoyment of the profits of its territorial revenues" (L. S. Sutherland, *The East India Company in Eighteenth-Century Politics,* 1952, p. 147). According to Donald Greene, SJ "may have been acting with the so-called Johnstone group, who were extremely active at this time in opposing the Chathamite 'raid'" (*The Politics of SJ,* 1960, p. 201).

Robert Chambers

THURSDAY 22 JANUARY 1767

MS: Hyde Collection.

ADDRESS: To Robert Chambers, Esqr., University College, Oxon. [*Re-addressed*] No. 6 Kings-Bench Walks, Inner Temple, London.

POSTMARKS: OXFORD, 24 IA, FREE.

FRANK: Hfreethrale.

ENDORSEMENT: Doctor Sam. Johnson, 22 Jan. 1767.

Dear Sir: London, Jan. 22, 1767

The affairs of the East Indies are to come at last before the parliament, and therefore we shall be glad of any information about them.[1] We are likewise desirous of the papers which have been laid before the House, which can be no longer se-

1. *Ante* To Robert Chambers, 11 Dec. 1766, n. 2.

cret, and therefore, I suppose may be easily granted us. We will pay for transcribing if that be any difficulty. What other papers shall be put into our hands, shall be used if they are used at all, in defence of the company. Help us, dear Sir, if you can.[2]

I hope you are soon to come again, and go to the old business, for which I shall expect great abundance of materials and to sit very close, and then there will be no danger, and needs to be no fear.[3] I am, Dear Sir, your most humble servant,

SAM. JOHNSON

2. In Dec. 1766 the House of Commons had passed a motion, introduced by Alderman William Beckford, that the Company's papers be tabled to assist with the impending enquiry. Then Parliament adjourned for a month, 16 Dec. 1766–16 Jan. 1767. When it reassembled, complex negotiations ensued among the Ministry, the Opposition, and the Company directors; these dragged on until May, when a compromise agreement was finally reached (L. S. Sutherland, *The East India Company in Eighteenth-Century Politics*, 1952, pp. 158–76). The roles of SJ and Chambers in the affair (and specifically the "we" of this paragraph) have never been satisfactorily explained.

3. *Ante* To Robert Chambers, 11 Dec. 1766, n. 1.

Sir James Caldwell[1]

THURSDAY 12 FEBRUARY 1767

MS: Rylands Library. A copy in the hand of Caldwell's clerk.

HEADING: Doctor Samuel Johnson to Sir Jas. Caldwell. Feby. 12th, 1767.

Dear Sir James,

Our friend Doctor Hawkesworth[2] acquaints me that you are very desireous to see a Paper reciting a Conversation with

1. Sir James Caldwell (*c.* 1720–84), fourth Bt., of Castle Caldwell, Fermanagh; diplomat, soldier, and author of *Debates Relative to the Affairs of Ireland* (1766). Caldwell, who had known SJ for at least five years, may well have been introduced by John Hawkesworth: see below, n. 2 (Frank Taylor, "Johnsoniana from the Bagshawe Muniments," *Bulletin of the John Rylands Library* 35, 1952–53, pp. 213–24).

2. *Ante* To Joseph Warton, 8 Mar. 1753, n. 2. "Hawkesworth served Caldwell as a literary and personal advisor for a number of years, assisting him in his personal and public writings" (J. L. Abbott, *John Hawkesworth*, 1982, p. 128).

which his Majesty was pleased to honour me last Tuesday in his Library.[3] The moment I left the King's presence I put it down in writing as nearly as I could recollect and send you a Copy of it inclosed.

The King's information of what is going on in the litera[r]y as well as Political world is much more Extensive than is Generally imagined.

I have read with pleasure what you have Wrote to honest George[4] in favour of poor Mrs. Williams's Subscription[5] and shall return it to you with a little Amendation. You have taken the Hints I gave you and Illucidated and enforced them with great ability. You know I never flatter. I am, my dear Sir, affectionately yours,

SAMUEL JOHNSON

Don't forget the party we made to Dine at the Mitre next Tuesday.[6] I have Engaged Hool, the Translator of Tas[s]o, to be with us.[7] Do not engage yourself and you and I will Drink Tea with Mrs. Williams and regale her with your Letter to Faulkner. I am in bed and I got Davis to write this.[8] I hope it will overtake you before you go to Bromley.[9]

3. JB's account of the conversation between SJ and George III (*Life* II.33–41) is based principally upon this "paper," the eight-page "Caldwell Minute," now in the John Rylands Library. For a transcript of the Minute, see Taylor, "Johnsoniana," pp. 235–38.

4. *Ante* To Samuel Richardson, 28 Mar. 1754, n. 8.

5. *Ante* To Elizabeth Montagu, 9 June 1759, n. 3. Copies of the *Miscellanies* were still for sale in 1770 (Hazen, p. 215).

6. The Mitre Tavern, Mitre Court, Fleet Street, was SJ's "place of frequent resort . . . where he loved to sit up late" (*Life* I.399).

7. John Hoole (1727–1803), dramatist and poet, "translated the works of Tasso, Ariosto, and Metastasio, if not with congenial fervour of imagination, yet with correctness, elegance, and taste" (*Lit. Anec.* II.407). SJ had written the dedication to Hoole's *Jerusalem Delivered* (1763).

8. Probably the Mrs. Davis who was a companion and assistant to Anna Williams (*Life* IV.239 n. 2). "This letter is, of course, twice removed from Johnson; not merely is it a copy, but the original from which it was made was in the hand of 'Davis'. Thus, the capitals and unusual spellings . . . may be due either to 'Davis' or Maguire [Caldwell's clerk]" (Taylor, "Johnsoniana," p. 232).

9. *Ante* To John Hawkesworth, Early Mar. 1756, n. 8.

Hester Salusbury[1]

SATURDAY 14 FEBRUARY 1767

MS: Hyde Collection.

Madam: February the 14th 1767

I hope it will not be considered as one of the mere formalities of life, when I declare that to have heard nothing of Mrs. Thrale for so long a time has given me pain. My uneasiness is sincere, and therefore deserves to be relieved. I do not write to Mrs. Thrale lest it should give her trouble at an inconvenient time.[2] I beg, dear Madam, to know how she does, and shall honestly partake of your grief if she is ill, and of your pleasure if she is well. I am, Madam, your most obliged and most humble servant,

SAM. JOHNSON

1. Hester Maria Cotton Salusbury (1707–73), Hester Thrale's mother. Her husband John had died in 1762, and she divided her time between the Thrales' and her own house (No. 24 Dean Street, Soho). At this early stage of their acquaintance, Mrs. Salusbury and SJ thoroughly disliked each other. "The basic cause was their jealousy over Mrs. Thrale, for each was convinced that the other had improper and too much influence" (Hyde, 1977, p. 32).

2. Henry Salusbury (1767–76), the Thrales' third child and first son, was born 15 Feb., "strong and lively at Southwark" (Hyde, 1977, p. 24).

William Drummond

TUESDAY 21 APRIL 1767

PRINTED SOURCE: JB's *Life*, 1791, I.288.

ADDRESS: To Mr. William Drummond.

Johnson's-Court,
Dear Sir: Fleet-street, April 21, 1767

That my letter should have had such effects as you mention, gives me great pleasure.[1] I hope you do not flatter me by imputing to me more good than I have really done. Those whom my arguments have persuaded to change their opinion, show such modesty and candour as deserve great praise.

1. *Ante* To William Drummond, 13 Aug. 1766.

I hope the worthy translator goes diligently forward.[2] He has a higher reward in prospect than any honours which this world can bestow. I wish I could be useful to him.

The publication of my letter, if it could be of use in a cause to which all other causes are nothing, I should not prohibit. But first, I would have you consider whether the publication will really do any good; next, whether by printing and distributing a very small number, you may not attain all that you propose; and, what perhaps I should have said first, whether the letter, which I do not now perfectly remember, be fit to be printed.[3]

If you can consult Dr. Robertson, to whom I am a little known, I shall be satisfied about the propriety of whatever he shall direct.[4] If he thinks that it should be printed, I entreat him to revise it; there may, perhaps, be some negligent lines written, and whatever is amiss, he knows well how to rectify.

Be pleased to let me know, from time to time, how this excellent design goes forward.

Make my compliments to young Mr. Drummond, whom I hope you will live to see such as you desire him.[5]

I have not lately seen Mr. Elphinston, but believe him to be prosperous.[6] I shall be glad to hear the same of you, for I am, Sir, Your affectionate humble servant, SAM. JOHNSON

2. *Ante* To William Drummond, 13 Aug. 1766, n. 9.

3. *Post* To William Drummond, 24 Oct. 1767.

4. William Robertson (1721–93), D.D., Principal of Edinburgh University and author of the *History of Scotland* (1759). SJ had met him through their common friend William Strahan (*Life* III.331).

5. *Ante* To William Drummond, 1 Oct. 1758, n. 4.

6. *Ante* To James Elphinston, 20 Apr. 1749, n. 1.

Hester Thrale

MONDAY 11 MAY 1767

MS: Hyde Collection.

ADDRESS: To Mrs. Thrale in Southwark.

POSTMARKS: OXFORD, 12 MA.

Madam: Oxford, May 11, 1767

I am very sorry to have been out of the way when I could have been of any use. I could not help going, and cannot help staying two days longer, without defeating the purpose for which I went.[1] I will come as soon as I can.[2]

Of the continuance of my dear little Girl's bathing I can determine nothing,[3] having no principles upon which I can reason. Mr. Sutton's art is wholly in his own custody, but in observing his directions you have all the security that his success and his interest can give, and I think you must trust him.[4]

I sincerely wish that the event may be happy. I am, Madam, your most humble servant, SAM. JOHNSON

1. SJ was continuing to help Chambers with his Vinerian lectures (*Ante* To Robert Chambers, 11 Dec. 1766 and n. 1).

2. Instead of returning to London, SJ hurried to Lichfield to attend the dying Catherine Chambers, and did not return until late October (*Post* To William Drummond, 24 Oct. 1767).

3. SJ refers to Hester Maria (1764–1857), the Thrales' eldest child, nicknamed "Queeney" after Queen Esther.

4. Daniel Sutton (*c.* 1735–1819), author of *The Inoculator* (1796), had just inoculated Queeney Thrale against smallpox. According to Horace Walpole, writing the same year, Sutton "inoculates whole counties, and it does not cause the least interruption to their business" (*Walpole's Correspondence*, Yale ed. XXII.562 and n. 18). Sutton reduced the danger of live inoculation by prescribing a "secret remedy" of antimony, mercury, and calomel (Hyde, 1977, p. 26).

Thomas Lawrence[1]

WEDNESDAY 17 JUNE 1767

MS: Houghton Library.

ADDRESS: To Dr. Laurence in Essex Street, London.

POSTMARKS: LITCHFIELD, 19 IV.

Dear Sir: Lichfield, June 17, 1767

I must beg the favour of your advice for an old Friend whom

1. *Ante* To Lewis Paul, 29 Dec. 1755, n. 2.

I am extremely desirous to keep alive whether her distress does or does not admit of cure.

The Case, as the Apothecary could relate it I have enclosed. The Disease is, if I have not read your book without profit, a[2] Dropsy in the Flesh.[3] She is extremely heavy, and between the soreness and cumbrousness of her legs, and the weight of her body, is not able to cross the room. In this state of total inactivity she has remained eight months. She has had a slight fever for about a month, and was not before that, more thirsty than others, nor drinks much even with this new cause of thirst. She has now and then a fit of coughing, but not often, and is sometimes short breathed. Her Urine is thick and in a very small quantity. On[4] one leg she has several small ulcers, and one large ulcer on the other. The sores run little. The large ulcer is about the Shin, and that leg a little below the calf distils thin water through cracks of the Skin. This likewise is in small quantities. She has sometimes a pain in the side, and sometimes fetches involuntary sighs.

If You can pick out the case from these two imperfect accounts, I hope some good may yet be done. I shall wait for your directions with hope that art is not yet vain.[5] I have great solicitude about it. I am, Dear Sir, your most affectionate and most humble servant,

SAM. JOHNSON

2. MS: "a" altered from "an"

3. SJ refers to Lawrence's *Hydrops* (1756), a treatise on dropsy.

4. MS: "On" altered from "One"

5. Catherine Chambers died on 3 Nov. 1767 (*Life* II.481).

Thomas Lawrence

SATURDAY 20 JUNE 1767

PRINTED SOURCE: Chapman I.197.

ADDRESS: To Dr. Laurence in Essex Street, London.

POSTMARK: 22 IV.

Dear Sir: Lichfield, June 20, 1767

I have made what further enquiries I could about Mrs. Chambers, but neither she nor her attendants are very good relators of a Case.[1] I do not know very well what questions to ask, and hope you will in your letter make such enquiries as are necessary to your information.

She is not commonly costive,[2] and when she is, a very gentle purgative relieves her. She has now sat totally inactive for more than eight months, yet her distemper has not gained very fast upon her. When by passing from her chair to her bed and helping to undress herself she is more weary than common she has, like those that are well, a gentle sweat. Her cough has been for some days troublesome but she has no other symptom that seems immediately formidable. She drinks about four pints in the day and night. She is very weak and helpless, but has been in nearly the same state for a long time. I am, Sir, Your most obedient and most humble servant,

SAM. JOHNSON

1. *Ante* To Thomas Lawrence, 17 June 1767.

2. *costive*: "'bound' or confined in the bowels; constipated" (*OED*).

Hester Thrale

MONDAY 20 JULY 1767

MS: Hyde Collection.

Madam: Lichfield, July 20, 1767

Though I have been away so much longer than I purposed or expected,[1] I have found nothing that withdraws my affections from the friends whom[2] I left behind, or which makes me less desirous of reposing in that place which your kindness and Mr. Thrale's allows me to call my *home*.[3]

1. *Ante* To Hester Thrale, 11 May 1767, n. 2.

2. MS: "whom" superimposed upon "which"

3. Streatham Park, Surrey, the Thrales' country house, approximately six miles south of London on Tooting Common.

Miss Lucy is more kind and civil than I expected, and has raised my esteem by many excellencies very noble and resplendent, though a little discoloured by hoary virginity. Every thing else recals to my remembrance years in which I purposed what, I am afraid, I have not done, and promised my self pleasures which I have not found. But complaint can be of no use, and why then should I depress your hopes by my lamentations? I suppose it is the condition of humanity to design what never will be done, and to hope what never will be obtained. But among the vain hopes let me not number the hope which I have, of being long, Dear Madam, Your most obedient and most humble servant, SAM. JOHNSON

George Colman[1]

WEDNESDAY 19 AUGUST 1767

PRINTED SOURCE: *Posthumous Letters Addressed to F. Colman and G. Colman*, 1820, pp. 137–38.

ADDRESS: To George Coleman, Esqr., at Mr. Davies's Bookseller in Russell Street, Covent Garden, London.[2]

Sir, Litchfield, Augt. 19, 1767

The omission of answering your Letter proceeded neither from inattention nor disrespect, but from fearfulness to promise, and unwillingness to refuse.[3] During this contest of my doubts and wishes which ill health made me less able to com-

1. George Colman (1732–94), essayist and playwright. For six years Colman had written a series of successful comedies and farces for Drury Lane, beginning with *Polly Honeycombe* in 1760. He and Garrick collaborated on *The Clandestine Marriage* (1766). But the association with Garrick and Drury Lane ended acrimoniously when Colman purchased Covent Garden, which opened under his management on 14 Sept. 1767.

2. Thomas Davies (?1712–85), actor, bookseller, and author of *Memoirs of David Garrick* (1780), "a man of good understanding and talents" with whom SJ lived "in as easy an intimacy . . . as with any family which he used to visit" (*Life* 1.390–91).

3. Colman had asked SJ to supply a prologue for the opening of Covent Garden in September. When SJ refused, Colman turned to the poet laureate, William Whitehead (*Memoirs of the Colman Family*, ed. R. B. Peake, 1841, 1.203–4).

pose, I intended every week to return to London, and make a letter unnecessary by telling you my purpose.[4] But ill health which has crusted me into inactivity, has by not permitting me to do my business, hitherto precluded my return.[5] I will not deny that I am glad to find my poetical civilities superseded, by a voluntary performance, for I knew not how to set about that which the desire of preserving your regard and of increasing your kindness would have made it very painful to decline. I am, Sir, Your most humble servant,

SAM. JOHNSON

My compliments to dear Mr. Davies.

4. *Ante* To Hester Thrale, 11 May 1767, n. 2.

5. SJ's diary entry for 2 Aug. 1767 records that "I have been disturbed and unsettled for a long time, and have been without resolution to apply to study or to business, being hindered by sudden snatches" (*Works*, Yale ed. I.114).

Hester Thrale

SATURDAY 3 OCTOBER 1767

MS: Hyde Collection.

Dear Madam: Lichfield, Oct. 3, 1767

You are returned, I suppose, from Brighthelmston and this letter will be read at Streatham.

—Sine me, liber, ibis in urbem.[1]

I have felt in this place something like the shackles of destiny. There has not been one day of pleasure, and yet I cannot get away. But when I do come, I perhaps shall not be easily persuaded to pass again to the other side of Styx, to venture myself on the irremeable road.[2] I long to see you and all those of whom the sight is included in seeing you. Nil mihi rescribas,

1. *Parve—nec invideo—sine me, liber, ibis in urbem*: "Little book, you will go without me—and I grudge it not—to the city" (Ovid, *Tristia* I.1, trans. A. L. Wheeler, Loeb ed.).

2. In the *Aeneid* Virgil describes the River Styx as *irremeabilis unda*, "that stream whence none return" (VI.425, trans. H. R. Fairclough, Loeb ed.). Writing to Hester Thrale on 8 July 1784, SJ translates the same phrase as "irremeable stream."

for though I have no right to say, Ipsa veni, I hope that Ipse veniam.[3] Be pleased to make my compliments. I am, Madam, your most humble servant,

SAM. JOHNSON

3. *Hæc tua Penelope lento tibi mittit, Ulixe; / nil mihi rescribas attinet: ipse veni!*: "These words your Penelope sends to you, O Ulysses, slow of return that you are; writing back is pointless: come yourself!" (Ovid, *Heroides* 1.1–2, trans. Grant Showerman, Loeb ed.).

Robert Chambers

c. TUESDAY 6 OCTOBER 1767[1]

MS: Hyde Collection.

ADDRESS: To Robert Chambers, Esqre., in the King's Bench Walks, Temple, London [*Readdressed in an unidentified hand*] at University College, Oxford.

POSTMARKS: LITCHFIELD, 8 OC.

Dear Sir: [Lichfield]

I was much delighted both with the poetry and prose of your affectionate letter.[2] The company of the Ladies will add much to the pleasure of our cohabitation at Oxford,[3] but you must put up a Bed for me in another Chamber.

I have passed this Summer very uneasily. My old melancholy has laid hold upon me to a degree sometimes not easily supportable. God has been pleased to grant me some remission for a few days past. ⟨ ⟩ that visit to be long, but there are some who will expect to see me.

1. The MS is badly mutilated, and lacks a date. 1767 was the only year when SJ visited Lichfield in October and Chambers had rooms at the Inner Temple.

2. The "poetry" consisted of an "Epistle from R. C. to Doctor Samuel Johnson on the Choice of Life." See H. W. Liebert, "'The Choice of Life': A Poem Addressed to Dr. Samuel Johnson," privately printed for The Johnsonians, 1969. "The probable impetus for these verses sprang from the recent offer of a political post as attorney-general of Jamaica, worth £9,000 a year" (Sir Robert Chambers, *A Course of Lectures on the English Law*, ed. T. M. Curley, 1986, p. 23). Chambers declined the offer.

3. It is likely that SJ refers to Chambers's mother Anne (*c.* 1713–82) and his only sister Hannah (1742–68) (information supplied by Professor T. M. Curley).

I do not design that it shall be longer than may consist with our necessary operations.[4] Let me therefore know immediately how soon it will be necessary for us to be together. If I cannot immediately go with you to Oxford, you must be content to stay a little while in London.[5]

The great enquiry which you make I am not[6] qualified to satisfy at present,[7] but we will endeavour to discuss it at leisure, and much ⟨ ⟩

4. *Ante* To Robert Chambers, 11 Dec. 1766, n. 1.

5. SJ arrived in Oxford on 17 Oct. and stayed for several days (*Post* To William Drummond, 24 Oct. 1767; *Post* To Edmund Hector, 3 Nov. 1767).

6. MS: "not not"

7. See above, n. 2.

Bennet Langton

SATURDAY 10 OCTOBER 1767

MS: Hyde Collection.

ADDRESS: To Bennet Langton, Esq., at Mr. Rothwel's, Perfumer in New Bond Street, London.

POSTMARK: 12 OC.

Dear Sir: Lichfield, Oct. 10, 1767

That you have been all summer in London is one more reason for which I regret my long stay in the country. I hope that you [do] not leave the town before my return. We have here only the chance of vacancies in the passing Carriages, and I have bespoken one that may if it happens, bring me to town on the fourteenth of this month, but this is not certain.[1]

It will be a favour if you communicate this to Mrs. Williams. I long to see all my Friends. I am, Dear Sir, your most humble servant,

SAM. JOHNSON

1. SJ did not leave Lichfield until 17 Oct. His return to London was further delayed by a visit with Robert Chambers in Oxford (*Post* To William Drummond, 24 Oct. 1767; *Post* To Edmund Hector, 3 Nov. 1767).

Hester Thrale

SATURDAY 10 OCTOBER 1767

MS: Johnson House, London.
ADDRESS: To Mrs. Thrale.

Madam: Lichfield, Oct. 10, 1767

I hope soon to return from exile, for I have this evening bespoke a place in the first vehicle that shall have a vacancy. We have no regular Carriage from this place. I shall see Streatham with great delight, but am afraid that I must for a time visit Oxford, but of this I am not certain.[1] Few things can please me more than [2] that Mr. Thrale and You desire the return of, Madam, Your most obliged servant,

SAM. JOHNSON

1. *Ante* To Bennet Langton, 10 Oct. 1767, n. 1.
2. MS: "than" altered from "that"

William Drummond

SATURDAY 24 OCTOBER 1767

PRINTED SOURCE: JB's *Life*, 1791, I.289.

Sir: London, Johnson's-court, Fleet-street, Oct. 24, 1767

I returned this week from the country, after an absence of near six months, and found your letter with many others, which I should have answered sooner, if I had sooner seen them.

Dr. Robertson's opinion was surely right. Men should not be told of the faults which they have mended.[1] I am glad the old language is taught, and honour the translator as a man whom God has distinguished by the high office of propagating his word.

I must take the liberty of engaging you in an office of char-

1. *Ante* To William Drummond, 21 Apr. 1767.

ity. Mrs. Heely,[2] the wife of Mr. Heely,[3] who had lately some office in your theatre, is my near relation, and now in great distress. They wrote me word of their situation some time ago, to which I returned them an answer which raised hopes of more than it is proper for me to give them. Their representation of their affairs I have discovered to be such as cannot be trusted; and at this distance, though their case requires haste, I know not how to act. She, or her daughters, may be heard of at Canongate Head.[4] I must beg, Sir, that you will enquire after them, and let me know what is to be done. I am willing to go to ten pounds, and will transmit you such a sum, if upon examination you find it likely to be of use. If they are in immediate want, advance them what you think proper. What I could do, I would do for the women, having no great reason to pay much regard to Heely himself.

I believe you may receive some intelligence from Mrs. Baker, of the theatre, whose letter I received at the same time with yours; and to whom, if you see her, you will make my excuse for the seeming neglect of answering her.[5]

Whatever you advance within ten pounds shall be immediately returned to you, or paid as you shall order. I trust wholly to your judgement. I am, Sir, &c.

SAM. JOHNSON

2. Elizabeth Ford Heeley (1712–68), SJ's first cousin. *Post* To Lucy Porter, 7 June 1768.

3. Humphrey Heeley (1714–?97), originally a Warwickshire ironmonger, whose "losses, and some indiscretions on his part, had driven him to Scotland" (Hawkins, p. 600; *Reades*, pp. 157–58; *Johns. Glean.* XI.214).

4. The westernmost section of Canongate (Edinburgh Old Town), which stretched from the Nether Bow Port to Holyrood.

5. Eliza Clendon Baker (d. 1778), widow of David Erskine Baker (1730–67), author of a *Companion to the Play House* (1764). Baker and his wife had "a most violent and infatuated turn for dramatic performance," which caused them to associate with "strolling companies, and provincial Theatres" (*Lit. Anec.* v.277).

Edmund Hector

TUESDAY 3 NOVEMBER 1767

MS: Houghton Library.

Johnson's Court,
Dear Sir: Fleetstreet, Nov. 3, 1767

Though on Oct. 17 I passed through Birmingham yet having not left Lichfield early, and thinking it fit to reach Oxford that night, I stopped only to change the Chaise, and could not without more delay call upon you to thank you for the Teaboard,[1] which is commended by those that have considered such things more than myself, and which I shall always value as the present of an old Friend whom I love with great affection.

I wished much that we had been permitted to pass a short time together, a few serious and a few jocund hours would have brought back a little of our former lives. Surely we shall meet some time again.[2]

Harry Jackson visited me several times.[3] He seems to be in great indigence. I should think that in a place like Birmingham rich and busy, some station might be found for him in which he might be out of want.

Be pleased to make my most respectful compliments to Mrs. Hector,[4] and tell her that I freely forgive you your absence, because you were detained by attendance upon her, and hope that the necessity of such attendance is now removed by her recovery. I am, Dear sir, your most affectionate, humble Servant,

SAM. JOHNSON

1. *teaboard*: "a tea-tray, esp. a wooden one" (*OED*).

2. *Post* To Hester Thrale, Early July 1770.

3. Harry Jackson (d. 1777), a former schoolmate of SJ, "whom he treated with much kindness, though he seemed to be a low man, dull and untaught. . . . He had tried to be a cutler at Birmingham, but had not succeeded; and now he lived poorly at home [Lichfield], and had some scheme of dressing leather in a better manner than common" (*Life* II.463; *Post* To JB, 1 Sept. 1777).

4. Mary Hector, daughter of Joseph Gibbons of Birmingham and Edmund Hector's second wife; they were married in 1742 (*Reades*, p. 151).

Elizabeth Aston[1]

TUESDAY 17 NOVEMBER 1767

MS: Hyde Collection.

Madam: Nov. 17, 1767

If you imputed to disrespect or inattention that I took no leave when I left Lichfield, you will do me great injustice. I know you too well not to value your friendship.

When I came to Oxford I enquired after the product of our Walnut tree, but it had like others born this year but very few nuts, and for those few I came too late. The tree, as I told you, Madam, we cannot find to be more than thirty years old, and upon measuring it, I found it, at about one foot from the ground, seven feet in circumference, and at the height of about seven feet the circumference is five feet and an half. It would have been, I believe, still bigger, but that it has been topped. The nuts are small, such as they call single nuts; whether this nut is of quicker growth than better, I have not yet enquired. Such as they are, I hope to send them next year.

You know, dear Madam, the liberty that I took of hinting that I did not think your present mode of life very pregnant with happiness.[2] Reflection has not changed my opinion.[3] Solitude excludes pleasure, and does not always secure peace. Some Communication of sentiments is commonly necessary, to give vent to the imagination, and discharge the mind of its own flatulencies.[4]

Some Lady surely might be found in whose conversation you might delight, and in whose fidelity you might repose. *The*

1. Elizabeth Aston (1708–85), third daughter of Sir Thomas Aston, third Bt., of Aston Hall, Cheshire, and the sister-in-law of SJ's friends Henry Hervey and Gilbert Walmesley (*Johns. Glean.* v.249). SJ had known her since *c.* 1736 (Clifford, 1955, p. 162).

2. MS: "i" superimposed upon "y"

3. Both of Elizabeth Aston's parents were dead, and she was the only one of eight sisters not to have married. Aston had built herself a house (Stowe Hill, near Lichfield) *c.* 1754, where she lived alone.

4. "Happiness is not found in self-contemplation; it is perceived only when it is reflected from another" (*Idler* No. 41, *Works*, Yale ed. II.130). Cf. *Rasselas*, chap. 21 ("The Happiness of Solitude. The Hermit's History").

world, says Locke, *has people of all sorts*.[5] You will forgive me this obtrusion of my opinion. I am sure, I wish you well.

Poor Kitty has done what we have all to do,[6] and Lucy has the world to begin anew. I hope she will find some way to more content than I left her possessing.

Be pleased to make my compliments to Mrs. Hinkley,[7] and Miss Turton.[8] I am, Madam, your most obliged and most humble servant,

SAM. JOHNSON

5. SJ, who quotes this maxim at the beginning of *Rambler* No. 160, may be echoing the first paragraph of Locke's *Some Thoughts Concerning Education* (*Works*, Yale ed. v.85 n. 1).

6. *Ante* To Thomas Lawrence, 17 June 1767, n. 5.

7. Presumably Blanche Pyott Hinckley (d. 1772), of Lichfield Close, the widow of Thomas Hinckley (*Johns. Glean.* IV.178, VII.155).

8. Catherine Turton (d. 1777), the daughter of John Turton of Alrewas (*Johns. Glean.* v.265).

Hester Thrale

MONDAY 29 FEBRUARY 1768

MS: Hyde Collection.

ADDRESS: To Mrs. Thrale.

Madam: New Inn Hall,[1] Febr. 29, 1768

Though I do not perceive that there is any need of help, I shall yet write another advertisement, lest you might suspect that my complaisance had more of idleness than sincerity.[2] I am, Madam, your most obliged and most humble servant,

SAM. JOHNSON

1. SJ was staying with Robert Chambers (Principal of New Inn Hall, Oxford) and helping him with the second series of Vinerian lectures. Originally a group of medieval buildings near St. Peter's in the Bailey, New Inn Hall was occupied in the sixteenth and seventeenth centuries by students of canon and civil law. "But in the 18th century the only part of the buildings remaining was a house for the principal, who, in the absence of any students, had no duties either of residence or of instruction" (H. W. Liebert, "'The Choice of Life': A Poem Addressed to Dr. Samuel Johnson," privately printed for The Johnsonians, 1969, p. 3).

2. In Nov. 1765 SJ had helped Henry Thrale compose an appeal to the electors of Southwark (Clifford, 1952, pp. 59–60). In Feb. 1768 Thrale was again campaigning for Parliament; on the reverse of this letter appears, in SJ's hand, "an

election address which was printed in the London papers of Mar. 3, 1768, signed by Thrale" (Clifford, 1952, p. 72 n. 1). In "a hotly contested election," Thrale was returned top of the poll on 23 Mar. (Namier and Brooke III.528).

Richard Penneck[1]

THURSDAY 3 MARCH 1768

MS: Hyde Collection.

ADDRESS: To the Reverend Mr. Pennick at the Museum.

ENDORSEMENT: Dr. Saml. Johnson—si cetera nescis quaere.

Sir: New Inn Hall, Oxford, March 3, 1768

I am flattered by others, with an honour with which I dare not presume to flatter my self, that of having gained so much of your kindness or regard, as that my recommendation of a Candidate for Southwark, may have some influence in determining your vote at the approaching election.

As a Man is willing to believe well of himself I now indulge my Vanity by soliciting your Vote and Interest for Mr. Thrale, whose encomium I shall make very compendiously by telling you, that You would certainly vote for him if you knew him.

I ought to have waited on You with this request, even though my right to make it, had been greater. But as the Election approaches, and I know not how long I may be detained here,[2] I hope you will not impute this unceremonious treatment, to any want of respect in, Sir, Your most obedient and most humble Servant, SAM. JOHNSON

1. The Rev. Richard Penneck (*c.* 1728–1803), F.R.S., Rector of St. John's, Southwark, and Keeper of the Reading Room at the British Museum (*Alum. Cant.* I.iii.341).

2. SJ stayed at Oxford until 30 Apr. (*Post* To Hester Thrale, 28 Apr. 1768).

Hester Thrale

THURSDAY 3 MARCH 1768

MS: Houghton Library.

Dear Madam: March 3, 1768

I thought Mr. Wesley[1] had been secured, since what I have done is ineffectual, I doubt the power of my solicitation, but to leave nothing undone, I have written to him.

Mr. Pennick I have seen, but with so little approach to intimacy that I could not have recollected, yet to him I have enclosed a letter which after this information you may use as you think is best.[2] I suppose it can do no harm.

Do You think there is any danger that you are thus anxious for a single vote?[3] Pray let me know as often as you can find a little time, for I love to see a Letter.

Be pleased to make my Compliments to Mr. Thrale, and Mrs. Salusbury,[4] and Miss Hetty,[5] and every Body. How does the poor little Maid?[6] I am, Madam, your most obliged and most humble servant,

SAM. JOHNSON

1. "Some Election Voter, I forget who" (Piozzi 1.6). It is highly unlikely that SJ refers to John Wesley the evangelist, since there is no evidence that Wesley owned property in Southwark or that he was an elector for the Borough (information supplied by Dr. Frank Baker, *The Bicentennial Edition of The Works of John Wesley*).

2. *Ante* To Richard Penneck, 3 Mar. 1768 and n. 1.

3. *Ante* To Hester Thrale, 29 Feb. 1768, n. 2.

4. *Ante* To Hester Maria Salusbury, 14 Feb. 1767, n. 1.

5. *Ante* To Hester Thrale, 11 May 1767, n. 3.

6. *Post* To Hester Thrale, 14 Mar. 1768.

Hester Thrale

MONDAY 14 MARCH 1768

MS: Hyde Collection.

Madam: March 14,[1] 1768

My last letter came a day after its time by being carried too late to the post. This I mention that you may not suspect me of negligence. I wrote at the same time to Mr. W—— in more

1. MS: "14" altered from "13"

forcible terms than perhaps he thinks I had a right to.[2] He has not answered me. He and his Wife are on such terms that I know not whether his inclination can be inferred from hers.

If I can be of any use I will come directly to London, but if Mr. Thrale thinks himself certain, I have no doubt.[3] That they all express the same certainty has very little effect on those who know how many Men are confident without certainty, and positive without confidence. We have not any reason to suspect Mr. Thrale of deceiving us or himself.

I hope all our friends at Streatham are well, and am glad to hope that the poor Maid will recover. When the mind is drawn toward a dying bed, how small a thing is an Election? But on Death we cannot be always thinking and, I suppose we need not.[4] The thought is very dreadful.

This little Dog does nothing, but I hope he will mend, he is now reading Jack the Giant killer.[5] Perhaps so noble a Narrative may rouse in him the Soul of enterprise. I am, Madam, your most obedient and most humble servant,

SAM. JOHNSON

2. *Ante* To Hester Thrale, 3 Mar. 1768, n. 1.

3. *Ante* To Hester Thrale, 29 Feb. 1768, n. 2.

4. "If one was to think constantly of death, the business of life would stand still" (*Life* v.316).

5. The earliest eighteenth-century version on record appeared in chapbook form (1711). SJ recommended *Jack the Giantkiller* and other such tales of "wonder" as the most suitable reading for children (*Life* iv.8 n. 3).

Thomas Apperley[1]

THURSDAY 17 MARCH 1768

MS: Oriel College, Oxford.

ADDRESS: To —— Apperley, Esq., at Sir. W. W. Wynne's, Bart.,[2] in Grosvenor Square, London.

POSTMARK: ⟨18⟩ MA, [Undeciphered].

1. Thomas Apperley (1730–?1816) of Leominster, Herefordshire, matriculated at Oriel College, Oxford, on 7 June 1766 (*Alum. Oxon.* II.i.27). *Ante* To Thomas Percy, 4 Oct. 1760, n. 3.

2. Sir Watkin Williams Wynn (1748–89), fourth Bt., of Wynnstay, Denbigh-

Sir: Oxford, March 17, 1768

I do not think that you can live any where without gaining influence, and therefore believing[3] that you cannot be without it in Oriel College, I take the liberty of entreating you to employ it at the approaching election of a fellow, in favour of Mr. Crofts a Gentleman of great merit both literary and social, and one to whom some such benefaction is necessary for the prosecution of his Studies.[4] This address to you I make merely from zeal to serve him, without any solicitation, and as he is a Man whom I have a desire to forward, You will, by doing what you can for him, and doing it speedily, bestow a very great favour upon, Sir, Your most obedient and most humble Servant,

SAM. JOHNSON

---

shire, had entered Oriel College in 1766. He went on to become M.P. for Shropshire (1772–74) and for Denbighshire (1774–89) (Namier and Brooke III.671–72).

3. MS: "believing" altered from "believe"

4. George Croft (1747–1809), D.D. (1780), had taken his B.A. from University College, Oxford, on 16 Feb. Croft was not elected to the Oriel fellowship; however, on 6 Dec. he was appointed master of Beverley Grammar School. In 1779 he was elected fellow of University College. SJ had described University as "almost filled with my friends" (*Ante* To William Strahan, 24 Oct. 1764); Croft was clearly one of that number.

Hester Thrale

FRIDAY 18 MARCH 1768

MS: Hyde Collection.

Madam: [Oxford] March 18, 1768

No part of Mr. Thrale's troubles would have been troublesome to me, if any endeavours of mine could have made them less.[1] But I know not that I could have done more for him, than in your approaching danger I can do for you.[2] I wish you bothe

1. *Ante* To Hester Thrale, 29 Feb. 1768, n. 2.

2. Anna Maria (1768–70), the Thrales' fourth child, was born at Streatham Park on 1 Apr. (Hyde, 1977, p. xii).

well, and have little doubt of seeing you both emerge from your difficulties.

When the Election is decided I entreat to be immediately informed; and when You retreat to Streatham if I shall not have returned to town, I hope that Mrs. Salusbury will favour me now and then with an account of you when you can less conveniently give it of yourself.[3] To be able to do nothing in the exigence of a Friend is an uneasy state, but in the most pressing exigenc[i]es it is the natural state of Humanity, and in all has been commonly that of, Dear Madam, Your most obedient and most humble Servant,

SAM. JOHNSON

3. Cf. *Ante* To Hester Maria Salusbury, 14 Feb. 1767.

James Boswell

WEDNESDAY 23 MARCH 1768

PRINTED SOURCE: JB's *Life*, 1791, I.303.

My dear Boswell, Oxford, March 23, 1768

I have omitted a long time to write to you, without knowing very well why.[1] I could now tell why I should not write, for who would write to men who publish the letters of their friends without their leave?[2] Yet I write to you in spite of my caution, to tell you that I shall be glad to see you, and that I wish you would empty your head of Corsica, which I think has filled it rather too long.[3] But, at all events, I shall be glad, very glad to see you.[4] I am, Sir, Yours affectionately,

SAM. JOHNSON

1. SJ had last written to JB on 21 Aug. 1766.

2. In his *Account of Corsica*, published on 18 Feb. 1768, JB had included the second and third paragraphs of SJ's letter of 14 Jan. 1766.

3. For JB's impassioned reply ("My noble-minded friend, do you not feel for an oppressed nation bravely struggling to be free?"), see *Life* II.58–59.

4. JB spent three days with SJ at Oxford, 26–28 Mar. 1768 (*Earlier Years*, p. 548).

Hester Thrale

THURSDAY 24 MARCH 1768

MS: Hyde Collection.

ADDRESS: To Mrs. Thrale in Southwark.

POSTMARKS: OXFORD, 26 MR.

Dear Madam: Oxford, March 24, 1768

You serve me very sorrily. You may write every day to this place, and yet I do not know what is the event of the Southwark Election, though I am sure, you ought to believe that I am very far from indifference about it.[1] Do; Let me know as soon as you can.

Our Election was yesterday. Every possible influence of hope and fear was, I believe, enforced on this occasion, the slaves of power, and the solicitors of favour were driven hither from the remotest corners of the Kingdom, but Iudex honestum praetulit utili.[2] The Virtue of Oxford has once more prevailed.

The death of Sir Walter Bagot a little before the Election left them no great time to deliberate,[3] and they therefore joined to Sir Roger Newdigate their old Representative,[4] one Mr. Page an Oxfordshire Gentleman of no name, no great interest, nor perhaps any other merit, than that of being on the right side.[5] Yet when [the] poll was numbered, it produced

1. *Ante* To Hester Thrale, 29 Feb. 1768 and n. 2.

2. *sed quotiens bonus atque fidus / iudex honestum prætulit utili*: "but so oft as, a judge righteous and true, thou preferrest honour to expediency" (Horace, *Odes* IV.ix.40–41, trans. C. E. Bennett, Loeb ed.).

3. Sir Walter Wagstaffe Bagot (1702–68), fifth Bt., of Blithfield, Staffordshire, M.P. for Oxford University from 16 Dec. 1762 until his death on 20 Jan. 1768 (Namier and Brooke II.37–38).

4. Sir Roger Newdigate (1719–1806), fifth Bt., of Arbury, Warwickshire, and Harefield, Middlesex, served as M.P. for Oxford University from 31 Jan. 1751 until his resignation in 1780. "He was vigilant in protecting the interests of his constituents; his political and religious attitude commended him to most of them; and his position was greatly strengthened by the benefactions he had made to the University (he was the founder of the Newdigate prize)" (Namier and Brooke III.198).

5. Francis Page (?1726–1803), of Middle Aston, Oxfordshire, remained M.P. for Oxford University until 1801 (Namier and Brooke III.242).

for Sir R. Newdigate		352
	Mr. Page	296
	Mr. Jenkinson[6]	198
	Dr. Hay[7]	62

Of this I am sure you must be glad, for without enquiring into the opinions or conduct of any party, it must be for ever pleasing to see men adhering to their principles against their interest, especially[8] when you consider that these Voters are poor, and never can be much less poor but by the favour of those whom they are now opposing.[9] I am, Madam, Your most obliged and most humble Servant,

SAM. JOHNSON

6. *Ante* To Charles Jenkinson, 26 Oct. 1765, n. 1.

7. *Ante* To George Hay, 9 Nov. 1759, n. 1. Hay, a graduate of St. John's College, "had kept up his connexion with Oxford University. Influential at St. John's, he had been talking of standing for the University since 1759; and encouraged by Thomas Frey, president of St. John's, an eccentric supporter of Wilkes and liberty, did so in 1768; but he found himself at the bottom of the poll" (Namier and Brooke II.600).

8. MS: "e" superimposed upon "a"

9. Both Charles Jenkinson and George Hay were supporters, in the main, of the Government's policies, and their careers prospered accordingly. Newdigate and Page, by contrast, were devoted primarily to Church and University. Newdigate in particular was "suspicious of a court which seemed to him alien and which pursued a foreign policy he regarded as un-English" (Namier and Brooke III.196).

Lucy Porter

MONDAY 18 APRIL 1768

MS: Pembroke College, Oxford. A copy in the hand of Thomas Harwood, collated with the text in JB's *Life*, 1804, II.59.

ADDRESS: To Mrs. Lucy Porter, in Lichfield.

My Dear Dear Love, Oxford, Apr. 18, 1768

You have had a very great loss.[1] To lose an old friend, is to be

1. Lucy Porter's aunt, Mrs. John Hunter, had just died (*Reades*, p. 245). *Ante* To Lucy Porter, 10 May 1759, n. 1.

cut off from a great part of the little pleasure that this life allows. But such is the condition of our nature, that as we live on we must see those whom we love drop successively, and find our circle of relation grow less and less, till we are almost unconnected with the world; and then it must soon be our turn to drop into the grave. There is always this consolation, that we have one Protector who can never be lost but by our own fault, and every new experience of the uncertainty of all other comforts should determine us to fix our hearts where true joys are to be found.[2] All union with the inhabitants of earth must in time be broken; and all the hopes that terminate here, must on one part or other end in disappointment.

I am glad that Mrs. Adey[3] and Mrs. Cobb[4] do not leave you alone. Pay my respects to them, and the Sewards,[5] and all my friends. When Mr. Porter comes, he will direct you.[6] Let me know of his arrival, and I will write to him.

When I go back to London, I will take care of your reading glass.[7] Whenever I can do any thing for you, remember, my dear darling, that one of my greatest pleasures is to please you.

The punctuality of your correspondence I consider as a proof of great regard. When we shall see each other, I know not, but let us often think on each other, and think with tenderness. Do not forget me in your prayers. I have for a long time back been very poorly; but of what use is it to complain?

2. "O Almighty God . . . Grant unto thy people, that they may love the thing which thou commandest, and desire that which thou dost promise; that so . . . our hearts may surely there be fixed, where true joys are to be found" (Collect for the Fourth Sunday after Easter, *Book of Common Prayer*).

3. Felicia Hammond Adey (1712–78) was the widow of Joseph Adey (1704–63), former Town Clerk of Lichfield (*Johns. Glean.* XI.5).

4. Mary Hammond Cobb (1718–93) was Felicia Adey's sister and the second wife of Thomas Cobb (d. 1772), a Lichfield mercer (*Johns. Glean.* XI.95).

5. *Ante* To John Taylor, 10 Aug. 1742, n. 4. Thomas Seward was married to Elizabeth Hunter (1712–80), daughter of SJ's schoolmaster; their one surviving child was Anna (1742–1809), "the Swan of Lichfield."

6. Joseph Porter (*c.* 1724–83), a merchant at Leghorn and Lucy's younger brother (*Reades*, pp. 238–40).

7. *reading glass*: "a large magnifying glass for use in reading" (*OED*). *Post* To Lucy Porter, 7 June 1768.

Write often, for your letters always give great pleasure to, My Dear, your most affectionate, and most humble servant,

SAM. JOHNSON

Hester Thrale

TUESDAY 19 APRIL 1768

MS: Houghton Library.

Madam: Oxford, Apr. 19, 1768

If I should begin with telling you what is very true that I have of late been very much disordered, you might perhaps think that in the next line I should [1] impute this disorder to my distance from you, but I am not yet well enough to contrive such stratagems of compliment. I have been really very bad, and am glad that I was not at Streatham, where I should have been troublesome to you, and You could have given no [2] help to me.[3]

I am not however without hopes of being better, and therefore hear with great pleasure of the welfare of those from [whom] I always expect to receive pleasure when I am capable of receiving it, and think myself much favoured that You made so much haste to tell me of your recovery.

I design to love little Miss Nanny very well, but you must let us have a Bessy some other time.[4] I suppose the Borough bells rung for the young Lady's arrival. I hope she will be happy.[5] I will not welcome her with any words of ill omen. She will cer-

1. MS: "should" altered from "shall" 2. MS: "no" altered from "not"

3. Earlier in the month Hester Thrale had been recovering from the birth of her fourth child, Anna Maria. *Ante* To Hester Thrale, 18 Mar. 1768, n. 2.

4. SJ's "desire to have a Thrale daughter named after his wife was somewhat unreasonable, as the Thrales had never known Mrs. Johnson, and what they might have heard about 'Tetty' from Garrick and others could not have stirred their enthusiasm" (Hyde, 1977, p. 28). The Thrales' next child was named "Lucy Elizabeth," and SJ was the godfather (*Post* To Henry Thrale, 29 June 1769).

5. "She *is* happy, poor Anna-Maria: She died before Two years old" (Piozzi 1.13).

tainly be happy, if she be as she and all friends are wished to be by, Madam, your most obliged and most humble servant,

SAM. JOHNSON

Phipps Weston[1]

FRIDAY 22 APRIL 1768

MS: British Library.

ADDRESS: To the Reverend Mr. Weston in Cleveland Row, St. James's, London.

POSTMARKS: OXFORD, 23 AP.

ENDORSEMENT: Oxford, April 22, 1768.

Dear Sir: New Inn Hall, Apr. 22, 1768

You will not expect that in[2] a few minutes which is all the time allowed me to answer your letter to Mr. Chambers, I should in any degree arrange and digest or perhaps even fully conceive and comprehend a plan like that which your Letter exhibits. It is a plan truly regal in its extent as well as its benevolence.[3] What the Poet says of Caesar that he was *indocilis privata loqui*, may now be applied a second time, and applied without any of the invidious adherences that then polluted the praise.[4]

What I can do in this great undertaking I yet know not, but hope you will not doubt, but that I will do what it is so high an honour to be employed in, to the best of my abilities.

If Mr. Barnard be not gone pay him my compliments, and

1. The Rev. Phipps Weston (*c.* 1738–94), Rector of Witney, Oxfordshire, and Fellow of Magdalen College, Oxford (1763–72). According to the Rev. Richard George Robinson, writing to JB in 1790, Weston was "an intimate friend of Dr. Johnson, by whose recommendation he had been appointed librarian to the king" (Waingrow, p. 320).

2. MS: "I should" del. before "in"

3. SJ refers to the development of the Royal Library and to Frederick Barnard's projected "expedition . . . for the importation of Literature." *Post* To Frederick Barnard, 28 May 1768 and n. 4.

4. *Sic fatur, quamquam plebeio tectus amictu / indocilis privata loqui*: "Thus he spoke; for though the garb he wore was humble, he knew not how to speak the language of a private man" (Lucan, *Pharsalia* v.539, trans. J. D. Duff, Loeb ed.).

if he be, when you write send after him my sincere wishes of all pleasure and prosperity.[5] I have been as Mr. Chambers will tell you, miserably disordered for some time but hope to be better, and whether I am as well as I wish, or not, shall endeavour to be with you in about ten days. I am, Dear Sir, Your most obedient and most humble Servant,

SAM. JOHNSON

5. *Post* To Frederick Barnard, 28 May 1768, n. 1.

Hester Thrale

THURSDAY 28 APRIL 1768

MS: Gerald M. Goldberg.

Madam: Oxford, April the 28th 1768

It is indeed a great alleviation of Sickness to be nursed by a Mother,[1] and it is a comfort in return to have the prospect of being nursed by a daughter, even at that hour when all human attention must be vain. From that social desire of being valuable to each other, which produces kindness and officiousness, it proceeds, and must proceed, that there is some pleasure in being [able] to give pain. To roll the weak eye of helpless anguish and see nothing on any side but cold indifference, will I hope happen to none whom I love or value; it may tend to withdraw the mind from life, but has no tendency to kindle those affections which fit us for a purer and a nobler state.

Yet when any Man finds himself disposed to complain with how little care he is regarded, let him reflect how little he contributes to the happiness of others, and how little for the most part he suffers from their pains. It is perhaps not to be lamented that those Solicitudes are not long nor frequent, which must commonly be vain, nor can we wonder that in a state in[2] which all have so much to feel of their own evils, very few have leisure for those of another. However, it is so or-

1. *Ante* To Hester Maria Salusbury, 14 Feb. 1767, n. 1.
2. MS: "in" repeated as catchword

dered, that few suffer for want of assistance, and that kindness which could not assist, however pleasing, may be spared.

These reflections do not grow out of any discontent at C——s behaviour;[3] he has been neither negligent nor troublesome, nor do I love him less, for having been ill in his house. This is no small degree of praise. I am better, having scarce eaten for seven days. I shall come home on Saturday. I am, Madam, Your most humble Servant,

SAM. JOHNSON

3. SJ had been staying with Robert Chambers since late February and possibly earlier. *Ante* To Hester Thrale, 29 Feb. 1768, n. 1.

Phipps Weston

THURSDAY 28 APRIL 1768

MS: British Library.

POSTMARKS: OXFORD, 29 AP.

Dear Sir: Oxf. April 28, 1768

I am something better, and shall come home on Saturday, but I would not delay so long to express the respectful pleasure with which I read your account of his Majesty's reception of my Service.[1] I cannot derive to my self much praise from that compliance which was enforced by interest⟨,⟩ by vanity,[2] by Duty to my King, by Gratitude to my Bene⟨factor, by⟩ all the motives which have power upon the Good the bad the foolish and the Wise.

That I may be able in any manner to promote so noble, so regal a design, you will easily believe me, earnestly to wish. In the mean time let us have the pleasure of comparing the King under whom we have the happiness to live, with Lewis the fourteenth, taking Lewis in his fairest character, as a patron of Learning. Lewis indeed employed Boileau and Racine to write a life, but that life was his own, his liberality was prompted by

1. *Ante* To Phipps Weston, 22 Apr. 1768.

2. MS: "vani" written above undeciphered deletion

his appetite of flattery.[3] But our King exerts his influence, and his bounty for the general illumination and improvement of mankind, his design is to mend the world by imitable examples, and to excite diligence by attainable praise. He leaves his own Character to vindicate itself, and those honours which he scorns to buy, will be paid by voluntary veneration. I am, Sir, Your most obedient and most humble servant,

SAM. JOHNSON

3. Jean Racine (1639–99) and Nicolas Boileau-Despréaux (1639–1711) were appointed Historiographers Royal in 1677. SJ would have known of their projected life of Louis XIV from Louis Racine's memoir of his father: "Les deux poètes, résolus de ne plus l'être, ne songèrent qu'à devenir historiens; et pour s'en rendre capables, ils passèrent d'abord beaucoup de temps à se mettre au fait et de L'Histoire générale de France, et de L'Histoire particulière du règne qu'ils avoient à écrire (*Oeuvres de Louis Racine*, 1808, v.92). No such "histoire particulière" has been recovered: most of Racine's historical manuscripts were destroyed by fire in 1726.

Phipps Weston

TUESDAY 3 MAY 1768

MS: Hyde Collection.

ADDRESS: To the Reverend Mr. Weston.

ENDORSEMENT: London, May 3, 1768.

Sir: May 3, 1768

As my disorder is principally upon my Spirits I am very suddenly better and worse, I therefore go out where I can be quite at liberty, for I know that diversity of objects is reckoned to do much towards the cure in cases like mine. If you will let me know when I may expect the favour that you mentioned yesterday, I will be at home, and we will shut out the rest of the world. My compliments to Mr. Barnard. I am, Sir, your most humble Servant,

SAM. JOHNSON

Hester Thrale

MONDAY 23 MAY 1768

MS: Hyde Collection.

Madam: May 23, 1768

Though I purpose to come home to morrow I would not omit even so long to tell you how much I think myself favoured by your notice.[1] Every Man is desirous to keep those Friends whom he is [2] proud to have gained, and I count the friendship of your house among the felicities of life.

I thank God that I am better,[3] and am at least within hope of being as well as you have ever known me. Let me have your prayers. I am, Madam, your most humble servant,

SAM. JOHNSON

1. By "home" SJ means Streatham Park (*Ante* To Hester Thrale, 20 July 1767). He had returned to London in time to visit JB on 2 May (*Earlier Years*, p. 549).

2. MS: "h" partially erased before "is"

3. *Ante* To Hester Thrale, 19 Apr. 1768.

Frederick Barnard[1]

SATURDAY 28 MAY 1768

MS: British Library.[2]

Sir, May 28, 1768

It is natural for a Scholar to interest himself in an expedition undertaken like yours for the importation of Literature, and

1. Frederick Augusta Barnard (1743–1830), F.S.A. (1789), F.R.S. (1790), K.C.H. (1828), librarian to George III and George IV (*Walpole's Correspondence*, Yale ed. XXX.319 n. 7). Though "presumed to be a natural son of Frederick Prince of Wales" (*GM* 1830, p. 571), Barnard was in fact "the son of John Barnard, a page of the backstairs, who was the son of another John Barnard, who had been page to Frederick Prince of Wales. . . . [He] was named after the Prince and Princess of Wales, who were probably his godparents" (John Brooke, "The Library of King George III," *Yale University Library Gazette* 52, 1977, p. 37 and nn. 3, 4).

2. This letter was first published in 1823, as part of a "Report of the Committee

therefore though, having never travelled myself, I am very little qualified to give advice to a traveller, yet that I may not seem inattentive to a design so worthy of regard, I will try whether the present state of my health will suffer me to lay before you what observation or report have suggested to me, that may direct your enquiries or facilitate your success.

Things of which the mere rarity makes the value, and which are prized at high rate by wantonness rather than by use, are always passing from poorer to richer countries, and therefore though Germany and Italy were principally productive of typographical curiosities, I do not much imagine that they are now to be found there in great abundance. An eagerness for scarce books and early Editions which prevailed among the English about half a century ago, filled our shops with all the Splendour and Nicety of Literature, and when the Harleian Catalogue was published many of the books were bought for the Library of the King of France.[3]

I believe however that by the diligence with which you have enlarged the Library under your care,[4] the present Stock is so nearly exhausted, that till new purchases supply the Booksellers with new Stores, you will not be able to do much more than glean up single books as accident shall produce them, this therefore is the time for visiting the continent.

What addition you can hope to make by ransacking other

---

on Papers Relating to the Royal Library which his Majesty has been Graciously pleased to Present to the British Nation" (*GM* 1823, pp. 347–50). In his preface to the *Bibliothecæ Regiæ Catalogus*, 1820–29, Barnard quotes SJ's "very friendly letter" in full, calling it "a necessary document, in an account of the progressive formation of the Royal Library" (I.ii, iii).

3. *Ante* To Theophilus Levett, 1 Dec. 1743, n. 2. The Bibliothèque Nationale contains no record of Louis XV's purchases from the Harleian Catalogue (information supplied by Mme. Nicole Masson, B.N.).

4. Barnard's name first appears in the Privy Purse accounts for June 1765. By 1768 he had been awarded a salary of £200 per annum and an allowance of £2,000. Barnard traveled abroad to add to a library that began with the purchase in 1762 of two major collections: George Thomason's materials relating to the Civil War, and the manuscripts assembled by Joseph Smith (1682–1770), British Consul at Venice. By 1769 the library had grown to almost ten thousand volumes (Brooke, "Library," p. 37).

countries we will now consider. English Literature you will not seek in any place but England. Classical Learning is diffused every where and is not except by accident more copious in one part of the polite world than in another. But every Country has literature of its own which may be best gathered on its native soil.

The studies of the Learned are influenced by forms of Government and modes of Religion, and therefore those books are necessary and common in some places, which where different opinions or different manners prevail are of little use and for that reason rarely to be found.

Thus in Italy you may expect to meet with Canonists[5] and Sch[o]lastick Divines, in Germany with Writers on the feudal Law, and in Holland with Civilians.[6] The Schoolmen[7] and Canonists must not be neglected for they are useful to many purposes, nor too anxiously sought, for their importance among us is much lessened by the Reformation. Of the Canonists at least a few eminent Writers may be sufficient. The schoolmen are of more general value. But the feudal and civil Law I cannot but wish to see complete. The feudal Constitution is the original of the law of property over all the civilised part of Europe, and the civil Law, as it is generally understood to include the law of Nations, may be called with great propriety a regal study.

Of those books which have been often published and diver[si]fied by various modes of impression, a royal Library should have at least the most curious Edition,[8] the most splendid, and the most useful.[9] The most curious Edition is commonly the

5. *canonist*: "a man versed in the ecclesiastical laws; a professour of the canon law" (SJ's *Dictionary*).

6. *civilian*: "one that professes the knowledge of the old Roman Law, and of general equity" (SJ's *Dictionary*).

7. *schoolman*: "a writer of scholastick divinity or philosophy" (SJ's *Dictionary*).

8. *curious*: "elegant; neat; laboured; finished" (SJ's *Dictionary*).

9. The King's library differed from those of earlier, private collectors in that it did not consist chiefly of rare editions. Rather, it was "a library which contained every book which an eighteenth-century scholar could desire. It was a library to be used, not simply to be admired" (Brooke, "Library," p. 41).

first and the most useful may be expected among the last. Thus of Tullys Offices, the Edition of Fust[10] is the most curious,[11] and that of Greevius[12] the most useful. The most splendid the eye will discover.

With the old Printers you are now become well acquainted. If you can find any collection of their productions to be sold you will undoubtedly buy it, but this can scarcely be hoped, and you must catch up single volumes where you can find them. Try every place, things often occur where they are least expected. I was shown a Welch Grammar written in Welch, and printed at Milan I believe before any Grammar of that language had been printed here.[13]

Of purchasing entire libraries I know not whether the inconvenience may not overballance the advantage. Of [a] Library collected with general views one will have many books in common with another. When you have bought two collections you will find that you have bought many books twice over, and many in each which you left at home and therefore did not want, and when you have[14] selected a small number you will have the rest to sell at a great loss,[15] or to transport hither at perhaps a greater. It will generally be more commodious to

10. Johann Fust (d. ?1466), a money broker of Mainz who advanced money to Gutenberg from 1450 to 1455, then operated his own printing business in partnership with Peter Schöffer (*fl.* 1449–1502). Fust and Schöffer published two editions of Cicero's *De officiis*, the first in 1465, the second in 1466. Barnard acquired the 1466 edition for the royal library (*Bibliothecæ Regiæ Catalogus* II.165).

11. Fust and Schöffer, celebrated for the beauty and technical distinction of their books, possessed a "skill in the art of printing which amazes all who examine their work. . . . They overcame difficulties which would prove formidable to a modern compositor" (Edwin Willoughby, *The Library Quarterly* 2, 1932, pp. 302–3).

12. Johann Georg Grævius (1623–1703), German classical scholar and professor at Utrecht, prepared numerous editions of Cicero. Two copies of his *De Officiis* (Amsterdam, 1688) are listed in the *Bibliothecæ Regiæ Catalogus* (II.160, 166).

13. Griffith Roberts, *Dosparth byrr ar y rhann gyntaf i ramadeg cymraeg*, Milan, 1567. The first Welsh grammar printed in London was John David Rhys, *Cambrobrytannicae Cymraecaeve linguae* . . . 1592, although William Salesbury added material on the Welsh and English languages in the various editions of his *Dictionary in Englyshe and Welshe*, London, 1547, 1550, 1567 (E. J. Dobson, *English Pronunciation: 1500–1700*, 1968, I.11).

14. MS: "have have"

15. MS: "loss" del. before "loss"

buy the few that you want at a price somewhat advanced, than to encumber yourself with useless loads.

But Libraries collected for particular studies will be very valuable acquisitions. The collection of an eminent Civilian, Feudist [16] or Mathemati[ci]an, will perhaps have very few Superfluities.

Topography or local History prevail much in many parts of the Continent. I have been told that scarcely a village of [Italy] wants its historian.[17] These books may be generally neglected, but some will deserve attention by the celebrity of the place, the eminence of the authour, or the beauty of the Sculptures.

Sculpture [18] has always been more cultivated among other nations than among us.[19] The old art of cutting on wood which decorated [20] the books of ancient impression, was never carried here to any excellence, and the practice of engraving on copper which succeeded have never been much employed among us in adorning books.[21] The old Books with wooden cuts [22] are to be diligently sought, the designs were often made by great Masters and the prints are such as cannot be made by any artist now living.

It will be of great use to collect in every place maps of the

16. *feudist*: "a writer or authority on Feuds, one versed in feudal law" (*OED*). "The whole system of ancient tenures is gradually passing away; and I wish to have the knowledge of it preserved adequate and complete. For such an institution makes a very important part of the history of mankind" (*Post* To JB, 31 Aug. 1772).

17. "There is scarce a village in Italy but there is a particular history of it" (Giuseppe Baretti, *Italian Library*, 1757, p. 177).

18. SJ's *Dictionary* defines sculpture as "the art of carving wood" and as "the art of engraving on copper"—both senses applicable to SJ's discussion of illustrated books.

19. "England's early contribution to the history of the illustrated book was negligible" (David Bland, *A History of Book Illustration*, 1958, p. 137). Until well into the eighteenth century, English bookmakers imported most of their engravings and illustrators from the Continent (p. 137).

20. MS: "filled" del. before "decorated"

21. In contrast to Continental practice, which involved the extensive use of copper engraving, English bookmakers tended to work in relief, using wood blocks and a simpler printing method (Bland, *History*, pp. 119, 144–47).

22. MS: "cat" del. before "cuts"

adjacent Country, and plans of towns, buildings, and gardens. By this care you will form a more valuable Body of Geography than can otherwise be had.[23] Many Countries have been very exactly surveyed, but it must not be expected that the exactness of actual mensuration will be preserved when the Maps are reduced by a contracted scale, and incorporated into a general System. The King of Sardinia's Italian Dominions are not large, yet the maps made of them in the reign of Victor,[24] fill two Atlantick folios.[25] This part of your design will deserve particular regard, because in this your success will always be proportionate to your diligence.

You are too well acquainted with literary history not to know that many books derive their value from the reputation of the printers. Of the celebrated printers you do not [need] to be informed, and if you did, you might consult Baillet's Jugemens des Sçavans.[26] The productions of Aldus[27] are enumerated in the Bibliotheca Graeca,[28] so that you may know when you have them all, which is always of use as it prevents needless searches.

The great ornaments of a Library furnished for Magnificence as well as use are the first Editions, of which therefore I would not willingly neglect the mention. You know, Sir, that the annals of typography begin with the Codex 1458 but there is great reason to believe that there are latent in obscure cor-

23. "The Collections of Geography and Topography . . . have increased to an extent not hitherto equalled" (Barnard, *Bibliothecæ Regiæ Catalogus* I.vii).

24. Victor Amadeus II (1666–1732), King of Sicily (1713) and of Sardinia (1720).

25. SJ refers to the *Théâtre des États du Duc de Savoie*, 2 vols., 1700. He takes the label "Atlantic folios" from the French "Atlantique," a bibliographical term designating folios of "Atlas" dimensions (*c.* 34″ x 26″) (E. J. Labarre, *Dictionary and Encyclopædia of Paper and Paper Making*, 1952, p. 10). The *OED* attributes the first and only use of "Atlantic" in this sense to SJ.

26. Adrien Baillet (1649–1706), *Jugemens des sçavans sur les principaux ouvrages des auteurs*, 4 vols., 1685–86. The first volume is concerned with printers.

27. Aldo Manuzio (1450?–1515), classical scholar and printer, founded the Aldine Press at Venice *c.* 1490.

28. *Bibliotheca Græca*, 1705–07, the work of Johann Albert Fabricius (1668–1736), German classical scholar.

ners books printed before it.[29] The secular[30] feast in memory of the invention of printing is celebrated in the fortieth year of the century,[31] if this tradition therefore be right the art had in 1458 been already exercised eighteen years. There prevails among typographical antiquaries a vague opinion that the Bible had been printed three times before the edition of 1462[32] which Calmet calls la premiére edition bien averée.[33] One of these editions has been lately discovered in a Convent, and transplanted into the french King's Library.[34] Another copy likewise has been found but I know not whether of the same impression or of another. These discoveries are sufficient to raise hope and instigate enquiry.

One hint more may deserve to be added, though it is not very likely that you will have any opportunity of turning it to profit. It is recorded by those that have with the greatest diligence examined the first essays of typography, and particularly by Naudaeus the Librarian of Cardinal Mazarine, that the stamp or insigne by which Fust marked his editions were

29. The "codex" to which SJ refers is the Mainz Psalter, printed by Fust and Schöffer in 1457. It is the first successful attempt at color printing, as well as the first printed book to contain a colophon (Geoffrey Glaister, *Glossary of the Book*, 1960, p. 190). Although SJ's date is incorrect, eighteenth-century bibliographers had correctly dated the Psalter.

30. MS: "secular" written above "secular" del.

31. In 1740 "the third hundred year's feast of the noble art and mystery of printing, discovered in 1440, was celebrated in Strasburg" (*GM* 1740, p. 95).

32. These three Bibles are the 42-line Mazarin Bible printed by Gutenberg, completed *c.* 1455; the 36-line Bible, whose printer is unknown, completed before 1461; and the 49-line Latin Bible printed by Johann Mentelin (*fl.* 1458–78), completed in 1460 (Glaister, *Glossary*, pp. 39, 320; *Life* II.524).

33. Augustin Calmet (1672–1757), *Dictionnaire historique ... de la Bible*, 2 vols., 1722, I.xvii.

34. Probably the 42-line Bible (*Life* II.524). See above, n. 32. It was acquired for the French Royal Library in 1739 by a curate of Annecy, "who literally dragged it out of the dust of a library belonging to the 'Cordeliers de Moutiers [Franciscans], the capital of Tarentaise'" (T. F. Dibdin, "On the Vulgate Bible of 1450–1455," *The Classical Journal* 4, 1811, p. 475). SJ saw this Bible when he visited Paris in Oct. 1775: "The Bible, supposed to be older than that of Mentz, in [14]62: it has no date; it is supposed to have been printed with wooden types.—I am in doubt; the print is large and fair, in two folios" (*Life* II.397).

Horns,[35] and I have read an advertisement of a Book offered to Sale in Holland that was so stamped. For these horns I have looked to no purpose in the books printed by Fust which are commonly known, yet since it cannot be doubted but that there are yet in the world books so marked I believe you may consider them, if ever you should find them, as printed before 1458, for those printed after that year I think, always want the stamp.

In the purchase of old books let me recommend to you to examine with great caution whether they are perfect. In the first editions the loss of a leaf is not easily observed. You remember how near we both were to purchasing a mutilated Missal at a high price.

All this perhaps you know already and therefore my Letter may be of no use. I am however desirous to show you that I wish prosperity to your undertaking.

One advice more I will give of more importance than all the rest, of[36] which I therefore hope you have still less need.[37] You are going into a part of the world divided, as it is said, between bigotry and atheism.[38] Such representations are always hyperbolical, but there is certainly enough of both to alarm any mind solicitous for piety and truth. Let not the contempt of Superstit[i]on precipitate you into infidelity,[39] nor the horrour of infidelity ensnare you in superstition.

I sincerely wish you successful and happy, for I am, Sir, Your affectionate, humble servant,

SAM. JOHNSON

35. "The Mark . . . consists of two shields hanging from a branch [which somewhat resembles antlers], each shield decorated with heraldic or pseudo-heraldic designs; but although conjectures have been advanced to explain them, the meaning of these emblems is still unknown" (Edwin Willoughby, "The Cover Design," *The Library Quarterly* 2, 1932, pp. 302–3).

36. MS: "and" del. before "of"

37. In his published copy of this letter Barnard calls attention to "the valuable admonition, so forcibly expressed, with which it concludes" (*Bibliothecæ Regiæ Catalogus* I.iii).

38. "Between July 1768 and Dec. 1771, Barnard visited Paris, Vienna, Rome, Strasbourg, Dresden, Berlin, Amsterdam, Brussels, and Spa" (Brooke, "Library," p. 38).

39. MS: undeciphered deletion before "infidelity"

Francis Barber

SATURDAY 28 MAY 1768

MS: Hyde Collection.

ADDRESS: To Mr. Francis Barber at Mrs. Clap's in Bishop Stortford, Hertfordshire.[1]

POSTMARK: 28 MA.

Dear Francis: May 28, 1768

I have been very much out of order. I am glad to hear that you are well, and design to come soon to see you. I would have you stay at Mrs. Clapp's for the present, till I can determine what we shall do.[2] Be a good Boy.

My compliments to Mrs. Clap and to Mr. Fowler.[3] I am, yours affectionately,

SAM. JOHNSON

1. Barber was attending the Grammar School of Bishop Stortford, whose headmaster from 1764 to 1767 had been the Rev. Joseph Clapp (*c.* 1725–67). He continued to board with Clapp's widow Mary (d. 1781), who lived at Windhill House, on High Street (*Johns. Glean.* II.16–19).

2. Barber remained at the Grammar School, boarding with Mrs. Clapp, until *c.* 1772 (*Johns. Glean.* II.21–22).

3. The Rev. Robert Fowler, who succeeded Joseph Clapp as headmaster on 1 Dec. 1767. Fowler resigned in 1769 (*Johns. Glean.* II.18–19).

Lucy Porter

TUESDAY 7 JUNE 1768

MS: Hyde Collection.

ENDORSEMENT: 1768.

My Dearest, London, June 7, 1768

You would have heard from me many times in these last weeks but that I have been very ill. I am now getting better. Do not forget to pray for me.

I hope you have had the Books and the Reading glass.[1] I

1. *Ante* To Lucy Porter, 18 Apr. 1768.

sent you the nicest glass that I could get, and hope you will find it fit, and think it pretty. Whatever I can do for you, I do with great willingness, and have much pleasure in thinking that I am remembred by you.

Mr. Heely whom you may perhaps remember to have married a cousin Betty Ford of mine,[2] is come up to town from Scotland very poor, his wife my Cousin died on the road, and I procured him money to bury her.

Poor Jos. Simpson is dead at last.[3] Every day Somebody dies, and it must soon be our turn. May we be fit for it.

When you write make your letters as long as you can, for I always think them too short. Let me know how you live, and how you supply the loss of your friends.[4] Be as cheerful as you can and pass some part of every day in reading, and a little part in thinking upon me. I wish we were nearer that I might sometimes see you. Let me know if your Glass fits you, for if it does not fit, it must be changed. I am, my dearest, your most humble servant,

SAM. JOHNSON

2. *Ante* To William Drummond, 24 Oct. 1767 and n. 2.

3. *Ante* To John Levett, 17 Mar. 1752, n. 3.

4. Two of these lost friends were her companion Catherine Chambers (d. Nov. 1767) and her aunt Lucy Hunter (d. Apr. 1768).

Hester Thrale

FRIDAY 17 JUNE 1768

MS: Hyde Collection.

Madam: June 17, 1768

I know that you were not displeased to find me gone abroad when you were so kind as to favour me with a visit. I find it usefull to be moving, but whithersoever I may wander, I shall not, I hope, leave behind me that gratitude and respect, with which your attention to my health and tenderness for my weakness have impressed my heart. May you be long before you want the kindness which you have shown to, Madam, your most obliged and most humble servant,

SAM. JOHNSON

Lucy Porter

SATURDAY 18 JUNE 1768

PRINTED SOURCE: Hill I.148–49.

My Love, June 18, 1768

It gives me great pleasure to find that you are so well satisfied with what little things it has been in my power to send you. I hope you will always employ me in any office that can conduce to your convenience. My health is, I thank God, much better; but it is yet very weak; and very little things put it in a troublesome state; but still I hope all will be well. Pray for me.

My friends at Lichfield must not think that I forget them. Neither Mrs. Cobb,[1] nor Mrs. Adey,[2] nor Miss Adey,[3] nor Miss Seward,[4] nor Miss Vise,[5] are to suppose that I have lost all memory of their kindness. Mention me to them when you see them. I hear Mr. Vise has been lately very much in danger. I hope he is better.

When you write again, let me know how you go on, and what company you keep, and what you do all day. I love to think on you, but do not know when I shall see you. Pray, write very often. I am, Dearest, Your humble Servant,

SAM. JOHNSON

1. *Ante* To Lucy Porter, 18 Apr. 1768, n. 4.

2. *Ante* To Lucy Porter, 18 Apr. 1768, n. 3.

3. Mary Adey (1742–1830), the daughter of Joseph and Felicia Adey of Lichfield; in 1794 she married John Sneyd (1734–1809), High Sheriff of Staffordshire (*Johns. Glean.* IV.145).

4. *Ante* To Lucy Porter, 18 Apr. 1768, n. 5.

5. Mary Vyse (1743–1827), younger daughter of the Rev. William Vyse (1709–70), Treasurer of Lichfield Cathedral, Archdeacon of Salop, and SJ's former classmate at Pembroke College (*Johns. Glean.* V.210–11).

Lucy Porter

TUESDAY 12 JULY 1768

MS: Birthplace Museum, Lichfield.

My Dearest: July 12, 1768

Do not you owe me a Letter? I have been too much disordered in my health to keep nice accounts. If you did not do it before you will owe me one now, and I hope you will not be long in paying it. I am grown something better, but am yet very weakly. I ride out, and believe I shall go to the seaside next month.[1] I hope it will please God that I shall recover. Pray write to me.

Let me know how you do, and how you go on, and whom you have with you. For I would willingly hear that you are well and happy. Make your Letter as long as you can, that I may read it the oftner. Do not neglect nor delay.

Make my compliments to Mr. Greene.[2] I am, my dear, yours etc.

SAM. JOHNSON

1. There is no record of such a visit, but in September SJ accompanied the Thrales on what Hester Thrale described as "a little Tour into Kent for the benefit of his health" (Clifford, 1952, p. 75).

2. Richard Greene (1716–93), Lichfield surgeon, apothecary, and antiquarian, who put together "a wonderful collection, both of antiquities and natural curiosities, and ingenious works of art" (*Life* II.465; *Reades*, p. 145).

Hester Thrale

FRIDAY 11 NOVEMBER 1768

PRINTED SOURCE: Piozzi, *Letters* I.16; collated with excerpt in Anderson Galleries Catalogue 1424, 23 Apr. 1919, Lot 532.

Madam: Nov. 11, 1768

I am sincerely sorry for you both; nor is my grief disinterested; for I cannot but think the life of Mrs. Salusbury some addition to the happiness of all that know her.[1] How much

1. Hester Maria Salusbury died of breast cancer on 18 June 1773 (*Thraliana*

soever I wish to see you, I hope you will give me no pleasure at the expence[2] of one to whom you have so much greater reason[3] to be attentive. I am, etc.

1.311 n. 2). However, her first recorded symptoms date from 1770 (Hyde, 1977, p. 42). This letter must therefore refer to a different illness.

2. "expense" (Anderson Galleries)

3. "so much reason" (Anderson Galleries)

Hester Thrale

FRIDAY 2 DECEMBER 1768

MS: Hyde Collection.

Madam: Dec. 2, 1768

I can readily find no paper that is not ruled for juridical use. You will wonder that I have not written, and indeed I wonder too; but I have been[1] oddly put by my purpose. If my omission has given you any uneasiness, I have the mortification of paining that mind which I would most wish to please. I am not, I thank God, worse than when I went, and you have no hope that I should grow better here. But I will show myself to morrow, and only write in hope that my letter will come before me and that you will have forgiven the negligence of, Madam, your most obliged and most humble servant,

SAM. JOHNSON

1. MS: "b" superimposed upon "p"

Hester Thrale

WEDNESDAY 14 DECEMBER 1768

MS: Hyde Collection.

Madam: [Oxford] Dec. 14, 1768

Before I went, I promised to see the rent paid, and left ten pounds towards it. At club I met Langton, and nobody else, he is no richer than he was, but he gave me a guinea, and enquired after Miss.[1]

Chambers has no heart, so I shall have the pleasure of seeing you on Saturday, and next week will be the end of the course.[2] If he had courage I think it might have been done by wednesday. I am, Madam, your most humble servant,

SAM. JOHNSON

1. *Ante* To Hester Thrale, 11 May 1767, n. 3.

2. SJ was hoping that, with his help, Chambers would finish Part III of the Vinerian lectures, the series on property law. However, "if by this time Chambers had come close to completing the course, he nevertheless did not deliver the required sixty lectures during the third reading, beginning on January 14, 1769" (*A Course of Lectures on the English Law*, ed. T. M. Curley, 1986, I.25).

George Colman[1]

TUESDAY 17 JANUARY 1769

MS: Hyde Collection.

ENDORSEMENT: from Dr. Johnson, Jan. 17, 1769–and ans.

Sir: Jan. 17, 1769

Since your kind promise of a benefit for Mrs. Williams,[2] my Friend Mr. Strahan has obtained the concurrence of all the other partners, except Mr. Powel to whom I have written,[3] and who delays his answer till he has consulted you. As You will not counsel him to refuse what you have yourself granted, I suppose, he will make no objection, and therefore entreat you to give us, as soon as you can, the play which you think most proper and appoint us the day which can first be spared. You

1. *Ante* To George Colman, 19 Aug. 1767, n. 1.

2. *Ante* To Thomas Birch, 9 Jan. 1756.

3. William Powell (1735–69), a prominent actor who specialized in tragic roles, appeared at Drury Lane from 1763 until his defection to Covent Garden in 1767. The other partners were Thomas Harris (*c.* 1738–1820), a soap manufacturer, who took over the management of Covent Garden when Colman retired in 1774; Henry Dagge (d. 1795) and his brother James, London solicitors; and a bookseller named "Leake," possibly James Leake of Bath (E. R. Page, *George Colman the Elder*, 1935, p. 138; *Letters of David Garrick*, ed. D. M. Little and G. M. Kahrl, 1963, II.595 n. 2).

can perhaps give us the choice of several plays, but we know not how to choose as well as you, and therefore hope that you will contrive to make your favour as efficacious as you can.

You will therefore, I hope, turn this business in your mind, and favour me as soon as you can with your determination.[4] I am, Sir, Your most humble servant, SAM. JOHNSON

4. There is no record of a benefit performance for Anna Williams.

Louise Flint[1]

FRIDAY 31 MARCH 1769

MS: H. W. Liebert. A copy in the hand of H. L. Piozzi.
ENDORSEMENT: Mr. Johnson's letter to Miss Flint.

Mademoiselle: a Londres, Mars 31, 1769

Il faut avouer que la lettre que vous m'avez fait l'honeur de m'ecrire, a ete long tems sans rêponse. Voici mon Apologie. J'ai eté affligé d'une Maladie de Violence peu supportable, et d'un lenteur bien ennuiant. Tout état a ses droits particuliers. On compte parmi les droits d'un Malade ce de manquer aux offices de respect, et aux devoirs de reconoissance. Gené par ses douleurs il ne scait veiller qu'a soimême. Il ne pense qu'a se soulager, et a se retablir, peu attentif a tout autre soin, et peu sensible á la gloire d'etre traduit d'une main telle que vôtre.

Neanmoins Mademoiselle votre merite auroit exige que je m'efforcasse a vous rendre graces de vos egards si je l'aurois pu faire sans y meler des querelles. Mais comment m'empescher de me plaindre de ces appas par lesquelles vous avez

1. Louise Flint (d. 1821), a friend of Frances Reynolds, identified by H. L. Piozzi as "a *very* young Lady who had translated his Strictures at the end of Shakespear's Plays" (MS note). She later married Antoine Rivarol (1753–1801), author of *De l'universalité de la langue française* (1797). Rivarol's royalist writings forced him to escape from France in 1792. He left behind his wife and son, who were imprisoned during the Terror (J. G. Alger, *Englishmen in the French Revolution*, 1889, p. 345).

gagne sur l'Esprit de Mademoiselle Reynolds jusqu'a ce qu'elle ne se souvient plus ni de sa patrie ni de ses amis.[2] C'est peu de nous louer, c'est peu de repandre nos ouvrages par des traductions les plus belles, pendant que vous nous privez du plaisir de voir Mademoiselle Reynolds et de l'êcouter.—Enfin Madamoiselle il faut etre moins aimable, afin que nous vous aimions plus. Je suis, Mademoiselle, Vôtre tres humble, et Obeissant Serviteur, SAM. JOHNSON

2. Frances Reynolds had traveled to Paris in 1768, with Louise Flint as her companion (James Northcote, *Life of Sir Joshua Reynolds*, 1819, 1.201).

Hester Thrale

THURSDAY 18 MAY 1769

MS: Houghton Library.

Madam: May 18, 1769

Now I know you want to be forgetting me, but I do not want to be forgotten, and would rather send you letters like *Presto's*, than suffer myself to slip out of your memory.[1] That I should forget you there is no danger, for I have time enough to think both by night and day, and he that has leisure for any thing that is not present, always turns his mind to that which he likes best.

One reason for thinking on You is, that I must for a while be content with thinking, for our affairs will not suffer me to come home,[2] till Saturday.[3] I am, Madam, your most humble servant, SAM. JOHNSON

1. In 1768 Deane Swift had published letters I–XL of the *Journal to Stella*. In his edition Swift omitted or translated all but a specimen of the "little language"; his substitutions included "Presto" for "pdfr," Jonathan Swift's alphabetical symbol for himself (*Journal to Stella*, ed. Harold Williams, 1948, I.lviii).

2. *Ante* To Hester Thrale, 23 May 1768, n. 1.

3. It is likely that SJ was continuing to help Chambers complete Part III of his Vinerian lectures. SJ had gone to Oxford in Feb. 1769 (*Life* 1.548), and was soon to leave for another visit, during the course of which he "appeared to be deeply engaged in some literary work" (*Life* II.68).

Thomas Warton

WEDNESDAY 31 MAY 1769

MS: Trinity College, Oxford.

ADDRESS: To the Reverend Mr. Warton.

Dear Sir: [Oxford][1] May 31, 1769[2]

Many years ago when I used to read in the library of your College I promised to recompense the College for that permission by adding to their[3] books a Baskervilles Virgil.[4] I have now sent it, and desire you to reposite it on the Shelves in my Name.[5]

If You will be pleased to let me know when You have an hour of leisure, I will drink tea with you.[6] I am engaged for the afternoon to morrow and on friday; all my mornings are my own. I am, Sir, your most humble Servant,

SAM. JOHNSON

1. "He was now staying at Oxford" (Warton's note).

2. MS: "1769" added by Warton

3. MS: "their" superimposed upon undeciphered erasure

4. *Ante* To Edmund Hector, 15 Apr. 1755, n. 6.

5. The presentation copy at Trinity College is inscribed by Warton, "Hunc librum D.D. Samuel Johnson, L.L.D., quod hic loci studiis interdum vacaret" (*Life* II.485).

6. *Ante* To Hester Thrale, 18 May 1769, n. 3. SJ stayed in Oxford until early July.

Hester Thrale

c. WEDNESDAY 21 JUNE 1769

MS: Hyde Collection.

Dear Madam: New Inn Hall,[1] June 27, 1769[2]

I had your note sent hither, and can easily spare the pineap-

1. *Ante* To Hester Thrale, 29 Feb. 1768, n. 1.

2. The letter is misdated: see below, n. 4.

ple,[3] and be satisfied with the reason for which it was sent. Though I hope I shall never want any new memorials to keep you in my mind yet I am glad to find you solicitous not to be forgotten, though I should not deserve to be remembred if there could be any reason for such solicitude.

The pain and sickness which you suffer, you may bear to feel and I to think on with less impatience on your part, and less grief on mine, because the crisis is within view.[4] I will not encrease your uneasiness with mine. I hope I grow better. I am very cautious and very timorous. Whether fear and caution do much for me I can hardly tell. Time will perhaps do more than both.

I purpose to come to town in a few days, but I suppose I must not see you. I will, however, call on Mr. Thrale in the borough, and shall hope to be soon informed that your trouble is over, and that you [are] well enough to resume your care for that which yet continues, and which your kindness may sometimes alleviate. I am, Madam, your most obedient and most humble servant,

SAM. JOHNSON

3. "Pineapple" and "strawberries and cream," which recur frequently in SJ's correspondence with Hester Thrale, stand for the special comforts and solicitude he found only at Streatham Park ("home").

4. Lucy Elizabeth (1769–73), the Thrales' fifth child, was born on 22 June (Hyde, 1977, p. 30).

Henry Thrale

THURSDAY 29 JUNE 1769

PRINTED SOURCE: Piozzi, *Letters* 1.23.

Sir: New Inn Hall, Oxford, June 29, 1769

That Mrs. Thrale is safely past through her danger is an event at which nobody but yourself can rejoice more than I rejoice. I think myself very much honoured by the choice that you have been pleased to make of me to become related to the little maiden.[1] Let me know when she will want me, and I will very punctually wait on her. I am, etc.

SAM. JOHNSON

1. *Ante* To Hester Thrale, 19 Apr. 1768, n. 4.

Hester Thrale

THURSDAY 29 JUNE 1769

MS: Hyde Collection.

Madam: Oxford, June 29, 1769

Hesiod, who was very wise in his time, though nothing to such wise people as we, says that the evil of the worst times has some good mingled with it.[1] Hesiod was in the right. These times are not much to my mind. I am not well, but in these times you are safe, and have brought a pretty little Miss.[2] I always wished it might be a Miss, and now that wish is gratified, nothing remains but that I entreat you to take care of yourself, for whatever number of Girls or Boys you may give us, we are far from being certain that any of them will ever do for us, what you can do, it is certain that they cannot now do it, and the ability which they want, they are not likely to gain, but by your precepts and your example, by an example of excellence, and by [the precepts][3] of truth.

Mr. Thrale tells me that my furlough is shortened, I am always ready to obey orders, I have not yet found any place from which I shall not willingly depart, to come back to you. I am, Dearest Lady, your most obedient and most humble servant,

SAM. JOHNSON

1. "But, notwithstanding, even these shall have some good mingled with their evils" (*Works and Days*, l. 179, trans. H. G. Evelyn-White, Loeb ed.).

2. *Ante* To Hester Thrale, *c.* 21 June 1769, n. 4.

3. "the admonitions" (Piozzi, *Letters* 1.22).

Hester Thrale

THURSDAY 6 JULY 1769

MS: Houghton Library.

Dearest Madam: July 6, 1769

Though I am to come home to morrow, I would not let the alarming letter which I received this morning be without notice. Dear Madam, take all possible care of your health. How near we always are to danger. I hope your danger is now past, but that fear which is the necessary effect of danger must remain always with us. I hope my little Miss is well.[1] Surely I shall be very fond of her. In a year and half she will run and talk. But how much ill may happen in a year and half. Let us however hope for the better side of possibility, and think that I may then and afterwards continue to be, Madam, Your most obedient servant, SAM. JOHNSON

1. *Ante* To Hester Thrale, *c.* 21 June 1769, n. 4.

Hester Thrale

MONDAY 14 AUGUST 1769

MS: Birthplace Museum, Lichfield.

Madam: Lichfield, August 14, 1769

I set out on Thursday Morning, and found my Companion, to whom I was very much a stranger, more agreeable than I expected. We went cheerfully forward, and passed the night at Coventry. We came in late and went out early, and therefore I did not send for my Cousin Tom,[1] but I design to make him some amends for the omission.

Next day we came early to Lucy who was, I believe, glad to

1. Thomas Johnson (1703–79), SJ's first cousin, a currier in Coventry (*Reades*, pp. 222–25). SJ defines *currier* in his *Dictionary* as "one who dresses and pares leather for those who make shoes."

see us.[2] She had saved her best gooseberries upon the tree for me, and, as Steele says, *I was neither too proud nor too wise* to gather them. I have rambled a very little inter fontes et flumina nota,[3] but I am not yet well. They have cut down the trees in George Lane.[4] Evelyn in his Book of Forest trees, tell[s] us of wicked men that cut down trees and never prospered afterwards,[5] yet nothing has deterred these audacious aldermen from violating the Hamadryads of George Lane. As an impartial traveller I must however tell that in Stow street where I left a draw-well, I have found a pump, but the lading well in this ill-fated George Lane lyes shamefully neglected.[6]

I am going to day or to morrow to Ashbourne, but I am at a loss how I shall get back in time to London.[7] Here are only chance Coaches, so that there is no certainty of a place. If I do not come, let it not hinder your journey. I can be but a few days behind you, and I will follow in the Brighthelmston Coach. But I hope to come.

I took care to tell Miss Porter, that I have got another Lucy.[8] I hope she is well. Tell Mrs. Salusbury that I beg her stay at Streatham, for little Lucy's sake. I am, Madam, your most obliged, humble servant,

SAM. JOHNSON

2. SJ refers to himself and Francis Barber.

3. *fortunate senex, hic inter flumina nota / et fontis sacros frigus captabis opacum*: "Happy old man! Here, amid familiar streams and sacred springs, you shall court the cooling shade" (Virgil, *Eclogues* 1.51–52, trans. H. R. Fairclough, Loeb ed.).

4. George Lane, in central Lichfield, connected Stowe Street to Castle Ditch. SJ's foster-mother lived there, and he "used to call . . . and eat fruit in the garden, which was full of trees" (*Johns. Misc.* 1.130; Clifford, 1955, p. 28).

5. "One might fill a just *volume* with the *Histories of Groves* that were violated by wicked Men, who came to fatal periods" (John Evelyn, *Sylva, or A Discourse of Forest-Trees*, 3d ed., 1679, p. 268).

6. The *OED* cites this sentence under def. 4 of *lading*; compounded thus, it signifies "the bailing or ladling out of water."

7. The Thrales were about to leave for their vacation house in Brighton. SJ joined them there on 21 Aug. (*Post* To John Taylor, 5 Oct. 1769; Clifford, 1952, pp. 81–82).

8. *Ante* To Hester Thrale, *c.* 21 June 1769, n. 4.

Elizabeth Aston

SATURDAY 26 AUGUST 1769

MS: Johnson House, London.

ENDORSEMENT in an unidentified hand: to Mrs. Aston, Augst. 69.

Madam: Brighthelmston, August 26, 1769

I suppose you have received the Mill. The whole apparatus seemed[1] to be perfect, except that there is wanting a little tin spout at the bottom, and some ring or knob on which the bag that catches the meal is to be hung. When these are added, I hope you will be able to grind your own bread, and treat me with a cake made by yourself of meal from your own corn of your own grinding.

I was glad, Madam, to see you so well, and hope your hea[l]th will long encrease, and then long continue. I am, Madam, your most obedient servant,

SAM. JOHNSON

1. MS: "med" written above undeciphered deletion

James Boswell

SATURDAY 9 SEPTEMBER 1769

MS: Beinecke Library. The transcript (in the hand of one of JB's children) used as copy for the *Life*.

ADDRESS in JB's hand: To James Boswell, Esqr.

Dear Sir: Brighthelmston, Septr. 9, 1769

Why do you charge me with unkindness?[1] I have omitted nothing that could do you good or give you pleasure unless it be that I have forborn to tell you my opinion of your Account of Corsica.[2] I believe my opinion if you think well of my judge-

1. JB had written to SJ on 5 Sept., en route to the Stratford Shakespeare Jubilee (*Boswell in Search of a Wife*, ed. Frank Brady and F. A. Pottle, 1957, p. 292).

2. *Ante* To JB, 23 Mar. 1768.

ment might have given you pleasure but when it is considered how much vanity is excited by praise I am not sure that it would have done you good. Your History is like other histories but your journal is in a very high degree curious and deligh[t]ful.[3] There is between the history and the journal that difference which there will always be found between notions borrowed from without, and notions generated within.[4] Your history was copied from books.[5] Your journal rose out of your own experience and observation. You[6] express images which operated strongly upon yourself and you have impressed them with great force upon your readers. I know not whether I could name any narrative by which curiosity is better excited or better gratified.

I am glad that you are going to be married[7] and as I wish you well in things of less importance wish you well with proportionate ardour in this crisis of your life. What I can contribute to your happiness I should be very unwilling to withhold for I have always loved and valued you and shall love you and value you still more as you become more regular and useful effects which a happy Marriage will hardly fail to produce.

I do not find that I am likely to come back very soon from this place.[8] I shall perhaps stay a fortnight longer and a fortnight is a long time to a lover absent from his Mistress. Would a fortnight ever have an end?[9] I am, Dear Sir, your most affectionate, humble servant,

SAM. JOHNSON

3. MS: "delighful" written above "entertaining" del. (perhaps reproducing SJ's alteration)

4. JB's *Account of Corsica* begins with "a largely unoriginal survey of the history, geography, climate, and natural resources" of the island (*Boswell on the Grand Tour*, ed. Frank Brady and F. A. Pottle, 1955, p. 146). The second part presents JB's own "Journal of a Tour to That Island, and Memoirs of Pascal Paoli."

5. For a discussion of JB's sources, see *Earlier Years*, p. 361.

6. MS: "observation you"

7. JB married his first cousin, Margaret Montgomerie (*c.* 1738–89), on 25 Nov. 1769 (*Earlier Years*, p. 441).

8. *Post* To John Taylor, 5 Oct. 1769.

9. MS: exclamation mark

John Taylor

THURSDAY 5 OCTOBER 1769

MS: Hyde Collection.

ADDRESS: To The Revd. Dr. Taylor at Ashburn, Derbyshire.

POSTMARKS: 5 OC, FREE.

FRANK: Hfreethrale.

ENDORSEMENT: 5 Octr. 69, 1769.

Dear Sir: Oct. 5, 1769

I got very well to London, and went on the next Monday to Brighthelmston, from which I am now returned.[1] I think you might write to me, and let me know what became of your demand of the living, and other occurrences of your life. I am not fully determined against coming this winter again into your corner of the world, but I have yet no settled plan.[2] Write to me however. I am, sir, your most etc.

SAM. JOHNSON

1. *Ante* To Hester Thrale, 14 Aug. 1769 and n. 7.

2. SJ did not visit Taylor until the following summer (*Post* To Hester Thrale, 20 July 1770).

Thomas Percy

SUNDAY 5 NOVEMBER 1769

MS: Victoria and Albert Museum.

ADDRESS: To the Reverend Mr. Percy.

Sir: Nov. 5, 1769

I am desired by some Ladies who support a Charity School on Snowhill, to solicite you for a Charity Sermon, to be preached either the last Sunday of this month, or the first of the next.[1]

1. The Ladies' Charity School, on King Street in the parish of St. Sepulchre, Holborn, was founded in 1702 for the purpose of training young girls to be domestics (Wheatley and Cunningham II.353–54). The School was "maintained by the charitable Contributions of 150 good Women who see to the management

This application had been made sooner if you had been in town, but I hope it is not yet too late, and that if you can comply without great inconvenience You will not refuse.[2] They meet on Wednesday, and desire to know your determination to morrow. I hope you will not refuse them, for I have a great esteem of some of them, and I think, You may appear with great propriety on such occasions. I am, Sir, Your most humble servant,

SAM. JOHNSON

Please to send your answer to Mrs. Williams, for I shall not be in town.

---

of it" (*Thraliana* I.115). It is probable that SJ's phrase "some Ladies" includes Anna Williams (who bequeathed her "little substance" to the School), Hester Thrale (a subscriber and manager), and Ann Gardiner (*c.* 1716–89), the wife of a tallow-chandler on Snow Hill and one of the School's most zealous supporters (*Life* IV.241, 246; Hill II.334 n. 3). In 1783 SJ "obtained for it a sermon from the late Bishop of St. Asaph, Dr. [Jonathan] Shipley" (*Life* IV.246).

2. Percy preached a sermon on Sunday, 26 Nov. 1769 (extract from the School's Minute Book, quoted in Hill I.157).

James Boswell

THURSDAY 9 NOVEMBER 1769

PRINTED SOURCE: JB's *Life*, 1791, I.331.

Dear Sir, [Streatham] Nov. 9, 1769

Upon balancing the inconveniencies of both parties, I find it will less incommode you to spend your night here, than me to come to town.[1] I wish to see you, and am ordered by the lady of this house to invite you hither.[2] Whether you can come or

1. "Being to set out for Scotland on the 10th of November, I wrote to him at Streatham, begging that he would meet me in town on the 9th; but if this should be very inconvenient to him, I would go thither" (*Life* II.109–10).

2. "I was detained in town till it was too late on the ninth, so went to him early in the morning of the tenth of November. . . . He was so good as to accompany me to London, and see me into the post-chaise which was to carry me on my road to Scotland" (*Life* II.110–11).

not, I shall not have any occasion of writing to you again before your marriage, and therefore tell you now, that with great sincerity I wish you happiness.[3] I am, dear Sir, Your most affectionate, humble servant,

SAM. JOHNSON

3. *Ante* To JB, 9 Sept. 1769 and n. 7.

Henry Bright

TUESDAY 9 JANUARY 1770

MS: British Library.

ENDORSEMENT in an unidentified hand: Addrest to the Revd. Henry Bright, then Masr. of Abingdon School.

Johnsons Court,
Fleetstreet, Jan. 9th 1770

Sir:

I would gladly be informed if you are willing to take another pupil, in the same manner as Mr. Strahan was taken.[1] You will I think have more trouble with him, and therefore ought to have a higher price.[2]

I shall [be] at Oxford on Fryday and Saturday next, where[3] if you cannot come over, I shall expect a letter from you. I am, Sir, Your most humble servant,

SAM. JOHNSON

1. *Ante* To Henry Bright, 12 Oct. 1762. The new pupil was Ralph Plumbe (?1754–76), Henry Thrale's nephew and the son of Alderman Samuel Plumbe (1717–84), a London sugar refiner.

2. Hester Thrale records various instances of Plumbe's dullness and "consummate Ignorance": "this was the Youth whom I asked who succeeded Romulus—and Johnson said I might as well enquire who phlebotomized Romulus" (*Thraliana* I.101–2). His family hoped that, with special tutoring at Abingdon, he might be admitted to Oxford.

3. MS: "where" written above "but" del.

Hester Thrale

SATURDAY 13 JANUARY 1770

MS: Hyde Collection.

ADDRESS: To Henry Thrale, Esq., in Southwark.

POSTMARKS: OXFORD, 15 IA.

Dear Madam: [Oxford] Jan. 13, 1770

We have so much to do, or do our little so lazily that I have been forced to delay my return to Tuesday.[1] I could not before I went send you any of the papers,[2] but will try to bring them when I come. I am, Madam, Your most obedient servant,

SAM. JOHNSON

1. It is possible that SJ was still helping Robert Chambers with his Vinerian lectures. "All that is certainly known is that Johnson virtually stopped going to New Inn Hall once Chambers delivered all the prescribed number of private lectures and received all his salary in the academic year ending in July 1770" (*A Course of Lectures on the English Law*, ed. T. M. Curley, 1986, p. 26).

2. "The papers he means were *the false Alarm*" (H. L. Piozzi's MS note). *The False Alarm*, SJ's political pamphlet on the John Wilkes affair, was written at the Thrales' Southwark house, 10–11 Jan. 1770, and published 17 Jan. (*Works*, Yale ed. x.313).

Henry Bright

SATURDAY 27 JANUARY 1770

MS: Hyde Collection.

ENDORSEMENT in an unidentified hand: To the Revd. Henry Bright.

Sir: Jan. 27, 1770

I expect that Mr. Alderman Plumbe will bring his son to you in a very few days.[1] I have told him on what terms you are to take him; and I believe Mr. Plumbe will not be hard to please about lodging and accommodations.

It will, I think be proper that you examine the young Gentleman in the presence of his father. Mr. Plumbe is a Scholar

1. *Ante* To Henry Bright, 9 Jan. 1770 and n. 1.

more than sufficient to perceive his sons deficiencies.[2] By knowing how much is wanting, a better Judgement will be made hereafter how much shall have been gained. I do not doubt your diligence, and sin[c]erely wish you success.[3] I am, Sir, your most humble servant,

SAM. JOHNSON

2. MS: "defienciencies"

3. Ralph Plumbe made very little progress under Bright's tutelage, and was withdrawn from the school by July 1771 (*Thraliana* I.102 and n. 2).

Joseph Smith[1]

THURSDAY 1 MARCH 1770

MS: Hyde Collection.

ADDRESS: To Mr. Joseph Smith, Ironmonger in Bishop Stortford, Hertfordshire.

ENDORSEMENTS in two unidentified hands: Dr. Johnson, Dr. Johnson to Mr. J. Smith.

Johnsons Court,
Sir: Fleetstreet, March 1, 1770

Mr. Hoole showed me your request, and I shall make it known to Mr. Thrale, though I do not expect much regard to be paid by him to my opinions about malt. Such things however sometimes proceed beyond expectation.

I have taken the liberty to inclose a Bill of £50 and by that you will take the trouble to examine and to satisfy Mrs. Clapp's account,[2] the remainder you will please to keep till I wait on you at Stortford. Pray let me know that you receive it. I am, Sir, your most humble servant,

SAM. JOHNSON

1. Joseph Smith, an ironmonger of Bishop Stortford whom SJ may have met through Anna Williams or John Hoole (*Johns. Glean.* II.23–24).

2. *Ante* To Francis Barber, 28 May 1768 and n. 1.

Richard Farmer[1]

WEDNESDAY 21 MARCH 1770

MS: Hyde Collection.

ENDORSEMENT in JB's hand: To The Rev. Dr. Farmer.

Johnson's Court,
Sir: Fleetstreet, March 21, 1770

As no Man ought to keep wholly to himself any possession that may be useful to the publick, I hope you will not think me unreasonably intrusive, if I have recourse to you for such information as you are more able to give me, than any other Man.

In support of an opinion which you have already placed above the need of any more support Mr. Steevens a very ingenious Gentleman lately of King's College,[2] has collected an account of all the translations which Shakespeare might have seen and used. He wishes his catalogue to be perfect, and therefore entreats that you will favour [him] by the insertion of such additions, as the accuracy of your enquiries has enabled you to make. To this request I take the liberty of adding my own solicitation.[3]

We have no immediate use for this catalogue, and therefore do not desire that it should interrupt or hinder your more important employments, but it will [be] kind to let us know

1. Richard Farmer (1735–97), D.D., F.S.A., Fellow of Emanuel College, Cambridge, and author of an *Essay on the Learning of Shakespeare* (1766), which SJ praised "as a most excellent performance; as a compleat and finished piece that leaves nothing to be desired in point of Argument" (*Correspondence of Thomas Percy and Richard Farmer*, ed. Cleanth Brooks, 1946, p. 121). SJ and Farmer first became acquainted at Cambridge in Feb. 1765, when SJ asked for Farmer's assistance with his forthcoming edition of Shakespeare (pp. 84–85). Farmer was elected to The Club in 1795.

2. *Ante* To Jacob Tonson, 9 Oct. 1765, n. 3.

3. Farmer sent Steevens his catalogue of "Ancient Translations from Classic Authors." The "Advertisement to the Reader" of the Johnson-Steevens Shakespeare (1773) thanks Farmer for correcting and amplifying the list of "the Greek and Roman poets, orators, etc., who had been rendered accessible to our author" (*Life* II.489–90).

that you receive it. I am, Sir, Your most obedient and most humble Servant, SAM. JOHNSON

Robert Chambers

SATURDAY 24 MARCH 1770

MS: Hyde Collection.

ADDRESS: To Robert Chambers, Esq., at Mr. Bell's in Coney Street, York.

POSTMARKS: [Undeciphered], 24 MR, ⟨BE⟩.

ENDORSEMENT: Mr. S. Johnston, 24 Mar. 70.

Dear Sir: March 24, 1770

I see nothing that needs hinder me from going with you for a few days to Oxford, and therefore intend to do it.[1] I am just now out of order with the Rheumatism, but hope to get over it. Though it is painful, it [is] an evil much more easily born than my former complaints. I am, Sir, your most humble servant, SAM. JOHNSON

1. *Ante* To Hester Thrale, 13 Jan. 1770, n. 1; *Post* To Hester Thrale, 6 Apr. 1770.

Hester Thrale

FRIDAY 6 APRIL 1770

MS: Hyde Collection.

Madam: [Oxford] Apr. 6, 1770

I have now been here two nights, the first was[1] but bad, the second was something better. I did not go out yesterday nor shall go out to day, and can therefore give no account of Mr. Coulson.[2]

1. MS: "was" superimposed upon "but" partially erased

2. The Rev. John Coulson (1719–88), Fellow of University College, Oxford. In 1774, the Thrales and SJ were entertained by Coulson "with liberality and with kindness" (*Life* v.459 n. 4).

I think to come back in the beginning of the week. I am, Madam, your most obliged and most humble servant,

SAM. JOHNSON

Mr. Chambers sends his compliments.[3]

3. *Ante* To Hester Thrale, 13 Jan. 1770, n. 1.

Lucy Porter

TUESDAY 1 MAY 1770

MS: Pembroke College, Oxford. A copy in the hand of Thomas Harwood.

ADDRESS: To Mrs. Lucy Porter in Lichfield.

Dearest Madam, May 1, 1770

Among other causes that have hindred me from answering your last kind letter is a tedious and painful Rheumatism, that has afflicted me for many Weeks, and still continues to molest me.

I hope you are well, and will long keep your health and your chearfulness.

One reason why I delayed to write was my uncertainty how to answer your letter. I like the thought of giving away the money very well,[1] but when I consider that Tom Johnson is my nearest relation,[2] and that he is now old and in great want, that he was my playfellow in childhood, and has never done any thing to offend me, I am in doubt whether I ought not rather to give it him, than any other.

Of this, my Dear, I would have your opinion. I would willingly please you, and I know that you will be pleased best, with what you think right.

Tell me your mind, and do not learn of me to neglect writing, for it is a very sorry trick, though it be mine.

Your Brother is well;[3] I saw him to-day; and thought it long

1. The source of this money has not been determined.
2. *Ante* To Hester Thrale, 14 Aug. 1769, n. 1.
3. *Ante* To Lucy Porter, 18 Apr. 1768, n. 6.

since I saw him before, but, it seems, he has called often and could not find me. I am, My Dear, your affectionate, humble Servant,

SAM. JOHNSON

Henry Bright

THURSDAY 24 MAY 1770

MS: Princeton University Library.

Sir: London, May 24, 1770

The young Gentleman whom the Lady that brings you this, designs to place under your care, has, I am afraid, already lost some time at a negligent or unskilful School, and must therefore be advanced as fast as you can properly do it.[1] He has an hereditary claim to good parts both from his Father and his Mother, and will, I hope, afford his Instructor pleasure by his goodnature and docility. The Lady is my friend, and therefore I recommend him to you with great earnestness. I am, Sir, Your most humble servant,

SAM. JOHNSON

Please to remember [me] to Mr. Plumbe.

1. Chapman (1.236) identifies the "young Gentleman" as Ralph Plumbe and the "Lady" as his mother. His note is based on a mistranscription of the MS and on insufficient information. The correct reading of SJ's postscript is not "Mr. J. Combe" but "Mr. Plumbe." Ralph Plumbe, who had gone to Eton, was already studying with Henry Bright, and his father, not his mother, had brought him to Abingdon (*Ante* To Henry Bright, 27 Jan. 1770; *Thraliana* 1.101).

Lucy Porter

TUESDAY 29 MAY 1770

MS: Loren Rothschild.

ADDRESS: To Mrs. Lucy Porter, Lichfield.

POSTMARKS: 30 MA, 31 MA, FREE.

FRANK: Hfreethrale.

My Dearest Dear: London, May 29, 1770

I am very sorry that your eyes are bad, take great [care] of them, especially by candlelight. Mine continue pretty good, but they are sometimes a little dim. My Rheumatism grows gradually better.

I have considered your Letter, and am willing that the whole money should go where you, my Dear, originally intended. I hope to help Tom. some other way. So that matter is over.[1]

Dr. Taylor has invited me to pass some time with him at Ashbourne, if[2] I come, you may be sure that I shall take you and Lichfield in my way.[3] When I am nearer coming I will send you word.

Of Mr. Porter I have seen very little, but I know not that it is his fault, for he says that he often calls and never finds me.[4] I am sorry for it, for I love him.

Mr. Mathias has lately had a great deal of money left him, of which you have probably heard already.[5] I am, My dearest, Your most affectionate Servant, SAM. JOHNSON

1. *Ante* To Lucy Porter, 1 May 1770 and n. 1; *Ante* To Hester Thrale, 14 Aug. 1769, n. 1.

2. MS: "I" del. before "if"

3. *Post* To Unidentified Correspondent, 25 June 1770; *Post* To Hester Thrale, 20 July 1770.

4. *Ante* To Lucy Porter, 18 Apr. 1768, n. 6.

5. James Mathias (*c.* 1710–82), a friend of Lucy's brother Joseph and a London merchant trading with Hamburg, who died possessed of a "well-acquired and ample fortune" (*GM* 1782, p. 311; *Reades*, pp. 240–41).

Hannah Horneck[1]

WEDNESDAY 13 JUNE 1770

MS: Free Library of Philadelphia.

ADDRESS: Mrs. Horneck.

1. Mrs. Hannah Horneck (d. 1803) was the widow of Captain Kane Horneck of the Royal Engineers, a close friend of Edmund Burke (*Burke's Correspondence* VII.64). As a young woman she was called "the Plymouth Beauty," whose "Devonshire family had connected her with Reynolds, and so introduced her to

Wednesday, June 13

Mr. Johnson sends Mrs. Horneck and the young Ladies his best wishes for their health and pleasure in their journey,[2] and hopes his Wife will keep him in her mind.[3]

Goldsmith" (John Forster, *Life and Times of Oliver Goldsmith,* 1871, II.147). Mrs. Horneck had two daughters, Catherine (*c.* 1750–99) and Mary (*c.* 1752–1840), both celebrated for their beauty and both painted by Reynolds (*Poems of Gray, Collins, and Goldsmith,* ed. Roger Lonsdale, 1969, p. 662).

2. In July the Hornecks and Goldsmith left for a trip to Paris (*Letters of Oliver Goldsmith,* ed. K. C. Balderston, 1928, p. 91).

3. This joking reference may be to Mary Horneck, whom Goldsmith had nicknamed "the Jessamy Bride" (Balderston, *Letters,* p. 81).

Edmund Burke

THURSDAY 21 JUNE 1770

MS: Sheffield City Libraries (Wentworth Woodhouse Muniments).

ADDRESS: To Edmund Burke, Esq.

ENDORSEMENT: Saml. Johnson; Dr. Johnson, June 21 1790.

Dear Sir: June 21, 1770

I promised a long time ago to lend you Cowley's Latin Works. If you have not yet seen them, be pleased to accept of this copy which I bought at Oxford, and which is of the best edition.[1] You may easily repay this little present by informing me that dear Mrs. Burke is better.[2] I am, Sir, Your most humble Servant,

SAM. JOHNSON

1. *Abrahami Couleii Angli, Poemata Latina* (1668), ed. Thomas Sprat, which "represents Cowley's collected Latin works" (M. R. Perkin, *Abraham Cowley: A Bibliography,* 1977, p. 49). A copy was in Burke's library at the time of his death (*Burke's Correspondence* II.146 n. 1). SJ also owned a copy (Greene, 1975, p. 51).

2. Jane Mary Nugent Burke (1734–1812), whom Burke married in 1757. In early August he wrote to Richard Shackleton: "My Wife has had a very long illness; it was a slow fever with frequent appearances of amendment, and frequent relapses. She was confined to her Bed for above two months, and reduced in strength and in flesh beyond any thing that can be imagined. But I thank God she is now up again" (*Burke's Correspondence* II.149).

Thomas Warton

SATURDAY 23 JUNE 1770

MS: Trinity College, Oxford.

Dear Sir: London, June 23, 1770

The readiness with which you were pleased to promise me some notes on Shakespeare was a new instance[1] of your Friendship. I shall not hurry you, but am desired by Mr. Steevens who helps me in this Edition to let you know, that we shall print the tragedies first, and shall therefore want first the notes which belong to them. We think not to incommode the reader with a supplement, and therefore what we cannot put into its proper page, will do us no good.[2] We shall not begin to print before the end of six weeks, perhaps not so soon. I am, Sir, your most obliged and most humble Servant,

SAM. JOHNSON

1. MS: "instrance"

2. Volume 10 of the Johnson-Steevens edition of 1773 concludes with three appendices. The first of these contains 36 notes by Warton.

Unidentified Correspondent[1]

MONDAY 25 JUNE 1770

MS: Salt Library, Stafford.

Dear Sir: June 25, [17]70

I have this afternoon received a Letter from the Housekeeper of my Friend Dr. Taylor in Derbyshire, informing me that he now lies dangerously sick of a fever. As[2] my Journey was undertaken in a great measure to pass some weeks with him, I would rather put it off till I can hear again, and till I know the event of his disorder. But still I will go with you at the time

1. The recipient may have been SJ's stepson, Joseph Porter. *Ante* To Lucy Porter, 18 Apr. 1768, n. 6; cf. *Post* To Unidentified Correspondent, 14 June 1771.

2. MS: "A" superimposed upon "a"

settled rather than disappoint you.[3] I am, Dear Sir, your affectionate, humble servant,

SAM. JOHNSON

Please to let me know what we shall do. If you have no particular reason for going I think we may stay some time longer.

3. *Post* To Hester Thrale, 20 July 1770.

John Taylor

MONDAY 2 JULY 1770

MS: Houghton Library.

ADDRESS: To the Reverend Dr. Taylor in Ashbourn.

ENDORSEMENTS: 2 July 70, 1770.

Dear Sir: Lichfield, July 2d 1770

I hope the danger that has threatened you is now over, and that you [have] nothing now to overcome but that languor which must necessarily succeed a disorder so violent as yours.[1] Recovery is a state which requires great caution, and I entreat you not to be negligent of yourself.

I am now at Lichfield, and if my company can afford you either help or entertainment I am ready to come to you.[2] If you can write let me know from yourself the state of your health, if writing be difficult, Let me hear by some other hand. Be very careful of yourself. I am, Dear sir, Your most humble servant,

SAM. JOHNSON

1. *Ante* To Unidentified Correspondent, 25 June 1770.
2. *Post* To Hester Thrale, 20 July 1770.

Hester Thrale

EARLY JULY 1770[1]

MS: Birthplace Museum, Lichfield.

1. Dated on the basis of the references to the four surviving Thrale children, especially "Lucy begins to walk."

Dear Madam: Lichfield, July [2]

Do not say that I never write to you, and do not think that I expected to find any friends here that could make me wish to prolong my stay. For your strawberries, however, I have no care. Mrs. Cobb has strawberries,[3] and will give me as long as they last, and she has cherries too. Of the Strawberries at Streatham I consign my part to Miss [4] and Harry.[5] I hope Susy grows,[6] and Lucy begins to walk,[7] though this rainy weather confines us all in the house. I have neither frolicked nor fretted.

In the tumult, whatever it was, at your house I hope my Countrywomen either had no part, or behaved well.[8] I told Mr. Heartwel [9] about three days ago how well Warren [10] was liked in her place.

I have passed one day at Birmingham with my old Friend Hector —there's a name—and his Sister, an old Love.[11] My Mistress is grown much older than my friend.

—O, quid habes illius, illius
Quae spirabat amores
Quae me surpuerat mihi.[12]

2. MS: rest of dateline erased

3. *Ante* To Lucy Porter, 18 Apr. 1768, n. 4.

4. *Ante* To Hester Thrale, 11 May 1767, n. 3.

5. Henry Thrale the younger (1767–76).

6. Susanna Arabella (1770–1858), the Thrales' sixth child, b. 23 May.

7. *Ante* To Hester Thrale, 19 Apr. 1768, n. 4.

8. "Mrs. Salusbury's house in town was robbed of goods and linen to a large amount, while she was absent at Streatham" (H. L. Piozzi's note). It is probable that "my Countrywomen" refers to servants from Staffordshire, one of whom was called "Warren." *Post* To Hester Thrale, 14 July 1770.

9. Possibly John Hartwell of Lichfield, dyer and woolen manufacturer (*Johns. Glean.* IV.27–29).

10. See above, n. 8.

11. Ann Hector Carless (1711–88), the widow of the Rev. Walter Carless (1714–57), of Standon, Staffordshire (*Johns. Glean.* III.46). "She was the first woman with whom I was in love. It dropt out of my head imperceptibly; but she and I shall always have a kindness for each other" (*Life* II.460).

12. "What dost thou retain of her, of her, I ask, who once breathed love, who stole me from myself" (Horace, *Odes* IV.xiii.18–20, trans. C. E. Bennett, Loeb ed.).

Time will impair the body, and uses us well if it spares the mind.[13] Dearest Madam, Your most humble Servant,

SAM. JOHNSON

13. MS: two lines heavily del. after "mind"

Hester Thrale

SATURDAY 7 JULY 1770

MS: Hyde Collection.

Dear Madam: Lichfield, July 7, 1770

I thought I should have heard some thing to day about Streatham, but there is no letter, and I need some consolation for Rheumatism is come again, though in a less degree than formerly. I reckon to go next week to Ashbourne,[1] and will try to bring you the dimensions of the great Bull. The Skies and the ground are all so wet, that I have been very little abroad and Mrs. Aston is from home, so that I have no motive to walk.[2] When she is at home she lives on the top of Stow Hill, and I commonly climb up to see her once a day. There is nothing there now but the empty Nest. I hope Streatham will long be the place.

To write to you about Lichfield is of no use for you never saw Stow pool,[3] nor Borowcop hill, I believe you may find Borow or Boroughcop hill in my Dictionary under cop or cob.[4] Nobody here knows what the name imports.[5]

1. SJ did not leave for Ashbourne until 18 July (*Post* To Hester Thrale, 20 July 1770). 2. *Ante* To Elizabeth Aston, 17 Nov. 1767, n. 1.

3. A pond close to the center of Lichfield, on whose marshy perimeter SJ's father constructed a parchment factory (Clifford, 1955, p. 28).

4. *Borowcop Hill* does not appear under *cop* or *cob* (both of which mean "head" or "top").

5. "At the end of St. John's-street, a short distance to the left, is Borrocop or Borough-Cop Hill. The words Borough, Burgh, Berry and Bury, were the common appellations given by the Saxons to small camps or elevated posts. . . . Upon this mount the martyrdom of the thousand Christians, in the tenth persecution, is said to have happened" (Thomas Harwood, *History and Antiquities of Lichfield*, 1806, p. 561).

I have taken the liberty to enclose a letter, for, though you do not know it, three groats make a Shilling.[6] I am, Dearest Madam, Your most obliged and most humble Servant,

SAM. JOHNSON

6. By enclosing a letter SJ is saving the postage from Lichfield to London, which was fourpence (or one groat).

Hester Thrale

WEDNESDAY 11 JULY 1770

MS: Hyde Collection.

Madam: Lichfield, July 11, 1770

Since my last letter nothing extraordinary has happened. Rheumatism which has been very troublesome is grown better. I have not yet seen Dr. Taylor and July runs fast away. I shall not have much time for him, if he delays much longer to come or send.[1] Mr. Grene the Apothecary[2] has found a book which tells who paid levies in our parish, and how much they paid, above an hundred years ago. Do you not think we study this book hard? Nothing is like going to the bottom of things. Many families that paid the parish rates are now extinct like the race of Hercules.[3] Pulvis et umbra sumus.[4] What is nearest us, touches us most. The passions rise higher at domestick than at imperial tragedies.[5] I am not wholly unaffected by the

1. *Post* To Hester Thrale, 20 July 1770.

2. *Ante* To Lucy Porter, 12 July 1768, n. 2.

3. SJ does not appear to have a specific literary source in mind here, but rather the status of Hercules as archetypal hero. Neither his descendants nor the burghers of Lichfield are safe from extinction.

4. *Pulvis et umbra sumus*: "We are but dust and shadow" (Horace, *Odes* IV.vii.16, trans. C. E. Bennett, Loeb ed.).

5. SJ here condenses one of the fundamental premises of his theory of biography: "Our passions are therefore more strongly moved, in proportion as we can more readily adopt the pains or pleasures proposed to our minds, by recognising them as once our own, or considering them as naturally incident to our state of life" (*Rambler* No. 60, *Works*, Yale ed. III.319).

revolutions of Sadler Street,[6] nor can forbear to mourn a little when old names vanish away, and new come into their place.

Do not imagine, Madam, that I wrote this letter for the sake of these philosophical meditations for when I began it, I had neither Mr. Grene nor his book in my thoughts, but was resolved to write and did not know what I had to send but my Respects to Mrs. Salusbury, and Mr. Thrale, and Harry and the Misses.[7] I am, Dearest Madam, Your most obliged and most humble servant,

SAM. JOHNSON

6. The Johnson family house stood at the corner of Sadler (later Market) and Breadmarket Streets.

7. *Ante* To Hester Thrale, Early July 1770 and nn. 4–7.

Hester Thrale

SATURDAY 14 JULY 1770

MS: Hyde Collection.

Dear Madam: Lichfield, July 14, 1770

When any calamity is suffered, the first thing to be remembred is, how much has been escaped. The house might have been entred by Ruffians when Mrs. Salusbury had [been] in it and who can tell what horrours might have followed.[1]

I thought you would in time compliment your compliments away. Nothing goes well when I am from you, for when I am from you the house is robbed. You must therefore suppose, that if I had been with you, the robbery would not have been. But it was not our gang.[2] I should have had no interest.

Your loss, I am afraid, is very great, but the loss of patience would have been greater.

My Rheumatism torments me very much, though[3] not as in

1. *Ante* To Hester Thrale, Early July 1770, n. 8.

2. To judge from Hester Thrale's response, 17 July 1770, this "gang," headed by SJ and Giuseppe Baretti, consisted of certain members of the Streatham Park circle.

3. MS: "though" altered from "thought"

the winter. I think I shall go to Ashbourne on Monday or Tuesday.[4]

You will be pleased to make all my compliments. I am, Madam, Your most obliged and most humble servant,

SAM. JOHNSON

4. In the event, SJ went to Ashbourne on Wednesday 18 July (*Post* To Hester Thrale, 20 July 1770).

Hester Thrale

FRIDAY 20 JULY 1770

MS: Hyde Collection.

Dear Madam: Ashbourne, July 20, 1770

I hope your complaint, however troublesome is without danger, for your danger involves us all,[1] when you [were] ill before, it was agreed that if you were lost, hope would be lost with you, for such another there was no expectation of finding.

I came hither on Wednesday, having staid one night at a Lodge in the forest of Nedewood.[2] Dr. Taylors is a very pleasant house with a lawn and a Lake,[3] and twenty deer and five fawns upon the Lawn. Whether I shall by any light see Matlock I do not yet know.[4]

Let us not yet have done rejoicing that Mrs. Salusbury was

1. In her letter of 17 July, Hester Thrale had complained of "an odious sore throat" (MS: Rylands Library).

2. Needwood Forest, in eastern Staffordshire, stretches along the River Trent at the boundary with Derbyshire. It covered about 10,000 acres and had "four wards and four keepers, with a handsome lodge to each" (Sampson Erdeswicke, *A Survey of Staffordshire*, ed. Thomas Harwood, 1844, p. 279).

3. Taylor had inherited The Mansion, Ashbourne, from his father in 1731. "The original house was built about 1680 by the grandfather of Dr. Taylor, an Ashbourne attorney; this was a smaller house in the Jacobean style, consisting of an oblong portion adjoining the street and two wings projecting into the garden" (*Life* III.499). In addition to extensive alterations and additions to The Mansion itself, Taylor had enclosed a large piece of wasteland to form a deer-park (Thomas Taylor, *Life of John Taylor*, 1910, p. 20).

4. Hester Thrale had concluded her letter of 17 July, "Mr. Thrale particularly

not in the house. The robbery will be a noble tale when we meet again.[5]

That Barettis book would please you all I made no doubt.[6] I know not whether the world has ever seen such travels before. Those whose lot it is to ramble can seldom write, and those who know how to write very seldom ramble. If Sidney had gone, as he desired, the great voyage with Drake, there would probably have been such a narrative as would have equally satisfied the Poet and Philosopher.[7]

I have learned since I left you that the names of two of the Pleiades were Coccymo and Lampado.[8] I am, Madam, Your humble Servant,

SAM. JOHNSON

Here are Strawberries.

---

vexes lest you should not see Matlock on a moonlight Night" (MS: Rylands Library). SJ and the Thrales visited Matlock (a town in the Peak District of Derbyshire) on their trip to Wales in 1774 (*Life* v.430).

5. *Ante* To Hester Thrale, Early July 1770, n. 8.

6. Giuseppe Baretti's *Journey from London to Genoa* had just been published; according to Hester Thrale, "tis a most pleasing performance, and meets with eager Readers in our house" (17 July 1770, MS: Rylands Library).

7. In 1585 Sir Philip Sidney helped Sir Francis Drake to organize and finance a naval expedition against the Spaniards in the West Indies. Sidney planned to accompany Drake, but he was forbidden to leave by the Queen, who sent him instead to the Netherlands as Governor of Flushing (Sir Fulke Greville, *Life of Sir Philip Sidney*, ed. Nowell Smith, 1907, pp. 70–77).

8. "The Allusion is to a search made at that Time by the Streatham Coterie, for female Names ending in O" (H. L. Piozzi's note). The Pleaides were the seven daughters of Atlas and Pleione. They were pursued by Orion until Zeus placed both hunter and hunted among the stars (Apollodorus, *The Library*, II.2–4, ed. J. G. Frazer, Loeb ed.).

Hester Thrale

MONDAY 23 JULY 1770

MS: Hyde Collection.

Dearest Madam: Ashbourne, July 23, 1770

There had not been so long an interval between my two last

letters,[1] but that when I came hither I did not at first understand the hours of the post.

I have seen the great Bull, and very great he is. I have seen likewise his heir apparent, who promises to inherit all the bulk and all the virtues of his Sire. I have seen the Man who offered an hundred guineas for the young Bull while he was yet little better than a Calf. Matlock I am afraid I shall not see,[2] but I purpose to see Dovedale,[3] and after all this seeing I hope to see You. I am, Madam, Your most obliged, humble servant,

SAM. JOHNSON

1. *Ante* To Hester Thrale, 14 July 1770; 20 July 1770.

2. *Ante* To Hester Thrale, 20 July 1770 and n. 4.

3. SJ did not see Dovedale until 1774, when he visited the Peak District of Derbyshire with the Thrales. He described it then as "a place that deserves a visit, but did not answer my expectation. The river is small, the rocks are grand. . . . I certainly expected a larger river where I found only a clear quick brook. I believe I had imaged a valley enclosed by rocks, and terminated by a broad expanse of water" (*Life* v.430–31).

Hester Thrale

SATURDAY 28 JULY 1770

MS: Beinecke Library.

Dear Madam: Ashbourne, July 28, 1770

I am very glad to think that you want me home. I have taken a place in the Coach, and shall be, I hope, in London on Fryday, and at Streatham on Saturday. The Journey to Brighthelmston makes no part of my felicity, but as I love those with whom I go, and those I shall love equally in any other place.[1] I am afraid Suzy[2] will overtake Lucy,[3] and then I shall be ashamed of my girl. We have here a great deal of Haymaking but the rain catches us. I had a sorry night last night, nor is the rheumatism well, but I am I think, rather better on the whole. I am, Madam, your most obedient servant,

SAM. JOHNSON

1. If the Thrales did visit Brighton, it was only for "a short trip" (Clifford, 1952, p. 83).

2. *Ante* To Hester Thrale, Early July 1770, n. 6.

3. *Ante* To Hester Thrale, 19 Apr. 1768, n. 4.

Francis Barber

TUESDAY 25 SEPTEMBER 1770

MS: Hyde Collection.

ADDRESS: To Mr. Barber at Mrs. Clapp's in Bishop Stortford, Hertfordshire.[1]

POSTMARKS: 26 SE, 27 SE.

Dear Francis: London, Sept. 25, 1770

I am at last sat down to write to you, and should very much blame myself for having neglected you so long, if I did not impute that and many other of my failures to want of health. I hope[2] not to be so long silent again. I am very well satisfied with your progress, if you can really perform the exercises which you are set, and I hope Mr. Ellis does not suffer you to impose on him or on yourself.[3]

Make my compliments to Mr. Ellis and to Mrs. Clapp, and Mr. Smith.[4]

Let me know what English books you read for your entertainment. You can never be wise unless you love reading.

Do not imagine that I shall forget or forsake you, for if when I examine you, I find that you have not lost your time, you shall want no encouragement, from, yours affectionately,

SAM. JOHNSON

1. *Ante* To Francis Barber, 28 May 1768 and n. 1.

2. MS: defective; "hope" in JB's hand

3. The Rev. William Ellis (b. ?1730), headmaster of the Bishop Stortford Grammar School, 1770–?72 (*Johns. Glean.* II.19–21; *Alum. Oxon.* II.ii.422).

4. *Ante* To Joseph Smith, 1 Mar. 1770, n. 1.

Joseph Warton

THURSDAY 27 SEPTEMBER 1770

MS: Hyde Collection.

Dear Sir: Sept. 27,[1] 1770

I am revising my Edition of Shakespeare and remember that

1. MS: "27" altered from "28"

I formerly misrepresented your opinion of Lear.[2] Be pleased to write the paragraph as you would have it, and send it.[3] If you have any remarks of your own upon that or any other play I shall gladly receive them.[4]

Make my compliments to Mrs. Warton.[5] I sometimes think of wandering for a few days to Winchester, but am apt to delay.[6] I am, Sir, your most humble servant,

SAM. JOHNSON

2. "My learned friend Mr. *Warton*, who has in the *Adventurer* very minutely criticised this play, remarks, that the instances of cruelty are too savage and shocking, and that the intervention of *Edmund* destroys the simplicity of the story" (SJ's *Shakespeare*, 1765, VI.158).

3. The note in the Johnson-Steevens edition of 1773 is unaltered from the version in 1765.

4. *Ante* To Thomas Warton, 23 June 1770 and n. 2. Appendix I of the Johnson-Steevens edition does not contain any notes by Joseph Warton.

5. *Ante* To Joseph Warton, 9 Oct. 1765, n. 1.

6. MS: "delay" altered from "delays"

Bennet Langton

WEDNESDAY 24 OCTOBER 1770

MS: Hyde Collection.

Dear Sir: London, Oct. 24, 1770

I have now so far done my work,[1] that if Lady Rothes shall be pleased to honour me with her commands,[2] I hope, I shall be able to obey them. Make my most respectful compliments to her and to all the Ladies.[3]

1. Chapman (I.240) suggests that SJ is referring to his *Thoughts on Falkland's Islands*, which was published the following March. This identification seems highly improbable, however, since the pamphlet discusses events and incorporates information from Dec. 1770 to Feb. 1771 (*Works*, Yale ed. X.358, 362, 366). A much likelier candidate is his revision of the 1765 Shakespeare (*Ante* To Joseph Warton, 27 Sept. 1770).

2. On 24 May 1770 Langton had married Mary, Dowager Countess of Rothes (*c.* 1743–1820), the widow of the tenth Earl (Fifer, p. lviii).

3. For Langton's mother and sisters, *Ante* To Bennet Langton, 9 Jan. 1759, nn. 3, 6.

Our club commenced again on last Monday. Dr. Goldsmith has been at Paris with the Hornecks not very delightfully to either side.[4] Chamier is come from France, but I have not seen him.[5] He is returned re infecta. Mrs. Burke is quite well.[6] And I am, for me, not amiss. I believe that I can set acorns, and hope to mend my breath by walking about. I am, Dear Sir, your most obliged and most humble Servant,

SAM. JOHNSON

4. *Ante* To Hannah Horneck, 13 June 1770 and n. 2. Writing to Sir Joshua Reynolds from Paris, 29 July 1770, Goldsmith complained that he could "find nothing on the continent so good as when I formerly left it. One of our chief amusements here is scolding at every thing we meet with" (*Letters of Oliver Goldsmith*, ed. K. C. Balderston, 1928, p. 94). Goldsmith also resented the expense of the trip, and, according to JB, the fact that more attention was paid to the Horneck sisters than to him (*Life* I.414 and n. 2).

5. Anthony Chamier (1725–80), a London financier, secretary to the commander-in-chief at the War Office, and one of the original members of The Club. He had been transacting business for the East India Company in Paris, and returned to England in early July (*Walpole's Correspondence*, Yale ed. IV.427, 453). Chamier went on to become Under Secretary of State (1775–80) and M.P. for Tamworth (1778–80) (Namier and Brooke II.207–8).

6. *Ante* To Edmund Burke, 21 June 1770 and n. 2.

Thomas Percy

TUESDAY 27 NOVEMBER 1770

MS: Hyde Collection.

ADDRESS: To the Revd. Dr. Percy at Easton Maudit, Northamptonshire, By Castle Ashby Bag.

ENDORSEMENT: Mr. Johnson, Novr. 27, 1770.

Dear Sir: Nov. the 27, 1770

Mrs. Williams and I heard last night of the death of poor little Miss Anne.[1] We hope the rest of [the] family are out of danger, and that the pretty people yet left you, will console you for the loss of her which has been taken away.[2]

1. Anne (b. 1760), Percy's daughter, died on 17 Nov. (*Correspondence of Thomas Percy and George Paton*, ed. A. F. Falconer, 1961, p. 39 n. 3).

2. Percy's surviving children were Barbara (b. 1761), Henry (b. 1763), Elizabeth

We shall be glad to hear something better of you, that you are yourself completely recovered,[3] and that Mrs. Percy's health is restored. We are both of us[4] pretty well. I am, Sir, Your most humble Servant, SAM. JOHNSON

(b. 1765), and Charlotte (b. 1767). Charlotte died four months later (Mar. 1771) of "the same dreadful disorder which had proved so fatal to her eldest sister" (A.C.C. Gaussen, *Percy*, 1908, p. 124).

3. Percy had been ill with the same fever that killed his daughter (Gaussen, *Percy*, p. 123).

4. MS: "us" superimposed upon "you"

Francis Barber

FRIDAY 7 DECEMBER 1770

MS: Hyde Collection.

ADDRESS: To Mr. Barber at Mrs. Clapp's in Bishop Stortford, Hertfordshire.[1]

POSTMARK: 8 DE.

Dear Francis: December 7, 1770

I hope you mind your business. I design you shall stay with Mrs. Clapp these[2] Holydays. If you are invited out you may go if Mr. Ellis gives leave. I have ordered you some cloaths which you will receive, I believe next week. My compliments to Mrs. Clapp and to Mr. Ellis,[3] and Mr. Smith[4] etc. I am your affectionate, SAM. JOHNSON

1. *Ante* To Francis Barber, 28 May 1768 and n. 1.
2. MS: "these" altered from "this"
3. *Ante* To Francis Barber, 25 Sept. 1770 and n. 3.
4. *Ante* To Joseph Smith, 1 Mar. 1770, n. 1.

Joseph Smith

TUESDAY 29 JANUARY 1771

MS: Hyde Collection.

ADDRESS: To Mr. Smith.

ENDORSEMENT in an unidentified hand: Dr. Johnson to Mr. Jh. Smith.

Sir: January 29, 1771

I beg leave to give you again the trouble which you were so kind as to take last year of cashing these bills and paying them.

Be pleased to send me some Irish Cloath[1] for 12 Shirts at 4 yards to a shirt, the price may be from 3s. 6d. to 4s. the yard. The piece which you sent in the Summer to Mrs. Williams, you may charge to me.

I inclose, as I did last year, a bill of 50£ which I beg to know whether you receive. You need send back no money, but a state of the account between us. I am, sir, your most humble servant,

SAM. JOHNSON

As I remember there was a surplus of about ten pounds in your hands last year.

1. Linen, "the staple of commerce" in eighteenth-century Ireland (*Walpole's Correspondence*, Yale ed. XXXIX.20 n. 16).

John Rivington[1]

SATURDAY 2 FEBRUARY 1771

MS: Hyde Collection.

ADDRESS: To Mr. Rivington, Bookseller.

Sir: Febr. 2, 1771

When Mr. Steevens treated with You about the new impression of Shakespeare, he agreed with [you that] the additions now made should be printed by themselves for the benefit of former purchasers.[2] As some of my subscribers may think themselves ill treated, it is proper to advertise our intention,

1. John Rivington (1720–92), prominent bookseller in St. Paul's Churchyard and one of the publishers of SJ's Shakespeare (*Lit. Anec.* III.400).

2. *Ante* To Thomas Warton, 23 June 1770 and n. 2. "No copy of the separately published additions is known, and they were probably never printed" (Arthur Sherbo, *SJ, Editor of Shakespeare*, 1956, p. 105).

and I shall be glad to see it done in one or more of the papers next week.[3] I am, Sir, Your humble servant,

SAM. JOHNSON

3. No such advertisement has been discovered.

Richard Farmer

MONDAY 18 FEBRUARY 1771

MS: Folger Shakespeare Library.

Johnson's Court,
Fleetstreet, Febr. 18, 1771

Sir:

Some time ago Mr. Steevens and I took the liberty of sending a catalogue in hope of some improvement and augmentation.[1] Mr. Steevens, who undertakes the whole care of this impression, begins to fancy that he wants it.

I have done very little to the book, but by the plunder of your pamphlet, and the authorities which Mr. Steevens has very diligently collected, I think, it will be somewhat improved. If you could[2] spare us any thing we should think your communication a great favour. I hope amongst us all Shakespeare will be better understood. You have already done your part, and when you have finished what I am told you are now projecting, will leave I believe much fewer difficulties to future criticks.[3] I am, Sir, your most humble servant,

SAM. JOHNSON

1. *Ante* To Richard Farmer, 21 Mar. 1770 and nn. 1, 3.

2. MS: "could" altered from "can"

3. Farmer had announced his intention to write "A series of Letters on the subject of Shakespear and his commentators," but the project was never completed (*Correspondence of Thomas Percy and Richard Farmer*, ed. Cleanth Brooks, 1946, p. 50 and n. 19).

Bennet Langton

WEDNESDAY 20 MARCH 1771

MS: Hyde Collection.

Dear Sir: March 20, 1771

After much lingering of my own, and much of the Ministry, I have at length got out my paper.[1] But delay is not yet at an end, not many had been dispersed before Lord North ordered the sale to stop.[2] His reasons I do not distinctly know you may try to find them in the perusal.[3] Before his order a sufficient number were dispersed to do all the mischief, though perhaps not to make all the sport that might be expected from it.

Soon after your departure I had the pleasure of finding all the danger past with which your navigation was threatned.[4] I hope nothing happens at home to abate your satisfaction, but that Lady Rothes, and Mrs. Langton and the young Ladies are all well.

I was last night at the club. Dr. Percy has written a long Ballad in many *Fits*; it is pretty enough.[5] He has printed, and will soon publish it. Goldsmith is at Bath with Lord Clare.[6] At Mr. Thrales, where I am now writing, all are well. I am, Dear Sir, Your most humble Servant,

SAM. JOHNSON

1. *Ante* To Bennet Langton, 24 Oct. 1770, n. 1.

2. Frederick North (1732–92), Viscount North, eldest son of the first Earl of Guildford, M.P. for Banbury (1754–90) and First Lord of the Treasury (1770–82).

3. The pamphlet was withdrawn in order to be "softened in one particular" (*Life* II.135). SJ originally wrote of George Grenville: "he had powers not universally possessed; if he could have got the money, he could have counted it." At the Ministry's insistence this was altered to read: "he had powers not universally possessed; and if he sometimes erred, he was likewise sometimes right" (*Works*, Yale ed. X.383). The pamphlet was re-released *c.* 27 Mar. (*Works*, Yale ed. X.349).

4. Langton's "navigation" was the Wey Canal in Surrey, a project in which he had invested along with the Earl of Portland (Fifer, pp. lix–lx; *Johns. Glean.* II.59).

5. SJ refers to *The Hermit of Warkworth. A Northumberland Ballad. In three fits or cantos* (1771). For SJ's three parodies of the ballad, see *Poems*, pp. 184–86.

6. Robert Nugent (1709–88), of Carlanstown, County Meath, and Gosfield, Essex, was created Viscount Clare in 1767 for his services to the administration. Lord Clare was "a friend of Pope; a patron of Goldsmith; and author of an *Ode to William Pulteney*, which was admired by Horace Walpole, quoted by Gibbon, and is now forgotten" (Namier and Brooke III.219). His only son, Lt.-Col. Edmund Nugent (1731–71), died at Bath on 26 Apr., attended by Goldsmith (*Letters of Oliver Goldsmith*, ed. K. C. Balderston, 1928, p. 100; Namier and Brooke III.218).

Henry Thrale

MARCH 1771

MS: Hyde Collection.

Dear Sir: March 1771[1]

In the Shrewsbury an Eastindia Ship commanded by Captain Jones,[2] there is one Thomas Coxeter who lately enlisted as a Soldier in the Company's service. He repents of his adventure, and has written to his sister,[3] who bring[s] this letter, to procure him his discharge. He is the Son of a Gentleman who was once my friend,[4] and the boy was himself a favourite with my wife. I shall therefore think it a great favour, if you will be pleased to use your influence with Sir George Colebrook,[5] that he may be discharged. The request is not great, for he is slight and feeble, and worth nothing, but to those who value him for some other merit than his own.[6] I am, Sir, your most obliged and most humble servant,

SAM. JOHNSON

1. MS: day of the month missing

2. The *Shrewsbury* (499 tons) set sail on its second voyage, to Bombay, on 1 May 1771. In command of the ship was Capt. Benjamin Jones (Charles Hardy, *Register of Ships Employed in the Service of the East India Company, 1760–1810*, 1811, p. 49).

3. The daughter of Thomas Coxeter the elder (see below, n. 4) was "much noticed, and occasionally assisted with money, by Dr. Johnson; and after the death of that benevolent Moralist, her latter days were in some degree cheered by the notice taken of her by the Committee of the Literary Fund. She died in November 1807" (*Lit. Anec.* II.513). She may have been the "Mrs. Coxeter" with whom Francis Barber boarded (Waingrow, p. 164).

4. Thomas Coxeter (1689–1747), a literary antiquarian "without any settled pursuit," who worked in Grub Street and "amassed materials for a Biography of our Poets" (*Lit. Anec.* II.512). Coxeter also "assisted Mr. Ames in his History of British Typography; had a curious collection of old plays; and pointed out to Theobald many of the black-letter books with which that Critick illustrated Shakspeare" (*Lit Anec.* II.512).

5. Sir George Colebrooke (1729–1809), second Bt., of Gatton, Surrey, M.P. for Arundel (1754–74). He served as director and chairman of the East India Company (1767–71, 1772–73) (Namier and Brooke II.235).

6. *Post* To Thomas Percy, 1 Dec. 1776; 2 Dec. 1776.

Robert Chambers

SATURDAY 6 APRIL 1771

MS: Hyde Collection.

ADDRESS: To Robert Chambers, Esq., at New inn Hall, Oxford.

POSTMARK: 6 AP.

ENDORSEMENT: Mr. Johnson, 6 Apr. 1771.

Dear Sir: Apr. 6, 1771

I am very much obliged by your kind invitation, but as You are to come hither so soon, why should we make journies for that which will be had without them.

Quadrigis petimus bene vivere; quod petis hic est.[1]

We can live together in town, and dine in chambers or[2] at the mitre, and do as well as at New inn hall.

My Friends tell me that I am pretty well, and I hope you are well too. Come hither as soon as You can. I am, Sir, your most humble servant,

SAM. JOHNSON

1. *Quadrigis petimus bene vivere. quod petis hic est*: "with cars we seek to make life happy. What you are seeking is here" (Horace, *Epistles* I.xi.29, trans. H. R. Fairclough, Loeb ed.).

2. MS: "or" superimposed upon "a"

Elizabeth Langton[1]

WEDNESDAY 17 APRIL 1771

PRINTED SOURCE: *GM* 1800, p. 915.

Madam: London, April 17, 1771

If I could have flattered myself that my letters could have given pleasure, or have alleviated pain, I should not have omitted to write to a lady to whom I do sincerely wish every increase of pleasure, and every mitigation of uneasiness.

1. *Ante* To Bennet Langton, 9 Jan. 1759, n. 3. Elizabeth Langton "possessed, among other valuable qualifications, great mental abilities, and was a particular favourite and correspondent of the late Dr. Samuel Johnson" (*GM* 1791, p. 91).

I knew, dear Madam, that a very heavy affliction had fallen upon you; but it was one of those which the established course of nature makes necessary, and to which kind words give no relief.[2] Success[3] is on these occasions to be expected only from time.

Your censure of me, as deficient in friendship, is therefore too severe. I have neither been unfriendly, nor intentionally uncivil. The notice with which you have honoured me, I have neither forgotten, nor remembered without pleasure.

The calamity of ill health, your brother will tell you that I have had, since I saw you, sufficient reason to know and to pity. But this is another evil against which we can receive little help from one another. I can only advise you, and I advise you with great earnestness, to do nothing that may hurt you, and to reject nothing that may do you good. To preserve health is a moral and religious duty: for health is the basis of all social virtues; and we can be useful no longer than while we are well.

If the family knows that you receive this letter, you will be pleased to make my compliments.

I flatter myself with the hopes of seeing Langton after Lady Rothes's recovery;[4] and then I hope that you and I shall renew our conferences, and that I shall find you willing as formerly to talk and to hear;[5] and shall be again admitted to the honour of being, Madam, your most obedient and most humble servant,

SAM. JOHNSON

2. It is possible that this "heavy affliction" was the death of Bennet Langton the elder in June 1769.

3. SJ may have written "Succour" (Chapman 1.251).

4. *Ante* To Bennet Langton, 24 Oct. 1770, n. 2. Lady Rothes was pregnant, but miscarried a few months later (*Post* To Bennet Langton, 29 Aug. 1771). The Langtons' first child was born the following March.

5. *Post* To Hester Thrale, 20 July 1771.

Mrs. Rolt[1]

TUESDAY 7 MAY 1771

MS: Hyde Collection.

ADDRESS: To Mrs. Rolt.

Madam, May 7, 1771

If I have any right notion of the School of which you have heard, it will not be worth your persuit;[2] but whatever it be, it is wholly in the power of Dr. Percy to obtain it, as he knows both you and Mrs. Williams. I am, Madam, your most humble servant,

SAM. JOHNSON

1. Mary Rolt (d. 1792), second wife and widow of Richard Rolt (?1725–70), author of a *Dictionary of Trade and Commerce* (1756), to which SJ had contributed a preface without reading the book (*Life* I.359; Hazen, pp. 198–99). She was a cousin of Thomas Percy, who made her an allowance after her husband's death (B. H. Davis, *Thomas Percy*, 1989, p. 282).

2. Perhaps the Ladies' Charity School, Holborn. *Ante* To Thomas Percy, 5 Nov. 1769, n. 1.

Madame de Boufflers[1]

THURSDAY 16 MAY 1771

MS: Hyde Collection.

Mai 16, 1771

Oui, Madame, le moment est arrivè, et il faut que je parte, mais pourquoi faut il partir? est ce que je m'ennuye? je m'ennuyerai ailleurs. Est ce que je cherche ou quelque plaisir ou quelque soulagement? Je ne cherche rien, je n'espere rien. Aller, voir ce que j'ai vû, être un peu rejouè, un peu degoutè,

1. Marie Charlotte Hippolyte (1724–1800), Comtesse de Boufflers-Rouverel, "*savante, galante*, a great friend of the Prince of Conti, and a passionate admirer *de nous autres Anglais*" (*Walpole's Correspondence*, Yale ed. XXII.135). According to Topham Beauclerk: "When Madame de Boufflers was first in England [1763] . . . she was desirous to see Johnson. I accordingly went with her to his chambers in the Temple, where she was entertained with his conversation for some time" (*Life* II.405). H. L. Piozzi identifies Madame de Boufflers as the recipient of this letter (Piozzi I.34).

me resouvenir que la vie se passe et qu'elle se passe en vain, me plaindre de moi, m'endu[r]cir aux dehors, voici le tout de ce qu'on compte pour les delices de l'année.

Que Dieu vous donne, Madame, tous les agremens de la vie, avec un esprit qui peut en jouir, sans s'y livrer trop.

Unidentified Correspondent[1]

FRIDAY 14 JUNE 1771

MS: Birthplace Museum, Lichfield. A copy in an unidentified hand.

Dear Sir: Johnsons Court, June 14, 1771

The time is now come when we used to go to Lichfield; if you have any design of the same Journey this year, and like my company as I like yours, I shall be glad to settle the Scheme of travelling with you, and shall be better pleased, the[2] sooner we go. I am, Dear Sir, your most humble Servant,

SAM. JOHNSON

1. The recipient may have been SJ's stepson, Joseph Porter. *Ante* To Lucy Porter, 18 Apr. 1768, n. 6; cf. *Ante* To Unidentified Correspondent, 25 June 1770.

2. MS: "they"

Hester Thrale

SATURDAY 15 JUNE 1771

MS: Hyde Collection.

Dear Madam: June 15, 1771

It seems strange that I should live a week so near you, and yet never see you. I have been once to enquire after you, and when I have written this note, am going again. The use of the pamphlet the Letter will show which lies at the proper page.[1] When Mr. Langton shows so much attention, it cannot become

1. *Experiments and Observations on the Malvern Waters* (1756, 1763), by John Wall (1708–76), M.D., Worcester physician and medical writer, who recommended the waters for a variety of ailments, including cancer. *Ante* To Hester Thrale, 11 Nov. 1768, n. 1.

me to show less.[2] What to think of the case I know not, the relation has all appearance of truth and one great argument is, that the only danger is in not believing. The water can, I think, do no harm, Dr. Wall thinks it may do good. If Mrs. Salusbury should think fit to go before you can go with her, I will attend her, if She will accept of my company, with great readiness at my own expence, and if I am in the Country will come back.[3]

I need not tell you, that I hope you are with the necessary exceptions all well,[4] or that I am, Madam, your most obliged and most humble servant, SAM. JOHNSON

2. Bennet Langton had written to SJ on 10 June, bringing Wall's pamphlet to his notice and recommending it to the Thrales: "One of the Cures, I see, was in a Case resembling, as I should imagine, that of poor Mrs. Salisbury" (MS: Hyde Collection). This case concerned a woman with "a schirrous Lump in her Breast of considerable Magnitude," which "in about 6 Month's Time . . . was considerably lessen'd in Size" (Wall, *Experiments and Observations*, 1763, pp. 110–11).

3. Mrs. Salusbury decided not to try the waters, and therefore declined SJ's offer.

4. SJ refers to chronic problems in the Thrale nursery (Queeney's worms, Lucy's infected ears) and to Hester's pregnancy, then far-advanced (Hyde, 1977, pp. 44–46). *Post* To Hester Thrale, 22 June 1771.

James Boswell

THURSDAY 20 JUNE 1771

PRINTED SOURCE: JB's *Life*, 1791, I.348.

Dear Sir: London, June 20, 1771

If you are now able to comprehend that I might neglect to write without diminution of affection, you have taught me, likewise, how that neglect may be uneasily felt without resentment. I wished for your letter a long time, and when it came, it amply recompensed the delay.[1] I never was so much pleased as now with your account of yourself; and sincerely hope, that

1. JB had written on 18 Apr. to renew "a correspondence which had been too long discontinued" (*Life* II.139). After apologizing for his silence, he gave SJ "an account of my comfortable life as a married man, and a lawyer in practice at the

between publick business, improving studies, and domestick pleasures, neither melancholy nor caprice will find any place for entrance. Whatever philosophy may determine of material nature, it is certainly true of intellectual nature, that it *abhors a vacuum*:[2] our minds cannot be empty; and evil will break in upon them, if they are not pre-occupied by good. My dear Sir, mind your studies, mind your business, make your lady happy,[3] and be a good Christian. After this,

——tristitiam et metus
Trades protervis in mare Creticum
Portare ventis.[4]

If we perform our duty, we shall be safe and steady, "*Sive per*," etc.[5] whether we climb the Highlands, or are tost among the Hebrides; and I hope the time will come when we may try our powers both with cliffs and water. I see but little of Lord Elibank, I know not why; perhaps by my own fault.[6] I am this day going into Staffordshire and Derbyshire for six weeks.[7] I am, dear Sir, Your most affectionate And most humble servant,

SAM. JOHNSON

Scotch bar; invited him to Scotland, and promised to attend him to the Highlands, and Hebrides" (*Life* II.140).

2. "Nature abhors a vacuum" has been traced back to a treatise (*De placitis philosophorum*) attributed to Plutarch. By the mid-sixteenth century, however, it had attained the status of a proverb (*Oxford Dictionary of Proverbs*, rev. F. P. Wilson, 1970, p. 555).

3. *Ante* To JB, 9 Sept. 1769, n. 7.

4. *tristitiam et metus / tradam protervis in mare Creticum / portare ventis*: "I will banish gloom and fear to the wild winds to carry o'er the Cretan Sea" (Horace, *Odes* I.xxvi.1–3, trans. C. E. Bennett, Loeb ed.).

5. *Integer vitæ scelerisque purus / non eget Mauris iaculis neque arcu / nec venenatis gravida sagittis, / Fusce, pharetra, / sive per Syrtes iter æstuosas. . . .* : "He who is upright in his way of life and unstained by guilt, needs not Moorish darts nor bow nor quiver loaded with poisoned arrows, Fuscus, whether his way shall be through the sweltering Syrtes . . ." (Horace, *Odes* I.xxii.1–5, trans. C. E. Bennett, Loeb ed.).

6. Patrick Murray (1703–78), fifth Baron Elibank, lawyer, army officer, and the author of a number of pamphlets on economic and historical subjects, including *An Inquiry into the Original of the Public Debt* (1753). SJ, who had known Elibank since at least 1765, praised his extensive knowledge, derived from "comparison of books with life" (*Life* v.570–72).

7. *Post* To Hester Thrale, 20 June 1771; *Post* To Bennet Langton, 29 Aug. 1771.

Hester Thrale

THURSDAY 20 JUNE 1771

MS: Birthplace Museum, Lichfield.

Dear Madam: Thursday, June 20, 1771

This Night a[t] nine o'clock Sam. Johnson and Francis Barber Esquires set out in the Lichfie[l]d stage. Francis is indeed rather upon it. What adventures we may meet with who can tell?

I shall write when I come to Lichfield, and hope to hear in return, that You are safe, and Mrs. Salusbury better, and all the rest as well as I left them.[1] I am, Madam, your most humble servant,

SAM. JOHNSON

1. *Ante* To Hester Thrale, 15 June 1771.

Hester Thrale

SATURDAY 22 JUNE 1771

MS: Hyde Collection.

Dear Madam: Lichfield, June 22, 1771

Last night I came safe to Lichfield, this day I was visited by Mrs. Cobb.[1] This afternoon I went to Mrs. Aston,[2] where I found Miss Turton,[3] and waited on her home. Miss Turton wears Spectacles, and can hardly climb the Stiles. I was not tired at all, either last night or to day. Miss Porter is very kind to me. Her Dog and Cats are all well.

In all this there is nothing very memorable, but *sands form the mountain*.[4] I hope to hear from Streatham of a greater

1. *Ante* To Lucy Porter, 18 Apr. 1768, n. 4.

2. *Ante* To Elizabeth Aston, 17 Nov. 1767, n. 1.

3. *Ante* To Elizabeth Aston, 17 Nov. 1767, n. 8.

4. "Think nought a trifle, though it small appear; / Small sands the mountain, moments make the year" (Edward Young, *Love of Fame* VI.205–6).

event, that a new Being is born that shall in time write such letters as this,[5] and that another Being is safe, that she may continue to write such. She can indeed do many other things, she can add to the pleasure of many Lives, and among others to that of her most obedient and most humble servant,

SAM. JOHNSON

5. Sophia (1771–1824), the Thrales' seventh child, was born on 23 July, approximately a month overdue (Hyde, 1977, p. 48).

Hester Thrale

TUESDAY 25 JUNE 1771

MS: Birthplace Museum, Lichfield.

Dear Madam: June 25, 1771

All your troubles, I hope, are now past, and the little stranger safe in the cradle.[1] You have then nothing to do but survey the lawn from your window, and see Lucy try to run after Harry.

Here things go wrong. They have cut down another tree,[2] but they do not yet grow very rich. I enquired of my Barber after another Barber. That Barber, says he is dead and his Son has left off, to turn Maltster.—Mal[t]sters, I believe do not get much money. The price of Barley, and the King's duty are known, and their profit is never suffered to rise high.[3]—But there is often a rise upon Stock.—There may as well be a fall—Very seldom. There are those in this town that have not a farthing less this year than fifty pounds by the rise upon

1. *Ante* To Hester Thrale, 22 June 1771, n. 5.

2. *Ante* To Hester Thrale, 14 Aug. 1769.

3. Despite the restraints mentioned by SJ, it was in fact possible for maltsters to make a substantial profit. From 1760 to 1780 the malt tax remained constant, at 9¼*d.* the bushel. Moreover, maltsters were able to evade the excise by such methods as sprinkling or compression of the grain. The primary factor in determining profit, however, was the price of barley, which fluctuated, sometimes dramatically, from season to season. Even when the price rose sharply, maltsters could and did pass some of their costs directly onto the brewers: from 1770 to 1771, for example, malt prices rose from 26*s.* 6*d.* per quarter to 33*s.*–34*s.* (Peter Mathias, *The Brewing Industry in England, 1700–1830*, 1959, pp. 266, 403–10).

Stock.[4] Did You think, there had been yet left a City in England, where the gain of fifty pounds in a year would be mentioned with Emphasis?

Has Mrs. Salusbury got her lawrel water?[5] It may perhaps do good, at least it may be tried. I am sure I wish it success. I am, Madam, your most obedient and most humble servant,

SAM. JOHNSON

4. The stock reports published in the *GM* for Jan.–June 1771 confirm a steady increase in all categories.

5. In his *Experiments and Observations on the Malvern Waters*, 1763, John Wall recommended that breast cancer be treated by applying to the patient's chest "a Cloth kept constantly wet" with an infusion of laurel leaves (p. 111). *Ante* To Hester Thrale, 15 June 1771.

Hester Thrale

WEDNESDAY 3 JULY 1771

MS: Hyde Collection.

Dear Madam: Ashbourn, July 3, 1771

Last Saturday I came to Ashbourn;[1] the dangers or the pleasures of the journey I have at present no disposition to recount. Else might I paint the beauties of my native plain, might I tell of "the smiles of Nature and the charms of art,"[2] else might I relate how I crossed the Staffordshire Canal one of the great efforts of human labour and human contrivance,[3]

1. MS: "Ashbourn" altered from "Ashburne"

2. "How has kind Heaven adorned the happy land, / And scattered blessings with a wasteful hand! / . . . With all the gifts that heaven and earth impart, / The smiles of nature, and the charms of art" (Joseph Addison, *A Letter from Italy*, ll. 105–6, 109–10).

3. "This Canal was begun in the year 1766, by virtue of an act of the 6th of George III, and is now nearly compleated from the mouth of the river Darwent in Derbyshire, to near Stone in Staffordshire, which is about forty-five miles, and is passable for barges of thirty tons burthen" ("Description of the Plan of the Grand Canal from the Trent to the Mersey," *GM* 1771, p. 296). The Canal was not completed until 1777 (*A Map of the County of Stafford by William Yates*, 1775, Introduction by A.D.M. Phillips, vol. 12 of *Collections for a History of Staffordshire*, 1984, p. xvi).

which from the bridge on which I viewed it, passd away on either side, and loses itself in distant regions uniting waters that Nature had divided, and dividing lands which Nature had united. I might tell how these reflections fermented in my mind till the chaise stopped at Ashbourne, at Ashbourne in the Peak. Let not the barren name of the peak terrify you; I have never wanted Strawberries and cream. The great Bull has no disease but age. I hope in time to be like the great Bull; and hope you will be like him too a hundred years hence.

In the mean time, dearest Madam, you have many dangers to pass. I hope the danger of this year is now over, and you are safe in Bed with a pretty little Stranger in the cradle.[4] I hope you do not think me indifferent about you, and therefore will take care to have me informed. I am, Madam, Your most obedient and most humble servant,

SAM. JOHNSON

4. *Ante* To Hester Thrale, 22 June 1771, n. 5.

Hester Thrale

SUNDAY 7 JULY 1771

MS: Hyde Collection.

Dear Madam: Ashbourn, July 7, 1771

No news yet of the little one. Our expectations were premature.[1]

Poor Dr. Taylor is ill, and under my government, you know that the art of government is learned by obedience, I hope I can govern very tolerably.

The old Rheumatism is come again into my face and mouth, but nothing yet to the Lumbago, however having so long thought it gone, I do not like its return.

Miss Porter was much pleased to be mentioned in your letter, and is sure that I have spoken better of her than she de-

1. *Ante* To Hester Thrale, 22 June 1771, n. 5.

sired. She holds that both Frank and his Master are much improved. The master she says is not half so *lounging* and *untidy* as he was, there was no such thing last year as getting him off his chair.

Strawberries and cream every day.

Taylor talks of killing a Buck. Don't let him do it, if you can help it. I protest against it.

I am willing to entertain some hope from Dr. Bromfield's infusion,[2] for where is the use of Despair? The lotion cannot I think do any thing, but the internal use may be efficacious.

Be pleased to make my compliments to every body. I am, Madam, your most obedient and most humble servant,

SAM. JOHNSON

2. Robert Bromfield (?1722–86), M.D., physician to the British Lying-in Hospital and the Thrales' family doctor (Hyde, 1977, p. 35).

Hester Thrale

MONDAY 8 JULY 1771

MS: Hyde Collection.

Dearest Madam: Ashbourne, July 8, 1771

Indifference is indeed a strange word in a Letter from me to you.[1] Which way could it possibly creep in? I do not remember any moment for a very long time past, when I could use it without contradiction from my own thoughts.

This naughty Baby stays so long that I am afraid it will be a Giant like King Richard. I suppose I shall be able to tell it, "Teeth hadst thou in thy head when thou wert born."[2] I wish your pains and your danger over.

1. *Ante* To Hester Thrale, 3 July 1771.

2. SJ alludes to the speech in which Henry VI taunts the future Richard III with his monstrous birth: "Thy mother felt more than a mother's pain, / And yet brought forth less than a mother's hope. / . . . Teeth hadst thou in thy head when thou wast born, / To signify thou cam'st to bite the world" (*3 Henry VI* v.vi.49–50, 53–54).

Dr. Taylor is better, and is gone out in the chaise. My Rheumatism is better too.

I would have been glad to go to Hagley in compliance with Mr. Littylton's kind invitation,[3] for beside the pleasure of his conversation I should have had the opportunity of recollecting past times, and wandering *per montes notos et flumina nota*,[4] of recalling the images of sixteen, and reviewing my conversations with poor Ford.[5] But this year will not bring this gratification within my power.[6] I promised Taylor a month. Every thing is done here to please me, and his ill health is a strong reason against desertion.

I return all the compliments, and hope I may add some at last to this wicked, tiresome, dilatory Bantling. I am, Dearest Madam, your most obedient and most humble servant,

SAM. JOHNSON

3. William Henry Lyttelton (1724–1808), of Little Hagley, Worcestershire, M.P. for Bewdley (1748–55, 1774–90), created Baron Westcote (1776) and Baron Lyttelton (1794) (Namier and Brooke III.76–77). He made the Grand Tour with Henry Thrale, and became godfather in 1773 to the Thrales' second son, Ralph. According to SJ, who had known the family for forty-five years, Lyttelton "had more Chaff than Grain in him" (*Thraliana* I.200). In her letter of 1 July, Hester Thrale had transmitted a warm invitation to visit during his time at Ashbourne (MS: Rylands Library).

4. *Ante* To Hester Thrale, 14 Aug. 1769, n. 3.

5. The Rev. Cornelius Ford (1694–1731), SJ's brilliant but profligate first cousin, "a Cambridge don, a gay London spark, a wit and man of fashion" (Clifford, 1955, p. 78). In 1725–26 SJ had spent nine months with Ford, who was "rusticating" on his property at Pedmore, Worcestershire. The Lytteltons of Hagley Park were neighbors and family friends (Clifford, 1955, p. 82).

6. In 1774 SJ visited Lyttelton at Little Hagley, together with the Thrales (*Life* V.456).

Hester Thrale

WEDNESDAY 10 JULY 1771

MS: Hyde Collection.

Dearest Madam: Ashbourne, July 10, 1771

Sure I shall hear to morrow some news from Mr. Thrale, for all that I can expect no good news of you. I am not sorry that opium is necessary, and sincerely wish your pain and your danger happily at an end.

I am obliged to my friend Harry for his remembrance, but think it a little hard that I hear nothing from Miss.

Here has been a Man here to day to take a farm. After some talk he went to see the Bull, and said that he had seen a bigger. Do you think he is likely to get the farm?

Toûjours strawberries and Cream.

Dr. Taylor is much better, and my Rheumatism is less painful. Let me hear in return as much good of you and of Mrs. Salusbury. You despise the Dog and Duck,[1] things that are at hand are always slighted. I remember that Dr. Grevil of Glocester sent for that water when his wife was in the same danger, but he lived near Malvern,[2] and you live near the Dog and Duck. Thus in difficult cases we naturally trust most what we least know.

Why Bromfield,[3] supposing that a lotion can do good, should despise laurel water in comparison with his own receipt I do not see, and see still less why he should laugh at that which Wall thinks efficacious.[4] I am afraid philosophy will not warrant much hope in a lotion.

Be pleased to make my compliments from Mrs. Salusbury to Susy.[5] I am, Dear Madam, your most humble servant,

SAM. JOHNSON

1. SJ refers to mineral springs in St. George's Fields, Lambeth, Surrey, which were called after an adjacent pub, *The Dog and Duck*. The water was considered efficacious in treating scrofula and cancer (Wheatley and Cunningham 1.509–10).

2. *Ante* To Hester Thrale, 15 June 1771, n. 1.

3. *Ante* To Hester Thrale, 7 July 1771, n. 2.

4. *Ante* To Hester Thrale, 15 June 1771, n. 1; 25 June 1771.

5. That is, from the eldest to the youngest member of the Thrale household.

Hester Thrale

MONDAY 15 JULY 1771

MS: Berg Collection, New York Public Library.
ADDRESS: To Mrs. Thrale.

Dear Madam: Ashbourne, July 15, 1771

When we come together to practice chymistry, I believe we shall find our furnaces sufficient for most operations.[1] We have a Gentleman here reading philosophical lectures, who performs the chymical part with furnaces of the same kind with ours, but much less, yet he says, that he can in his little furnace raise a fire that will melt iron. I saw him smelt lead, and shall bring up some oar for our operations. The carriage will cost more than the lead perhaps will be worth but a Chymist is very like a Lover

"And sees those dangers which he cannot shun."[2]

I will try to get other oar both of iron and copper, which are all which this country affords, though feracissima metallorum regio.[3]

The Doctor has no park, but a little enclosure behind his house, in which there are about thirty Bucks and Does, and they take bread from the hand. Would it not be [a] pity to kill them? It seems to be now out of his head.

This day we had no strawberries. I am, Madam, Your most obliged and most humble servant,

SAM. JOHNSON

1. "It was about this Time that a Laboratory was fitted up at Streatham for Mr. Johnson's Amusement" (H. L. Piozzi's note). *Post* To Hester Thrale, 24 July 1771. "But the danger Mr. Thrale found his friend in one day when I was driven to London, and he had got the children and servants round him to see some experiments performed, put an end to all our entertainment" (*Johns. Misc.* I.307).

2. "I know the Bite, yet to my ruin run, / And see the Folly which I cannot shun" (Lady Mary Wortley Montagu, *The Bassette Table*, ll. 70–71).

3. Perhaps an echo of Pliny the Elder's description of Spain as *feracem . . . metallorum omnium generum*: "rich in every kind of ore" (*Historia Naturalis* XXXVII.lxxvii.203, trans. D. E. Eichholz, Loeb ed.).

Joshua Reynolds

WEDNESDAY 17 JULY 1771

MS: Hyde Collection.[1]

ADDRESS: To Sir Joshua Reynolds in Leicester Fields, London.

POSTMARK: 19 IY.

Dear Sir: Ashbourn in Derbyshire, July 17, 1771

When I came to Lichfield I f⟨ound that my⟩ portrait had been much visited and mu⟨ch admired.⟩[2] Every man has a lurking wish to appear ⟨considerable in⟩ his native place, and I was pleased with ⟨the dignity⟩ confered by such a testimony of your regard.

Be pleased therefore to accept the thanks of, Sir, Your most obliged and most humble servant,

SAM. JOHNSON

Compliments to Miss Reynolds.

1. MS: mutilated; material in angle brackets from text in JB's *Life*

2. SJ refers to a studio variant, painted for Lucy Porter, of the Reynolds portrait completed in 1769 and exhibited in 1770. The original was purchased by the third Duke of Dorset (*Life* IV.449; K. K. Yung, *Samuel Johnson*, 1984, p. 103).

Hester Thrale

WEDNESDAY 17 JULY 1771

MS: Birthplace Museum, Lichfield.

Madam: Ashbourn, July 17, 1771

At Lichfield I found little to please me. One more of my few s[c]hoolfellows is dead, upon which I might make a[1] new reflection and say Mors omnibus communis.[2] Miss Porter was rather better than last year, but I think Miss Aston grows

1. MS: "th" del. before "a"

2. *Mors omnibus communis*: "Death is common to all." This adage can be traced back to Cicero's *De Senectute* (XIX.68). By the sixteenth century, however, it had attained proverbial status, as SJ's "new reflection" ironically suggests.

rather worse. I took a walk in quest of juvenile images, but caught a cloud instead of Juno.[3]

I longed for Taylor's chaise,[4] but I think Lucy did not long for it, though she was not sorry to see it. Lucy is a Philosopher, and considers me as one of the external and accidental things that are to be taken and left without emotion. If I could learn of Lucy would it be better? Will you teach me?

I would not have it thought that I forget Mrs. Salusbury but nothing that I can say will be of use, and what comfort she can have, your duty will not fail to give her.

What is the matter that Queeny uses me no better, I should think she might have written to me, but she has never sent, a message nor a compliment. I thank Harry for remembring me.

Rheumatism teazes me yet, but Dr. Taylor is got well. I am, Madam, Your most obedient and most humble servant,

SAM. JOHNSON

3. Zeus deceived Ixion, who was attempting to rape Hera, with a cloud-image of the goddess (Pindar, second Pythian ode).

4. Dr. Taylor possessed "an equipage properly suited to a wealthy well-beneficed clergyman": a "large roomy post-chaise, drawn by four stout plump horses, and driven by two steady jolly postillions" (*Life* II.473).

Hester Thrale

SATURDAY 20 JULY 1771

MS: Hyde Collection.

Dear Madam: Ashbourn, July 20, 1771

Sweet meat and sower sauce.—With your letter which was kind, I received another from Miss Langton to let me know with what *frigidity* I have answered her and to tell me that she neither hopes nor desires to excite greater warmth.[1] That my first salutation *Madam* surprised her as if an old friend newly meeting her, had thrown a glass of cold water in her face, and

1. *Ante* To Elizabeth Langton, 17 Apr. 1771.

that she does not design to renew our conversations when I *condescend* to visit them after Lady Rothes gets up.[2]

'Tis not for nothing that we Life persue.[3]

I have certainly now such a letter as I never had before, and such as I know not how to answer. I dare neither write with *frigidity* nor with fire. Our intercourse is something

> Which good and bad does equally confound
> And either horn of fate's dilemma wound.[4]

There was formerly in France a Cour de l'Amour, but I fancy nobody was ever summoned before it after threescore, yet in this court if it now subsisted I seem likely to be non-suited.[5]

I am not very sorry that she is so far off. There can be no great danger in writing to her.

Of long walks I cannot tell you,[6] for I have no companion, and the rheumatism has taken away some of my courage, but last night I slept well.

To Strawberries and cream which still continue, we now add custard and bilberry pye.

Our two last fawns are well, but one of our swans is sick. Life, says Foresight, is chequerwork.[7] I am, Madam, your most obedient and most humble servant,

SAM. JOHNSON

2. *Ante* To Elizabeth Langton, 17 Apr. 1771 and n. 4.

3. " 'Tis not for nothing that we life pursue; / It pays our hopes with something still that's new" (Dryden, *Aureng-Zebe* IV.i.45–46).

4. "Whom Good or Ill does equally confound / And both the Horns of Fates Dilemma wound" (Cowley, *The Mistress*, "Against Hope," ll. 3–4).

5. *nonsuit*: "to deprive of the benefit of a legal process for some failure in the management" (SJ's *Dictionary*).

6. In her letter of 17 July, Hester Thrale had asked him about "the long walks you take" (MS: Rylands Library).

7. "Our Lives are checquer'd: Mirth and Sorrow, Want and Plenty, Night and Day, make up our Time" (Congreve, *Love for Love* II.i.35–37).

Hester Thrale

MONDAY 22 JULY 1771

MS: Hyde Collection.

Dear Madam: [Ashbourne] July 22, 1771

Nothing new has happened, and yet I do not care to omit writing. Last post I had four letters all female; besides yours, I had one from Mrs. Hervey,[1] Miss Langton, and Mrs. Williams. Mrs. Hervey must stay, and what to say to Miss Langton I cannot devise.[2]

My Rheumatism continues to persecute me most importunately, and how to procure ease in this place where there are no hot rooms I do not see, but I always hope next day or next night will be better, and am not always disappointed.

Queeny has not written yet, perhaps she designs that I should love Harry best. I am, Dear Madam, your most obliged and most humble Servant, SAM. JOHNSON

1. Catherine Aston Hervey (*c.* 1705 – *c.* 1780), eldest daughter of Sir Thomas Aston (1666–1725), third Bt., and the widow of SJ's friend Henry Hervey (1701–48), whom she married in 1730 (*Johns. Glean.* v.245–46).

2. *Ante* To Hester Thrale, 20 July 1771.

Hester Thrale

WEDNESDAY 24 JULY 1771

MS: Hyde Collection.

Dear Madam: Ashbourn, July 24, 1771

We have no news here but about health and sickness. I am miserably harrassed. Dr. Taylor is quite well. The sick Swan is dead, and dead without an elegy either by himself or his Friends.[1] The other swan swims about solitary, as Mr. Thrale, and I, and others should do, if we lost our Mistress.

1. "So, on Maeander's banks, when death is nigh, / The mournful Swan sings her own Elegie" (John Dryden, "Dido to Aeneas," ll. 1–2, *Ovid's Epistles*; quoted under *elegy* in SJ's *Dictionary*).

The great Bull and his four Sons are all well, we call the first of the young Bulls the Dauphin, so you see, non deficit alter—aureus.[2] Care is taken of the breed.

Naughty Queeny! no better yet. I hope we shall teach little Lucy better.

Be pleased to make my compliments to Mr. Thrale and desire that his builders will leave about a hundred loose bricks. I can at present think of no better place for Chimistry in fair weather, than the pump side in the kitchen Garden.[3] I am, Dear Madam, your most obedient and most humble servant,

SAM. JOHNSON

My paper lay wrong and I did not perceive it.

2. *primo avolso non deficit alter / aureus*: "When the first is torn away, a second fails not, golden too" (Virgil, *Aeneid* VI.143–44, trans. H. R. Fairclough, Loeb ed.).

3. *Ante* To Hester Thrale, 15 July 1771 and n. 1.

Frances Reynolds[1]

THURSDAY 25 JULY 1771

MS: Hyde Collection. A copy in the hand of Frances Reynolds.

Dearest Madam: Ashbourn, July 25, 1771

As the business relating to young Mr.——was transacted between you and me,[2] I think it more proper to communicate to you than to Sir Joshua, a letter which I have received this day from Dr. Griffith of Pembroke College.[3]

"Your Friend——when he took leave for the vacation left me two bills of ten pounds each, to pay his Debts. To my great surprise they are neither of them accepted. I have unluckily

1. *Ante* To Bennet Langton, 9 Jan. 1759, n. 21.

2. The young man in question was probably Frances's nephew Samuel Johnson (*c.* 1754–78), son of William Johnson of Torrington, Devon, and her sister Elizabeth. Lack of money forced Samuel to leave Oxford in 1772. He returned in 1776 and entered Exeter College, thanks to an exhibition established by his great-uncle (S. M. Radcliffe, *Sir Joshua's Nephew*, 1930, p. x).

3. Thomas Griffith (b. *c.* 1724), D.D., Fellow of Pembroke College, Oxford.

forgot to take his address, and I shall be much obliged to you if you will acquaint me how I may direct to him or to his Friends."

I am sorry about it, and cannot judge here what can be done. If you could immediately send the twenty pounds, before I write to the Doctor, it would save the young gentleman's credit. If his Father cannot pay; I think I must be five pounds and you five pounds, and Sir Joshua ten. Perhaps the whole difficulty proceeds from accident or mistake, but the present state of the affair is disreputable, and though the money shall at last be paid, there will still be[4] loss of credit, which a speedy remittance will effectually prevent.

This will come to you on Saturday. Be pleased to write to me on Saturday night, I will not answer Dr. Griffith till I have heard from you. You must not wonder, my Dearest, that I seem more in earnest than the value of twenty pounds may seem to deserve. There is little money at Oxford, and therefore small sums are there of great importance. If you write on Saturday direct to the Reverend Dr. Taylor's in Ashbourn Derbyshire, if you stay longer, to Mrs. Porters in Litchfield.

I am, my Dearest Dear, Your most obedient and most humble servant,

SAM. JOHNSON

4. MS: "there will be still be"

Frances Reynolds

MONDAY 29 JULY 1771

MS: Hyde Collection. A copy in the hand of Frances Reynolds.

My Dearest Dear: July 29th, 1771

I received your letter and Bill, and have written to Dr. Griffith, so that there is an end of the whole business.[1]

I expect to be in Town within ten days, or a fortnight, and to drink tea with Dear Miss Renny. Neither Dr. Taylor nor I

1. *Ante* To Frances Reynolds, 25 July 1771.

have been very well since I came, but we are both now better, and now we are better, we are going to part. I am, Dearest Madam, Your most humble servant, SAM. JOHNSON

Hester Maria Thrale

MONDAY 29 JULY 1771

MS: The Earl of Shelburne.

My sweet, dear, pretty, little Miss: Ashbourn, July 29, 1771

Please to tell little Mama, that I am glad to hear, that she is well, and that I am going to Lichfield, and shall come soon to London.[1] Desire her to make haste and be quite well, for, You know, that You and I are to tye her to the tree, but we will not do it while she is weak. Tell dear Grandmama that I am very sorry for her pain. Tell Papa that I wish him joy of his new Girl,[2] and tell Harry that you have got my heart, and will keep it, and that I am, Dearest Miss, your most obedient servant,

SAM. JOHNSON

1. *Post* To Hester Thrale, 3 Aug. 1771.
2. *Ante* To Hester Thrale, 22 June 1771, n. 5.

Henry Thrale

WEDNESDAY 31 JULY 1771

MS: Rosenbach Museum and Library.

Dear Sir: [Lichfield] July 31, 1771

I am this morning come to Lichfield, a place which has no temptations to prolong my stay, but if it [had] more, would not have such as could withold me from your house when I am at liberty to come to it. I hope our dear Mistress is got up and recovering, pray tell her to mind whether I am not got quite wild for want of government. My thoughts are now about getting to London, I shall watch for a place, for our carriages are only such as pass through the place sometimes full, and sometimes vacant.

Be pleased to frank the inclosed, which contains a Bill, to The Reverend Dr. Griffith at Pembroke College, Oxford.[1] I am, Sir, Your most humble Servant, SAM. JOHNSON

1. *Ante* To Frances Reynolds, 25 July 1771 and n. 3.

Hester Thrale

SATURDAY 3 AUGUST 1771

MS: Current location unknown. Transcribed from photostat supplied by F. B. Bemis.

Dear Madam: Lichfield, Saturday, August 3, 1771

If you were well enough to write last tuesday, you will surely be well enough to read on Monday, and therefore I will now write to you as before.

Having stayed my month with Taylor I came away on Wednesday, leaving him, I think, in a disposition of mind not very uncommon, at once weary of my stay, and grieved at my departure.

My purpose was to have made haste to You and Streatham, and who would [have] expected that I should be stopped by Lucy? Hearing me give Francis orders to take us places, she told me that I should not go till after next week. I thought it proper to comply for I was pleased to find that I could please, and proud of showing you that I do not come an universal outcast. Lucy is likewise a very peremptory Maiden, and if I had gone without permission, I am not very sure that I might have been welcome at another time.

When we meet we may compare our different uses of this interval. I shall charge you with having[1] lingred away in expectation and disappointment, two months which are both

1. MS: "have"

physically and morally considered as analogous to the fervid and vigorous part of human life, two months in which Nature exerts all her powers of benefaction, and graces the liberality of her hand by the elegance of her smile; two months which, as Doodle says, you[2] never saw before,[3] and which, as la Bruyere says, you shall never see again.

But complaints are vain, we will try to do better another time.—to morrow and to morrow.[4]—A few designs and a few failures, and the time of designing will be past.

Mr. Seward left Lichfield yesterday,[5] I am afraid, not much mended by his opium. He purposes to wait on you—and if envy could do much mischief, he would have much to dread, since he will have the pleasure of seeing you sooner than, Dear Madam, your most obliged and most humble servant,

SAM. JOHNSON

2. MS: "you" altered from "your"

3. "Sure such a day as this was never seen!" (Fielding, *Tom Thumb the Great* I.i.1).

4. "To-morrow, and to-morrow, and to-morrow, / Creeps in this petty pace from day to day" (*Macbeth* v.v.19–20).

5. *Ante* To John Taylor, 10 Aug. 1742, n. 4.

Hester Thrale

MONDAY 5 AUGUST 1771

MS: Birthplace Museum, Lichfield.

Dear Madam: Lichfield, Aug. 5, 1771

Though I have now been two posts without hearing from you, I hope no harm has befallen you. I have just been with the old Dean, if I may call him old who is but seventy eight, and find him as well both in mind and body as his younger neighbours.[1] I went with my Lucy this morning to a philosophical lecture, and have been this evening to see Mr. Green's curiosities, both natural and artificial,[2] and I am come home to write to my dear Lady.

1. John Addenbrooke (*c.* 1690–1776), D.D., who became Dean of Lichfield in 1745.

2. *Ante* To Lucy Porter, 12 July 1768, n. 2.

So rolls the world away.[3]

The days grow visibly shorter—Immortalia ne speres monet annus[4]—I think it time to return. Do you think, that after all this roving you shall be able to manage me again? I suppose, like Scrace,[5] that you[6] are thinking how to reduce me, but you may spare your contrivances, and need not fear that I find any reception that gives me pleasure equal to that of being, Madam, your most obedient and most humble servant,

SAM. JOHNSON

3. "Thus runs the world away" (*Hamlet* III.ii.268).

4. *immortalia ne speres, monet annus et almum / quæ rapit hora diem*: "The year and the hour that rob us of the gracious day warn thee not to hope for unending joys" (Horace, *Odes* IV.vii.7–8, trans. C. E. Bennett, Loeb ed.). SJ translated this ode in 1784 (*Poems*, pp. 264–65).

5. Charles Scrase (1709–92), London solicitor, a family friend and legal adviser of the Thrales. Hester Thrale found Scrase "a Man of more acute Parts, and keen Penetration than I think I ever yet saw" (*Thraliana* I.364). *Post* To Hester Thrale, 14 Nov. 1778.

6. MS: "your"

Bennet Langton

THURSDAY 29 AUGUST 1771

MS: Hyde Collection.

ADDRESS: To Benet Langton, Esq., at Langton near Spilsby, Lincolnshire.

POSTMARK: 29 AV.

Dear Sir: August 29, 1771

I am lately returned from Staffordshire and Derbyshire. The last Letter mentions two others which you have written to me since you received my pamphlet.[1] Of these two I never had but one, in which you mentioned a design of visiting Scotland,[2] and by consequence put my Journey to Langton out of my thoughts. My summer wanderings are now over, and I am

1. *Thoughts on the Late Transactions Respecting Falkland's Islands*, published 16 Mar. 1771 (*Works*, Yale ed. X.349).

2. This trip eventually took place in the autumn of 1772 (*Boswell for the Defence*, ed. W. K. Wimsatt and F. A. Pottle, 1959, p. 139). The Langtons stayed in Edinburgh for over two months, visiting relatives of Lady Rothes (Fifer, p. lix).

engaging in a very great work the revision of my Dictionary from which I know not at present how to get loose.[3]

If you have observed or been told any errors or omissions, you will do me a great favour by letting me know them.

Lady Rothes, I find, has disappointed You and Herself.[4] Ladies will have these tricks. The Queen,[5] and Mrs. Thrale, both Ladies of experience, yet both missed their reckoning this Summer.[6] I hope, a few months will recompense your uneasiness.

Please to tell Lady Rothes how highly I value the honour of her invitation, which it is my purpose to obey as soon as I have disengaged my self.[7] In the mean time I shall hope to hear often of her Ladyship and every day better news and better, till I hear that you have both[8] the happiness, which to both is very sincerely wished, by, Sir, your most affectionate and most humble servant,

SAM. JOHNSON

3. SJ was at work on the fourth edition, which, "unlike the second and third folios . . . was considerably revised" (Sledd and Kolb, p. 114). In the "Advertisement" to this edition SJ claimed, "Many faults I have corrected, some superfluities I have taken away, and some deficiencies I have supplied" (*Bibliography*, p. 56). In Oct. 1771 he sent it to the press; it was published early in 1773 (Sledd and Kolb, p. 115). *Post* To JB, 24 Feb. 1773.

4. *Ante* To Elizabeth Langton, 17 Apr. 1771, n. 4.

5. MS: "Q" superimposed upon "L"

6. Ernest Augustus (1771–1851), eighth child and fifth son of George III and Queen Charlotte, was born 5 June. For Sophia Thrale, *Ante* To Hester Thrale, 22 June 1771, n. 5.

7. There is no record that this projected visit ever took place.

8. MS: "both" altered from "bothe"

James Beattie[1]

FRIDAY 30 AUGUST 1771

MS: Aberdeen University Library.

ADDRESS: To Mr. Beattie.

1. James Beattie (1735–1803), Scots poet, essayist, and philosopher, Professor of Moral Philosophy in Marischal College, Aberdeen, and author of *An Essay on*

Dear Sir: August 30, 1771

I have inclosed an invitation from a very valuable family, with which, I think, you will, when you know it, have reason to be pleased.[2] You shall be waited on thither, by, Sir, your most humble servant, SAM. JOHNSON

the Nature and Immutability of Truth (1770). Beattie, who was traveling for his health, had arrived in London at the end of July, equipped with a letter of introduction from JB (*Life* II.141–42). On 28 Aug. Beattie wrote to Dr. John Gregory: "I waited on Dr. Samuel Johnson as soon as he came to town, and gave him Mr. Boswell's letter. He received me with the utmost kindness and affection, and desired me to be with him as much as possible" (Margaret Forbes, *Beattie and his Friends*, 1904, p. 60).

2. The invitation was from the Thrales, who rapidly became devoted friends. In Mar. 1772 SJ told JB: "We all love Beattie. Mrs. Thrale says, if ever she has another husband, she'll have Beattie" (*Life* II.148).

David Garrick

THURSDAY 12 DECEMBER 1771

MS: Berg Collection, New York Public Library.

ADDRESS: To David Garrick, Esq.

ENDORSEMENT: Dr. Johnson's Letter about Hogarth's Epitaph.[1]

Dear Sir: Streatham, Decr. 12, 1771

I have thought upon your Epitaph, but without much effect. An Epitaph is no easy thing.

Of your three stanzas, the third is utterly unworthy of you.[2]

1. William Hogarth (1697–1771) was buried in Chiswick Churchyard, where a monument had been erected in his memory. Mrs. Hogarth requested Garrick to "write an Epitaph for her Husband our most Excellent friend" (*Letters of David Garrick*, ed. D. M. Little and G. M. Kahrl, 1963, II.782).

2. This "third" stanza has not been recovered. The two discussed in this letter read:

If thou hast Genius, Reader, stay,
If thou hast feeling, drop a tear,
If thou hast neither, hence, away,
For Hogarth's dear remains lye here[.]

The first and third together give no discriminative character. If the first alone were to stand, Hogarth would not be distinguished from any other man of intellectual eminence.

Suppose you worked upon something like this.

The Hand of Art here torpid lies
That traced[3] th'essential form of Grace,[4]
Here death has clos'd the curious eyes
That saw the manners in the face.[5]

If Genius warm thee, Reader, stay,
If Merit[6] touch thee, shed a tear,
Be Vice and Dulness far away
Great Hogarth's honour'd Dust is here.

In your second stanza *pictured Morals* is a beautifull expression which I would wish to retain. But *learn* and *mourn* cannot stand for rhymes. *Art and Nature* have been seen together too often. In the first stanza is *feeling* in the second *feel. Feeling* for *tenderness* or *sensibility* is a word merely colloquial of late introduction, not yet [confident] enough of its own existence to claim a place upon a stone.[7] *If thou hast neither,* is quite prose, and prose of the familiar kind.

Go seek the Works he left mankind,
His pictur'd Morals read, and learn,
Let *Art* and *Nature* charm thy mind,
Then with thy Country feel, and mourn.

(I. A. Williams, "Bibliographical Notes," *The London Mercury* 6, 1922, pp. 182–83).

3. MS: "wav'd" inserted above "traced"

4. SJ alludes to the S-shaped curve first engraved by Hogarth in "Columbus Breaking an Egg" (Mar. 1752), the subscription ticket for *The Analysis of Beauty,* 1753 (Ronald Paulson, *Hogarth,* 1971, II.155). The "line of beauty" is a perfectly proportioned "waving-line"; the "line of grace" is the same line made three-dimensional—"changed from the waving into the serpentine-line." According to Hogarth, the line of grace "gives [more] play to the imagination" than the line of beauty (*The Analysis of Beauty,* ed. Joseph Burke, 1955, p. 68). SJ's variant ("wav'd" for "traced") makes the allusion more explicit.

5. For a variant form of the first stanza, see *Thraliana* I.41.

6. MS: "Merit" written above "History" del.

7. In his *Dictionary,* however, SJ offers "perception; sensibility" as the third definition of *feeling,* and illustrates its use with passages from Bacon and Watts.

Thus easy is it to find faults, but it is hard to make an Epitaph.

When you have reviewed it, let me see it again,[8] you are welcome to any help that I can give, on condition that you make my compliments to Mrs. Garrick. I am, Dear sir, your most etc.

SAM. JOHNSON

8. On 22 Dec. 1771, Garrick responded to SJ's criticisms: "I shall certainly tire You, for I am tired myself—the following alterations are submitted to you—shall I beg yr opinion once more?" (*Letters of Garrick*, ed. D. M. Little and G. M. Kahrl, 1963, II.778). For the text as it appears on the monument in Chiswick Churchyard, see *Poems*, p. 181.

Joseph Smith

THURSDAY 12 DECEMBER 1771

MS: Houghton Library.

ADDRESS: To Mr. Joseph Smith, Ironmonger in Bishop Stortford, Hertfordshire.

POSTMARK: 12 DE.

Johnson's court,
Fleetstreet, Dec. 12, 1771

Dear Sir:

I am ashamed and sorry that I have so long forgotten Mrs. Clap. I had really let it slip out of my thoughts. If you will be pleased to pay her I will settle with you, and remit what shall be due to you. I am, Sir, Your most humble Servant,

SAM. JOHNSON

Unidentified Correspondent

SUNDAY 16 FEBRUARY 1772

MS: British Museum, Department of Prints and Drawings.

Madam: Febr. 16, 1772

By taking no notice at all of me, I do not think that you behave in a proper manner to Your humble servant,

SAM. JOHNSON

Joseph Banks[1]

THURSDAY 27 FEBRUARY 1772

MS: Hyde Collection. A copy in the hand of Joshua Reynolds, written on the verso of To Joshua Reynolds, 27 Feb. 1772.[2]

Johnson's Court, Fleetstreet, Feb. 27, 1772

Perpetui, ambitâ bis terrâ, præmia lactis
Hæc habet, altrici Capra secunda Jovis.[3]

Sir:

I return thanks to you and to Dr. Solander for the pleasure which I received in yesterday's conversation.[4] I could not recollect a Motto for your Goat, but have given her a ⟨distich.⟩[5] You, Sir, may perhaps sometime have an epic poem, from some happier pen, than of,[6] Sir, Your most humble Servant,

SAM. JOHNSON

1. Joseph Banks (1743–1820), F.R.S., Bt. (1781), the celebrated naturalist who accompanied Capt. James Cook on his voyage to Australia and New Zealand in 1768–71. In 1778 Banks was elected President of the Royal Society and a member of The Club.

2. Collated with the text in the *European Magazine*, 1789, p. 5, and the lithographic facsimile at the Wellcome Historical Medical Library. See *Poems*, p. 183; *Life* II.492.

3. For the translation procured by JB, see *Life* II.144. The motto was "engraved upon a splendid collar" worn by the goat (Thomas Byerley, *Relics of Literature*, 1823, p. 310). According to H. L. Piozzi, Banks's goat had gone with him "on two of his adventurous expeditions" (*Johns. Misc.* I.195). The goat's first expedition, however, was not with Banks and Cook on the *Endeavour* but with Capt. Samuel Wallis on the *Dolphin*, 1766–68 (Byerley, *Relics*, p. 310).

4. Daniel Charles Solander (1736–82), a Swedish botanist trained by Linnæus, had been working in England since 1760. He catalogued the natural history collections in the British Museum, and was employed there as an assistant librarian when he was engaged by Banks to accompany him on the *Endeavour*. After their return to England in 1771, Solander served as Banks's librarian and secretary.

5. MS: mutilated: "distich" from text in *European Magazine* and Wellcome Library facsimile

6. "may some time have an epic poem from some happier hand than that of" (*European Magazine*); "may perhaps sometime have an epic poem, from some happier pen, than that of" (Wellcome facsimile).

Joshua Reynolds

THURSDAY 27 FEBRUARY 1772

MS: Hyde Collection.

ADDRESS: To Sir Joshua Reynolds.

Febr. 27, 1772

Be pleased to send to Mr. Banks whose place of residence I do not know this note, which I have sent open, that if you please, you may read it.[1]

When you seal it, do not use your own seal. I am, Sir, your most humble servant,

SAM. JOHNSON

1. *Ante* To Joseph Banks, 27 Feb. 1772.

Bennet Langton

SATURDAY 14 MARCH 1772

MS: Hyde Collection.

ADDRESS: To Benet Langton, Esq., near Spilsby, Lincolnshire.

POSTMARK: 14 MR.

Dear Sir: March 14, 1772

I congratulate You and Lady Rothes on your little Man,[1] and hope you will all be many years happy together.

Poor Miss Langton can have little part in the joy of her family.[2] She this day called her Aunt Langton to receive the Sacrament with her, and made me talk yesterday on[3] such subjects as suit her condition. It will probably be her *viaticum.* I surely need not mention again that she wishes to see her Mother.[4] I am, Sir, Your most humble servant,

SAM. JOHNSON

1. George (1772–1819), the Langtons' first child, born 8 Mar. (Fifer, p. lviii n. 29).
2. Elizabeth Langton may have thought she was dying, but she lived until 1791.
3. MS: "on" altered from "in"
4. *Ante* To Bennet Langton, 9 Jan. 1759, n. 6.

James Boswell

SUNDAY 15 MARCH 1772

PRINTED SOURCE: JB's *Life*, 1791, I.352.

Dear Sir: March 15, 1772

That you are coming so soon to town I am very glad; and still more glad that you are coming as an advocate.[1] I think nothing more likely to make your life pass happily away, than that consciousness of your own value, which eminence in your profession will certainly confer. If I can give you any collateral help, I hope you do not suspect that it will be wanting. My kindness for you has neither the merit of singular virtue, nor the reproach of singular prejudice. Whether to love you be right or wrong, I have many on my side: Mrs. Thrale loves you, and Mrs. Williams loves you, and what would have inclined me to love you, if I had been neutral before, you are a great favourite of Dr. Beattie.[2]

Of Dr. Beattie I should have thought much, but that his lady puts him out of my head: she is a very lovely woman.[3]

The ejection which you come hither to oppose, appears very cruel, unreasonable, and oppressive.[4] I should think there could not be much doubt of your success.[5]

1. JB was defending John Hastie, schoolmaster of Campbeltown, Argyll, "who had been dismissed from his £20-a-year job for brutality and irregular attendance" (*Later Years*, p. 26). The case, which Hastie had won in the Court of Session, was appealed to the House of Lords. JB arrived in London on 19 Mar. (*Boswell for the Defence*, ed. W. K. Wimsatt and F. A. Pottle, 1959, p. 33).

2. *Ante* To James Beattie, 30 Aug. 1771, n. 1.

3. Beattie had married Mary Dun, daughter of Dr. James Dun of Aberdeen, in 1767. She was "a few years younger than Dr. Beattie . . . tolerably handsome, and lively in conversation" (Sir William Forbes, *Life of Beattie*, 1824, I.97). However, Mrs. Beattie had "inherited from her mother that most dreadful of all human evils, a distempered mind; which . . . in a few years after their marriage, showed itself in caprices that embittered every hour of his life" (pp. 97–98). Mary Beattie had accompanied her husband to London the preceding summer (*Ante* To James Beattie, 30 Aug. 1771; Margaret Forbes, *Beattie and His Friends*, 1904, p. 59).

4. In his letter of 3 Mar., JB had told SJ only that Hastie "was deprived of his office for being somewhat severe in the chastisement of his scholars" (MS: Beinecke Library).

5. On 14 Apr. JB defended Hastie in the House of Lords, but despite briefing

My health grows better, yet I am not fully recovered. I believe it is held, that men do not recover very fast after threescore. I hope yet to see Beattie's College:[6] and have not given up the western voyage.[7] But however all this may be or not, let us try to make each other happy when we meet, and not refer our pleasure to distant times or distant places.

How comes it that you tell me nothing of your lady? I hope to see her some time, and till then shall be glad to hear of her.[8] I am, dear Sir, etc. SAM. JOHNSON

---

by SJ (*Life* II.183–85), and JB's own best efforts, the Court of Session's decision was reversed (Wimsatt and Pottle, *Defence*, pp. 113–16).

6. SJ and JB visited Marischal College, Aberdeen, on 23 Aug. 1773 (*Hebrides*, pp. 64–65).

7. JB had written to SJ on 3 Mar., hoping "to fix our voyage to the Hebrides or at least our journey through the highlands of Scotland" (MS: Beinecke Library).

8. SJ and Margaret Boswell met in Aug. 1773, at the beginning of the Hebridean tour. "As no man could be more polite when he chose to be so, his address to her was most courteous and engaging, and his conversation soon charmed her into a forgetfulness of his external appearance" (*Hebrides*, p. 12).

Samuel Paterson[1]

MONDAY 6 APRIL 1772

MS: Salt Library, Stafford.

ADDRESS: To Mr. Paterson in Essex Street.

ENDORSEMENT: Dr. Sam. Johnson, Apr. 6, 1772.

Sir: Apr. 6, 1772

I have inclosed two projects of two friends, for translations from the German Language. I think bothe promising and believe neither Translator will think on a very high price. Leave is obtained to dedicate the Book of two volumes to the Queen.

1. Samuel Paterson (1728–1802), London bookseller and auctioneer, author of *Another Traveller* (1767–69) and subsequently librarian to the first Marquis of Lansdowne. According to John Nichols, "Few men of this country had so much bibliographical knowledge; and perhaps we never had a Bookseller who knew so much of the contents of books generally" (*Lit. Anec.* III.439). SJ was the godfather of Paterson's son Charles.

I will beg the favour of you to mention them to Mr. Johnson[2] or any other Bookseller to whom you think they may be acceptable. I am, sir, your humble servant,

SAM. JOHNSON

2. *Ante* To William Strahan, 20 Jan. 1759, n. 5.

Robert Chambers

SATURDAY 11 APRIL 1772

MS: Hyde Collection.

ADDRESS: To Robert Chambers, Esq., at New Inn Hall, Oxford.

POSTMARK: 11 AP.

Dear Sir: London, April 11, 1772

I found my desire of your company excited by your kind letter, but a little business in which I am now engaged puts it out of my power to gratify myself without more inconvenience than you desire me to incur.[1] We must therefore be content for some time to live apart. I am detained here as you are detained at Oxford. In the mean time you need not forget me. I shall be glad to hear any good of my old friends at University College, or[2] any other house.

I think nothing has happened here, but that Boswel is come up gratis with an appeal to the Lords.[3] While I am writing I expect to hear him come in, with his noisy benevolence.[4] I am, Sir, your most humble servant,

SAM. JOHNSON

1. SJ may be referring to preparations for the fourth edition of his *Dictionary*. *Ante* To Bennet Langton, 29 Aug. 1771 and n. 3.

2. MS: "or" superimposed upon "an"

3. *Ante* To JB, 15 Mar. 1772, nn. 1, 5.

4. "On Saturday, April 11, he appointed me to come to him in the evening, when he should be at leisure to give me some assistance for the defence of Hastie, the schoolmaster of Campbelltown, for whom I was to appear in the House of Lords" (*Life* II.183).

Bennet Langton

MONDAY 13 APRIL 1772

MS: Fitzwilliam Museum.

Monday, Apr. 13, 1772

Mr. Johnson sends his compliments and will pass wednesday Evening with Mr. Langton at whatever place he shall appoint. He hopes that Lady Rothes and little George are well.[1]

1. *Ante* To Bennet Langton, 14 Mar. 1772, n. 1.

John Taylor

FRIDAY 17 APRIL 1772

MS: Hyde Collection.

ADDRESS: To the Reverend Dr. Taylor.

ENDORSEMENT: 17 April 1772.

Dear Sir: April 17, 1772

When I promised to dine with You to morrow I did not sufficiently consider what I was promising. On the last day of Lent I do not willingly go out,[1] and shall be glad to change to morrow for Monday or any other day except thursday next week. I am, Sir, your most etc. SAM. JOHNSON

1. In 1772 Easter fell on Sunday, 19 Apr. On Saturday afternoon JB called on SJ "and found him in solemn mood, with the great New Testament open again" (*Boswell for the Defence*, ed. W. K. Wimsatt and F. A. Pottle, 1959, p. 127). For SJ's Easter prayers and resolutions, see *Works*, Yale ed. 1.146–49.

John Taylor

SATURDAY 15 AUGUST 1772

PRINTED SOURCE: *The Reliquary* 14, 1873–74, p. 97.

Dear Sir: August 15, 1772

That neither of us can in all these months find time to write to the other is very strange. We seem to try who can forbear longest. You see I have yielded at last.

My hope of coming down in the sunshiny months has been long over. My work will, I am afraid, hold me here to the end of September.[1] I am held, however, by no other impediment, for I know not when I have been so well for many years past.

Of your health I expected that you would have given me some account. Have you been at Kedlestone?[2] And are you better for it? Is your head easy and your appetite good? All this I wish I could come to examine, but must be for the present content to hear, if you will be content to tell me.

Nothing very memorable has happened since your departure from London, except the failure of Fordice, who has drawn upon him a larger ruin than any former Bankrupt.[3] Such a general distrust and timidity has been diffused through the whole commercial system, that credit has been almost extinguished and commerce suspended. There has not since the year of the South Sea been, I believe, such extensive distress or so frightful an alarm. It can however be little more that a panick terrour from which when they recover, many will wonder why they were frighted.

Do not be long without writing me a letter and let me know very fully how you do. I am, Dear Sir, Yours, etc.

SAM. JOHNSON

1. *Ante* To Bennet Langton, 29 Aug. 1771 and n. 3.

2. The park of Kedleston Hall, Lord Scarsdale's seat outside of Derby, contained "a mineral spring which is regarded very efficacious in scorbutic diseases" (Charles Knight, *Derbyshire*, 1841, p. 63).

3. Alexander Fordyce (1729–89), a banker from Aberdeen, became the leading partner in the London house of Neale, James, Fordyce, and Down. During the 1760s, Fordyce speculated irresponsibly in East India stock, and when the dispute over the Falkland Islands caused a fluctuation in the market, his bank's assets began to dwindle. Losses continued until finally the bank stopped payment on 10 June 1771. According to the *GM*: "It is beyond the power of words to describe the general consternation of the metropolis at this instant. No event for 50 years past has been remembered to have given so fatal a blow both to trade and public credit. An universal bankruptcy was expected, the stoppage of almost every banker's house in London was looked for. The whole city was in an uproar; many of the first families in tears" (*GM* 1772, p. 293). In July Horace Walpole told Sir Horace Mann, "Four more bankers are broken; and two men, ruined by these failures (which are computed to amount to four millions) shot themselves the day before yesterday" (*Walpole's Correspondence*, Yale ed. XXIII.420).

James Boswell

MONDAY 31 AUGUST 1772

PRINTED SOURCE: JB's *Life*, 1791, I.387.

Dear Sir: August 31, 1772

The regret has not been little with which I have missed a journey so pregnant with pleasing expectations, as that in which I could promise myself not only the gratification of curiosity, both rational and fanciful, but the delight of seeing those whom I love and esteem, * * * * * * * * * * *. But such has been the course of things, that I could not come; and such has been, I am afraid, the state of my body, that it would not well have seconded my inclination. My body, I think, grows better, and I refer my hopes to another year; for I am very sincere in my design to pay the visit, and take the ramble. In the mean time, do not omit any opportunity of keeping up a favourable opinion of me in the minds of any of my friends. Beattie's book is, I believe, every day more liked; at least, I like it more, as I look more upon it.[1]

I am glad if you got credit by your cause, and am yet of opinion, that our cause was good, and that the determination ought to have been in your favour. Poor Hastie, I think, had but his deserts.[2]

You promised to get me a little Pindar,[3] you may add to it a little Anacreon.[4]

1. *Ante* To James Beattie, 30 Aug. 1771, n. 1. SJ particularly admired Beattie's *Essay on Truth* for its attack on Hume: "Sir, he has written like a man conscious of the truth, and feeling his own strength. Treating your adversary with respect, is giving him an advantage to which he is not entitled" (*Life* v.29). During the summer of 1772 SJ was almost certainly selecting quotations from the *Essay* to use as illustrations in the fourth edition of the *Dictionary* (information supplied by Professor Allen Reddick).

2. *Ante* To JB, 15 Mar. 1772 and nn. 1, 5.

3. SJ refers to the miniature (32°) edition of Pindar's *Works* published in four volumes by the Foulis Press between 1754 and 1758 (Philip Gaskell, *A Bibliography of the Foulis Press*, 2d ed. 1986, p. 190). SJ owned a set at the time of his death (Greene, 1975, p. 91).

4. The miniature (32°) edition of Anacreon's *Odes* published by the Foulis Press

The leisure which I cannot enjoy, it will be a pleasure to hear that you employ upon the antiquities of the feudal establishment. The whole system of ancient tenures is gradually passing away; and I wish to have the knowledge of it preserved adequate and complete. For such an institution makes a very important part of the history of mankind. Do not forget a design so worthy of a scholar who studies the laws of his country, and of a gentleman who may naturally be curious to know the condition of his own ancestors.[5] I am, dear Sir, Yours with great affection,

SAM. JOHNSON

in 1761 (Gaskell, *Bibliography*, p. 238). SJ owned a copy at the time of his death (Greene, 1975, p. 28).

5. One of JB's projected works was a collection of feudal tenures and charters of Scotland (*Lit. Car.*, p. 307). *Post* To JB, 27 Oct. 1779.

John Taylor

MONDAY 31 AUGUST 1772

MS: Berg Collection, New York Public Library.

ADDRESS: To The Revd. Dr. Taylor in Ashbourn, Derbys.

FRANK: Hfreethrale.

POSTMARKS: 31 AV, 1 SE, FREE.

ENDORSEMENTS: 1772, 31 Augt. 72 very fine.

Dear Sir: August 31, 1772

I am sorry to find both from your own letter and from Mr. Langley that your health is in[1] a state so different from what might be wished.[2] The Langleys impute a great part of your complaints to a mind unsettled and discontented. I know that you have disorders, though I hope not very formidable, inde-

1. MS: "fr" del. before "in"

2. William Langley (d. 1795), rector of Fenny Bentley, Derbyshire, and headmaster of Ashbourne Grammar School. According to JB, who visited Ashbourne in 1777, "Mr. Langley, a clergyman, the Head Master . . . lives just on the opposite side of the street to Dr. Taylor's. But they are not on good terms" (*Boswell in Extremes*, ed. C. M. Weis and F. A. Pottle, 1970, p. 152).

pendent of the mind, and that your complaints do not arise from the mere habit of complaining. Yet there is no distemper, not in the highest degree acute, on which the mind has not some influence, and which is not better resisted by a cheerful than a gloomy temper. I know that you do not much ⟨*two words*⟩, yet[3] I would have you read when you can settle your attention but that perhaps will be not so often as is necessary to encrease the general cheerfulness of Life. If you could get a little apparatus for chimistry or experimental philosophy it would offer you some diversion, or if you made some little purchase at a small distance, or took some petty farm into your own hands, it would break your thoughts when they become tyrannous and troublesome, and supply you at once with exercise and amusement.

You tell me nothing of Kedlestone, which you went down with a design of visiting, nor of Dr. Butter who seems to be a very rational Man,[4] and who told you with great honesty that your cure must in the greatest measure depend upon yourself.

Your uneasiness at the misfortunes of your Relations, I comprehend perhaps too well. It was an irresistible obtrusion of a disagreeable image, which you always wished away but could not dismiss, an incessant persecution of a troublesome thought neither to be pacified nor ejected. Such has of late been the state of my own mind. I had formerly great command of my attention, and what I did not like could forbear to think on. But of this power which is of the highest importance to the tranquillity of life, I have for some time past been so[5] much exhausted, that I do not go into a company towards night in which I foresee anything disagreeable, nor enquire after any thing to which I am not indifferent, lest some-thing, which I know to be nothing, should fasten upon my imagination, and hinder me from sleep. Thus it is that the progress of life brings often with it diseases not of the body only, but of the mind. We must endeavour to cure both the one[6] and the

3. MS: "I" through "yet" heavily del.

4. William Butter (1726–1805), M.D., a Scots physician practicing in Derby.

5. MS: "some"

6. MS: "only" del. before "one"

other. For our bodies we must ourselves do a great part, and for the mind it is very seldom that any help can be had, but what prayer and reason shall supply.

I have got my work so far forward that I flatter my self with concluding it this month, and than shall do nothing so willingly as come down to Ashbourne. We will try to make October a pleasant month. I am, Sir, yours affectionately,

SAM. JOHNSON

I wish we could borrow of Dr. Bentley[7] the Preces in usum Sarum.[8]

7. Richard Bentley (*c.* 1704–86), D.D., Rector of Nailstone, Leicestershire (1746–48).

8. "Sarum Rite" or "Sarum Use," the form of the Roman Liturgy, codified by St. Osmund (d. 1099), Bishop of Sarum or Salisbury (1078–99), and observed in southern England until the Reformation. The Sarum Missal and other liturgical manuals included many prayers that were removed from the Roman Breviary after the Council of Trent.

John Taylor

TUESDAY 6 OCTOBER 1772

MS: Berg Collection, New York Public Library.

ADDRESS: To The Revd. Dr. Taylor at Ashbourne, Derbys.

FRANK: Hfreethrale.

POSTMARKS: 6 OC, FREE.

ENDORSEMENTS: 1772, 6 Octr. 72, A very good Hint to Professional Men.

Dear Sir: Oct. 6, 1772

Now you find yourself better consider what it is that has contributed to your recovery, and do it over again. Keep what health you have and try to get more.

I am now within a few hours of being able to send the whole dictionary to the press,[1] and though I often went sluggishly to the work, I am not much delighted at the con⟨clusion.⟩ My

1. *Ante* To Bennet Langton, 29 Aug. 1771 and n. 3.

purpose is to come down to Lichfield next week, I will send you word when I am to set out, and hope you will fetch me.[2] Miss Porter will be satisfied with a very little of my company. I am, Dear Sir, Your affectionate servant,

SAM. JOHNSON

2. On 15 Oct. SJ left for Lichfield, where he stayed for approximately ten days. He then went on to Ashbourne, returned to Lichfield 2 Dec., and came back to London 11 Dec.

William Strahan

THURSDAY 8 OCTOBER 1772

PRINTED SOURCE: Clement Shorter, *Unpublished Letters of Dr. Samuel Johnson*, 1915, p. 3.

ADDRESS: To William Strahan, Esq.

Sir: October 8, 1772

I am now within about two hours or less of the end of my work.[1] I purpose to go into the country for a month.[2] I shall desire you to help me to twenty pounds which I shall take with me, and shall leave a note of fifteen for you to pay for me. You will receive the money while I am away. I shall leave you my letter for that purpose. I am, Sir, your humble servant,

SAM. JOHNSON

1. *Ante* To John Taylor, 6 Oct. 1772; *Ante* To Bennet Langton, 29 Aug. 1771 and n. 3.

2. *Ante* To John Taylor, 6 Oct. 1772, n. 2.

John Taylor

TUESDAY 13 OCTOBER 1772

MS: Houghton Library.

ADDRESS: To the Reverend Dr. Taylor in Ashbourne, Derbyshire.

POSTMARK: 13 OC.

ENDORSEMENTS: 1772, 13 Octr. 72.

Dear Sir: London, Oct. 13, 1772

Francis has just taken places in the Stage, and we expect to be at Lichfield on Fryday. How soon you will think it proper to fetch us away must be left to your determination.[1] We shall stay I am afraid longer than we are welcome if we stay long. I am, Sir, your most humble servant,

SAM. JOHNSON

1. *Ante* To John Taylor, 6 Oct. 1772, n. 2.

Hester Thrale

THURSDAY 15 OCTOBER 1772

MS: Hyde Collection.

Madam: Oct. 15, 1772

I am about to set out at nine to night. The chair is very valuable both as your work, and as Mrs. Salusbury's present.[1] I am glad that Malt can be had, but the price is very formidable.[2] Do not be dejected, send for me, if I can do you either service or pleasure, and make no doubt of success equal to your wishes, if your wishes are seconded by vigour.[3] I believe I need not tell any of You that I am Your most obliged and most humble servant,

SAM. JOHNSON

1. Mrs. Salusbury had just given SJ "a Chair of Mrs. Thrale's Work when She was a good little Girl and minded her Book and her Needle" (MS: Rylands Library).

2. Mrs. Salusbury ended her letter, "Mr. Thrale has got some Malt at 38s." *Ante* To Hester Thrale, 25 June 1771, n. 3; *Post* To Hester Thrale, 19 Oct. 1772.

3. Tempted into reckless speculation, Henry Thrale had nearly gone bankrupt the previous summer. He collapsed into a deep depression, but by borrowing money from family and friends, his wife was able to keep the brewery going. However, "since the price of grain continued to rise, conditions remained precarious" (Clifford, 1952, pp. 93–94).

John Taylor

MONDAY 19 OCTOBER 1772

MS: Hyde Collection.

ADDRESS: To the Reverend Dr. Taylor in Ashbourne, Derbyshire.

POSTMARK: LITCHFIELD.

ENDORSEMENTS: 1772, 9 Octr. 72.

Dear Sir: [Lichfield] Monday, Oct. 19, 1772

If You are so unwilling to be detained at Lichfield, it had been better if you had told me the day on which you would come, else I am in a state of uncertainty. I have so little entertainment here that I think of making some excursion; and if that should happen You may come when I am away. I will therefore fix the Meeting thus. I will be here ready for You on Tuesday the twenty seventh of this month. I do not mean that you need come on Tuesday but that you are not to come sooner. I am, Sir, your affectionate Servant, SAM. JOHNSON

Hester Thrale

MONDAY 19 OCTOBER 1772

MS: Hyde Collection.

Dear Madam: [Lichfield] Octr. 19th 1772

I set out on thursday night at nine, and arrived at Lichfield, on fryday night at eleven, no otherwise incommoded than with want of sleep, which however I enjoyed very comfortably the first night. I think a stage coach is not the worst bed.

I am here at present a little windbound, as the paper will show you,[1] and Lichfield is not a place of much entertainment, yet, though I have some thoughts of rambling a little, this is to be my home long enough to receive a letter, which will I hope tell me that you are busy in reformation, that dear Mrs. Salusbury is easy, that all the young people are well, and that Mr.

1. The available newspapers for this period do not mention high winds in Staffordshire.

Thrale brews at less expence than fourteen shillings a quarter.[2] They have had in this country a very prosperous Hay harvest, but malt is five and sixpence a strike,[3] or two pounds four shillings a quarter.[4] Wheat is nine and six pence a bushel.[5] These are prices which are almost descriptive of a famine. Flesh is likewise very dear.

In this wide extended calamity let us try what alleviation can be found in our kindness to each other. I am, Madam, your most obliged and most humble servant, SAM. JOHNSON

2. Four months later the manager of the brewery reported to Hester Thrale that the cost of production could not "easily be reduced" below 10*s*. a quarter (Hester Thrale to SJ, 20 Feb. 1773; MS: Rylands Library).

3. *strike*: "a bushel; a dry measure of capacity; four pecks" (SJ's *Dictionary*).

4. *Post* To Hester Thrale, 24 Oct. 1772.

5. According to the *GM*, the average price of wheat in Staffordshire, 5–10 Oct., was 7*s*.7*d*., the highest in all of England (*GM* 1772, p. 442).

Hester Thrale

SATURDAY 24 OCTOBER 1772

MS: Hyde Collection.

Madam: Lichfield, Oct. 24, 1772

I would have you consider whether it will not be best to write to Sir Thomas,[1] not taking notice of any thing proposed to Mr. Bridge,[2] and only letting him know that the report which terrified you so much has had little effect, and that You have now no particular need of his money.[3] By this You will free him from solicitude, and having nothing to fear from you he

1. Sir Thomas Salusbury (1708–73), Kt., Hester Thrale's uncle, from whom she had expected to inherit the estate of Offley Place in Hertfordshire. Though Sir Thomas's remarriage in 1763 impaired her prospects, there was always "a possibility that, with reconciliation, she might again take the position which she had been brought up to consider her rightful due" (Clifford, 1952, p. 107).

2. Edward Bridge (d. 1792), the steward who looked after Mrs. Salusbury's Welsh properties (*Thraliana* 1.292). He was dismissed in 1774 (*The Piozzi Letters*, ed. E. A. Bloom and L. D. Bloom, 1989, 1.378–79 n. 4).

will love you as before. It will abate any triumph of your enemies, and dispose them less to censure, and him less to regard censure.

When you wrote the letter which you call injudicious, I told you that it would bring no money, but I do not see how in that tumult of distress you could have forborn it without appearing to be too tender of your own personal connections, and to place your unkle above your family. You did what then seemed best, and are therefore not so reasonable as I wish my Mistress to be, in imputing to yourself any unpleasing consequences. Your Unkle, when he knows that you do not want, and mean not to disturb him, will probably subside in silence to his former stagnation of unactive kindness.

Do not suffer little things to disturb you. The Brewhouse must be the scene of action, and the subject of Speculation. The first consequence of our late trouble ought to be, an endeavour to brew at a cheaper rate,[4] an endeavour not violent and transient, but[5] steady and continual, prosecuted with total contempt of censure or wonder, and animated by resolution not to stop while more can be done.[6] Unless this can be done nothing can help us, and if this be done, we shall not want help.

Surely there is[7] something to be saved; there is to be saved whatever is the difference between vigilance and neglect, between parcimony and profusion.

The price of malt has risen again. It is now two pounds eight shillings the quarter.[8] Ale is sold in the publick houses, at sixpence a quart, a price which I never heard of before.[9]

3. It was rumored that the second Lady Salusbury "had insisted on some Will being made to bar my Succession" (*Thraliana* 1.313). When Sir Thomas died the following October, Hester Thrale's fears proved well founded (Clifford, 1952, p. 107).

4. *Ante* To Hester Thrale, 15 Oct. 1772, n. 3.

5. MS: "b" superimposed upon "c"

6. *Ante* To Hester Thrale, 19 Oct. 1772.

7. MS: "there is" written above "this" del.

8. *Ante* To Hester Thrale, 19 Oct. 1772.

9. The standard London retail price was 3½*d.* per quart (H. A. Monckton, *A History of English Ale and Beer*, 1966, p. 151).

This weather, if it continues, will certainly save hay,[10] but it can but little ballance the misfortune of the scanty harvest. This however is an evil which we only share with the whole nation, and which we did not bring upon ourselves.

I fancy the next letter may be directed to Ashbourne. Pray write word how long I may have leave to stay.

I sincerely wish Mrs. Salusbury continuance and increase of ease and comfort, and wish all good to you all. I am, Madam, your most obliged and most humble servant,

SAM. JOHNSON

10. On 11 Aug. 1772, Horace Walpole reported to Sir Horace Mann, "We have had and have the summerest summer that I have known these hundred years" (*Walpole's Correspondence*, Yale ed. XXIII.426).

Hester Thrale

THURSDAY 29 OCTOBER 1772

MS: Hyde Collection.

Dear Madam: Ashbourn, Oct. 29, 1772

In writing to your Unkle you certainly did well, but your letter was hardly confident enough.[1] You might have ventured to speak with some degree of indifference, about money which you know, that you shall not have. I have no doubt of the present perverseness of his intention, but if I mistake not his character his intention and execution are not very near each other; and as he acts by mere irritation when the disturbance is over, he will lye still.

What have I committed that I am to be left behind on Saturdays?[2] The coach, I think, must go twice with the rest, and at one of the times you might make room for me if you cared for me.[3] But so am I served, that sit thinking and thinking of you, and all of you.

1. *Ante* To Hester Thrale, 24 Oct. 1772.

2. When the Thrales were based in Southwark, Saturday was the usual day for going out to Streatham.

3. On 7 Nov. Hester Thrale replied: "What can you mean by the Coach going

Poor dear Mrs. Salusbury; is the place then open?[4] I am however glad to hear that her vigour of mind is yet undiminished. I hope she will now have less pain.

We are here as we used to be; our Bulls and Cows if there is any change, seem to grow bigger.

That you are to go to the other house I am inwardly pleased however I may pretend to pity you;[5] and I am of Mamma's opinion that you may find yourself something to do there, and something of importance.[6] I am, Madam, your most obedient and most humble servant, SAM. JOHNSON

---

twice on Saturdays? It holds my Master the three Children and myself at once well enough, but where is any room for our dear Mr. Johnson?" (MS: Rylands Library).

4. Mrs. Salusbury was so ill with cancer that she had been forced to give up her house on Dean Street, Soho, and move permanently to Streatham Park. *Post* To Hester Thrale, 9 Nov. 1772.

5. On 3 Nov. the Thrales, in order to economize more effectively, moved from Streatham Park to their house in Southwark, which Mrs. Thrale thoroughly disliked.

6. *Post* To Hester Thrale, 9 Nov. 1772.

Hester Thrale

SATURDAY 31 OCTOBER 1772

MS: Hyde Collection.

Madam: [Ashbourne] Oct. 31, 1772

Though I am just informed that by some accidental negligence, the letter which I wrote on Thursday was not given to the post, yet I cannot refuse myself the gratification of writing again to my Mistress. Not that I have any thing to tell, but that by showing how much I am employed upon you, I hope to keep you from forgetting me.

Doctor Taylor asked me this morning on what I was thinking, and I was thinking on Lucy. I hope Lucy is a good girl. But she cannot yet be so good as Queeny. I have got nothing yet for Queeny's Cabinet.[1]

1. "It was probably at his [SJ's] suggestion that Queeney began her collection

I hope dear Mrs. Salusbury grows no worse. I wish any thing could be found that would make her better. You must remember her admonition, and bustle in the Brewhouse. When I come you [2] may expect to have your hands full with all of us.

Our Bulls and Cows are all well, but we yet hate the man that had seen a bigger Bull. Our Deer have died, but many are left. Our waterfal at the garden makes a great roaring this wet weather.

And so no more at present from, Madam, your most obedient, humble servant,

SAM. JOHNSON

---

of natural specimens, since he saw to it that she had a special cabinet made to hold the treasures, and on every trip tried to secure some new object to add to them" (Clifford, 1952, p. 112). The cabinet is now in the Bowood Collection (Hyde, 1977, p. 51).

2. MS: "you" altered from "your"

Hester Maria Thrale

MONDAY 2 NOVEMBER 1772

MS: The Earl of Shelburne.

ADDRESS: To Miss Thrale.

Dear Sweeting: Ashbourn, Nov. 2, 1772

Your pretty letter was too short. If Lucy is not good, you must try to mend her by good advice, and good example, for all the little girls will try to be like you. I am glad to hear of the improvement and prosperity of my hen. Miss Porter has buried her fine black Cat. So things come and go. Generations, as Homer says, are but like leaves;[1] and you now see the faded leaves falling about you.

You are sorry to come to town, and I am sorry for dear Grandmamma that will be left in the Country,[2] be sure that you make my compliments to her. I am, Dear Miss, your most obedient servant,

SAM. JOHNSON

1. "As is the generation of leaves, so is the generation of men" (*Iliad* VI.146, trans. A. T. Murray, Loeb ed.).

2. *Ante* To Hester Thrale, 29 Oct. 1772, nn. 4, 5.

Hester Thrale

WEDNESDAY 4 NOVEMBER 1772

MS: Hyde Collection.

Dear Madam: Ashbourn, Nov. 4, 1772

We keep writing to each other when by the confession of both there is nothing to be said, but on my part I find it very pleasing to write, and what is pleasing is very willingly continued.

I hope your prescriptions have been successful, and Mr. Thrale is well. What pity it is that we can not do something for the dear Lady. Since I came to Ashbourne I have been out of order. I was well at Lichfield. You know sickness will drive me to You. So perhaps you very heartily wish me better. But you know likewise that health will not hold me away, and I hope you think that sick or well I am, Madam, Your most humble servant,

SAM. JOHNSON

Hester Thrale

SATURDAY 7 NOVEMBER 1772

MS: Hyde Collection.

Dear Madam: Ashbourn, Nov. 7, 1772

So many days and never a letter. Fugere fides, pietasque pudorque.[1] This is Turkish usage. And I have been hoping and hoping. But you [are] so glad to have me out of your mind.

I think you were quite right in your advice about the thousand pounds, for the payment could not have been delayed long, and a short delay would have lessened credit with-

1. SJ seems to have conflated two lines from Ovid's *Metamorphoses*: *fugere pudor verumque fidesque* (I.129) and *et ante oculos rectum pietasque pudorque* (VII.72): "modesty and truth and faith fled the earth"; "before her eyes righteousness, filial affection, and modesty" (trans. F. J. Miller, Loeb ed.).

out advancing interest. But in great matters you are hardly ever mistaken.

We have here very rainy weather, but it makes the grass grow; and makes our waterfal roar; I wish Queeny heard it, she would think it very pretty. I go down to it every day, for I have not much to do, and have not been very well; but by physick am grown better. You and all your train may be supposed to keep me company in my walks. I wish I could know how you brew, and how you go on, but you tell me nothing. I am, Madam, Your most humble servant,

SAM. JOHNSON

Hester Thrale

MONDAY 9 NOVEMBER 1772

PRINTED SOURCE: Piozzi, *Letters* 1.48–49.

Dear Madam: [Ashbourne] Nov. 9, 1772

After I had sent away my last letter, I received your's, which was an answer to it; but, being not fully directed, had lain, I think, two days at the office.[1]

I am glad that you are at last come home, and that you exert your new resolution with so much vigour.[2] But the fury of housewifery will soon subside; and little effect will be produced but by methodical attention and even frugality; nor can these powers be immediately attained. You have your own habits, as well as those of others, to combat: you have yet the skill of management to learn, as well as the practice to establish. Do not be discouraged either by your own failures, or the perverseness of others; you will, by resolution frequently renewed, and by perseverance properly excited, overcome in time both them and yourself.

Your letter to Sir Thomas will, I doubt not, have the effect intended. When he is not pinched he will sleep.[3]

1. Hester Thrale's letter of 4 Nov. responds to SJ's of 31 Oct.

2. *Ante* To Hester Thrale, 29 Oct. 1772 and n. 5.

3. *Ante* To Hester Thrale, 24 Oct. 1772 and nn. 1, 3; 29 Oct. 1772.

Mr. Thrale's money, to pay for all, must come from the sale of good beer. I am far from despairing of solid and durable prosperity. Nor will your success exceed my hopes, or my opinion of your state, if, after this tremendous year, you should annually add to your fortune three thousand pounds. This will soon dismiss all incumbrances; and, when no interest is paid, you will begin annually to lay up almost five thousand. This is very splendid; but this, I think, is in your power.[4]

Dear mamma, I hope, continues to be cheerful. Do the Plumbes take her house furnished?[5] I think it a very proper habitation for them, out of the smoke of the city, and yet not in the blaze of the court.

I am much obliged to you for your desire of my return; but if I make haste, will you promise not to spoil me? I do not much trust yet to your new character, which I have had only from yourself.[6]

Be pleased to direct your next letter to Lichfield; for I shall, I think, be contriving to find my way back.[7] I am, etc.

SAM. JOHNSON

4. In addition to the money Hester Thrale had borrowed from family and friends, "the total indebtedness of the brewery in trade . . . was said to be £130,000—most of it in the form of inescapably extended credit to tradesmen supplying raw materials. . . . It took the house almost nine years to pay off these debts completely" (Peter Mathias, *The Brewing Industry in England 1700–1830*, 1959, p. 267).

5. *Ante* To Hester Thrale, 29 Oct. 1772, n. 4. In her letter of 4 Nov., Hester Thrale had mentioned that Alderman Plumbe and his family "have a fancy to take her [Mrs. Salusbury's] house in Dean Street" (MS: Rylands Library).

6. Hester Thrale had described her industrious, cost-cutting, managerial role in the Southwark establishment as that of a "Skin Flint" (4 Nov. 1772; MS: Rylands Library).

7. SJ did not return to Lichfield until 2 Dec. (*Post* To Hester Thrale, 27 Nov. 1772; 3 Dec. 1772).

Hester Thrale

SATURDAY 14 NOVEMBER 1772

MS: Hyde Collection.

Madam: [Ashbourne] Nov. 14, 1772

It was my intention to have [made] more haste home than will be easily permitted. I talked to Dr. Taylor of going away this week, and he is moody and serious and says I promised to stay with him a month. I know not how to get away, without leaving him clandestinely. I did not come hither till the 27 of last month, but I was delayed, as you may remember, by his detention among his people.[1]

If I am wanted at the Borough I will immediately come, if not,[2] be pleased to give me leave to stay the month with him.[3] Let me know next post, and direct to Ashbourne. I am, Madam, your most obedient servant,

SAM. JOHNSON

1. *Ante* To John Taylor, 19 Oct. 1772.

2. MS: semicolon

3. *Ante* To Hester Thrale, 9 Nov. 1772, n. 7.

Hester Thrale

THURSDAY 19 NOVEMBER 1772

MS: Hyde Collection.

Dear Madam: [Ashbourne] Nov. 19, 1772

I longed for your letter to day, for till that came I could not make any promises, or form any determinations. You need not doubt my readiness to return, but it is impossible to foresee[1] all occasions of interruption or all necessities of compliance.

Be pleased to tell poor dear Mrs. Salusbury, that I wish her better, and to wish is all the power that we have. In the greatest exigencies we can only regret our own inability. I think Mrs. Queeney might write again.

This year will undoubtedly be an year of Struggle and difficulty. But I doubt not of getting through it, and the difficulty

1. MS: "foresee" altered from "foreseen"

will grow yearly less and less.[2] Supposing that our former mode of life kept us on the level, we shall by the present contraction of expence, gain upon fortune a thousand a year, even though no improvements can be made in the conduct of the trade. Every two thousand pounds saves an hundred pound interest, and therefore as we gain more we pay less. We have a rational hope of success; we have rather a moral certainty, with life and health. Let us therefore not be dejected. Continue to be a housewife, and be as[3] frolicksome with your tongue as you please.[4] I am, Dearest Lady, Your most humble servant,

SAM. JOHNSON

2. *Ante* To Hester Thrale, 9 Nov. 1772, n. 4.

3. MS: "as as"

4. In her letter of 7 Nov., Hester Thrale had claimed that, until SJ's return, "there is no chance for me to do anything except by a little inneffectual teizing to keep my tongue in Tune" (MS: Rylands Library).

Hester Thrale

SATURDAY 21 NOVEMBER 1772

MS: Birthplace Museum, Lichfield.

Madam: [Ashbourne] Nov. 21, 1772

This is saturday, and while I am writing, you are going or gone to see dear Mrs. Salusbury,[1] I hope your company does her good. Your letters always do me good, I was hoping for one to day. I have had however no reason to complain of you, but Queeny is a naughty Puss; pray let her write me word what became of the poor Clerk.

Since I came into the country we have had no considerable occurrences. The Doctor stays at home and I stay with him, sometimes reading, and sometimes talking, not sleeping much, for I have not of late slept well, and some nights have been very troublesome, but I think myself now better.

I am afraid I shall be able to bring home no[thing] for Miss's

1. *Ante* To Hester Thrale, 29 Oct. 1772, nn. 2, 4.

cabinet,[2] for I have met with no natural curiosities, but where should I find them sitting always in the house. I use no exercise, and therefore desire that no mortification may be spared to, Madam, Your most obedient, most humble servant,

SAM. JOHNSON

2. *Ante* To Hester Thrale, 31 Oct. 1772, n. 1.

Hester Thrale

MONDAY 23 NOVEMBER 1772

MS: Hyde Collection.

Dear Madam: [Ashbourne] Nov. 23, 1772

I am sorry that none of your letters bring better news of the poor dear Lady. I hope her pain is not great.[1] To have a disease confessedly incurable and apparently mortal is a very heavy affliction; and it is still more grievous when pain is added to despair.

Every thing else in your letter pleased me very well, except that when I come, I entreat I may not be flattered, as your letters flatter me. You have read of heroes and princes ruined by flattery, and I question if any of them had a flatterer so dangerous as you. Pray keep strictly to your character of governess.[2]

What I told you of your power to advance your affairs, I am persuaded to be much less than the truth, and less than it will be found, when you come to experience the effect of diligence and prudence.

I cannot yet get well, my nights are flatulent, and unquiet, but my days are tolerably easy, and Taylor says that I look much better than when I came hither. You will see when I come, and I can take your word.

Our house affords no revolutions. The great Bull is well. But I write not merely to think on you, for I do that without

1. *Ante* To Hester Thrale, 29 Oct. 1772.

2. *Ante* To Hester Thrale, 9 Nov. 1772 and n. 6.

writing, but to keep you a little thinking on me. I perceive that I have taken a broken piece of paper, but that is not the greatest fault that [you] must forgive in, Madam, Your most humble servant,

SAM. JOHNSON

Hester Thrale

FRIDAY 27 NOVEMBER 1772

MS: Hyde Collection.

Dear Madam: [Ashbourne] Nov. 27, 1772

If you are so kind as to write to me on saturday, the day on which[1] you will receive this, I shall have it before I leave Ashbourn. I am to go to[2] Lichfield on Wednesday, and purpose to find my way to London through Birmingham and Oxford.

I was yesterday at Chatsworth. It is a very fine house.[3] I wish you had been with me to see it, for then, as we are apt to want matter of talk, we should have gained something new to talk on. They complimented me with playing the fountains, and opening the cascade.[4] But I am of my Friend's opinion, that when one has seen the Ocean, Cascades are but little things.[5]

I am in hope of a letter to day from You or Queeny, but the

1. MS: "w" superimposed upon "th"

2. MS: "to" altered from "th"

3. Chatsworth, the seat of the Dukes of Devonshire, was built by the first Duke as a replacement for the original Elizabethan mansion. The principal architects were William Talman and Thomas Archer. Work began in 1687, and continued until the Duke's death in 1707 (Nikolaus Pevsner and Elizabeth Williamson, *Derbyshire*, 1978, pp. 126–38).

4. The first Duke of Devonshire was largely responsible for the gardens and grounds at Chatsworth, which included waterworks and a cascade, begun in 1694. Both cascade and fountains were designed by Grillet, a pupil of Le Nôtre (Pevsner and Williamson, *Derbyshire*, pp. 138–39).

5. As H. L. Piozzi explains in a letter to Richard Duppa, 26 Sept. 1816, SJ is making mild fun of Thomas Percy, who wrote to his wife when she was staying with the Thrales at Brighton: "'I am enjoying the fall of a murmuring Stream . . . but to you who reside close to the roaring Ocean, such Scenery would be insipid'. *This* our Doctor laughed at, as ridiculous Affectation" (MS: Hyde Collection).

Post has made some blunder, and the packet is not yet distributed. I wish it may bring me a little good of you all. I am, Madam, your most obedient and most humble servant,

SAM. JOHNSON

Hester Maria Thrale

SATURDAY 28 NOVEMBER 1772

MS: The Earl of Shelburne.

Dear Miss: [Ashbourne] Nov. 28, 1772

Mamma used us both very sorrily when she hindered you from writing to me.[1] She dos not know how much I should love to read your letters, if they were a little longer. But we shall soon, I hope, talk matters all over. I have not had the luck this journey to pick up any curiosities for the cabinet.[2] I would have been glad to bring you something, if I could have found it.

I hope You go often to see dear Grandmamma.[3] We must all do what we can to help her and please her, and take great care now she is so bad, not to make her worse.

You said nothing of Lucy, I suppose she is grown a pretty good scholar, and a very good play fellow; after dinner we shall have good sport playing all together, and we will none of us cry.

Make my compliments to Grandmamma, and Papa, and Mamma, and all the young ones. I am, Dearest Miss, Your most humble servant,

SAM. JOHNSON

1. Queeney had written to SJ on 24 Nov., "Mama knows I would have written sooner but she said you would be troubled with no more of my Stuff" (MS: Rylands Library).

2. *Ante* To Hester Thrale, 31 Oct. 1772, n. 1.

3. *Ante* To Hester Thrale, 29 Oct. 1772, n. 4.

Robert Chambers

THURSDAY 3 DECEMBER 1772

MS: Hyde Collection.

ADDRESS: To Robert Chambers, Esq., at New Inn Hall, Oxford [*Re-addressed in an unidentified hand*] No. 6 Kings Bench Walks, Inner Temple, London.

POSTMARKS: LITCHFIELD, 9 DE.

ENDORSEMENT: Mr. Johnson.

Dear Sir: Lichfield, Dec. 3, 1772

By your advertisement I guess that you are at Oxford.[1] I shall come through Oxford next week and if you leave it, beg the favour of you to order beds for me and Francis at your Hall.[2] I am, Sir, your most humble servant, SAM. JOHNSON

1. Chambers began his seventh and final series of Vinerian lectures on 1 Dec. 1772. As with the previous series, it was advertised in *Jackson's Oxford Journal* (E. L. McAdam, "Dr. Johnson's Law Lectures for Chambers, II," *RES* 16, 1940, pp. 160–61).

2. It is likely that SJ and Francis Barber stayed at Oxford for three nights, 8–10 Dec. (*Post* To Edmund Hector, 5 Dec. 1772; 12 Dec. 1772).

Hester Thrale

THURSDAY 3 DECEMBER 1772

MS: Hyde Collection.

Dear Madam: Lichfield, Dec. 3, 1772

I found two letters here to recompense my disappointment at Ashbourne. I shall not now be long before I hope to settle, for it is a fine thing to be settled. When one parts from friends it is uncertain when one shall come back, and when one comes back it is not very certain how long one shall stay. But hope, you know was left in the box of Prometheus.[1]

1. It was Prometheus' brother Epimetheus who owned the box from which Pandora released "all the Spites that might plague mankind" (Robert Graves, *The Greek Myths*, 1955, I.145).

Miss Aston claims kin to you, for she says she is somehow akin to the Cottons.[2] In a little time you shall make them all yet prouder of their kindred. Do[3] not be depressed. Scarce years will not last for ever, there will sometime be good harvests.[4] Scarcity itself produces plenty by inciting cultivation. I hope we shall soon talk these matters over very seriously, and that we shall talk of them again much less seriously many years hence.

My Love to all
Both great and small.

These verses I made myself, though perhaps they have been made by others before me. I am, Dear Madam, your most obedient servant,

SAM. JOHNSON

2. Elizabeth Aston's first-cousin-once-removed, Elizabeth Aston Cotton (d. 1795), was married to Hester Thrale's first cousin, Rowland Cotton (d. 1794), Admiral R.N. (*Johns. Glean.* v.242, xi.107).

3. MS: "Don"

4. *Ante* To Hester Thrale, 19 Oct. 1772; 24 Oct. 1772.

Edmund Hector

SATURDAY 5 DECEMBER 1772

MS: Houghton Library.

ADDRESS: To Mr. Hector in Birmingham. Turn at Colshil.

POSTMARK: LITCHFIELD.

Dear Sir: Lichfield, Dec. 5, 1772

When I came down into this country, I proposed to myself the pleasure of a few days passed in your company, but it has happened now as at many former times that I proposed enjoyments which I cannot obtain. I have a hasty summons to London,[1] and can hope for little more than to pass a night with you and Mrs. Careless.[2]

I purpose to come to you on Monday, and to go away next day, if I can get a place in the Oxford coach. If by this notice

1. *Post* To Hester Thrale, 5 Dec. 1772.

2. *Ante* To Hester Thrale, Early July 1770, n. 11.

you can secure a place for tuesday to Oxford, it will be a favour. I hope we shall meet again with more leisure, and revive past images, and old occurrences. I am, Dear Sir, Your faithful, humble servant,

SAM. JOHNSON

Hester Thrale

SATURDAY 5 DECEMBER 1772

MS: Hyde Collection.

Madam: Lichfield, Dec. 5, 1772

When your last Letter came, Lucy had just been wheedling for another week. Lucy seldom wheedles. I had not promised her, and therefore was not distressed by your summons. I have ordered the chaise for Monday and hope to get a place in the Oxford coach at Birmingham on Tuesday, and on Wednesday or Thursday to lye in my old habitation, under your government.

I have just taken leave of Mrs. Aston who has given me some shells for Miss, if I can contrive to bring them.[1]

Mr. Thrale needs not fear my loitering, but it pains me to think that my coming[2] can be of any consequence. We will set all our understandings to work, and surely we have no insuperable difficulties. Spirit and Diligence will do great things.

Please to make my compliments to dear Mrs. Salusbury. I am, Madam, Your most humble servant,

SAM. JOHNSON

1. *Ante* To Hester Thrale, 31 Oct. 1772, n. 1.

2. MS: "c" superimposed upon "p"

Edmund Hector

SATURDAY 12 DECEMBER 1772

PRINTED SOURCE: *Notes and Queries*, sixth series, May 1881, III.361. Collated with text in Sotheby's Catalogue, 5 June 1929, Lot 618.

ADDRESS: To Mr. Hector, in Birmingham.

Dear Sir: Dec. 12, 1772

I got hither last night, full of your kindness and that of Mrs. Careless, and full of the praises of[1] Banstay,[2] which though I had not many days before seen Chatsworth,[3] keeps, I think, the upper place in my imagination. I return all my friends sincere thanks for their attention and civility.

Yet perhaps I had not written so soon had I not had another favour to solicite. Your case of the cancer and mercury has made such impression upon my friend, that we are very impatient for a more exact relation than I could give, and I therefore entreat, that you will state it very particularly, with the patient's age, the manner of taking mercury, the quantity taken, and all that you told or omitted to tell me.[4] To this request I must add another that you will write as soon as you can. I am, Dear Sir, your affectionate servant,

SAM. JOHNSON

1. "full of praise of" (Sotheby)

2. "Banstay," a conjectural reading, may be a mistake for "Borsley." Bordesley Hall, on the outskirts of Birmingham, was the home of John Taylor the manufacturer (*Ante* To Edmund Hector, 7 Dec. 1765, n. 3). The mansion was burnt down in the Riots of 1791 (R. K. Dent, *Old and New Birmingham,* 1880, 1972, II.233).

3. *Ante* To Hester Thrale, 27 Nov. 1772 and n. 3.

4. SJ and Hester Thrale were continuing to search for a treatment that might cure or alleviate Mrs. Salusbury's breast cancer. *Ante* To Hester Thrale, 15 June 1771.

James Granger[1]

TUESDAY 15 DECEMBER 1772

MS: Hyde Collection.

Sir: Dec. 15, 1772

When I returned from the country I found your letter, and

1. The Rev. James Granger (1723–76), collector and historian, whose *Biographical History of England* (1769), printed with blank leaves for the reception of engraved portraits, created a long-lasting vogue for "grangerized" volumes. According to SJ, Granger's *History* was "full of curious anecdote, but might have been better done" (*Life* V.255).

would very gladly have done what you desire had it been in my power. But Mr. Farmer[2] is, I am confident, mistaken in supposing that he gave me any such pamphlet or cut.[3] I should as soon have suspected myself as Mr. Farmer of forgetfulness, but that I do not know except from your Letter the name of Arthur o'Toole, nor recollect that I ever heard it before.[4] I think it impossible that I should have suffered such a total obliteration, from my mind, of any thing which was ever there. This at least is certain, that I do not know of any such pamphlet, and equally certain I desire you to think it, that if I had it, you should immediately receive it, from, Sir, Your most humble Servant,

SAM. JOHNSON

2. *Ante* To Richard Farmer, 21 Mar. 1770, n. 1.

3. *cut*: "a picture cut or carved upon a stamp of wood or copper, and impressed from it" (SJ's *Dictionary*).

4. The third edition of Granger's *History* (1779) contains a print of "Arthurus Severus Nonesuch O'Toole. *Aet.* 80. 1618" (1.397). The print was prefixed to John Taylor's pamphlet, *To the Honor of the Noble Captaine OToole* (1622). According to Taylor, O'Toole was the heir to Powerscourt, south of Dublin, and had fought for Elizabeth's forces both in Ireland and abroad (*Captain OToole*, A3).

INDEX

This is an index of proper names alone; the comprehensive index to the entire edition appears in Volume v. The following abbreviations are used: Bt. (Baronet), Kt. (Knight), ment. (mentioned). Peers are listed under their titles, with cross-references from the family name.

Entries for each of SJ's correspondents begin with a comprehensive listing of all letters to the individual in question. Page numbers for footnotes refer to pages on which the footnotes begin, although the item which is indexed may be on a following page.

The index was compiled mainly by Phyllis L. Marchand with the assistance of Marcia Wagner Levinson and Judith Ann Hancock.

F

G

J

K

L

Q

R

S

T

V

W

X

Y

Z